MODEL JURY INSTRUCTIONS

S0-AXT-371

Business Torts Litigation

FOURTH EDITION

SECTION OF LITIGATION
American Bar Association

The
MODEL JURY INSTRUCTIONS
Series

Business Torts Litigation

Construction Litigation

Employment Litigation

Patent Litigation

Securities Litigation

Defending Liberty
Pursuing Justice

SECTION OF LITIGATION
American Bar Association

MODEL JURY INSTRUCTIONS

Business Torts Litigation

FOURTH EDITION

Business Torts Litigation Committee
SECTION OF LITIGATION
AMERICAN BAR ASSOCIATION

Defending Liberty
Pursuing Justice

Cover design by ABA Publishing

The materials contained herein represent the opinions and views of the authors and/or the editors, and should not be construed to be the views or opinions of the law firms or companies with whom such persons are in partnership, associated with, or employed by, nor of the American Bar Association or the Section of Litigation unless adopted pursuant to the bylaws of the Association.

Nothing contained in this book is to be considered as the rendering of legal advice for specific cases, and readers are responsible for obtaining such advice from their own legal counsel. This book and any forms and agreements herein are intended for educational and informational purposes only.

© 2005 American Bar Association. All rights reserved. No part of this publication may be reproduced, stored in a retrieval system, or transmitted in any form or by any means, electronic, mechanical, photocopying, recording, or otherwise, without the prior written permission of the publisher. For permission contact the ABA Copyrights & Contracts Department, copyright@abanet.org or via fax at (312) 988-6030.

09 08 07 06 05 5 4 3 2 1

Library of Congress Cataloging-in-Publication Data

Model jury instructions: business torts litigation / Ian H. Fisher, Bradley P. Nelson, editors—4th ed.
    p. cm.
    Includes index
    ISBN 1-59031-486-7
    1. Instructions to juries—United States—Forms. 2. Competition, Unfair—United States. 3. Tort liability of corporations—United States. I. American Bar Association. II. Fisher, Ian H., 1969- . III. Nelson, Bradley P., 1960- .

KF8984.A65M64 2005
347.73'758—dc22   2005004579

Discounts are available for books ordered in bulk. Special consideration is given to state bars, CLE programs, and other bar-related organizations. Inquire at Book Publishing, ABA Publishing, American Bar Association, 321 North Clark Street, Chicago, Illinois 60610.

www.ababooks.org

Table of Contents

Preface

Those of us who practice in the areas of business and commercial litigation know firsthand the difficulties of drafting jury instructions, even for trials involving common business torts. Many state and federal model instructions focus heavily on criminal and personal tort and contract cases, with only limited attention paid to the typical business torts that populate our case loads.

Almost 25 years ago, the American Bar Association Litigation Section's Business Torts Committee began to fill this gap with the creation of the first edition of *Model Jury Instructions: Business Torts Litigation*. The second and third editions followed, each with new chapters covering additional and evolving business torts, along with revised and updated coverage of prior chapters. One major focus of the instructions, which continues in this fourth edition, is to point out in the commentary the differences in the law as applied among jurisdictions and to provide citations to a broad range of state and federal authorities to support the individual instructions. Over the years, these model instructions have been an invaluable reference for business litigators and courts across the country.

The Business Torts Committee is proud to sponsor this fourth edition of the business torts model jury instructions. Robert Schaberg and R. Wayne Byrd, past co-chairs of the Business Torts Committee, initiated the work on this edition. Their initiative and leadership made this edition possible. This edition continues a tradition of excellence established with the prior three. Among the major revisions reflected in this fourth edition are new instructions relating to punitive damages in light of the Supreme Court's recent decisions in *State Farm Mut. Auto Ins. Co. v. Campbell*, 538 U.S. 408 (2003) and *BMW of N. Am., Inc. v. Gore*, 517 U.S. 559 (1996). Those cases establish that many traditional punitive damage instructions, which give wide latitude and little guidance to juries, may not withstand constitutional scrutiny. The revised punitive damage instructions in this edition attempt to cure the deficiencies found in many of the standard traditional instructions.

This fourth edition is built on the work produced in the prior three. We gratefully acknowledge the authors of the prior editions, many of whom also revised and updated their chapters for this edition. Those authors new to this edition also share our gratitude for their hard work and invaluable contributions.

We are confident that business and commercial litigators in all parts of the country will find this book and the accompanying instructions on CD-ROM valuable resources for use in preparing and trying business tort cases.

Bradley P. Nelson*
Ian H. Fisher
Editors

* Bradley P. Nelson and Ian H. Fisher are partners at Schopf & Weiss LLP, 312 W. Randolph, Suite 300, Chicago, Illinois 60606, www.sw.com. Mr. Nelson can be reached at (312) 701-9313 or nelson @sw.com. Mr. Fisher can be reached at (312) 701-9316 or fisher@sw.com.

Foreword to Model Jury Instructions Series

Jury instructions: that is where the rubber hits the road in the law. At their best, jury instructions summarize cogently, clearly, and distinctly the contours of the law that a jury must apply to the facts. At their worst, jury instructions are tangled, arcane, incomprehensible legalese masquerading as a guide for the jury.

The jury instructions in this volume pertain to business torts litigation. They are for those among us who, every once in a while, fail to settle a case and therefore must go to trial. When a case is tried to a judge, that judge is presumed to know the law. When the case is tried to a jury of laypeople, they are presumed not to know the law. Therefore, they must be provided with a legal road map. These jury instructions are intended to serve that purpose. They can be used as such a guide not only in court before a jury, but also for evaluating and preparing a case for trial. These jury instructions are designed to tell a jury, and therefore you, what you must prove to prevail in your case. We hope you will find the guidance provided here enlightening and useful at the multiple stages of taking, preparing, and trying a case.

Each jury instruction is intended to be party-neutral. However, because ours is an adversary system of justice, lawyers may try to rewrite these neutral instructions in a manner that better presents the case for their clients. We wish those lawyers luck in convincing a court that the proposed reformulation conforms to the status of the law. Obviously, because the law is rarely static, the success of such reformulation will closely track any developments in the law.

In the notes that follow each instruction, you will find discussion of cases from which the instruction is derived, whether plaintiffs and defendants disagree on its use, and how it might be modified depending upon the individual circumstances. These model jury instructions do not incorporate standard form instructions dealing with generalized burdens of proof, credibility of witnesses, or other such background matters that every set of jury instructions is presumed to include. The instructions here do include instructions on a wide range of issues and causes of action that arise in the context of business torts litigation. The table of contents spells these out for the reader and is intended to assure ease of use.

As the Section of Litigation of the American Bar Association, we can imagine few more useful tools to provide our colleagues than cogent, clear, and distinct jury instructions. We have designated these jury instructions as "model" ones because we hope that, in time, that is what they will become. To that end, we invite the readers and users of these proposed model jury instructions to share their reactions with us. Let us know which of the instructions work and which do not. Let us know which of the instructions you believe could be more clearly written. Let us know which of the instructions a court has refused to give and why. In a future revision, we will try to incorporate your feedback so that these proposed "model" jury instructions in fact become model in use.

This volume is one of five that the Section of Litigation has produced on jury instructions, including volumes on employment, securities, construction, patent, and now this, the latest edition of business tort instructions. All of these have been provided to the entire federal judiciary. We hope that this volume will be accorded the same acceptance received by the prior jury instruction volumes. The profession certainly owes a large debt of gratitude to those individual lawyers who have given so unstintingly and so generously of their time to produce these jury instructions.

We hope that all of the ABA Section of Litigation jury instructions now in print constitute a respectable body of work, but it is only a beginning. Other volumes are in the drafting or planning stages. In time, we plan to present model jury instructions for many other areas of the law that often form the underlying basis for cases tried in the federal courts.

Book Publishing Board
Section of Litigation

Chapter One
Inducing Breach of and Tortious Interference with Contract

Neal C. Baroody*

* Neal C. Baroody is a partner at Baroody & O'Toole (www. baroodyotoole.com), 201 North Charles Street, Suite 2208, Baltimore, MD 21201, nbaroody@aol.com.

1.1 Introduction

The model jury charges in these first two chapters reflect common law liability for inducing a breach of contract or interfering with contractual relations. The broad tort category of "interference" encompasses not only those situations in which an existing contract is breached or interfered with, but also those situations involving no contract. Examples of such situations include: (a) when a contract is in the formative stages, though incomplete; (b) when there is an ongoing business relationship; and (c) when a business relationship has not yet been established but is reasonably probable.

This chapter covers only the situation in which a third party induces the breach of an existing contract. Chapter Two, "Interference with Prospective Advantage," covers the situation in which no contract exists. The tort of inducing a breach of contract or interference with contractual relations also is referred to as "interference with business relations."

Jurisdictions differ on a number of fundamental issues related to the tort of inducing breach of contract. Notwithstanding these differences, the courts of almost all jurisdictions generally require at least the following criteria:

1. the existence of a valid contract;

2. knowledge of the contract on the part of the defendant or that it was readily apparent to the defendant;

3. an intentional interference that causes a breach of the contract; and

4. economic damages suffered by the plaintiff as a result of the defendant's interference.

The development of the tort has been plagued by doctrinal inconsistency, within and among jurisdictions. *See* Harvey Perlman, *Interference with Contract and Other Economic Expectancies: A Clash of Tort and Contract Doctrine*, 49 U. Chi. L. Rev. 61 (1982) [hereinafter Perlman] and Gary Myers, *The Differing Treatment of Efficiency and*

Competition in Antitrust and Tortious Interference Law, 77 Minn. L. Rev. 1097 (1993) [hereinafter Myers]. Courts have disagreed on such fundamental matters as the type of contract to be protected, the kind of interference that will be actionable, and the defenses that can be asserted. *See id.*; W. Page Keeton, *Prosser & Keeton on the Law of Torts* § 129 (5th ed. 1984) [hereinafter Keeton]. For example, Louisiana recognizes the tort only when a corporate officer interferes with the corporation's contract with the plaintiff. See *Matrix Essential v. Emporium Drug Mart*, 756 F. Supp. 280 (W.D. La. 1991) (citing *9 to 5 Fashions v. Spurney*, 538 So. 2d 228 (La. 1989)). And Missouri recognizes the tort only if the interference is based upon an "independently wrongful" act. See *Community Title Co. v. Roosevelt Federal Savs. & Loan Ass'n*, 796 S.W.2d 369 (Mo. 1990).

The most significant difference among the courts considering this tort involves the plaintiff's burden of proof. *See* Perlman, *supra* at 65. The traditional view requires the plaintiff to prove that the defendant intentionally interfered with the contract and the interference caused damages. The defendant has the burden to prove any justification or privilege. An increasing number of courts, however, have applied the test set forth in the *Restatement (Second) of Torts* § 766 (1979). This test requires the plaintiff to prove that the defendant intentionally *and improperly* interfered with the contract. Although the comments to section 766 acknowledge the split of authority and do not purport to determine conclusively the burden-of-proof issue, the addition of the "improper" element has had a significant impact on the development of the law. Most states now require the plaintiff to prove, as an element of the tort, that the defendant's conduct was the result of either an improper motive or improper means.

Sections 766 and 767 of the *Restatement (Second) of Torts* (1979) have heavily influenced the developing law.

§ 766 *Intentional Interference with Performance of Contract by Third Person*

One who intentionally and improperly interferes with the performance of a contract (except a contract to marry) between another and a third person by inducing or otherwise causing the third person not to perform the contract is subject to liability to the other for the pecuniary loss resulting to the other from the failure of the third person to perform the contract.

§ 767 *Factors in Determining Whether Interference Is Improper*
In determining whether an actor's conduct in intentionally interfering with a contract or a prospective contractual relation of another is improper or not, consideration is given to the following factors:

(a) the nature of the actor's conduct,

(b) the actor's motive,

(c) the interests of the other with which the actor's conduct interferes,

(d) the interests sought to be advanced by the actor,

(e) the social interests in protecting the freedom of action of the actor and the contractual interests of the other,

(f) the proximity or remoteness of the actor's conduct to the interference, and

(g) the relations between the parties.

Today, a majority of jurisdictions have adopted the *Restatement*'s approach and require some showing of intentional wrongful conduct or motive. *See, e.g., Sturdza v. United Arab Emirates*, 281 F.3d 1287 (D.C. Cir. 2002); *LaSalle Nat'l Bank v. Perelman*, 82 F. Supp. 2d 279 (D. Del. 2000); *Kand Med., Inc. v. Freund Med. Prods., Inc.*, 963 F.2d 125 (6th Cir. 1992), *rehearing denied* (1992) (applying Ohio law); *Allen & O'Hara, Inc. v. Barrett Wrecking, Inc.*, 898 F.2d 512 (7th Cir. 1990) (applying Wisconsin law); *H.J., Inc. v. Int'l Tel. & Tel. Corp.*, 867 F.2d 1531 (8th Cir. 1989) (applying Connecticut law); *Q.E.R., Inc. v. Hickerson*, 880 F.2d 1178 (10th Cir. 1989) (applying Colorado law); *Brownsville Golden Age Nursing Home, Inc. v. Wells*, 839 F.2d 155 (3d Cir. 1988) (applying Pennsylvania law); *Davis v. West Cmty. Hosp.*, 755 F.2d 455 (5th Cir. 1985) (applying Texas law); *V.C. Video, Inc. v. Nat'l Video, Inc.*, 755 F. Supp. 962 (D. Kan. 1990); *United Truck Leasing Corp. v. Geltman*, 551 N.E.2d

20 (Mass. 1990); *Roy v. Coyne*, 630 N.E.2d 1024 (Ill. App. Ct. 1994); *Mason v. Wal-Mart Stores, Inc.*, 333 Ark. 3, 969 S.W.2d 160 (1998); *Hodges v. Buzzeo*, 193 F. Supp. 2d 1279 (M.D. Fla. 2002)

Because not all states have adopted the *Restatement,* the jury issues in this chapter are prepared in the alternative to make them easily adaptable to the legal requirements of the various jurisdictions.

1.2   Inducing Breach of Contract: Generally

The theory underlying the broad tort of interference with contract balances a party's freedom to enter into business relationships with the sometimes competing interests of other parties coexisting in the marketplace. The development of the common law demonstrates the attempts courts have made to delineate the boundaries within which a party may conduct its own affairs without interfering with the business relationships of others.

Thus, courts impose liability for inducing a breach of contract when a party, who is a stranger to a contract, induces its breach while acting in a manner other than in the legitimate exercise of the party's own rights. Moreover, the injured party's cause of action extends not only to conduct that results in an actual breach of the contract, but also to conduct that results in substantial interference with the performance or diminution of the value of the contract. *See Arkansas v. Texas,* 346 U.S. 368 (1953). The basic theory is that the right to perform a contract and to reap the profits resulting therefrom, and also the right to performance by the other party, are property rights entitled to protection. *See* Keeton, *supra* at 991; M.C. Dransfield, Annotation, *Liability for Procuring Breach of Contract,* 26 A.L.R.2d 1227 § 1 (1952 & Supp. 2003); 64 P.O.F. 3d 273 *Tortious Interference with Real Estate Contract* § 2 (2001 & Supp. 2002); 45 Am. Jur. 2d *Interference* § 1 (1999 & Supp. 2003). For an alternative explanation of the intellectual context in which the tort may be understood, see Richard Epstein, *Inducement of Breach of Contract as a Problem of Ostensible Ownership,* 16 J. Legal Stud. 1 (1987).

1.3　Inducing Breach of Contract: Elements of Liability

1.3.1　Generally

For the plaintiff to recover on its claim against the defendant, the plaintiff must prove, by a preponderance of the evidence, each of the following five [six] elements:

1. that at the time of the acts of the defendant, [name], the plaintiff, [name], was a party to a valid contract with [name of breaching party] to [state purpose of contract];

2. that the defendant either knew of the existence or, under the circumstances, should have known of the existence, of that contract;

3. that the acts of the defendant in inducing [name of breaching party] to breach its contract with the plaintiff were intentional within the meaning of the word *intent*, which I will provide you with later in my instructions;

4. [optional—depending upon law of jurisdiction] that the conduct of the defendant was improper under the factors I will instruct you to consider;

5. that, as a proximate result of the acts of the defendant, [name of breaching party] was induced to breach its contract with the plaintiff; and

6. that, as a direct and proximate result of the defendant's conduct, the plaintiff was damaged.

If you find from your consideration of all of the evidence that the plaintiff has proved each of these elements by a preponderance of the evidence, then you will consider the question of the amount of money damages that may be awarded under instructions I will give you.

If you find, however, from your consideration of all of the evidence that the plaintiff has not proved any one or more of these elements by a preponderance of the evidence, then the defendant is not liable, and your verdict should be against the plaintiff and for the defendant.

COMMENT

This charge reflects the traditional standard for establishing liability and includes the optional element of improper conduct on the part of the defendant. A majority of jurisdictions now require the plaintiff to prove this element. For a more detailed discussion, see Section 1.1 and the cases cited therein.

Note that in jurisdictions that do not require the plaintiff to prove that the defendant's conduct was improper (sometimes referred to as requiring the conduct itself or the motive to be unjustified, malicious, inherently tortious, or unlawful), the charge should not include either optional element 4 above or the instruction in Section 1.4 (option A), regarding factors used to determine whether interference is improper. Instead, the charge requiring the defendant to prove its conduct was justified or privileged should be submitted. *See* § 1.1, *supra*; § 1.4 (option B), *infra*.

1.3.1.a   Requirement of a Contract

For you to find for the plaintiff on its claim against the defendant, you must find that the plaintiff was a party to a valid contract in full force and effect at the time of the actions complained of and that the contract was breached as a result of the defendant's conduct.

A contract may be defined simply as an oral or written agreement, which the law will enforce, to do or not to do a particular thing in exchange for adequate consideration. If all of the basic elements required by law for there to be a contract are present, a contract is deemed to be valid if it is not illegal, in restraint of trade, or otherwise opposed to public policy. A contract is considered to be in full force and effect if, at the time in question, the agreement was in effect between the parties and not terminated, expired, or otherwise rendered void.

Hence, in order for you to find the existence of a contract sufficient to meet the plaintiff's burden of proof, you must find that there was in effect, at the time of the actions complained of, an agreement between the plaintiff and [name of breaching party] to [state purpose of contract], which agreement was neither illegal nor in restraint of trade nor otherwise opposed to public policy.

[If the jurisdiction is one that does not require that the breached contract be enforceable—and counsel should note the lack of uniformity on this question among the various states—then the following additional paragraph should be added here.]

Should you find that all of the above conditions for a contract have been proved by a preponderance of the evidence, the fact that the contract may have been unenforceable by the plaintiff against [name of breaching party] by virtue of [insert any claimed reason(s)] will not render that contract insufficient to meet the plaintiff's burden of proof as to the existence of a valid contract.

COMMENT

The last (optional) paragraph of this charge assumes there is no dispute about the existence of basic contractual elements, such as capacity or consideration. The charge speaks only to the immateriality of enforceability. If basic contract law issues are to be decided, a series of paragraphs explaining each of the elements of a contract must be inserted in this charge. Such instructions concerning basic contract principles are omitted here as being beyond the scope of these instructions.

To commit a tort of interference with contractual relations, the defendant must have interfered with a valid contract existing between two parties. One who interferes with an illegal, invalid, or void contract will not be held liable in tort. *See Restatement (Second) of Torts* § 774 (1979). Pursuant to comment (f) to section 766, the contract need not be legally *enforceable* as to third persons for a cause of action for tortious interference to lie. *See Restatement (Second) of Torts* § 766 cmt. f (1979). The *Restatement* takes the view that, *until* a party to the contract raises a defense that would permit the party to avoid the contract (for example, formal defects, statute of frauds, lack of mutuality, unconscionability, indefiniteness), a defendant may not interfere improperly with the performance of that contract. *See id.* Most courts have adopted the *Restatement*'s approach and allow a party to sue for tortious interference of a contract even though the breached contract was voidable. *See* James O. Pearson, Annotation, *Liability for Interference with Invalid or Unenforceable Contract,* 96 A.L.R.3d 1294 (1979 & Supp. 2003); 64 P.O.F. 3d 273 *Tortious Interference with Real Estate Contract* § 3 (2001 & Supp. 2002); 45 Am. Jur. 2d *Interference* § 5 (1999 & Supp. 2003).

For example, courts usually hold that a contract voidable because of the statute of frauds can afford a basis for a tort action when the defendant interferes with the contract's performance. *See Frantz v. Parke,* 729 P.2d 1068 (Idaho Ct. App. 1986); *Winternitz v. Summit Hills,* 532 A.2d 1089 (Md. Ct. Spec. App. 1987), *cert. denied,* 538 A.2d 778 (Md. 1988); *Keenan v. Artintype, Inc.,* 546

N.Y.S.2d 741 (N.Y. Sup. Ct. 1989). *But see; United Magazine Co. v. Murdoch Magazines Distribution, Inc.*, 146 F. Supp. 2d 385 (S.D.N.Y. 2001); *Kopp, Inc. v. U.S. Technologies, Inc.*, 539 A.2d 309 (N.J. Super. Ct. App. Div. 1988) (dictum) (other grounds would have precluded action based on interference with contract, when contract apparently had not been agreed to by anyone authorized to bind party, even orally).

Similarly, more courts are following the trend toward allowing recovery for the breach of a contract terminable at will. Although a party to the contract may terminate it at will, courts reason that the interference of another party that induces the wrongful termination is a tort for which recovery may be had. *See Restatement (Second) of Torts* § 766 cmt. g (1979); 45 Am. Jur. 2d *Interference* § 22 (1999 & Supp. 2003); Keeton, *supra* at 995-96; *Nat'l Right to Life Political Action Comm. v. Friends of Bryan*, 741 F. Supp. 807 (D. Nev. 1990); *Leaco Enter., Inc. v. Gen. Elec. Co.*, 737 F. Supp. 605 (D. Or. 1990); *Beyda v. USAir, Inc.*, 697 F. Supp. 1394 (W.D. Pa. 1988); *Lockheed Martin Corp. v. Aatlas Commerce Inc.*, 725 N.Y.S.2d 722 (N.Y. App. Div. 2001); *Sterner v. Marathon Oil Co.*, 767 S.W.2d 686 (Tex. 1989); *Duggin v. Adams*, 360 S.E.2d 832 (Va. 1987). *See generally* M.C. Dransfield, Annotation, *Liability for Procuring Breach of Contract*, 26 A.L.R.2d 1227 § 1 (1952 & Supp. 2003).

Courts have remained split, however, when the breached contract was unenforceable for want of consideration, mutuality, or certainty. Although a number of courts have held that a cause of action may lie for the inducement of breach of such contracts, other courts have disagreed. Compare cases where liability was found (*Gallipo v. City of Rutland*, 656 A.2d 635 (Vt. 1994); *Cook v. MFA Livestock Ass'n*, 700 S.W.2d 526 (Mo. Ct. App. 1985) (indefiniteness); *Carman v. Heber*, 601 P.2d 646 (Colo. Ct. App. 1979) (lack of mutuality); *Allen v. Leybourne*, 190 So. 2d 825 (Fla. Dist. Ct. App. 1966) (lack of consideration)) with cases where no liability was found (*Wedgewood Carpet Mills, Inc. v. Color-Set, Inc.*, 254 S.E.2d 421 (Ga. Ct. App. 1979) (indefiniteness and lack of mutuality); *Grimm v. Baumgart*, 97 N.E.2d 871 (Ind. Ct. App. 1951) (lack of certainty and mutuality)). *See generally* James O. Pearson, Annotation, *Liability for Interference with Invalid or Unenforceable Contract*, 96 A.L.R.3d 1294 (1979 & Supp. 2003).

1.3.1.b   Contracts Terminable at Will

A contract that has no specified term or duration is said to be terminable at will by either party. The liability of a third person for inducing a breach of contract is not affected by the fact that the contract is terminable at will. Therefore, in making your determination about the defendant's liability to the plaintiff, the fact that the contract in question may have been terminable at will by [name of breaching party] may not be a factor in your decision.

COMMENT

Although there is authority to the contrary, a number of courts have held that a defendant charged with inducing breach of contract is not shielded from liability simply because the contract breached was terminable at will by either party. *See* § 1.3.1.a, *supra. See generally* James O. Pearson, Annotation, *Liability for Interference with At Will Business Relationship,* 5 A.L.R.4th 9 (1981 & Supp. 2002).

Note: Even though the evidence that the contract in question is terminable at will may not affect liability, it may be relevant in assessing damages allegedly suffered by the plaintiff. *See Restatement (Second) of Torts* § 766 cmt. g (1979). It also is relevant when determining the applicability of competition as justification for interference. *See* § 1.4.5, *infra.*

1.3.2   Requirement of Knowledge

To find for the plaintiff, you must also find that the defendant knew of the existence of the contract between the plaintiff and [name of breaching party]. The requirement of knowledge may be found to exist if, from the facts and circumstances of which defendant had knowledge, the defendant should have known of the existence of the contractual relationship between the plaintiff and [name of breaching party]. This is sometimes referred to as "constructive knowledge."

COMMENT

This charge represents the generally accepted definition of the extent of knowledge required to meet the burden of proof for this tort. *See Restatement (Second) of Torts* § 766 cmt. i (1979); 64 P.O.F. 3d 273 *Tortious Interference with Real Estate Contract* § 8 (2001 & Supp. 2002); 45 Am. Jur. 2d *Interference* § 9 (1999 & Supp. 2003); Keeton, *supra* at 982; *Moloney v. Centner*, 727 F. Supp. 1232 (N.D. Ill. 1989); *Hanley v. Cont'l Airlines, Inc.*, 687 F. Supp. 533 (D. Colo. 1988); *Kennedy v. William R. Hudson, Inc.*, 659 F. Supp. 900 (D. Colo. 1987); *Yiakas v. Savoy*, 526 N.E.2d 1305 (Mass. App. Ct.), *review denied*, 529 N.E.2d 1346 (Mass. 1988); *DiBasio v. Brown & Sharpe Mfg. Co.*, 525 A.2d 489 (R.I. 1987).

Courts have held that if a party knows the facts that give rise to the plaintiff's contractual rights against another, a party has sufficient knowledge for liability, even though a party is mistaken about the legal significance of the facts or the contract means something other than what it is judicially held to mean. *See* 45 Am. Jur. 2d *Interference* § 9 (1999 & Supp. 2003); *Piedmont Cotton Mills, Inc. v. H. W. Ivey Constr. Co.*, 137 S.E.2d 528 (Ga. Ct. App. 1964); *Texaco, Inc. v. Penzoil Co.*, 729 S.W.2d 768 (Tex. App. 1987), *cert. dismissed*, 485 U.S. 994 (1988); *Calbom v. Knudtzon*, 396 P.2d 148 (Wash. 1964). If the defendant merely enters into an agreement with another knowing that the other cannot perform both the agreement and the contract with the third person, the defendant is not liable for inducing the other to commit a breach of

contract with the third person. *See Restatement (Second) of Torts* §
766 cmt. n (1979); 45 Am. Jur. 2d *Interference* § 9 (1999 & Supp.
2003); *Enercomp, Inc. v. McCorhill Publ'g, Inc.*, 873 F.2d 536 (2d
Cir. 1989); *NCC Sunday Inserts, Inc. v. World Color Press, Inc.*, 759
F. Supp. 1004 (S.D.N.Y. 1991); *Seven Star Shoe Co., Inc. v. Strictly
Goodies, Inc.*, 657 F. Supp. 917 (S.D.N.Y. 1987).

Proof of the defendant's knowledge of the contractual rights at
issue may be predicated on circumstantial evidence. *See Am. Cyanamid Co. v. Elizabeth Arden Sales Corp.*, 331 F. Supp. 597 (S.D.N.Y.
1971); *Texaco, Inc. v. Penzoil Co.*, 729 S.W.2d 768 (Tex. App. 1987),
cert. dismissed, 485 U.S. 994 (1988). In a minority of jurisdictions,
"it is enough to show that defendant had knowledge of facts,
which, if followed by reasonable inquiry, would have led to a
complete disclosure of the contractural relations and rights of
the parties." *See, e.g., ACT, Inc. v. Sylvan Learning Sys., Inc.*, 296
F.3d 657 (8th Cir. 2002) (applying Iowa law); *Cont'l Research, Inc.
v. Cruttenden, Podesta & Miller*, 222 F. Supp. 190 (D. Minn. 1963)
(Applying Minnesota law, the court noted its doubt whether a
defendant's negligent failure to inquire about a contract constituted constructive knowledge.). *But see* 45 Am. Jur. 2d *Interference* § 9 (1999 & Supp. 2003).

1.3.3 Requirement of Intent

1.3.3.a Generally

The plaintiff also must prove that the defendant intended to induce [name of breaching party] to breach its contract with the plaintiff. Conduct is intentional if done deliberately, with the purpose of inducing [name of breaching party] to breach its contract with the plaintiff. If you find that the defendant's conduct was not intentional, then you must find for the defendant.

COMMENT

Courts generally have held that inducing breach of contract is an intentional tort. Therefore, there is no liability for interference unless the act or acts in question were committed with the intent to interfere. *See* Keeton, *supra* at 982; 45 Am. Jur. 2d *Interference* § 8 (1999 & Supp. 2003). For cases discussing the general rule, see *Misany v. United States*, 873 F.2d 160 (7th Cir. 1989); *NCC Sunday Inserts, Inc. v. World Color Press, Inc.*, 759 F. Supp. 1004 (S.D.N.Y. 1991); *1301 Connecticut Ave. Assocs.*, 126 B.R. 823 (Bankr. D.D.C. 1991); *Funk v. Sara Lee Corp.*, 699 F. Supp. 1365 (E.D. Wis. 1988); *Liston v. Home Ins. Co.*, 659 F. Supp. 276 (S.D. Miss. 1986).

Generally, negligent interference with an existing contract is not actionable as a tort. *See Restatement (Second) of Torts* § 766C (1979). There is limited authority, however, recognizing liability for negligent interference with contract rights when the resultant damage is physical harm rather than pure economic harm. *See* Keeton, *supra* at 997; *Restatement (Second) of Torts* § 766C (1979); *Getty Ref. & Mktg. Co. v. MT Fadi B*, 766 F.2d 829 (3d Cir. 1985).

1.3.3.b   Intent Defined

Intent is defined by the law as that purpose or aim or state of mind with which a person acts or fails to act. Ordinarily, it is reasonable to infer that a person intends the natural and probable consequences of his or her acts.

COMMENT

The term "intent" is used throughout the *Restatement (Second) of Torts* to denote that the actor desires to cause the consequences of the actor's acts, or that the actor believes the consequences are substantially certain to result from the acts. *Restatement (Second) of Torts* § 8A (1965). This charge reflects the established definition of intent. *See, e.g., City Nat'l Bank of Fort Smith v. Unique Structures, Inc.,* 929 F.2d 1308 (8th Cir. 1991); *Liston v. Home Ins. Co.,* 659 F. Supp. 276 (S.D. Miss. 1986).

1.3.3.c Proof of Intent

Intent may be proved by indirect or circumstantial evidence. Although witnesses may see and hear, and may be able to give direct evidence of what a person does or fails to do, they do not likewise see and hear what a person intends to do or intends to refrain from doing.

Thus, in making your determination about whether the defendant's actions were intentional, you may look at the defendant's objective conduct and, in the absence of contrary evidence, draw an inference that the defendant, by defendant's conduct, intended the natural and probable consequences of defendant's act.

COMMENT

Cf. Piedmont Cotton Mills, Inc. v. H. W. Ivey Constr. Co., 137 S.E.2d 528 (Ga. Ct. App. 1964). *See generally* M.C. Dransfield, Annotation, *Liability for Procuring Breach of Contract*, 26 A.L.R.2d 1227 § 4 (1952 & Supp. 2003).

1.3.3.d   Requirement of "Malice" [Optional]

To find for the plaintiff, you must find that the defendant acted with malice. Malice, as used in this sense, refers to the intentional doing of a harmful act, without justification or excuse—that is, the willful violation of a known right. It is not necessary for the plaintiff to prove malice in the popular sense of hatred, ill will, or spite.

COMMENT

In jurisdictions that require that "malice" be shown, this charge may be used. It is superfluous in jurisdictions where intent need only be proved as defined in Section 1.3.3.6. This charge includes the traditional distinctions between actual malice and legal malice. *See Restatement (Second) of Torts* § 766 cmts. r, s (1979); 45 Am. Jur. 2d *Interference* § 7 (1999 & Supp. 2003); *see, e.g., Labus v. Navistar Int'l Transp. Corp.*, 740 F. Supp. 1053 (D.N.J. 1990); *Sweeney v. Athens Reg'l Med. Ctr.*, 709 F. Supp. 1563 (M.D. Ga. 1989); *Roy v. Woonsocket Inst. for Sav.*, 525 A.2d 915 (R.I. 1987); *Dussouy v. Gulf Coast Inv. Corp.*, 660 F.2d 594 (5th Cir. 1981) (applying Louisiania law); *Shea v. Emmanuel College*, 425 Mass. 761, 682 N.E.2d 1348 (1997) ("Actual malice is any 'spiteful, malignant purpose, unrelated to the legitimate corporate interest'.").

Due to the confusion engendered by the use of the word "malice," Keeton suggests avoiding the use of this term. *See* Keeton, *supra* at 983-84. The proposed jury instructions can be simplified by replacing this section with the definition of legal malice included in the definition of intent.

Although only legal malice need be established to prove the necessary intent, actual malice in the sense of spite, hostility, or ill will is relevant in all jurisdictions in two senses: (1) proof of legal malice may be made by proof of actual malice; and (2) actual malice must generally be proved to obtain an award of punitive damages. *See* 45 Am. Jur. 2d *Interference* § 62 (1999 & Supp. 1999); *see also* § 1.6.3, *infra*.

Note that it is important to distinguish the concept of actual malice as defined above (spite, hostility, or ill will) from the constitutional doctrine of "actual malice" developed by the United States Supreme Court in *New York Times Co. v. Sullivan*, 376 U.S. 254 (1964), and later defamation cases.

1.3.3.e   Summary of Requirement of Intent

In determining whether the defendant intentionally interfered with the contract between the plaintiff and [name of breaching party], you may look at the defendant's conduct. In the absence of evidence to the contrary, you may infer from the defendant's conduct, or lack of conduct, that the defendant intended those natural and probable consequences that one standing in like circumstances and possessing like knowledge should expect. If you thereby find that the defendant's conduct was in willful violation of a known right of the plaintiff, then the requisite intent was present.

COMMENT

This charge is recommended to collect and reinforce for the jury the various elements of the requirement that intent be proved as an element of the tort.

1.3.3.f   Unlawful Acts [Optional]

Should you find that the defendant's conduct in interfering with the plaintiff's contractual relationship with [name of breaching party] was itself unlawful, you may find the necessary intent, without anything more.

COMMENT

In appropriate cases when the conduct complained of may have been unlawful, counsel may include this charge, which incorporates the traditional view that a person must be presumed to intend the consequences of his or her unlawful conduct. Therefore, if the defendant interferes with the plaintiff's contract by violence, threats and intimidation, defamation, misrepresentation, unfair competition, bribery, or some other independently tortious means, the requisite intent and improper conduct are established. *See* Keeton, *supra* at 992, 45 Am. Jur. 2d *Interference* § 8 (1999 & Supp. 2003); *H.J., Inc. v. Int'l Tel. & Tel. Corp.*, 867 F.2d 1531 (8th Cir. 1989); *Seven Stars Shoe Co., Inc. v. Strictly Goodies, Inc.*, 657 F. Supp. 917 (S.D.N.Y. 1987); *Nazeri v. Mo. Valley Coll.*, 860 S.W.2d 303 (Mo. 1993); *Wells Fargo Bank v. Ariz. Laborers*, 38 P.3d 12 (Ariz. 2002)(violation of statute constitutes improper interference).

1.3.4 Requirement That the Breach Be Proximately Caused by the Defendant's Conduct

1.3.4.a Breach Defined

Breach of contract means the failure of a party to a contract, in the absence of legal excuse or impossibility of performance, to perform any promise that forms the whole or part of the contract. A breach may occur with regard to either an express or implied provision of the contract. An express provision is one that is specifically agreed to by the parties either orally or in writing. An implied provision is one that is recognized by the parties to exist and bind them in their actions despite the fact that it was not specifically spelled out or agreed to by the parties to the contract. An implied provision often arises out of terms that were expressly set forth in the contract and agreed to by the parties, and an implied promise constitutes a valid part of the contract.

COMMENT

This charge is based upon the traditional definition of breach of contract. General contract law, including an analysis of what constitutes breach of contract and the related concepts of materiality and substantial performance, is beyond the scope of these instructions. These definitions are included only because a requisite element of this tort is some form of breach of, or interference with, a contract. State law must be reviewed for peculiarities on this basic instruction.

For a detailed analysis of conduct that constitutes breach of contract, counsel should consult one of the standard texts or treatises in the area of contract law. *E.g.,* John D. Calamari & Joseph M. Perillo, *Law of Contracts* (3d ed. 1987); E. Allan Farnsworth, *Contracts* (1982).

1.3.4.b Breach Required

For the plaintiff to prevail on its claim against the defendant, you must find that the contract in question has been breached. This means you must find that [name of breaching party] failed to perform as agreed under the contract, either by virtue of the express provisions of the contract or as may be implied from the express provisions, in accordance with the definitions of express and implied contractual provisions for which I have already instructed you.

COMMENT

For the definitions of breach, express provision, and implied provision, see § 1.3.4.a and the comment thereto, *supra*. It is axiomatic that breach is a requisite element of the tort of inducing breach of contract. *See, e.g., Int'l Union, United Mine Workers of Am. v. Covenant Coal Group*, 759 F. Supp. 1204 (W.D. Va. 1991); *Price v. Sorrell*, 784 P.2d 614 (Wyo. 1989). For a discussion of the requirement that the contract in question be valid (which this instruction implicitly assumes), see § 1.3.1.a and comment thereto.

Restatement (Second) of Torts § 766 (1979) requires non-performance or a breach of the contract for liability to attach. On the other hand, *Restatement (Second) of Torts* § 766A (1979) does not require a breach or non-performance, but only that performance became more expensive and burdensome. Courts have been reluctant to adopt Section 766A because the element of proof for the dimunition in performance is too speculative and subject to abuse to provide a meaningful basis for a cause of action. *See CMI, Inc. v. Intoximeters, Inc.*, 918 F. Supp. 1068 (W.D. Ky. 1995); *Windsor Sec., Inc. v. Hartford Life Ins. Co.*, 986 F.2d 655 (3d Cir. 1993); Price v. Sorrell, 784 P.2d 614 (Wyo. 1989); *see generally* J. Hennessey, 10 *Business Tort Journal* 1 (Fall 2002).

1.3.4.c   Causal Relationship: Generally

You, the jury, must determine whether the defendant was responsible for the refusal of [name of breaching party] to perform the contract with the plaintiff. This means that, before you can decide in favor of the plaintiff, you must find, by a preponderance of the evidence, that, but for the actions of the defendant, the contract that was not performed would have otherwise been performed.

COMMENT

This general causation charge, containing the traditional "but for" test, finds wide support among the courts. *See, e.g., Sharma v. Skaarup Ship Management Corp.,* 916 F.2d 820 (2d Cir. 1990), *cert. denied,* 111 S. Ct. 1109 (1991); *Fitzpatrick v. Catholic Bishop of Chicago,* 916 F.2d 1254 (7th Cir. 1990); *Caudill v. Farmland Indus., Inc.,* 919 F.2d 83 (8th Cir. 1990); *Tomson v. Stephan,* 696 F. Supp. 1407 (D. Kan. 1988); *Merrill Lynch Futures, Inc. v. Miller,* 686 F. Supp. 1033 (S.D.N.Y. 1988); *Neterer v. Slabaugh,* 548 N.E.2d 832 (Ind. Ct. App. 1990). *See also* Keeton, *supra* at 989; 45 Am. Jur. 2d *Interference* § 10 (1999 & Supp. 2003) ("it must be shown that by reason of defendant's act, a contract which would otherwise have been performed was abandoned").

1.3.4.d   Proximate Cause

If you find that the plaintiff did suffer the losses claimed, you must then determine whether the defendant's conduct was the proximate cause of the plaintiff's loss or damage.

In this regard, the defendant's conduct will be considered to be the proximate cause of the plaintiff's loss or damage if you find that it was a substantial factor in causing that loss or damage. It need not be the *only* cause. The conduct will be a substantial factor in causing the loss or damage if it had such an effect in producing the loss that reasonable men and women would regard it as a cause of the loss or damage, considering a number of other contributing factors, such as whether defendant's conduct created a condition or chain of events that was continuous and active up to the time of the damage to the plaintiff, and the lapse of time between the defendant's conduct and the damage to the plaintiff.

COMMENT

This charge is based upon *Acme Cigarette Serv., Inc. v. Gallegos*, 577 P.2d 885 (N.M. Ct. App. 1978), and reflects the traditional definition of proximate cause. *See Restatement (Second) of Torts* § 433 (1977). The requirement of causal effect may be stated in somewhat different terms depending upon the jurisdiction. *See generally* Keeton, *supra* at 989.

Although there is some overlap between this instruction and the charge set forth in section 1.3.4.c, instructing the jury with both charges should not lead to confusion or inconsistent verdicts. The first charge is designed to inform the jury that the plaintiff has the burden of proving that, except for the defendant's actions, the plaintiff more likely than not would have received the benefits of its contract with the third party. Instructing the jury with this charge will make it clear to the jury that the defendant's conduct must have been more than merely a contributing cause, it must be a *substantial* factor in inducing the breach. If the latter instruction is not accepted in a certain jurisdiction, the charge set forth in Section 1.3.4.c may be given alone with no adverse impact.

Note that in *Eltolad Music, Inc. v. April Music, Inc.*, 188 Cal. Rptr. 858 (Cal. Ct. App. 1983), the Court of Appeals of California granted the defendant-appellant a new trial based upon the trial court's instruction to the jury that proximate cause constituted "a" moving cause of the breach. The California court held that the correct instruction, as requested by the defendant, was that proximate cause is "the" moving cause of the breach. Such an interpretation, apparently, is not the majority view. *See Fitzpatrick v. Catholic Bishop of Chicago*, 916 F.2d 1254 (7th Cir. 1990).

1.3.4.e Nonliability of Contractual Parties

Even if you find that the plaintiff's contract was breached and that, but for the defendant's conduct, the contract would otherwise have been performed, the plaintiff cannot prevail on the claim against the defendant if the defendant was a party to the contract with the plaintiff because the defendant may not be held liable to the plaintiff for inducing defendant's own breach of contract.

COMMENT

As a general rule, no action for inducing breach of contract may lie against another party to the contract at issue. *See* 45 Am. Jur. 2d *Interference* § (1999 & Supp. 2003); *see, e.g., Farmland Indus., Inc. v. Grain Bd. of Iraq*, 904 F.2d 732 (D.C. Cir. 1990); *Dow Chem. Corp. v. Weevil-Cide Corp., Inc.*, 897 F.2d 481 (10th Cir. 1990); *Knight v. Sharif*, 875 F.2d 516 (5th Cir. 1989); *Northwest Acceptance Corp. v. Lynnwood Equip., Inc.*, 841 F.2d 918 (9th Cir. 1988); *Michelson v. Exxon Research & Eng'g Co.*, 808 F.2d 1005 (3d Cir. 1987); *Powell v. Feroleto Steel Co., Inc.*, 659 F. Supp. 303 (D. Conn. 1986); *Applied Equip. Corp. v. Litton Saudi Arabia Ltd.*, 869 P.2d 454 (Cal. 1994); *Howard v. Youngman*, 81 S.W.3d 101 (Mo. Ct. App. 2002).

1.3.4.f Nonliability of Corporate Officers, Directors, and Employees

If you find that the defendant was a[n] [officer, director, employee—choose one] of a corporation at the time of the conduct at issue here, and was acting within the scope of defendant's official capacity when doing the acts complained of, then defendant is not *personally* liable to the plaintiff. This is so even though the defendant's conduct may have induced the breach of contract and the corporation itself may be liable to the plaintiff for the defendant's conduct.

COMMENT

A corporation, albeit a separate and distinct legal entity, can transact business only through its officers, directors, and employees. In many cases, a plaintiff asserting a cause of action for inducing breach of contract will name as defendants the corporate entity *and* various officers, directors, and/or employees. This charge is based on such a scenario and reflects the general rule that such individual defendants are not liable to the aggrieved party. *See, e.g., Piekarski v. Home Owners Sav. Bank, F.S.B.*, 759 F. Supp 542 (D. Minn. 1991); *Litchie v. U.S. Home Corp.*, 655 F. Supp. 1026 (D. Utah 1987); *Energy Constr. v. Georgia Metal Sys. & Eng'g*, 367 S.E.2d 324 (Ga. Ct. App. 1988); *Feaheny v. Caldwell*, 437 N.W.2d 358 (Mich. Ct. App. 1989). *See generally* Thomas G. Fischer, Annotation, *Liability of Corporate Director, Officer, or Employee for Tortious Interference with Corporation's Contract with Another*, 72 A.L.R.4th 492 (1989 & Supp. 2002); 45 Am. Jur. 2d *Interference* § 54 (1999 & Supp. 2003).

Notwithstanding the general rule, personal liability can be imposed for a myriad of reasons. For example, if the actions complained of are detrimental to the corporation and outside the scope of the agent's authority, there is no shield of immunity. *See, e.g., Presto v. Sequoia Sys., Inc.*, 633 F. Supp. 1117 (D. Mass. 1986). Likewise, if the conduct of the individual defendant is otherwise improper or unjustified (that is, based upon personal malice or ill will toward the plaintiff), liability also may be imposed. *See Stafford v. Puro*, 63 F.3d 1436 (7th Cir. 1995); *Grosvenor Properties Ltd. v. Southmark Corp.*, 896 F.2d 1149 (9th Cir. 1990); *Stanford v. Kraft Foods, Inc.*, 88 F. Supp. 2d 854 (N.D. Ill. 1999); *Traum v. Equitable Life Assur. Soc'y of the United States*, 240 F. Supp. 2d 776 (N.D. Ill. 2002); *Piekarski v. Home Owners Sav. Bank, F.S.B.*, 759 F. Supp. 542 (D. Minn. 1991); *Citylink Group, Ltd. v. Hyatt Corp.*, 729 N.E.2d 869 (Ill. App. 1st Dist. 2000). Similarly, a parent corporation acting contrary to its wholly owned subsidiary's economic interests can be considered a third party to its subsidiary's contractual relationship and can be held liable for tortiously interfering with that relationship. *See, e.g., Waste Conversion Sys., Inc. v. Greenstone Indus., Inc.*, 33 S.W.3d 779 (Tenn. 2000).

1.3.4.g   Joint and Several Liability

Should you find by a preponderance of the evidence that one or more persons other than the defendant [name of the defendant] also induced [name of breaching party] to breach the contract with the plaintiff, that finding will in no way change your finding as to [name of the defendant]. Under the law of this jurisdiction, each person is liable separately, and all persons who are found to have induced a breach of a contract are liable collectively.

COMMENT

As is the case throughout the law of torts, the general rule is that all persons who unite to induce a breach of contract are jointly and severally liable for the damages inflicted upon the party injured thereby. *See* M.C. Dransfield, Annotation, *Liability for Procuring Breach of Contract*, 26 A.L.R.2d 1227 § 42 (1952 & Supp. 2003); 45 Am. Jur. 2d *Interference* § 54 (1999 & Supp. 2003); *see also Wilson & Co. v. United Packinghouse Workers of Am.*, 181 F. Supp. 809 (N.D. Iowa 1960); *Hornstein v. Podwitz*, 173 N.E. 674 (N.Y. 1930); *Crowe v. Domestic Loans, Inc.*, 130 S.E.2d 845 (S.C. 1963); *Lien v. Northwestern Eng'g Co.*, 39 N.W.2d 483 (S.D. 1949).

1.4   Proper or Improper Interference

1.4.1   Burden of Proof

As is the case with the tort of interference with prospective advantage, courts are divided about whether the plaintiff must prove, as an element of the tort, that the defendant's conduct or motive was improper, or whether the burden is upon the defendant to demonstrate that the conduct was privileged and/or justified (that is, an affirmative defense). *See* § 2.9.1, *infra*. Some courts, although including absence of justification or the like as an element of the tort, nevertheless hold that justification is an affirmative defense to be pleaded and proved by the defendant. Practically speaking, "improper conduct" and "justification" are opposite sides of the same coin. In *Gross v. Lowder Realty Better Homes & Gardens*, 494 So. 2d 590, 597 n.3 (Ala. 1986), the Supreme Court of Alabama explained as follows:

> The Restatement utilizes the term "improper" to describe actionable conduct by a defendant. Non-justification is synonymous with "improper." If a defendant's interference is unjustified under the circumstances of the case, it is improper. The converse is also true.

A related issue concerns the burden of proof in a case involving a cause of action for inducing breach of contract. Depending upon the jurisdiction, different instructions are in order concerning the plaintiff's burden of proving improper motive or the defendant's burden of proving justification. *See HPI Health Care v. Mt. Vernon Hosp.*, 545 N.E.2d 679 (Ill. 1989); *see also* § 2.1 and comment thereto, *infra*. The *Restatement (Second) of Torts* does not take a position on the burden-of-proof issue. *See Restatement (Second) of Torts* ch. 37, Introductory Note (1979). By combining the charges on specific conduct set forth in Sections 1.4.2 through 1.4.8 with the burden-of-proof instructions set forth below as Options A and B, the model instructions can conceivably fit the law of any jurisdiction.

- *Option A: Plaintiff's Burden to Show Defendant's Conduct Improper*
  For the plaintiff to prevail on the claim against the defendant, you must find, by a preponderance of the evidence, that the plaintiff has demonstrated that the defendant's conduct was improper. The law recognizes that certain kinds of conduct under certain circumstances are *not* improper. The following instructions are intended to guide you in deciding whether the plaintiff has satisfied its burden to show that the defendant's conduct was improper.

- *Option B: Defendant's Burden to Show Conduct Proper*
  If you find that the plaintiff has met its burden of proof with respect to all of the elements of the tort of inducing breach of contract as to which I have previously instructed you, you must find for the plaintiff and against the defendant, unless you find that the defendant's conduct with respect to the contract in question was proper. The defendant must demonstrate, by a preponderance of the evidence, that the conduct in question was *not* improper.

COMMENT

The latter option takes into account the affirmative duty of the defendant to prove justification (that is, that defendant's conduct was not improper). This charge reflects that the burden of proof shifts to the defendant once the prima facie tort is demonstrated by the plaintiff. The affirmative defense of proper conduct must automatically fail, though, if the defendant's actions in inducing the breach of contract are inherently unlawful. *See* §§ 1.4.3, *supra,* and 2.9.1, *infra.*

1.4.2   Proper or Improper Interference Defined

The determination of whether the defendant's conduct was or was not improper depends upon your consideration of all the facts and circumstances of the case, and a balancing of the following factors:

1. the nature of the defendant's conduct;

2. the defendant's motive;

3. the interests of the plaintiff with which the defendant's conduct interfered;

4. the interests sought to be advanced by the defendant;

5. the social interests in protecting the freedom of action of the defendant and the contractual interests of the plaintiff;

6. the proximity or remoteness of the defendant's conduct to the interference claimed by the plaintiff; and

7. the relationship among the plaintiff, [name of breaching party], and the defendant.

COMMENT

This charge is generally based upon *Restatement (Second) of Torts* § 767 (1979). The comments to this *Restatement* section explain the significance of the various factors in depth and should be consulted by counsel. By and large, a majority of jurisdictions are approaching the issue of whether a defendant's interference is proper through an analysis of the seven specific factors set forth by the *Restatement. See, e.g., Allen & O'Hara, Inc. v. Barrett Wrecking, Inc.*, 898 F.2d 512 (7th Cir. 1990); *Q.E.R., Inc. v. Hickerson*, 880 F.2d 1178 (10th Cir. 1989); *Redies v. Nationwide Mut. Ins. Co.*, 711 F. Supp. 570 (D. Colo. 1989); *Reazin v. Blue Cross & Blue Shield of Kan.*, 663 F. Supp. 1360 (D. Kan 1987), *aff'd in part and remanded in part*, 899 F.2d 951 (10th Cir.), *cert. denied*, 110 S. Ct. 3241 (1990).

The lack of improper interference on the part of the defendant—that is, justification for the defendant's conduct (§ 1.4.1)—is by far the most popular defense advanced by defendants in actions for inducing breach of contract. *See* 45 Am. Jur. 2d *Interference* § 24 (1999 & Supp. 2003) (and cases cited therein).

Regarding the means employed by the defendant in inducing the breach of contract, see § 1.3. Regarding the defendant's motive in inducing the breach, see § 1.4.4. Although improper interference is a question of fact for the jury to determine in accordance with the several factors set forth in this instruction, the existence and exercise of a superior or an absolute right on the part of the defendant is a question of law for the court. For a discussion on the distinction between absolute and ordinary rights, see § 1.4.4 and the corresponding comment and note.

1.4.3 Unlawful Means Employed

Should you find that the means employed by the defendant to induce the breach of contract between the plaintiff and [name of breaching party] were unlawful in and of themselves, then you must find that the defendant's conduct was improper, regardless of any justification that the defendant may claim.

COMMENT

The tort of inducing breach of contract, as well as that of interference with prospective economic advantage, has been consistently applied when the means employed by the defendant are independently unlawful. *See Restatement (Second) of Torts* § 767 cmt. c (1979); Perlman, *supra* at 69-78. Stated another way, inducement based upon unlawful means on the part of the defendant destroys any claim of justification. *See* § 1.4.2, *infra*. Examples of such unlawful means are libel, slander, physical violence or threats, intentional infliction of emotional distress, wrongful discharge, and constitutional violations. *See, e.g., Pony Express Cab & Bus, Inc. v. Ward,* 841 F.2d 207 (8th Cir. 1988); *Deem v. Lockheed Corp.,* 749 F. Supp. 1230 (S.D.N.Y. 1989); *Duggin v. Adams,* 360 S.E.2d 832 (Va. 1987); *Hensen v. Truman Med. Ctr., Inc.,* 62 S.W.3d 549 (Mo. Ct. App. 2001); *Albert v. Loksen,* 239 F.3d 256 (2d Cir. 2001); *Warner v. Buck Creek Nursery, Inc.,* 149 F. Supp. 2d 246 (W.D. Va. 2001); *Lockheed Martin Corp. v. Aatlas Commerce Inc.,* 725 N.Y.S.2d 722 (N.Y. App. Div. 2001); *Garrett v. Langley Fed. Credit Union,* 121 F. Supp. 2d 887 (E.D. Va. 2000); *see generally* Keeton, *supra* at 982, 992-93. The variations and nuances on this subject, however, are numerous, and counsel must carefully check the law of the forum jurisdiction to tailor this charge appropriately to the case at bar.

1.4.4 Defendant's Motive

Should you find that the defendant acted *solely* to injure the plaintiff (that is, purely out of a sense of spite and a desire to harm the plaintiff for its own sake, and not to further any legitimate interest of defendant's own that falls within the instructions I will give you later), then you must find that the defendant's conduct was improper, regardless of any justification the defendant may claim. *Some* ill will on the part of the defendant is permissible, *providing* the defendant acted in substantial part with a proper purpose in mind.

COMMENT

This instruction is recommended, in appropriate jurisdictions (*see* § 1.4.1, *infra*), to forewarn the jury of the shift of the burden of proof when the defense to be considered is the affirmative defense of justification rather than that consisting solely of denials of matters constituting the plaintiff's case in chief. *See* James O. Pearson, Annotation, *Liability for Interference with At Will Business Relationship*, 5 A.L.R.4th 9 (1981 & Supp. 2002); Keeton, *supra* at 984; § 1.5.2, *infra*.

Note that motive is irrelevant when the defendant is exercising an absolute right. In such a case, the instruction regarding the defendant's motive would not be given. *See, e.g., Caven v. Am. Fed. Sav. & Loan Ass'n*, 837 F.2d 427 (10th Cir. 1988); *Mac Enter., Inc. v. Del E. Webb Dev. Co.*, 645 P.2d 1245 (Ariz. Ct. App. 1982); *Langeland v. Farmers State Bank of Trimont*, 319 N.W.2d 26 (Minn. 1982). The existence of an absolute right is a question of law for the court to decide. *See* M.C. Dransfield, Annotation, *Liability for Procuring Breach of Contract*, 26 A.L.R.2d 1227 § 23 (1952 & Supp. 2003); 45 Am. Jur. 2d *Interference* § 25 (1999 & Supp. 2003).

Note further that absolute rights are to be contrasted with common law and qualified rights. Absolute rights include rights incident to the ownership of property and rights growing out of contractual relationships. *See* 45 Am. Jur. 2d *Interference* § 24 (1999 & Supp. 2003). Such absolute rights may be exercised by the defendant without liability for interference and without reference to the defendant's motive, whereas the defendant's motive *does* play a role in the exercise of ordinary rights. *See id.*

Also note that preliminary Draft No. 1 of *Restatement (Third) of Unfair Competition* would change the present law to provide that if defendant was, in fact, competing with plaintiff, the defendant's motives are irrelevant to the issue of liability.

1.4.5   Self-Interest as Proper or Improper Interference

Should you find that the defendant acted lawfully and to protect a present, existing economic interest of its own, then you may find that defendant's conduct in inducing the breach of contract between the plaintiff and [name of breaching party] was not improper. Examples of such present economic interests include property interests, contract rights, and financial interests in the affairs of the person induced. Should you find, however, that the defendant acted improperly in pursuit of defendant's own prospective advantage, not yet realized, then you cannot find that defendant's interference was proper.

The fact that the defendant acted only in the pursuit of generalized competition, even if defendant acted solely by lawful means and without an improper purpose, is not alone sufficient to justify conduct which induced a breach of the plaintiff's contract, when the defendant had no present economic rights of defendant's own to protect.

COMMENT

Regarding the interests of the defendant, see *Restatement (Second) of Torts* § 767, cmts. d, f (1979); 45 Am. Jur. 2d *Interference,* § 28 (1999 & Supp. 2003). Keeton states that "[t]he defendant is . . . permitted to interfere with another's contractual relations to protect his own present existing economic interests, such as the ownership or condition of property, or a prior contract of his own, or a financial interest in the affairs of the person persuaded. He is not free, under this rule, to induce a contract breach merely to obtain customers or other prospective economic advantage; but he may do so to protect what he perceives to be existing interests. . . . But where the defendant's interest is merely one of prospective economic advantage, not yet realized, he has no such justification." Keeton, *supra* at 986-87. Thus, Keeton draws a clear distinction between prospective and current interests, and only interference based upon the latter may be considered proper.

Regarding financial interests in the affairs of others, the *Restatement (Second) of Torts,* section 769 and comment (b) thereto, provide that a defendant having a financial interest in the business of the person induced to breach defendant's contract with another is automatically shielded from liability, provided that the defendant does not employ wrongful means and acts to protect defendant's own interests. This automatic immunity, though, applies only to the tort of interference with prospective economic advantage, and *not* to inducing breach of contract. Rather, the general provisions of section 767 of the *Restatement (Second) of Torts* apply in such cases when determining whether the defendant's interference is improper. *See* § 1.4.2, *supra.*

Turning to competition, under the approach adopted by the drafters of the *Restatement,* competition (in the absence of unlawful means or acts) fully immunizes a defendant from liability for interference with prospective economic advantage. The same immunity applies when defendant, a competitor, causes the termination of a third party's contract with plaintiff when the contract in question is terminable at will. *See, e.g., Reazin v. Blue Cross & Blue Shield of Kan., Inc.,* 663 F. Supp. 1360 (D. Kan. 1987), *aff'd in part and remanded in part,* 899 F.2d 951 (10th Cir.), *cert. denied,* 497 U.S. 1005 (1990). When the contract is terminable at will, a defendant is entitled to a jury instruction to the effect that competition justifies the interference, as long as the means and acts of the defendant in bringing about the termination are not improper in and of themselves. *See id.*

The *Restatement,* however, is somewhat ambiguous about whether the privilege of competition extends to interference with existing enforceable contractual relations. Some statements in the *Restatement* indicate that any attempt to interfere with an existing contract for competitive reasons would be tortious. *See Restatement (Second) of Torts* § 767 cmts. e, f. Other statements, however, would seem to permit the following argument: Although competition might not be recognized as a justification, it might be an affirmative defense because only "improper" interference with a contract is tortious under the *Restatement. Cf. Restatement (Second) of Torts* § 768 cmt. h (competition not necessarily improper). For a competitor to send its regular advertising or to solicit business with the knowledge that the potential customer is under contract to a competitor might not necessarily constitute an improper inducement of breach. *See Restatement (Second) of Torts* § 766 cmts. m, n; § 768 cmt. a.

Traditionally, courts have held that the mere offer of better terms to a potential customer constitutes liable conduct for interference with a contract without any further showing as to impropriety. Keeton, *supra* at 987; 45 Am. Jur. 2d *Interference* § 29 (1999 & Supp. 2003) (and cases cited therein). Nevertheless, the *Restatement* itself restricts liability to inducements involving improper means. Therefore, fair and legal competition should not support liability for tortious interference with contractual relations. There is some authority for the latter position. *See, e.g., Ocean State Physicians Health Plan v. Blue Cross,* 883 F.2d 1101 (1st Cir. 1989), *cert. denied,* 494 U.S. 1027 (1990); *Reazin v. Blue Cross & Blue Shield of Kan.,* 663 F. Supp. 1360 (D. Kan. 1987), *aff'd in part and remanded in part,* 899 F.2d 951 (10th Cir.), *cert. denied,* 497 U.S. 1005 (1990); *Pino v. Prudential Ins. Co. of Am.,* 689 F. Supp. 1358 (E.D. Pa. 1988); *E.D. Lacey Mills, Inc. v. Keith,* 359 S.E.2d 148 (Ga. Ct. App. 1987). Even if competition is not considered justification for breaching an existing contract, the defendant may still prevail if defendant is able to justify defendant's conduct based upon the various factors set forth in the *Restatement. See Restatement (Second) of Torts* § 768 (1979).

1.4.6   Defendant Responsible for Welfare of Another

The defendant's conduct was not improper if you find that the defendant was charged with responsibility for the welfare of [name of breaching party] and that the defendant used reasonable means in a good faith attempt to protect the welfare of [name of breaching party].

COMMENT

This charge is based on section 770 of the *Restatement (Second) of Torts. See* 45 Am. Jur. 2d *Interference* § 31 (1999 & Supp. 2003); *Reazin v. Blue Cross & Blue Shield of Kan.,* 663 F. Supp. 1360 (D. Kan. 1987), *aff'd in part and remanded in part,* 899 F.2d 951 (10th Cir.), *cert. denied,* 497 U.S. 1005 (1990); *Calbom v. Knudtzon,* 396 P.2d 148 (Wash. 1964).

The existence of a confidential relationship between the defendant and the nonplaintiff contracting party is often the key to establishing the propriety of the defendant's conduct. *See Los Angeles Airways, Inc. v. Davis,* 687 F.2d 321 (9th Cir. 1982); *Hopper v. Lennen & Mitchell,* 52 F. Supp. 319 (S.D. Cal. 1943), *aff'd in part and rev'd in part on other grounds,* 146 F.2d 364 (9th Cir. 1944); *Aalgaard v. Merchants Nat'l Bank, Inc.,* 274 Cal. Rptr. 81 (Cal. Ct. App. 1990).

1.4.7 Advice as Proper or Improper Interference

The defendant's conduct was not improper if you find that the defendant provided truthful information to [name of breaching party] or provided honest advice to [name of breaching party] within the scope of a request for the advice.

COMMENT

This charge is based on section 772 of the *Restatement (Second) of Torts. See* 45 Am. Jur. 2d *Interference* § 32 (1999 & Supp. 2003); *Air Shells, Inc. v. Harrington,* 697 F. Supp. 896 (W.D. Pa. 1988); *C.N.C. Chem. Corp. v. Pennwalt Corp.,* 690 F. Supp. 139 (D.R.I. 1988); *C.R. Bard, Inc. v. Wordtronics Corp.,* 561 A.2d 694 (N.J. Super. Ct. Law Div. 1989); *Four Nines Gold, Inc. v. 71 Constr. Inc.,* 809 P.2d 236 (Wyo. 1991); *Prazma v. Kaehne,* 768 P.2d 586 (Wyo. 1989).

1.4.8 Protection of the Public Welfare

The defendant's conduct was not improper if you find that defendant acted in furtherance of the public welfare. To find that the defendant acted in furtherance of the public welfare, you must find that the defendant sought to further an established public policy that has a greater social value than ensuring the stability of the contract that was breached. An example of such a situation would be when the contract would have injured the public health, safety, or morals.

COMMENT

Determining whether the defendant's conduct was proper by virtue of having been undertaken in furtherance of the public welfare requires a balancing of the public interest served against the private interest violated. *See, e.g.,* 45 Am. Jur. 2d *Interference* § 27 (1999 & Supp. 2003); *Brownsville Golden Age Nursing Home, Inc. v. Wells,* 839 F.2d 155 (3d Cir. 1988); *Feminist Women's Health Ctr., Inc. v. Mohammed,* 586 F.2d 530 (5th Cir. 1978), *cert. denied,* 444 U.S. 924 (1979); *Stitzell v. York Mem'l Osteopathic Hosp.,* 754 F. Supp. 1061 (M.D. Pa. 1991); *W. Technologies v. Sverdrup & Parcel, Inc.,* 739 P.2d 1318 (Ariz. Ct. App. 1986); *Nat'l Collegiate Athletic Ass'n v. Hornung,* 754 S.W.2d 855 (Ky. 1988).

1.5   Compensatory Damages

1.5.1   Generally

Should you find that the defendant is liable for procuring or causing a breach of the plaintiff's contract, and that defendant's actions were neither justified nor privileged, then you may award such damages as will reasonably compensate the plaintiff for the actual losses plaintiff has sustained from that breach of its contract.

COMMENT

The general rule regarding damages recoverable for inducing the breach of a contract is that the broad tort principle for damages is applicable: damages are limited to compensation for the actual loss incurred. *See Restatement (Second) of Torts* § 774A (1979); 45 Am. Jur. 2d *Interference* § 58 (1999 & Supp. 2003); M.C. Dransfield, Annotation, *Liability for Procuring Breach of Contract*, 26 A.L.R.2d 1272 § 43 (1952 & Supp. 2003).

Keeton notes that courts have typically taken one of three approaches for awarding damages in interference with contractual relations cases:

1. *Contract method*: recovery is limited to damages within the contemplation of the parties when the original contract was created;

2. *Tort standard*: damages are limited to those which are "proximate" to the injury about which the complaint is made (that is, analogous to damages in negligence actions); and

3. *Intentional tort standard*: recovery is allowed for unforeseen expenses, damage to reputation, and mental suffering, in addition to punitive damages. Keeton, *supra* at 1002-03.

The *Restatement* has adopted the third standard. Section 744A provides that one can recover the pecuniary loss, consequential losses, and mental distress damages in an action for interference with a contract. *See Restatement (Second) of Torts* § 744A

(1979). Numerous courts have likewise adopted the *Restatement*'s approach. *See Lake Shore Investors v. Rite Aid Corp.,* 461 A.2d 725 (Md. Ct. Spec. App. 1983) (adopting Section 774A and citing other jurisdictions that also have done so), *aff'd,* 471 A.2d 735 (Md. 1984). For the recoverable elements of compensatory damages, see Section 1.5.3.

1.5.2   Damages: Impossibility of Precise Calculation No Bar to Recovery

If you find that the plaintiff has in fact suffered damage to its business or property, the fact that the precise amount of damage may be difficult to ascertain does not impair plaintiff's right to recover damages. Although you may not render a verdict based upon mere speculation or guesswork, the plaintiff is allowed some reasonable leeway in its method and proof of damage.

Although the law places a burden upon the plaintiff to prove such facts as will enable you, the jury, to arrive at the amount of damages with reasonable certainty, it is not necessary that the plaintiff prove the amount of those damages with mathematical precision. It is required that the plaintiff present only such evidence as might reasonably be expected to be available under the circumstances.

You are permitted to determine the amount of damage by estimation or approximation, as long as a reasonable basis for such estimate or approximation is shown with reasonable certainty. You may use any formula or theory for determining damages that is based upon the evidence in the case and that you believe to be reasonable; you are not bound to reject a formula or theory simply because it does not measure damages to the exact dollar and cent.

COMMENT

This instruction reflects the established rule that absolute precision is not required for an award of damages, even though total speculation may not be used. Estimation is permitted as long as its method is justified by the record admitted into evidence. *See Restatement (Second) of Torts* § 774A cmt. c (1979); 45 Am. Jur. 2d *Interference* § 58 (1999 & Supp. 2003); *Selby v. Pelletier,* 472 A.2d 1285 (Conn. App. Ct. 1984); *Daly v. Nau,* 339 N.E.2d 71 (Ind. Ct. App. 1975); *Steitz v. Gifford,* 19 N.E.2d 661 (N.Y. 1939). *See also Restatement (Second) of Torts* § 912 (1979).

1.5.3 Recoverable Elements of Damages

In determining the amount of compensatory damages, you may consider whether the plaintiff suffered any measurable loss of profits by reason of the defendant's conduct. You should be guided by the rule that the plaintiff is entitled to any profits that plaintiff would, with reasonable certainty, have enjoyed, were it not for the breach of plaintiff's contract. In arriving at the amount of profits lost by the plaintiff, you are entitled to consider the plaintiff's past earnings in its business and, in particular, those past earnings resulting from contracts of the nature of the contract in this case. You should also consider all of the other evidence concerning general economic and competitive conditions that you may find to have a bearing on the issue of lost profits.

In addition to lost profits, the plaintiff is entitled to recover any reasonable costs it incurred in an effort to mitigate or reduce plaintiff's damages and to recover business plaintiff lost due to the defendant's wrongful conduct. As a result, you may consider the plaintiff's expenses in determining the amount of compensatory damages.

COMMENT

Many authorities address the issue of lost profits. *See* 45 Am. Jur. 2d *Interference* §§ 58, 59 (1999 & Supp. 2003); *Marcus, Stowell & Beye Gov't Sec., Inc. v. Jefferson Inv. Corp.*, 797 F.2d 227 (5th Cir. 1986); *R.E. Davis Chem. Corp. v. Diasonics, Inc.*, 826 F.2d 678 (7th Cir. 1987); *Central Telecomms., Inc. v. TCI Cablevision, Inc.*, 800 F.2d 711 (8th Cir. 1986), *cert. denied*, 480 U.S. 910 (1987); *Upjohn Co. v. Riahom Corp.*, 650 F. Supp. 485 (D. Del. 1986); *see also* Charles S. Marvel, Annotation, *Recovery Based on Tortfeasor's Profits in Action for Procuring Breach of Contract*, 5 A.L.R.4th 1296 (1981 & Supp. 2002). Concerning recovery of costs of mitigation or recoupment, see M.C. Dransfield, Annotation, *Liability for Procuring Breach of Contract*, 26 A.L.R.2d 1227 § 43 (1952 & Supp. 2003).

Damages may be recovered in some jurisdictions for mental distress arising out of the interference of contractual relations. *See Restatement (Second) of Torts* § 774A (1979); *Westfield Dev. Co. v.*

Rifle Inv. Assocs., 786 P.2d 1112 (Colo. 1990) (mental distress may be sole element of damages); *Mooney v. Johnson Cattle, Inc.*, 634 P.2d 1333 (Or. 1981).

Although the measure of damages recoverable in an action for inducing a breach of contract varies among jurisdictions, it is generally said that the defendant should be held responsible for all of the quantifiable consequences of defendant's tortious conduct. *E.g.*, 45 Am. Jur. 2d *Interference* § 58 (1999 & Supp. 2003); *Restatement (Second) of Torts* § 774A (1979). Counsel should examine the case law in each jurisdiction to determine the extent of damages to which the plaintiff may be entitled.

1.5.4   Plaintiff's Burden of Proof

The law distinguishes between the measure of proof necessary to establish the fact that the plaintiff sustained an injury and that which is required to enable you to fix the amount of that damage. As I have instructed you, the fact of injury by reason of the alleged violation must be established by a preponderance of the evidence. This is a higher or more strict degree of proof than is required in proving the amount of damages. In proving the amount of damages, the law requires only that the plaintiff prove such facts as will enable you to arrive at the amount of damages with reasonable certainty. Moreover, the plaintiff is not required to prove the exact amount of damages, but to present only such evidence as might reasonably be expected to be available under the circumstances.

COMMENT

This instruction represents the general rule imposing a lesser burden of proof on the plaintiff concerning the amount of damage than for the fact of some damage or for establishing the defendant's liability. *See, e.g., H.L. Hayden Co. v. Siemens Med. Sys., Inc.,* 879 F.2d 1005 (2d Cir. 1989); *Franklin Music Co. v. Am. Broad. Co.,* 616 F.2d 528 (3d Cir. 1979).

1.6 Punitive Damages

1.6.1 Decision to Award Punitive Damages

If you find for the plaintiff and against the defendant and you have determined that the defendant must pay damages, then you should consider whether the conduct that led to your decision also subjects the defendant to punitive damages. To award punitive damages, you must find that the defendant's conduct that proximately caused actual [or nominal] damages to the plaintiff was the result of actual malice, wanton conduct, or oppressive conduct, as measured by the instructions I will give you.

COMMENT

This charge represents the modern view of damages. *See, e.State Farm Mut. Auto. Ins. Co. v. Campbell*, 538 U.S. 408 (2003); *Rabun v. Kimberly-Clark Corp.*, 678 F.2d 1053 (11th Cir. 1982); *Christman v. Voyer*, 595 P.2d 410 (N.M. Ct. App. 1979); *Wussow v. Commercial Mechanisms, Inc.*, 279 N.W.2d 503 (Wis. Ct. App. 1979); *Restatement (Second) of Torts* § 908 (1979); 45 Am. Jur. 2d *Interference* § 62 (1999 & Supp. 2003). The *Restatement* makes clear that under appropriate circumstances, punitive damages may be awarded for the tort of contractual interference. *Restatement (Second) of Torts* § 774A cmt. a (1979). *See generally* Sara L. Johnson, Annotation, *Punitive Damages for Interference with Contract or Business Relationship*, 44 A.L.R.4th 1078 (1986 & Supp. 2002). Counsel should note that although generally punitive damages will be awarded upon a showing of malice, wantonness, or oppressiveness, this principle is not universal and may well be affected by statute in a particular jurisdiction.

Most states require that the jury find liability and actual, or at least nominal, damages before punitive damages are allowed. *See* Richard C. Tinney, Annotation, *Showing of Actual Damages to Support Award of Punitive Damages*, 40 A.L.R.4th 11 (1985 & Supp. 2002); 45 Am. Jur. 2d *Interference* § 62 (1999 & Supp. 2003); *Am. Bus. Interiors, Inc. v. Haworth, Inc.*, 798 F.2d 1135 (8th Cir. 1986).

But see Platte v. Whitney Realty Co., 538 So. 2d 1358 (Fla. Dist. Ct. App. 1989) (punitive damages recoverable although actual damages could not be proved). For a discussion of the prerequisite of a verdict for actual damages, see the comment to Section 1.6.2. For the requirement of malicious, wanton, or oppressive conduct, see Sections 1.6.3, 1.6.4, and 1.6.5.

If the jurisdiction has a heightened standard for punitive damages, it should be given after this instruction. *See generally* Lee H. Russ, Annotation, *Standard of Proof As to Conduct Underlying Punitive Damage Awards—Modern Status,* 58 A.L.R.4th 878 (1987 & Supp. 2002).

1.6.2   Nominal Damages

The award of only a nominal sum with respect to the specific losses claimed by the plaintiff will not prevent your awarding punitive damages if you find that the award of punitive damages is justified under these instructions.

COMMENT

In most states the jury must make a finding of liability and actual, or at least nominal, damages before punitive damages are allowed. *See* Richard C. Tinney, Annotation, *Showing of Actual Damages to Support Award of Punitive Damages,* 40 A.L.R.4th 11 (1985 & Supp. 2002); 45 Am. Jur. 2d *Interference* § 62 (1999 & Supp. 2003); *Am. Bus. Interiors, Inc. v. Haworth, Inc.,* 798 F.2d 1135 (8th Cir. 1986). *But see Platte v. Whitney Realty Co.,* 538 So. 2d 1358 (Fla. Dist. Ct. App. 1989) (punitive damages recoverable although actual damages could not be proved).

In most jurisdictions, an award of nominal damages will suffice for this purpose. *See, e.g., Taylor v. Sandoval,* 442 F. Supp. 491 (D. Colo. 1977); *Tennant v. Vazquez,* 389 So. 2d 1183 (Fla. Dist. Ct. App. 1980); *Christman v. Voyer,* 595 P.2d 410 (N.M. Ct. App. 1979). *But see Wussow v. Commercial Mechanisms, Inc.,* 279 N.W.2d 503 (Wis. Ct. App. 1979). *See generally* Richard C. Tinney, Annotation, *Showing of Actual Damages to Support Award of Punitive Damages—Modern Cases,* 40 A.L.R.4th 11 (1985 & Supp. 2002).

1.6.3 Actual Malice

You may find the defendant's conduct to have been undertaken with actual "malice" sufficient to enable you to award punitive damages if you find it to have been prompted or accompanied by personal ill will, spite, or hatred, either toward the plaintiff individually or toward all persons in one or more groups or categories of which the plaintiff is a member.

COMMENT

Generally, courts require proof of facts tending to establish actual, as opposed to legal, malice to justify an award of punitive damages. *See* 45 Am. Jur. 2d *Interference* § 62 (1999 & Supp. 2003); *Norwood Easthill Assocs. v. Norwood Easthill Watch*, 536 A.2d 1317 (N.J. Super. Ct. App. Div. 1988); *Anthony Pools, Inc. v. Charles & David, Inc.*, 797 S.W.2d 666 (Tex. App. 1990); *Bellefonte Underwriters Co., Inc. v. Brown*, 663 S.W.2d 562 (Tex. App. 1984). Even if not required, actual malice is always an important factor in an award of punitive damages. *See, e.g., Universal City Studios, Inc. v. Nintendo Co.*, 615 F. Supp. 838 (S.D.N.Y. 1985), *aff'd*, 797 F.2d 70 (2d Cir.), *cert. denied*, 479 U.S. 987 (1986); *Int'l Wood Processors Corp. v. Power Dry, Inc.*, 593 F. Supp. 710 (D.S.C. 1984); *Edward Vantine Studios, Inc. v. Fraternal Composite Serv., Inc.*, 373 N.W.2d 512 (Iowa Ct. App. 1985).

1.6.4 Wanton Conduct

You may also award punitive damages if you find that the defendant's conduct was "wanton"; that is, that the conduct was undertaken in reckless or callous disregard of, or indifference to, the rights of one or more persons, including the plaintiff.

COMMENT

See King v. G.D. Van Wagenen Co., 717 F. Supp. 667 (D. Minn. 1989); *Liston v. Home Ins. Co.*, 659 F. Supp. 276 (S.D. Miss. 1986); *Universal City Studios, Inc. v. Nintendo Co.*, 615 F. Supp. 838 (S.D.N.Y. 1985), *aff'd*, 797 F.2d 70 (2d Cir.), *cert. denied*, 479 U.S. 987 (1986); *Ramona Manor Convalescent Hosp. v. Care Enterprises*, 225 Cal. Rptr. 120 (Cal. Ct. App. 1986).

1.6.5   Oppressive Conduct

You also may award punitive damages if, from all of the evidence, you find that the defendant's conduct was "oppressive"; that is, that it was done in a way or manner that injured, damaged, or otherwise violated the rights of the plaintiff with unnecessary harshness or severity, as by misuse or abuse of authority or power, or by taking advantage of some weakness, disability, or misfortune of the plaintiff.

COMMENT

See Barnes Group, Inc. v. C & C Prod., Inc., 716 F.2d 1023 (4th Cir. 1983); *Rabun v. Kimberly-Clark Corp.,* 678 F.2d 1053 (11th Cir. 1982); *Int'l Wood Processors Corp. v. Power Dry, Inc.,* 593 F. Supp. 710 (D.S.C. 1984), *aff'd,* 792 F.2d 416 (4th Cir. 1986).

1.6.6 Amount of Punitive Damages Award

If you decide that punitive damages are appropriate in this case based upon my prior instructions, you should award the amount of punitive damages that, in your sound judgment, will justly punish the defendant for its behavior and dissuade the defendant and others from acting the same way in future, similar situations.

In fixing the amount of punitive damages, you may consider the following factors:

1. the character of the defendant's act(s);

2. the nature and extent of the harm to the plaintiff that the defendant caused or intended to cause; and

3. the defendant's financial condition.

The amount of any punitive damages should bear a reasonable relationship to the injury, harm, or damage caused by the defendant. You must also keep in mind that the amount of such punitive damages, when awarded, must be fixed with calm discretion and sound reason. Punitive damages must not be awarded, or fixed in amount, based upon any sympathy, bias, or prejudice you may feel toward any party in the case.

[If evidence of "other acts" or harm against other parties has been allowed, add the following:] Some of the evidence you have heard concerned conduct by the defendant that was not the proximate cause of the damages claimed by the plaintiff in this case. Although you may consider this evidence for any bearing upon the defendant's state of mind in causing damages claimed by the plaintiff in this case, you are not to punish the defendant for conduct relating only to parties other than the plaintiff.

[If evidence of the defendant's financial condition has been allowed, add the following:] You have heard evidence of the defendant's financial condition. You are not to consider the defendant's financial condition in deciding whether to award punitive damages, but you may consider it in fixing the amount of punitive

damages to the extent that the actual [or nominal] damages are insufficient to justly punish the defendant for its behavior or dissuade the defendant or others from acting the same way in future, similar situations.

COMMENT

See State Farm Mut. Auto. Ins. Co. v. Campbell, 538 U.S. 408 (2003); *Cooper Indus., Inc. v. Leatherman Tool Group, Inc.*, 121 S. Ct. 1678 (2001); *BMW of N. Am., Inc. v. Gore*, 116 S. Ct. 1589, 1595 (1996); *Jannotta v. Subway Sandwich Shops, Inc.*, 125 F.3d 503 (7th Cir. 1997); *Fed. Deposit Ins. Corp. v. W.R. Grace & Co.*, 877 F.2d 614 (7th Cir. 1989), *cert. denied*, 110 S. Ct. 1524 (1990); *Aldrich v. Thomson McKinnon Sec., Inc.*, 756 F.2d 243 (2d Cir. 1985); Damages—Modern Cases, 40 A.L.R.4th 11 (1985 & Supp. 2002).

A state may not impose damages on a defendant for actions undertaken in other states that do not violate the other states' laws. *BMW*, 116 S. Ct. at 1597 (1996). Similarly, a "defendant's dissimilar acts, independent from the acts upon which liability was premised, may not serve as the basis for punitive damages." *State Farm*, 123 S. Ct. 1523.

A defendant's financial condition as a factor in setting punitive damages is generally accepted. *See, e.g., Miller v. Rukoff-Sexton, Inc.*, 845 F.2d 209 (9th Cir. 1988) (the defendants' net worth was admissible for setting punitive damages); *Hollins v. Powell*, 773 F.2d 191 (8th Cir.) (reducing punitive damage award in light of defendant's limited resources), *cert. denied*, 475 U.S. 1119 (1985); *Rupert v. Sellers*, 368 N.Y.S.2d 904 (N.Y. App. Div. 1975) (in bifurcated trial, evidence of the defendant's net worth should be considered after special verdict). *See generally* Annotation, *Punitive Damages: Relationship to Defendant's Wealth As a Factor in Determining Propriety of Award*, 87 A.L.R.4th 141 (1991 & Supp. 2002). Some states, such as Hawaii, even have statutes making the financial condition of the defendant relevant to the amount of punitive damages awardable. Others, like New York, protect the defendant from possible prejudice at trial through the use of a bifurcated trial procedure. *See Aldrich v. Thomson McKinnon Sec., Inc.,* 589 F. Supp. 683 (S.D.N.Y. 1984). However, the Supreme Court has cautioned that the financial condition of the defendant may not be used to create bias against big businesses or to permit an award that is unrelated to the actual damages. *State Farm,* 123 S. Ct. at 1525 ("[T]he wealth of a defendant cannot justify an otherwise unconstitutional punitive damage award."). Recent commentators have argued that the defendant's financial condition is only relevant in cases involving non-economically motivated torts. *See, e.g.,* Andrew L. Frey, *No More Blind Man's Bluff on Punitive Damages: A Plea to the Drafters of Pattern Jury Instructions,* 29 Litig. 24 (Summer 2003). In cases where the defendant was motivated by profits, they argue, compensatory damages are sufficient to act as a deterrent. *Id.*

Chapter Two
Interference with Prospective Advantage

Gary C. Crapster & Jessica C. Smith*

---

* Gary C. Crapster is a partner at Strasburger & Price, L.L.P., 901 Main Street, Suite 4300, Dallas, Texas 75202, and can be reached at (214) 651-4300, gary.crapster@strasburger.com. Jessica C. Smith is an associate at Strasburger & Price and can be reached at jessica.smith@strasburger.com.

2.1   Introduction

This chapter discusses the model jury charges for the tort of interference with another's reasonable expectations of economic advantage. This cause of action is also known as interference with prospective advantage or interference with business relations, and continues to develop. Its limitations are flexible and unclear, and accordingly this business tort may provide a remedy for a person in business who has been injured by conduct that does not fit other, more clearly defined business torts.

This chapter concentrates on jury charges for tortious interference with economic relationships that do not involve completed contracts. This chapter, together with the preceding one, discusses the torts of inducing breach of contract and interference with prospective advantage, which are generally recognized as subcategories of the broader theory of interference with advantageous economic relations. Both torts have long been recognized at common law, but the expanding law on the subject continues to be profoundly influenced by the *Restatement (Second) of Torts*, which places both torts under the broader category of interference with advantageous economic relations. After discussing the tort of interference with contractual relations in sections 766 and 766A, the *Restatement (Second)*, in section 766B, sets forth the elements of tortious interference with prospective contractual relations. The *Restatement (Second)* then discusses legal principles related to both torts in sections 767 and 774A. The torts are similar, but the plaintiff can recover more easily when there is an existing contract, rather than only the potential for a contract or relationship. This is because public policy favors protecting relationships that have legally enforceable rights. *Pac. Gas & Elec. v. Bear Stearns & Co., et al.*, 791 P.2d 587 (Cal. 1990).

One key issue involved in the tort of interference with prospective economic advantage is whether, given the particular factual situation, the defendant's interference is "improper." Unfortunately, the tests used in determining "improper" conduct are unavoidably vague because of the countless factual scenarios in which such conduct can arise. According to the *Restatement (Second)*, the "real question is whether the actor's conduct was fair and reasonable under the circumstances. Recognized standards of business ethics, business customs and practices are pertinent, and consideration is given to concepts of fair play and whether the defendant's interference is not sanctioned by the 'rules of the game.'" *Restatement (Second) of Torts* § 767(g) cmt.

The majority view protects reasonable expectations of future economic advantage—not just those evidenced by contract—from improper interference. Thus, liability may be imposed for "interfering with an existing noncontractual relationship, with relations, generally." 17 P.O.F.2d 517, 524-25 *Tortious Interference with At Will Business Relationship* (1978); 45 Am. Jur. 2d *Interference* § 49 (1969). Some examples are interference with the prospect of acquiring employment or employees; the opportunity of purchasing or selling goods or services; the opportunity for brokerage commissions, leasing opportunities or lending relationships; and practically any other commercial relationship imaginable that would probably lead to economic benefits. *See generally* Note, *Tortious Interference with Conduct of a Business,* 56 Yale L.J. 885 (1947); William L. Prosser, *The Law of Torts* § 130 (4th ed. 1971).

Most courts require the plaintiff to prove the following elements:

1. The plaintiff had a business relationship or reasonable expectancy;

2. The defendant knew or should have known of the relationship or expectancy;

3. The defendant's conduct caused the loss of the relationship or expectancy;

4. The defendant acted intentionally to either discontinue the relationship or prevent the expectancy; and

5. The defendant's conduct proximately caused the plaintiff's damages.

A notable distinction among the various jurisdictions involves the procedural treatment given by the courts to the issue of whether the defendant's conduct under the particular circumstances is the type of conduct that society should discourage. Although there is a consensus that only "improper" or "tortious" conduct should be compensable, courts in different jurisdictions disagree about the burden of proof on this issue. For example, some states allow the defense to assert affirmative defenses of justification or privilege for the conduct. On the other hand, some courts require plaintiffs to prove that the defendant's conduct was independently tortious or "improper."

Thus, the jurisdictions are split on the issue of whether the plaintiff has the burden to show that the defendant's conduct itself was improper as an additional element to those listed above, or whether the defendant must assert any possible justification or privilege as an affirmative defense. The majority of the cases that followed the original *Restatement of Torts* held that once the plaintiff showed an intentional interference, the defendant had the burden to prove any justification or privilege. The *Restatement (Second)*, however, requires as an element of the tort that the defendant intentionally *and improperly* interfere with the plaintiff's prospective advantage. Although the comments to the *Restatement (Second)* acknowledge the split of authority and do not purport to determine the burden-of-proof issue conclusively, the addition of the "improper" element in the *Restatement (Second)* has significantly affected the development of the law. Most states now place the burden on the plaintiff to prove, as an element of the cause of action, that the defendant's conduct was based upon improper motive or means.

The two sections of the *Restatement (Second)* that have heavily influenced the development of the law are sections 766B and 767:

> *Restatement (Second)*'s section 766B, *Intentional Interference with Prospective Contractual Relation*
> An interloper who intentionally and improperly interferes with another's prospective contractual relation (except a contract

to marry) is liable to the other for the economic injury suffered from the loss of the benefits of the association, whether the interference consists of:

(a) inducing or otherwise causing a third person not to enter into or continue the prospective relation or

(b) preventing the other from acquiring or continuing the prospective relation.

Restatement (Second)'s section 767, *Factors in Determining Whether Interference Is Improper*
The fact-finder will consider the following seven factors when deciding whether the defendant's conduct was "improper":

(a) the nature of the actor's conduct,

(b) the actor's motive,

(c) the interests of the other with which the actor's conduct interferes,

(d) the interests sought to be advanced by the actor,

(e) the social interests in protecting the freedom of action of the actor and the contractual interests of the other,

(f) the proximity or remoteness of the actor's conduct to the interference, and

(g) the relations between the parties.

Examples of cases that recognize the tort without requiring proof of malicious, inherently tortious, or otherwise improper conduct are: *Cherry, Bekaert & Holland v. Brown*, 582 So. 2d 502 (Ala. 1991); *Alyeska Pipeline Serv. Co. v. Aurora Air Serv., Inc.*, 604 P.2d 1090 (Alaska 1979), *but see Geolar, Inc. v. Gilbert Commonwealth, Inc. of Mich.*, 874 P.2d 937 (Alaska 1994) (suggesting improper conduct usually issue for jury); *Antwerp Diamond Exch. of Am., Inc. v. Better Bus. Bureau of Maricopa County, Inc.*, 637 P.2d 733 (Ariz. 1981); *United Bilt Homes, Inc. v. Sampson*, 832 S.W.2d 502 (Ark. 1992) (but also noting that conduct was unjustified); *Blank v. Kirwan*, 703 P.2d 58 (Cal. 1985); *Aalgaard v. Merchants Nat'l Bank, Inc.*, 274 Cal. Rptr. 81 (Cal. Ct. App. 1990); *Fellhauer v. City of Geneva*, 568

N.E.2d 870 (Ill. 1991); *Eisenbach v. Esformes*, 582 N.E.2d 196 (Ill. 1991); *Macke Laundry Serv. Ltd. Partnership v. Mission Assocs., Ltd.*, 873 P.2d 219 (Kan. 1994); *Owen v. Williams*, 77 N.E.2d 318 (Mass. 1948); *Joba Constr. Co. v. Burns & Roe, Inc.*, 329 N.W.2d 760 (Mich. Ct. App. 1982); *Rusk Farms, Inc. v. Ralston Purina Co.*, 689 S.W.2d 671, 679 (Mo. Ct. App. 1985); *Mike Pratt & Sons, Inc. v. Metalcraft, Inc.*, 383 N.W.2d 758 (Neb. 1986); *Victoria Bank & Trust Co. v. Brady*, 811 S.W.2d 931 (Tex. 1991) (involving interference with contract rights, but specifically removing lack of justification as element of plaintiff's claim); *Mitchell v. Aldrich*, 163 A.2d 833 (Vt. 1960); *Catercorp., Inc. v. Catering Concepts, Inc.*, 431 S.E.2d 277 (Va. 1993); *Sea-Pac Co., Inc. v. United Food and Commercial Workers Local Union*, 699 P.2d 217 (Wash. 1985); *Cherberg v. Peoples Nat'l Bank of Wash.*, 564 P.2d 1137 (Wash. 1977); *Calbom v. Knudtzon*, 396 P.2d 148 (Wash. 1964); *C. W. Dev., Inc. v. Structures, Inc. of W. Va.*, 408 S.E.2d 41 (W. Va. 1991); *Board of Trustees of Weston County Sch. Dist. No. 1, Weston County v. Holso*, 584 P.2d 1009 (Wyo. 1978); *Daniels v. Dean*, 833 P.2d 1078 (Mont. 1992).

The following cases require the plaintiff to show, as part of its prima facie case, that the defendant's conduct was independently tortious or "improper" as discussed in section 766B of the *Restatement (Second) of Torts*: *Geolar, Inc. v. Gilbert Commonwealth, Inc. of Mich.*, 874 P.2d 937 (Alaska 1994); *Fantaco Enter., Inc. v. Iavarone*, 555 N.Y.S.2d 921 (N.Y. App. Div. 1990); *Int'l Mining Co. v. Allen & Co., Inc.*, 567 F. Supp. 777 (S.D.N.Y. 1983) (citing New York law); *Ellis v. City of Valdez*, 686 P.2d 700 (Alaska 1984); *Envtl. Plan. v. Superior Court (Detmold Publ'g)*, 680 P.2d 1086 (Cal. 1984); *Rickel v. Schwinn Bicycle Co.*, 192 Cal. Rptr. 732 (Cal. Ct. App. 1983); *Solomon v. Aberman*, 493 A.2d 193 (Conn. 1985); *Blake v. Levy*, 464 A.2d 52 (Conn. 1983); *Green v. Johnston Realty*, 442 S.E.2d 843 (Ga. 1994); *Lykins v. Nationwide Mut. Ins. Co.*, 448 S.E.2d 716 (Ga. Ct. App. 1994); *Harsha v. State Sav. Bank*, 346 N.W.2d 791 (Iowa 1984); *Nesler v. Fisher & Co.*, 452 N.W.2d 191 (Iowa 1990); *Fischer v. UNIPAC Serv. Corp.*, 519 N.W.2d 793 (Iowa 1994); *Travelers Indem. v. Merling*, 605 A.2d 83 (Md. 1992); *United Wild Rice, Inc. v. Nelson*, 313 N.W.2d 628 (Minn. 1982); *Buller v. Pulitzer Publishing Co.*, 684 S.W.2d 473 (Mo. Ct. App. 1984); *Am. Bus. Interi-*

ors v. Haworth, Inc., 798 F.2d 1135 (8th Cir. 1986) (Missouri law required plaintiff to show no justification, but noted that innocent conduct might suffice); *Killian Constr. Co. v. Jack D. Ball & Assocs.*, 865 S.W.2d 889 (Mo. Ct. App. 1993); *Bolz v. Myers*, 651 P.2d 606 (Mont. 1982); *M&M Rental Tools, Inc. v. Milchem, Inc.*, 612 P.2d 241 (N.M. Ct. App. 1980); *Embree Constr. Group, Inc. v. Rafcor, Inc.*, 411 S.E.2d 916 (N.C. 1992); *Cameron v. New Hanover Memorial Hosp., Inc.*, 293 S.E.2d 901 (N.C. Ct. App. 1982); *Spartan Equip. Co. v. Air Placement Equip. Co.*, 140 S.E.2d 3 (N.C. 1965); *Top Serv. Body Shop v. Allstate Ins. Co.*, 582 P.2d 1365 (Or. 1978); *Willamette Dental Group, P.C. v. Oregon Dental Serv. Corp.*, 882 P.2d 637 (Or. Ct. App. 1994); *Thompson v. Tel. & Data Sys., Inc.*, 881 P.2d 819 (Or. Ct. App. 1994); *Yaindl v. Ingersoll-Rand Co.*, 422 A.2d 611 (Pa. 1980); *Triffin v. Janssen*, 626 A.2d 571 (Pa. Super. Ct. 1993); *Schulman v. J.P. Morgan Inv. Mgmt., Inc.*, 35 F.3d 799 (3d Cir. 1994) (applying Pennsylvania law); *Adler, Barish, Daniels, Levin and Creskoff v. Epstein*, 393 A.2d 1175 (Pa. 1978); *Glenn v. Point Park Coll.*, 272 A.2d 895 (Pa. 1971); *Cloverleaf Dev., Inc. v. Horizon Fin., F.A.*, 500 A.2d 163 (Pa. Super. Ct. 1985); *State Nat'l Bank of El Paso v. Farah Mfg. Co., Inc.*, 678 S.W.2d 661, 688 (Tex. Ct. App. 1984); *Deauville Corp. v. Federated Dep't Stores*, 756 F.2d 1183 (5th Cir. 1985); *Leigh Furniture and Carpet Co. v. Isom*, 657 P.2d 293 (Utah 1982); *Quadra Enter., Inc. v. R.A. Hanson Co., Inc.*, 667 P.2d 1120 (Wash. Ct. App. 1983); *Torbett v. Wheeling Dollar Sav. & Trust Co.*, 314 S.E.2d 166 (W. Va. 1983); *Liebe v. City Fin. Co.*, 295 N.W.2d 16 (Wis. Ct. App. 1980); *Four Nines Gold, Inc. v. 71 Constr., Inc.*, 809 P.2d 236 (Wyo. 1991).

Many of the decisions, particularly those published before the *Restatement (Second) of Torts*, do not focus on the procedural distinctions among the various jurisdictions. Cases with a more specific discussion of the split of authority are: *Aalgaard v. Merchants Nat'l Bank, Inc.*, 274 Cal. Rptr. 81 (Cal. Ct. App. 1990); *Ramona Manor Convalescent Hosp. v. Care Enter.*, 225 Cal. Rptr. 120 (Cal. Ct. App. 1986); *Harsha v. State Sav. Bank*, 346 N.W.2d 791 (Iowa 1984); *United Wild Rice, Inc. v. Nelson*, 313 N.W.2d 628 (Minn. 1982); *Yaindl v. Ingersoll-Rand Co.*, 422 A.2d 611 (Pa. 1980); *Adler, Barish, Daniels, Levin and Creskoff v. Epstein*, 393 A.2d 1175

(Pa. 1978); *Victoria Bank & Trust v. Brady,* 811 S.W.2d 931 (Tex. 1991); *Leigh Furniture and Carpet Co. v. Isom,* 657 P.2d 293 (Utah 1982).

The jury instructions in this chapter are prepared in the alternative to make them more easily adaptable to the legal requirements of the various jurisdictions.

2.2   General Instructions

2.2.1   Theory of Interference with Prospective Advantage

In this case the plaintiff, [name], seeks to recover money damages from the defendant, [name], for alleged interference with plaintiff's prospective advantage. That is, the plaintiff contends that, because of the defendant's conduct, plaintiff was prevented from [state what plaintiff would have acquired], and as a result plaintiff suffered monetary loss.

The law recognizes that everyone has a right to establish and conduct a lawful business, free from unjustified interference, and is entitled to the protection of organized society, through its courts, whenever that right is unlawfully invaded. Generally speaking, the question for you to decide is whether the plaintiff's right to such an expectancy has in fact been invaded, and whether, under all of the factors I will instruct you to consider, any such invasion was improper.

In these charges, I will give you the applicable legal principles upon which you are to determine this question.

COMMENT

This charge is based upon language from *Buxbom v. Smith*, 145 P.2d 305 (Cal. 1944). *See also* Fowler V. Harper, *Law of Torts* § 6.11 (2d ed. 1986).

2.2.2   Elements of Liability

To find liability for interference with prospective advantage, you, the jury, must find from a preponderance of evidence:

1. The plaintiff had a business relationship or reasonable expectancy;

2. The defendant knew or should have known of the relationship or expectancy;

3. The defendant's conduct caused the loss of the relationship or expectancy;

4. The defendant acted intentionally to either end the relationship or prevent the expectancy; and

5. [optional—depending upon law of jurisdiction] that the conduct of the defendant was improper under the factors I will instruct you to consider; and

6. The defendant's conduct proximately caused the plaintiff's damages.

If you find that the plaintiff has proved each of these elements by a preponderance of the evidence, then you will consider the question of the amount of money damages under instructions I will give you.

COMMENT

This charge reflects the traditional standard articulated in *Restatement of Torts* for establishing liability, and includes the optional element of improper conduct on the part of the defendant. An increasing number of jurisdictions are beginning to require the plaintiff to prove "improper" conduct as an element of its prima facie case, as discussed in the *Restatement (Second) of Torts*. Some states require this issue to be raised by the defendant in the form of a justification or privilege affirmative defense. In jurisdictions of this latter variety, item (5) listed above should be omitted, and the propriety of the defendant's conduct should be framed defensively with the burden of proof on the defendant. *See* section 2.9, *infra*.

2.3   Existence of Relationship

2.3.1   Generally

The plaintiff contends that at the time of the defendant's conduct, there existed a [state business relationship or expectancy, whichever is applicable]. You must first determine whether there existed such a [business relationship or expectancy—choose one].

In determining this question, the [business relationship or expectancy—choose one] need not be evidenced by a contract. It is sufficient if you find from the evidence that there were either prior dealings or a prior course of conduct between plaintiff and [name of third party] from which there would be a reasonable expectation of future economic benefit. The plaintiff must show this expected benefit with some degree of specificity, such that it is a realistic expectation, but it need not be shown with certainty, because prospective things in nature are necessarily uncertain. The law requires more than a mere hope or optimism; what is required is a reasonable likelihood or probability.

COMMENT

The damaged relationship plaintiff complains of must be between the plaintiff and some third party other than the defendant. However, triangular relationships are treated differently among the various courts. For a discussion involving insurer-agent-insured, see *Travelers Indemnity v. Merling*, 605 A.2d 80, 83 (Md. 1992).

Before the jury can find liability, it must first find that there was a reasonable likelihood of a financial benefit to the plaintiff. If a contract once existed but has since expired, this quite possibly may demonstrate no current relationship exists. *See, e.g., Ice Bros., Inc. v. Bannowsky*, 840 S.W.2d 57 (Tex. App. 1992); *Macke Laundry Serv. Ltd. Partnership v. Mission Assocs., Ltd.*, 873 P.2d 219 (Kan. 1994); *Ontap Premium Quality Waters, Inc. v. Bank of N. Ill., N.A.*, 634 N.E.2d 425 (Ill. App. Ct. 1994); *Am. Bus. Interiors v. Haworth, Inc.*, 798 F.2d 1135 (8th Cir. 1986); *see also Verkin v. Melroy*, 699 F.2d 729 (5th Cir. 1983); *Youst v. Longo*, 729 P.2d 728 (Cal. 1987);

North v. State, 400 N.W.2d 566 (Iowa 1987); *Joba Constr. Co. v. Burns & Roe, Inc.*, 329 N.W.2d 760 (Mich. Ct. App. 1982); *Thompson Coal Co. v. Pike Coal Co.*, 412 A.2d 466 (Pa. 1979); *Mobil Oil Corp. v. Cook*, 494 S.W.2d 926 (Tex. App. 1973); *Sea-Pac Co., Inc. v. United Food and Commercial Workers Local Union*, 699 P.2d 217 (Wash. 1985). The plaintiff necessarily must plead the existence of an identifiable relationship with a specific third party rather than speculate using inconclusory terms that some potential relationship might have formed had the defendant not interfered. *DuPage Aviation Corp. v. DuPage Airport Auth.*, 594 N.E.2d 1334 (Ill. App. Ct. 1993); *Cont'l Mobile Tel. Co., Inc. v. Chicago SMSA Ltd. P'ship*, 587 N.E.2d 1169 (Ill. App. Ct. 1992); *Eisenbach v. Esformes*, 582 N.E.2d 196 (Ill. 1991).

The above charge is based on a "valid" business association or future expectancy. *See* 45 Am. Jur. 2d *Interference* §§ 7, 50 (1969). If a question arises regarding the illegal nature of the relationship or expectancy, the charge should be modified to reflect this. Relationships terminable at will that involve unenforceable covenants not to compete, for example, cannot form the basis for an action for tortious interference. *Travel Masters, Inc. v. Star Tours, Inc.*, 827 S.W.2d 830 (Tex. 1992). An opinion excluding all competitive contests or sporting contests is found in *Youst v. Longo*, 729 P.2d 728 (Cal. 1987).

2.4 Knowledge

2.4.1 Generally

To find for the plaintiff, you must also find that the defendant knew of the existence of this [business relationship or expectancy—choose one]. To have knowledge means that the defendant has information concerning the [business relationship or expectancy—choose one], which was discovered by the defendant or was brought to defendant's attention by others.

In this regard, knowledge may be found to exist if, from the facts and circumstances of which the defendant had knowledge, the defendant should have known of the existence of such [business relationship or expectancy—choose one].

COMMENT

Because the action is an intentional tort, virtually all courts require the element of knowledge, i.e., that the defendant knew of the existence of the relationship. *See Southwestern Bell Tel. Co. v. John Carlo Tex., Inc.,* 843 S.W.2d 470 (Tex. 1992); *Macke Laundry Serv. Ltd. Partnership v. Mission Assocs., Ltd.,* 873 P.2d 219 (Kan. 1994); *Blank v. Kirwan,* 703 P.2d 58 (Cal. 1985); *O'Fallon Dev. Co., Inc. v. City of O'Fallon,* 356 N.E.2d 1293 (Ill. App. Ct. 1976); *Witte Transp. Co. v. Murphy Motor Freight Lines, Inc.,* 193 N.W.2d 148 (Minn. 1971); *Chaves v. Johnson,* 335 S.E.2d 97 (Va. 1985); *Bd. of Trustees of Weston County Sch. Dist. No. 1, Weston County v. Holso,* 584 P.2d 1009 (Wyo. 1978). Of course, this also requires a finding of liability if the defendant, under the circumstances, should have discovered the existence of the relationship. *See Cont'l Research, Inc. v. Cruttenden, Podesta & Miller,* 222 F. Supp. 190 (D. Minn. 1963).

An interesting phenomenon may occur when the claim involves a defendant corporation being imputed with knowledge because one of its employees was aware of the relationship. Whether that employee's knowledge can be attributed to the employer would be a hotly litigated issue. In that situation, the law of the applicable jurisdiction should be applied and incorporated into this charge.

2.5   Causation

2.5.1   Generally

You, the jury, must determine whether the defendant was responsible for preventing the plaintiff from entering into the relationship with [name of third party]. In other words, you must decide whether, except for the interference of the defendant, the plaintiff was reasonably certain to have entered into the relationship or fulfilled the expectancy with [name of third party].

COMMENT

Causation is theoretically similar to the instruction in section 2.3.1 regarding whether the plaintiff had a reasonable expectancy before the alleged interference. However, the two questions are distinct and should be submitted separately. First, the plaintiff must show it had a reasonable expectancy and then show that the defendant interfered in a way that caused the expectancy to fail or otherwise be damaged. Of course, the causation element may be submitted in various ways among the jurisdictions. *See* 17 P.O.F.2d 517, 529 *Tortious Interference with At Will Business Relationship* (1978); section 2.8.1 cmt., *infra.* Some jurisdictions instruct the jury that "but for" the improper interference by the defendant, the expectancy would not have failed or been damaged. *Lyon v. Campbell*, 120 Md. App. 412, 707 A.2d 850 (1998).

2.5.2   Substantial Factor

The defendant's conduct will be deemed to be responsible for the plaintiff's failure to enter into the relationship if it was a substantial factor in causing the third party not to enter into the relationship or to fulfill the expectancy with the plaintiff.

COMMENT

This instruction should be used along with the definition of "substantial factor" found at section 2.8.3, but only if it is consistent with the causation requirement of the applicable jurisdiction. *See Restatement (Second) of Torts* section 433. The instruction in section 2.5.1 essentially explains to the jury that the plaintiff's burden is to show that, but for the defendant's conduct, the plaintiff was reasonably certain to have obtained the prospective benefit.

If the substantial-factor instruction and definition in this section and in section 2.8.3 are not recognized by the jurisdiction, they should be omitted. A defendant's conduct that satisfies the "but for" causation requirement in section 2.5.1 would undoubtedly also constitute a substantial factor. However, conduct that might be found a substantial factor in section 2.5.2 might not necessarily pass the "but for" causation requirement in section 2.5.1, because circumstances other than the defendant's conduct might have caused the plaintiff's loss, regardless of the defendant's conduct. Therefore, the substantial-factor instruction may present a much less rigorous causation requirement for a plaintiff. *See Doupnik v. Gen. Motors Corp.,* 275 Cal. Rptr. 715 (Cal. Ct. App. 1990).

2.6   Intentional Interference

2.6.1   Generally

You, the jury, must determine whether the defendant intended to prevent the plaintiff from continuing or acquiring this [business relationship or expectancy—choose one]. Conduct is intentional if done with the desire to interfere with plaintiff's [business relationship or expectancy—choose one] or with the belief that interference is substantially certain to result. If you find that the defendant's conduct was not intentional, then you must find for the defendant.

COMMENT

Because interference with prospective economic advantage is an intentional tort and requires intentional conduct on the part of the defendant, calculated to damage or ruin the plaintiff's business relationship or expectancy, this instruction must be given. In some cases there may be a similarity in the requirement of intent and the need to specifically define a relationship with a third party. For example, in *J. Eck & Sons, Inc. v. Reuben H. Donnelley Corp.*, 572 N.E.2d 1090 (Ill. App. Ct. 1991), the court found that an intentional refusal by the defendant to sell an advertisement to plaintiff did not involve the intent to harm a particular relationship with a third party. *See Ellis v. City of Valdez*, 686 P.2d 700 (Alaska 1984); *Ramona Manor Convalescent Hosp. v. Care Enter.*, 225 Cal. Rptr. 120 (Cal. Ct. App. 1986); *O'Fallon Dev. Co., Inc. v. City of O'Fallon*, 356 N.E.2d 1293 (Ill. App. Ct. 1976); *Witte Transp. Co. v. Murphy Motor Freight Lines, Inc.*, 193 N.W.2d 148 (Minn. 1971); *Ice Bros., Inc. v. Bannowsky*, 840 S.W.2d 57 (Tex. App. 1992); *C. W. Dev., Inc. v. Structures, Inc. of W. Va.*, 408 S.E.2d 41 (W. Va. 1991); 45 Am. Jur. 2d *Interference* § 50 (1969).

An enlightening discussion of the distinction between intent to do the act that allegedly caused the interference and the actual intent to interfere is found in *Southwestern Bell Telephone Co. v. John Carlo Tex., Inc.*, 843 S.W.2d 470 (Tex. 1992). In this case, the Texas Supreme Court reversed because the jury instructions did not specifically require the jury to find an intent to interfere with plaintiff's contract.

Note that some forums have additionally required that the intentional act be independently tortious. *E.g., Kecko Piping Co., Inc. v. Town of Monroe,* 374 A.2d 179 (Conn. 1977). Others require the defendant to have acted maliciously, such as being guilty of fraud, misrepresentation, or intimidation. *See Verkin v. Melroy,* 699 F.2d 729 (5th Cir. 1983); *Lash v. State,* 14 So. 2d 229 (Ala. 1943); *Blake v. Levy,* 464 A.2d 52 (Conn. 1983); *Jones v. O'Connell,* 458 A.2d 355 (Conn. 1983); *Spartan Equip. Co. v. Air Placement Equip. Co.,* 140 S.E.2d 3 (N.C. 1965); *Bray v. Squires,* 702 S.W.2d 266 (Tex. App. 1985); *State Nat'l Bank of El Paso v. Farah Mfg. Co., Inc.,* 678 S.W.2d 661 (Tex. App. 1984); *Exxon Corp. v. Allsup,* 808 S.W.2d 648 (Tex. App. 1991); *Deauville Corp. v. Federated Dep't Stores,* 756 F.2d 1183 (5th Cir. 1985). Still others require the plaintiff to show that the defendant had a motive to bring financial injury or destruction on the plaintiff. *Page County Appliance Ctr., Inc. v. Honeywell, Inc.,* 347 N.W.2d 171 (Iowa 1984); *Fischer v. UNIPAC Serv. Corp.,* 519 N.W.2d 793 (Iowa 1994).

However, not all courts require a showing of malice. *KMS Rest. Corp. v. Wendy's Int'l, Inc.* 361 F.3d 1321 (11th Cir. 2004); *Chaves v. Johnson,* 335 S.E.2d 97 (Va. 1985); *Martin v. Wing,* 667 P.2d 1159 (Wyo. 1983). In several cases, particularly those decided prior to the *Restatement (Second) of Torts*, questions surrounding the nature and means of the defendant's interference and objective came into play only after the affirmative defense of justification or privilege was raised. In such cases, the showing of actual malice may be required to overcome a privilege otherwise recognized. *Ray Dancer, Inc. v. DMC Corp.,* 594 N.E.2d 1344 (Ill. App. Ct. 1992).

The proposed charges found in optional item (5) of section 2.2.2 and in section 2.7 should be used in states that require the plaintiff to prove more than that the defendant intended the conduct but also intended the interference that resulted from the conduct. See the comments at sections 2.1, 2.2.2, and 2.7 for lists of authorities that will assist in researching the law of various states.

See Restatement (Second) of Torts § 767. Possible additional support for actual malice to overcome privilege can be found in the following cases: *King v. Levin*, 540 N.E.2d 492, 494 (Ill. App. Ct. 1989) (deals with prospective advantage); *Arlington Heights Nat'l Bank v. Arlington Heights Fed. Sav. & Loan Ass'n*, 229 N.E.2d 514 (Ill. 1967); *Huskie v. Griffin*, 74 A. 595 (N.H. 1909).

2.6.2 Proof of Intentional Interference

Intent ordinarily may not be proved directly, because there is no way of scrutinizing the operations of the human mind. You may infer a person's intent from conduct substantially certain to interfere with the plaintiff's business expectation, but you are not required to infer it and should consider all of the circumstances. You may consider any statement made or act done or omitted by a party whose intent is an issue, and all of the facts and circumstances that indicate the party's state of mind. Furthermore, in determining the defendant's intention, the law assumes that every person intends the natural consequences of one's knowingly done acts. Thus, if you find that the defendant's conduct was knowingly done or knowingly omitted, you may draw the inference and find, unless the contrary appears from the evidence, that the defendant intended all the natural and probable consequences of defendant's conduct.

COMMENT

See Fischer v. UNIPAC Serv. Corp., 519 N.W.2d 793 (Iowa 1994); *Southwestern Bell Tel. Co. v. John Carlo Tex., Inc.*, 843 S.W.2d 470 (Tex. 1992); *DeVoto v. Pac. Fid. Life Ins. Co.*, 618 F.2d 1340 (9th Cir. 1980); *Baker v. United States*, 310 F.2d 924 (9th Cir. 1962) (criminal case), *cert. denied*, 372 U.S. 954 (1963); *Golden v. Sommers*, 56 F.R.D. 3 (M.D. Pa. 1972), *aff'd*, 481 F.2d 1398 (3d Cir. 1973); *Ramona Manor Convalescent Hosp. v. Care Enter.*, 225 Cal. Rptr. 120 (Cal. Ct. App. 1986); *Martin v. Wing*, 667 P.2d 1159 (Wyo. 1983); 3 Devitt, Blackmar & Wolff, *Federal Jury Practice and Instructions* § 81.03 (4th ed. 1992).

2.6.3   Conduct Knowingly Done

An act (or omission) is done knowingly if done purposefully and voluntarily, and not because of mistake, inadvertence, or other innocent reason.

COMMENT

See section 2.6.2; *Hayes v. Irwin*, 541 F. Supp. 397 (N.D. Ga. 1982); *Am. Sanitary Serv., Inc. v. Walker*, 554 P.2d 1010, (Or. 1976).

2.7 Factors Determining Whether Interference Is Improper

In your deliberations, you should consider the following factors in determining whether the conduct of the defendant was improper:

1. The nature of the defendant's conduct;

2. The defendant's motive;

3. The interests of the plaintiff with which the conduct interfered;

4. The interests sought to be advanced by the defendant;

5. The interest of our society in balancing the need to protect the freedom of the defendant to engage in such conduct with the need to protect prospective advantages such as sought by the plaintiff;

6. The proximity or remoteness of the defendant's conduct to the interference about which the plaintiff complains; and

7. The nature of the relationship between the plaintiff and defendant.

COMMENT

This instruction is limited in use to those jurisdictions that require that the defendant's interference be improper. See section 766B of the *Restatement (Second) of Torts* and the comments and lists of authorities in various states in sections 2.1 and 2.2.2. There is a split of authority on whether the plaintiff must prove either improper motives or means on the part of the defendant as part of a prima facie case, or whether such matters are relevant only if the defendant attempts to prove a justification or privilege for defendant's intentional conduct. In some states, including Texas, the plaintiff has the burden to show that the defendant's "conduct would be actionable under a recognized tort," such as defamation or fraud, not just that the conduct was unfair. *Wal-Mart*

Stores, Inc. v. Sturges, 52 S.W.3d 711 (Tex. 2001); *see also Trade 'N Post, L.L.C. v. World Duty Free Americas, Inc.*, 628 N.W.2d 707 (N.D. 2001). Similarly, the California Supreme Court has held that the plaintiff must show the defendant's actions, other than the mere interference, were wrongful in order to prevail. *See Dellas Penna v. Toyota Motor Sales, U.S.A.*, 902 P.2d 740 (Cal. 1995). If the plaintiff is successful, the defendant then has the burden to show it was justified in its actions.

This preceding instruction should be given if item (5) of the general instructions in section 2.2.2 is used. If it is not given, the propriety of the defendant's conduct may be submitted as an affirmative defense as discussed in section 2.9.

The language follows section 767 of the *Restatement (Second) of Torts*. A great many jurisdictions have essentially adopted the *Restatement (Second)* factors for determining if conduct is improper. *See Green v. Interstate United Mgmt. Serv. Corp.*, 748 F.2d 827 (3d Cir. 1984); *Int'l Mining Co. v. Allen & Co., Inc.* 567 F Supp. 777 (S.D.N.Y. 1983); *Harsha v. State Sav. Bank*, 346 N.W.2d 791 (Iowa 1984); *Adler, Barish, Daniels, Levin and Creskoff v. Epstein*, 393 A.2d 1175 (Pa. 1978); *Leigh Furniture and Carpet Co. v. Isom*, 657 P.2d 293 (Utah 1982); *Glass v. Glass*, 321 S.E.2d 69 (Va. 1984); *Liebe v. City Fin. Co.*, 295 N.W.2d 16 (Wis. Ct. App. 1980); *C. W. Dev., Inc. v. Structures, Inc. of W. Va.*, 408 S.E.2d 41 (W. Va. 1991). *See also Employer's Fire Ins. Co. v. Love It Ice Cream Co.*, 670 P.2d 160 (Or. 1983); *Hughes v. Houston Northwest Med. Ctr., Inc.*, 680 S.W.2d 838 (Tex. App. 1984) (suggesting unfounded litigation, knowingly brought, can constitute improper interference). *But cf. Pac. Gas & Elec. v. Bear Stearns*, 791 P.2d 587 (Cal. 1990); *Village Supermarket, Inc. v. Mayfair Supermarkets, Inc.*, 634 A.2d 1381 (N.J. Super. Ct. Law Div. 1993) (holding that merely inducing party to seek judicial determination of its rights is privileged as matter of law).

2.8 Damage to Plaintiff Proximately Resulting from Conduct

2.8.1 Generally

You must also consider whether the defendant's conduct was the proximate cause of damage to the plaintiff. If you find that the defendant's conduct was not the proximate cause of damage to the plaintiff, your verdict will be for the defendant.

COMMENT

In order to prevail in an action for interference with prospective advantage, most courts require that the plaintiff be damaged as a result of the interference. The above instruction would satisfy the requirement for a showing of damage, but it duplicates the issue of causation found in section 2.5. Depending upon the law of the jurisdiction, either the charge in section 2.8.1 or the one in section 2.5 may be used.

2.8.2　Monetary Loss

The plaintiff claims to have suffered monetary loss in the following respects: [set forth plaintiff's claims].

If you find that the plaintiff did not suffer such a loss, your verdict will be for the defendant.

COMMENT

Again, this instruction reflects the well-established rule that the plaintiff must in fact suffer some damage to establish a prima facie case in tort.

2.8.3 Substantial Factor

If you find that the plaintiff did suffer the losses it claims, you must then determine whether the defendant's conduct was the proximate cause of the plaintiff's loss or damage.

In this regard, the defendant's conduct will be deemed to be the proximate cause of the plaintiff's loss or damage if you find that it was a substantial factor in causing that loss or damage. It need not be the *only* cause. The conduct will be a substantial factor in causing the loss or damage if it had such an effect in producing the loss that reasonable people would regard it as a cause of the loss or damage. In resolving this issue, you may consider the number of other contributing factors, whether the defendant's conduct created a condition or chain of events that was continuous and active up to the time of the damage to plaintiff, and the lapse of time between the defendant's conduct and the damage to the plaintiff.

COMMENT

See section 2.5.1, *supra.*

This charge reflects the traditional definition of proximate cause, which uses the substantial-factor element. It is adapted from section 433 of the *Restatement (Second) of Torts*. Regarding conflict between the "but for" and substantial-factor tests, see the comment accompanying section 2.5.2. *See also* 1 James A. Dooley, *Modern Tort Law* § 8.03 (1977).

2.9   Defenses: Justifications and Privileges

2.9.1   Generally

As discussed in sections 2.1, 2.2.2, and 2.7, the procedural treatment of defenses of justification and privilege varies in the different states. As stated by the California Supreme Court in 1984:

> The factors enumerated by this court in *Herron* were patterned closely after those listed in the original Restatement of Torts section 767. The Restatement (Second) abandons use of the term "privilege" or "justification" in favor of the term "improperly interferes," so as to avoid questions of burden of pleading or proof (*id.*, at p. 5), but the factors to be used in determining whether interference is "improper" (§ 767) are essentially the same. *Envtl. Plan. v. Superior Court (Detmold Publ'g)*, 680 P.2d 1086, 1090 (Cal. 1984).

Because some states have increasingly considered whether the defendant's conduct was improper, they have placed decreasing emphasis on the justification and privilege affirmative defenses. However, some states have moved in the opposite direction, removing the "improper" element from the plaintiff's burden and shifting it to the defendant's burden as an affirmative defense. *See Victoria Bank & Trust v. Brady*, 811 S.W.2d 931 (Tex. 1991); *Gonzalez v. San Jacinto Methodist Hosp.*, 880 S.W.2d 436 (Tex. App. 1994). In *Southwestern Bell Tel. Co. v. John Carlo Tex., Inc.*, 843 S.W.2d 470 (Tex. 1992), the court reversed a plaintiff's verdict because the trial court failed to define "justification" for the jury as follows: "Interference is privileged when it results from the exercise of a party's own bona fide rights or when the party possesses an equal or superior interest to that of the plaintiff." For a more specific discussion and list of cases from various states on the burden-of-proof issue, see sections 2.1, 2.2.2, and 2.7. The Texas Supreme Court has further held that:

> [J]ustification and privilege are defenses in a claim for tortious interference with prospective relations only to the extent that they are defenses to the independent tortiousness of the defendant's conduct. Otherwise, the plaintiff need not prove

that the defendant's conduct was not justified or privileged, nor can a defendant assert such defenses.

Wal-Mart Stores, Inc. v. Sturges, 52 S.W.3d 711, 727 (Tex. 2001). Thus, if the plaintiff is able to show that the method defendant has used to interfere was independently tortious, then the issue of privilege or justification never arises. *See Prudential Ins. Co. of Am.*, 29 S.W.3d 74 (Tex. 2000).

The following two charges are optional, depending upon the rule regarding burden of proof in the particular forum. Option A is for use in states where the plaintiff must show the defendant's conduct or motive was improper. Option B places the burden of proof on the defendant to establish a specific affirmative defense.

The *Restatement (Second) of Torts*, in sections 768-74, discusses conduct traditionally recognized as "privileged." The instructions in sections 2.9.2 through 2.9.5 reflect those principles but do not include a position on burden of proof. Therefore, a combination of any of the instructions on specific conduct in sections 2.9.2 through 2.9.5, with the burden-of-proof instruction in either choice A or B in the following section, could be used to fit the appropriate law of any jurisdiction.

- *Option A: Plaintiff's Burden to Show Defendant's Conduct Improper*
  You have been instructed that to recover, the plaintiff has the burden to prove various facts by a preponderance of the evidence. One of those facts was that the defendant's conduct was improper. The law recognizes that certain kinds of conduct under certain circumstances are not improper. The following instructions are intended to guide you in deciding whether the plaintiff has satisfied its burden to show the defendant's conduct was improper under the facts as you find them.

- *Option B: Defendant's Burden to Show Conduct Proper Because It Was Justified or Privileged*
  The defendant claims [state basis of claimed justification and/or privilege]. The plaintiff denies [state disputed fact or facts].

If you find that the defendant has not sustained its burden of proving that [state disputed fact or facts], then the conduct was not justified or privileged, and your verdict will be for the plaintiff, provided you find that the plaintiff has met its burden of proof on what plaintiff must establish to prove liability. If you find that the defendant has sustained its burden of proving that [state disputed fact or facts], your verdict will be for the defendant.

COMMENT

The court must determine whether the defendant has established a legal right to interfere. If the court finds that the defendant does not possess this right, the court must then determine if a mistaken but colorable legal right was asserted. If it was, the jury will decide whether the right was exercised in good faith. *Texas Beef Cattle Co. v. Green*, 921 S.W.2d 203 (Tex. 1996). In Texas, the justification or privilege instruction is submitted as an affirmative defense with the burden on the defendant. *Texas Beef Cattle Co. v. Green*, 921 S.W.2d 203 (Tex. 1996); *see also Wal-Mart Stores, Inc. v. Sturges*, 52 S.W.3d 711 (Tex. 2001); *Southwestern Bell Telephone Co. v. John Carlo Tex., Inc.*, 843 S.W.2d 470 (Tex. 1992); *Victoria Bank & Trust Co. v. Brady*, 811 S.W.2d 931 (Tex. 1991); *Sterner v. Marathon Oil Co.*, 767 S.W.2d 686 (Tex. 1989). Note that the defense of justification or privilege will be present in the case only if conduct constituting the interference is not "unlawful." *See, e.g.*, William L. Prosser, *The Law of Torts* § 130 (4th ed. 1971); 1 Fowler V. Harper, et al., *Law of Torts* § 6.11 (2d ed. 1986). *Cf. Lowell v. Mother's Cake & Cookie Co.*, 144 Cal. Rptr. 664 (Cal. Ct. App. 1978). Because whether the defendant's conduct is "unlawful" is a question of law, when the defendant asserts a justification or privilege defense, the court must first determine whether the defendant's conduct is unlawful. *Tuttle v. Buck*, 119 N.W. 946 (Minn. 1909). If the court does so, and the other circumstances surrounding the invoking of the justification or privilege, if proved, are such to make the conduct justified or privileged, the existence of the circumstances on which the justification or privilege is based becomes a question of fact for the jury. *Restatement*

(Second) of Torts § 767 cmt. l (1977); *Gianelli Distrib. Co. v. Beck & Co.*, 219 Cal. Rptr. 203 (Cal. Ct. App. 1985). In Texas, courts submit this instruction but include questions regarding whether the defendant's actions were in good faith and further, if there was a contract involved, whether the jury believes a party should be able to "interfere with the execution of the contract where there is a bona fide doubt as to his rights under it." *Texas Beef Cattle Co. v. Green*, 921 S.W.2d 203, 211 (Tex. 1996). If the jury answers yes for both of these questions, then a malice finding is irrelevant and the defense of justification has been successful.

2.9.2   Competition as Proper or Improper Interference

The defendant asserts that its conduct was proper because it occurred during the course of competition between the defendant and the plaintiff. The law recognizes that one is justified or privileged to cause a third party not to enter into or continue a business relationship or expectancy with one's competition as long as the conduct relates to competition between the two competitors and the party is acting, at least in part, to advance its own interests in such competition, and as long as the party does not use wrongful means to compete.

You must first determine, then, whether the conduct of the defendant relates to competition between the defendant and the plaintiff for the business of [name of third party]. If you find that it does, then you will determine whether the defendant's purpose was, at least in part, to advance defendant's interest in competing with the plaintiff. For example, if you should find that the defendant was seeking to acquire the business diverted from the plaintiff for itself, then as long as the defendant's conduct was at least in part directed to that end, the fact that you may find it was also motivated by other reasons will not render it improper in the eyes of the law. But if you find that the defendant's conduct was motivated solely by bad faith or ill will, and not at all for the advancement of competitive interests, you must find that the conduct was not justified and that it was improper.

COMMENT

One of the most frequently used defenses is competition. It is widely recognized as a stronger defense in cases involving interference with prospective advantage, as contrasted with contracts. The elements are set out in section 768 of the *Restatement (Second) of Torts*. The facts of each case may require some modification to the instruction. See discussions of the defense in *C. E. Servs., Inc. v. Control Data Corp.*, 759 F.2d 1241 (5th Cir. 1985); *Northwest Airlines v. Am. Airlines*, 853 F. Supp. 1110 (D. Minn.

1994); *DEFCO, Inc. v. Decatur Cylinder, Inc.*, 595 So. 2d 1329 (Ala. 1992); *Public Sys., Inc. v. Towry,* 587 So. 2d 969 (Ala. 1991); *Edwards v. Anaconda Co.*, 565 P.2d 190 (Ariz. Ct. App. 1977); *A-Mark Coin Co. v. Gen. Mills, Inc.*, 195 Cal. Rptr. 859 (Cal. Ct. App. 1983); *Rickel v. Schwinn Bicycle Co.*, 192 Cal. Rptr. 732 (Cal. Ct. App. 1983); *Bowl-Mor Co., Inc. v. Brunswick Corp.*, 297 A.2d 61 (Del. Ch. 1972); *Doliner v. Brown,* 489 N.E.2d 1036 (Mass. App. Ct. 1986); *United Wild Rice, Inc. v. Nelson,* 313 N.W.2d 628 (Minn. 1982); *Embree Constr. Group, Inc. v. Rafcor, Inc.,* 411 S.E.2d 916 (N.C. 1992); *Crockett v. Sahara Realty Corp.*, 591 P.2d 1135 (Nev. 1979); *Fantaco Enter., Inc. v. Iavarone,* 555 N.Y.S.2d 921 (N.Y. App. Div. 1990); *Consol. Petroleum Indus., Inc. v. Jacobs,* 648 S.W.2d 363-67 (Tex. Ct. App. 1983); *Quadra Enter., Inc. v. R.A. Hanson Co.*, 667 P.2d 1120 (Wash. Ct. App. 1983). Several courts have adopted Prosser's statement:

> So long as the plaintiff's contractual relations are merely contemplated or potential, it is considered to be in the interest of the public that any competitor should be free to divert them to himself by all fair and reasonable means.

William L. Prosser, *Law of Torts* § 130 at 954 (4th ed. 1971).

Whether the defendant has utilized "wrongful means" may be an issue for the court or for the jury. As noted above, unlawful conduct would defeat any privilege. However, a fact question may exist about whether unlawful or wrongful conduct occurred. The comments to section 767(a) of the *Restatement (Second)* list various circumstances that may be adapted to particular cases for instructions on conduct or means used by a party. *Restatement (Second) of Torts* § 767(a) cmts. at 29-32. Most "unlawful" conduct in the cases falls into tortious or even criminal categories. However, a garden variety breach of contract, if done for improper purposes, may be found actionable in tort under certain circumstances. In *Am. Nat'l Petroleum Co. v. Transcon. Gas Pipe Line Corp.*, 798 S.W.2d 274 (Tex. 1990), the court rejected the defense that standard contract remedies were exclusively applicable when the only action taken was to breach the defendant's own contract.

The California Supreme Court noted that because it is actionable to interfere with a relationship that is purely prospective, it would be illogical not to protect a contractual relationship, even if it were terminable at will, or unenforceable. However, the court drew the line and found it not actionable for an interloper merely to induce or cause another to file suit for the purpose of seeking a declaration of the parties' rights. *Pac. Gas & Elec. Co. v. Bear Stearns & Co.*, 791 P.2d 587 (Cal. 1990).

2.9.3 Financial Interest

Interference with a prospective business relationship of another is not improper if the person interfering has a financial interest in the prospective relationship and acts in a reasonable way to protect that person's financial interest from being prejudiced by the prospective contract or business relation.

If you find that, before the defendant's conduct, defendant had a financial interest connected to [state the prospective relationship alleged by the plaintiff], and that defendant's conduct was a reasonable attempt exercised in good faith to protect that interest, then the defendant's conduct is not improper even if it did interfere with [state the prospective relationship].

COMMENT

This instruction is based on sections 769, 771, and 773 of the *Restatement (Second) of Torts. See also Geolar, Inc. v. Gilbert Commonwealth, Inc. of Mich.*, 874 P.2d 937 (Cal. 1994); *Alyeska Pipeline Serv. Co. v. Aurora Air Serv., Inc.*, 604 P.2d 1090 (Alaska 1979); *Envtl. Plan. v. Superior Court (Detmold Publ'g)*, 680 P.2d 1086 (Cal. 1984); *Asia Inv. Co., Ltd. v. Borowski*, 184 Cal. Rptr. 317 (Cal. Ct. App. 1982); *Travelers Indem. v. Merling*, 605 A.2d 83 (Md. 1992); *Doliner v. Brown*, 489 N.E.2d 1036 (Mass. App. Ct. 1986); *Schulman v. J.P. Morgan Inv. Mgmt., Inc.*, 35 F.3d 799 (3d Cir. 1994) (applying Pennsylvania law); *Victoria Bank & Trust Co. v. Brady*, 811 S.W.2d 931 (Tex. 1991) (recognizing equal interest only if exercised in good faith); *Lone Star Ford, Inc. v. McCormick*, 838 S.W.2d 734 (Tex. App. 1992); *Brown v. Safeway Stores, Inc.*, 617 P.2d 704 (Wash. 1980); *Roy v. Cunningham*, 731 P.2d 526 (Wash. Ct. App. 1986); *Quadra Enter., Inc. v. R.A. Hanson Co., Inc.*, 667 P.2d 1120 (Wash. Ct. App. 1983).

Sometimes it may appear obvious that the defendant has its own legitimate financial interest in the matter such that a summary judgment appears proper on this point. Deciding whether fact questions exist about whether this interest was exercised properly and in good faith is important. In *Hopkins v. Highlands Ins.*

Co., 838 S.W.2d 819 (Tex. Civ. App. 1992), the court reversed a summary judgment in favor of an insurance company that claimed it had a proper financial interest in refusing to insure a particular driver employed by the insured. Although the insurer clearly asserted a valid financial interest, the court found factual questions regarding whether the driving record requirements were uniformly applied in good faith to all other drivers. For a discussion of the application of governmental immunity to this tort, see *North v. State*, 400 N.W.2d 566 (Iowa 1987).

Generally, there should be a presumption that corporate officers, directors, and shareholders have a qualified privilege to interfere with prospective economic relations between the corporation and a third party. *Lone Star Ford v. McCormick*, 838 S.W.2d 734 (Tex. App. 1992). However, that presumption may be overcome when the means used or motives are found to be improper. *Ray Duncer, Inc. v. DMC Corp.*, 594 N.E.2d 1344 (Ill. App. Ct. 1992). *See also Embree Constr. Group, Inc. v. Rafcor*, 411 S.E.2d 916 (N.C. 1992); *Sammon v. Watchung Hills Bank for Sav.*, 611 A.2d 674 (N.J. Super. Ct. Law Div. 1992). Even partners may face liability if it is found that a relationship terminable at will is harmed by one using improper means or motives. *Wilensky v. Blalock*, 414 S.E.2d 1 (Ga. 1992).

The interest of a manager or agent in recommending against the continuation of a relationship between a third party and the principal is similar. A number of cases have debated whether a privilege for such a manager is absolute or qualified, but in the absence of clear evidence of improper motives or self-dealing, it is difficult for a plaintiff to overcome. *See Aalgaard v. Merchants Nat'l Bank, Inc.*, 274 Cal. Rptr. 81 (Cal. Ct. App. 1990); *Geick v. Kay*, 603 N.E.2d 121 (Ill. App. Ct. 1992); *Am. Med. Int'l v. Giurintano*, 821 S.W.2d 331 (Tex. App. 1991). A bankruptcy trustee has been held to be immune from a tortious interference suit. *Clements v. Barnes*, 834 S.W.2d 45 (Tex. 1992). A franchisor's right to select its franchisees has been held sufficient to preclude an action for interference. *Roberts v. Gen. Motors Corp.*, 643 A.2d 956 (N.H. 1994).

2.9.4 Defendant Responsible for Welfare of Another

Interference with [state prospective business relationship] is not improper if you find that the defendant is charged with the responsibility for the welfare of [state the third person with whom the plaintiff intended to enter into the relationship] and the defendant used reasonable means in a good-faith attempt to protect the welfare of [the third person with whom the plaintiff intended to enter into the relationship].

COMMENT

This charge is based on section 770 of the *Restatement (Second) of Torts*. For support: *Gott v. Berea College*, 161 S.W. 204 (Ky. Ct. App. 1913); *Dehnert v. Arrow Sprinklers, Inc.*, 705 P.2d 846 (Wyo. 1985) (dealing with defense in interference with contractual relations action).

2.9.5   Truthful Information or Advice

Interference with [state the prospective business relationship] is not improper when the only conduct of the party interfering is to provide truthful information or to provide honest advice in good faith within the scope of a request for the advice.

If you find that the defendant's only conduct interfering with [state the prospective advantage] was to provide truthful information, then the defendant's conduct was not improper. Likewise, if you find that the defendant's only conduct was to provide honest advice that was within the scope of advice requested by [state the third party with whom the plaintiff desired to have a business relationship], then the defendant's conduct was not improper.

COMMENT

This charge is based on section 772 of the *Restatement (Second) of Torts*. The question of whether the advice is given in good faith or for other motives may be a jury question. See *Weller v. Seton Hall Univ.*, 579 A.2d 332 (N.J. Super. Ct. App. Div. 1990), for an interesting discussion about whether the employment rights of certain nuns were violated or harmed due to "honestly held . . . [and] truly religiously motivated" beliefs, or were the subject of other nonreligious goals.

2.10   Damages

2.10.1   Generally

I am turning now to the question of damages and what can be considered in determining an award of money in this case. By including damages in these instructions, I do not wish to suggest or imply anything about the issue of liability or about whether any damages have been proved in this case.

Two kinds of damages can be considered in this case. They are compensatory damages and punitive damages.

Compensatory damages will consist of the plaintiff's direct economic losses and out-of-pocket expenses resulting from the defendant's conduct. In other words, the defendant is liable for all damages suffered by the plaintiff that were caused by the defendant's conduct.

Punitive damages, which I will discuss later, are damages that you may award, not as compensation to the plaintiff, but to justly punish the defendant for its behavior and to dissuade the defendant and others from acting the same way in future, similar situations.

COMMENT

In an action for interference with prospective advantage, the plaintiff generally may be awarded compensatory damages as well as punitive damages. *See, e.g., Elsbach v. Mulligan,* 136 P.2d 651 (Cal. Ct. App. 1943); 45 Am. Jur. 2d *Interference* §§ 58, 61 (1969). Some states, however, do prohibit or restrict the award of punitive damages, and the standard of proof is often higher for an award of exemplary damages.

2.10.2 Compensatory Damages

If, after considering the evidence in this case and the instructions of the court, you should find the issues in favor of the plaintiff, then it is my duty to tell you what damages the plaintiff would be entitled to recover. It would be such a sum as you believe, from the evidence, will fairly and reasonably compensate the plaintiff for any damage the plaintiff has suffered by reason of the defendant's acts complained of and for the anticipated profits of which the plaintiff was deprived, provided they are of such a nature to be beyond the speculative stage.

In determining compensatory damages, you may consider whether the plaintiff suffered any measurable loss of profits as a result of the defendant's conduct. In this case, the plaintiff claims that its business was affected because of loss of profits plaintiff might have earned but for the defendant's conduct.

For lost profits to be recovered, there must be a reasonable basis for computing them. Ordinarily, it is sufficient for this purpose to show actual past profits and losses; that is, past receipts and expenses in the plaintiff's business. Although they cannot be taken as an exact measure of future or anticipated profits, you, the jury, should consider those past profits and losses together with the uncertainties and contingencies by which they probably would have been affected. It would be proper for you to consider any normal increase in business that might have been reasonably expected in the light of past developments and existing conditions in the plaintiff's business. You may also take into consideration future uncertainties, such as increased competition, increased operating costs, and changes in economic trends. Losses and profits that are mere guesses, speculative, remote, or uncertain, or unwarranted estimates of witnesses, should not be considered.

Damages, if any, should be restricted to such losses, if any, as are proved by facts from which their existence is logically and legally inferable. The general rule on the subject of damages is that all damages resulting necessarily, immediately, and directly from the wrong are recoverable, and not those that are contingent and uncertain or mere speculation.

Although a qualified person may make estimates concerning probable profits or losses of a going business, you should, in weighing all such evidence, take into consideration, among other things, the truth or falsity of the basis of such estimates; the knowledge or lack of knowledge of the witnesses of all of the conditions on which the estimate is based; whether the facts assumed as a basis for an estimate rest upon actual accounts and records kept in the ordinary course of business rather than in uncertain recollections; and knowledge of the witness in the particular line of business about which the witness testifies. From all of the evidence in this case bearing on the subject, you should determine for yourselves the probability or improbability, and the amount, of profits anticipated by the plaintiff.

The difficulty or uncertainty in ascertaining or measuring the precise amount of any damages does not preclude recovery, and you, the jury, should use your best judgment in determining the amount of such damages, if any, based upon the evidence.

In determining compensatory damages, you may consider whether the plaintiff suffered any measurable loss to its goodwill. The goodwill of a company is an intangible business asset that reflects the basic human tendency to do business with a merchant who offers products of the type and quality the customer desires and expects. Service to the customer and a willingness to stand behind a warranty and other representations about the quality of the products sold by a merchant are factors in the goodwill of that business.

The goodwill attached to a product is a part of the overall business value that is the goodwill of the company. It is possible, therefore, that the general goodwill of a corporation may be damaged by the loss of goodwill to a particular product. Whether this has occurred is a question of fact for you to determine.

If you find that the plaintiff's goodwill has been damaged either by injury to the goodwill associated with a particular product or by injury to the plaintiff's general business reputation, you may assess such compensatory damages as you may find shown by the evidence. The measure of the plaintiff's damage is the difference between the value of such goodwill before and after the acts of the defendant.

[Other losses for which the plaintiff seeks recovery can be inserted here.]

That the defendant did not actually anticipate or contemplate that these losses would occur is not a relevant factor for you to consider.

If you find that the plaintiff is entitled to a verdict in accordance with these instructions, but you do not find that the evidence before you is sufficient to show that the plaintiff has sustained any substantial damages, then you may return a verdict for the plaintiff on one or more of the theories of liability and fix the amount of the compensatory damages in a nominal sum such as one dollar. Such a verdict would determine the rights of the parties, and the court can then issue orders directing their future conduct.

COMMENT

The plaintiff can recover for "all losses legally caused by the defendant's interference, if they are reasonably ascertainable." 17 P.O.F.2d 517, 545 *Tortious Interference with At Will Business Relationship* (1978). For support: *Wheeler v. Woods*, 723 P.2d 1224 (Wyo. 1986).

Among losses that the plaintiff can recover are lost profits, general loss to its business, and harm to goodwill. *See, e.g., Buxbom v. Smith*, 145 P.2d 305 (Cal. 1944); *Elsbach v. Mulligan*, 136 P.2d 651 (Cal. Ct. App. 1943). These losses are simply illustrative and should not be interpreted as excluding other kinds of losses.

The lost-profits part of the charge is from *F. L. Mendez & Co. v. Gen. Motors Corp.*, 161 F.2d 695 (7th Cir. 1947), an antitrust case. The goodwill part is from *Big O Tire Dealers, Inc. v. Goodyear Tire & Rubber Co.*, 408 F. Supp. 1219 (D. Colo. 1976), *modified on other grounds*, 561 F.2d 1365 (10th Cir. 1977).

2.10.3 Punitive Damages

2.10.3.a Decision to Award Punitive Damages

If you find for the plaintiff and against the defendant and you have determined that the defendant must pay damages, then you should consider whether the conduct that led to your decision also subjects the defendant to punitive damages. To award punitive damages, you must find that the defendant's conduct that proximately caused actual [or nominal] damages to the plaintiff was the result of actual malice, wanton conduct, or oppressive conduct, as measured by the instructions I will give you.

COMMENT

As noted in section 1.6.1, in jurisdictions where punitive damages are allowable in actions for tortious interference with contract, they are also permitted in actions for interference with prospective advantage. Because the standard for the award of punitive damages varies from state to state, counsel should insert the appropriate standard in the charge. If the jurisdiction has a heightened standard for punitive damages, it should be given after this instruction. *See generally* Lee H. Russ, Annotation, *Standard of Proof As to Conduct Underlying Punitive Damage Awards—Modern Status,* 58 A.L.R.4th 878 (1987 & Supp. 2002).

This charge represents the modern view of damages. *See, e.g., State Farm Mut. Auto. Ins. Co. v. Campbell,* 538 U.S. 408 (2003); *Rabun v. Kimberly-Clark Corp.,* 678 F.2d 1053 (11th Cir. 1982); *Christman v. Voyer,* 595 P.2d 410 (N.M. Ct. App. 1979); *Wussow v. Commercial Mechanisms, Inc.,* 279 N.W.2d 503 (Wis. Ct. App. 1979); *Restatement (Second) of Torts* § 908; 45 Am. Jur. 2d *Interference* § 62 (1999 & Supp. 2003). Counsel should note that although punitive damages generally will be awarded upon a showing of malice, wantonness, or oppressiveness, this principle is not universal and may well be affected by statute in a particular jurisdiction.

Most states require that the jury find liability and actual, or at least nominal, damages before punitive damages are allowed. *See* Richard C. Tinney, Annotation, *Showing of Actual Damages to Support Award of Punitive Damages,* 40 A.L.R.4th 11 (1985 & Supp. 2002); 45 Am. Jur. 2d *Interference* § 62 (1999 & Supp. 2003); *Am. Bus. Interiors, Inc. v. Haworth, Inc.,* 798 F.2d 1135 (8th Cir. 1986). *But see Platte v. Whitney Realty Co.,* 538 So. 2d 1358 (Fla. Dist. Ct. App. 1989) (punitive damages recoverable although actual damages could not be proved). For a discussion of the prerequisite of a verdict for actual damages, see the comment to section 2.10.3.b. For the requirement of malicious, wanton, or oppressive conduct, see sections 2.10.3.c, 2.10.3.d, and 2.10.3.e.

2.10.3.b   Nominal Damages

The award of only a nominal sum with respect to the specific losses claimed by the plaintiff will not prevent your awarding punitive damages if you find that the award of punitive damages is justified under these instructions.

COMMENT

In most states the jury must make a finding of liability and actual, or at least nominal, damages before punitive damages are allowed. *See* Richard C. Tinney, Annotation, *Showing of Actual Damages to Support Award of Punitive Damages,* 40 A.L.R.4th 11 (1985 & Supp. 2002); 45 Am. Jur. 2d *Interference* § 62 (1999 & Supp. 2003); *Am. Bus. Interiors, Inc. v. Haworth, Inc.,* 798 F.2d 1135 (8th Cir. 1986). *But see Platte v. Whitney Realty Co.,* 538 So. 2d 1358 (Fla. Dist. Ct. App. 1989) (punitive damages recoverable although actual damages could not be proved).

In most jurisdictions, an award of nominal damages will suffice for this purpose. *See, e.g., Taylor v. Sandoval,* 442 F. Supp. 491 (D. Colo. 1977); *Tennant v. Vazquez,* 389 So. 2d 1183 (Fla. Dist. Ct. App. 1980); *Christman v. Voyer,* 595 P.2d 410 (N.M. Ct. App. 1979). *But see Wussow v. Commercial Mechanisms, Inc.,* 279 N.W.2d 503 (Wis. Ct. App. 1979). *See generally* Richard C. Tinney, Annotation, *Showing of Actual Damages to Support Award of Punitive Damages—Modern Cases,* 40 A.L.R.4th 11 (1985 & Supp. 2002).

2.10.3.c   Actual Malice

You may find the defendant's conduct to have been undertaken with actual "malice" sufficient to enable you to award punitive damages if you find it to have been prompted or accompanied by personal ill will, spite, or hatred, either toward the plaintiff individually or toward all persons in one or more groups or categories of which the plaintiff is a member.

COMMENT

Generally, courts require proof of facts tending to establish actual, as opposed to legal, malice to justify an award of punitive damages. *See* 45 Am. Jur. 2d *Interference* § 62 (1999 & Supp. 2003); *Norwood Easthill Assocs. v. Norwood Easthill Watch*, 536 A.2d 1317 (N.J. Super. Ct. App. Div. 1988); *Anthony Pools, Inc. v. Charles & David, Inc.*, 797 S.W.2d 666 (Tex. App. 1990); *Bellefonte Underwriters Co., Inc. v. Brown*, 663 S.W.2d 562 (Tex. Ct. App. 1984). Even if not required, actual malice is always an important factor in an award of punitive damages. *See, e.g., Universal City Studios, Inc. v. Nintendo Co.*, 615 F. Supp. 838 (S.D.N.Y. 1985), *aff'd*, 797 F.2d 70 (2d Cir.), *cert. denied*, 479 U.S. 987 (1986); *Int'l Wood Processors Corp. v. Power Dry, Inc.*, 593 F. Supp. 710 (D.S.C. 1984); *Edward Vantine Studios, Inc. v. Fraternal Composite Serv., Inc.*, 373 N.W.2d 512 (Iowa Ct. App. 1985).

2.10.3.d   Wanton Conduct

You may also award punitive damages if you find that the defendant's conduct was "wanton;" that is, that the conduct was undertaken in reckless or callous disregard of, or indifference to, the rights of one or more persons, including the plaintiff.

COMMENT

See King v. G.D. Van Wagenen Co., 717 F. Supp. 667 (D. Minn. 1989); *Liston v. Home Ins. Co.*, 659 F. Supp. 276 (S.D. Miss. 1986); *Universal City Studios, Inc. v. Nintendo Co.*, 615 F. Supp. 838 (S.D.N.Y. 1985), *aff'd*, 797 F.2d 70 (2d Cir.), *cert. denied*, 479 U.S. 987 (1986); *Ramona Manor Convalescent Hosp. v. Care Enterprises*, 225 Cal. Rptr. 120 (Cal. Ct. App. 1986).

2.10.3.e   Oppressive Conduct

You also may award punitive damages if, from all of the evidence, you find that the defendant's conduct was "oppressive"; that is, that it was done in a way or manner that injured, damaged, or otherwise violated the rights of the plaintiff with unnecessary harshness or severity, as by misuse or abuse of authority or power, or by taking advantage of some weakness, disability, or misfortune of the plaintiff.

COMMENT

See Barnes Group, Inc. v. C & C Prod., Inc., 716 F.2d 1023 (4th Cir. 1983); *Rabun v. Kimberly-Clark Corp.,* 678 F.2d 1053 (11th Cir. 1982); *Int'l Wood Processors Corp. v. Power Dry, Inc.,* 593 F. Supp. 710 (D.S.C. 1984), *aff'd,* 792 F.2d 416 (4th Cir. 1986).

2.10.3.f   Amount of Punitive Damages Award

If you decide that punitive damages are appropriate in this case based upon my prior instructions, you should award the amount of punitive damages that, in your sound judgment, will justly punish the defendant for its behavior and dissuade the defendant and others from acting the same way in future, similar situations.

In fixing the amount of punitive damages, you may consider the following factors:

1. The character of the defendant's act(s);

2. The nature and extent of the harm to the plaintiff that the defendant caused or intended to cause; and

3. The defendant's financial condition.

The amount of any punitive damages should bear a reasonable relationship to the injury, harm, or damage caused by the defendant. You must also keep in mind that the amount of such punitive damages, when awarded, must be fixed with calm discretion and sound reason. Punitive damages must not be awarded, or fixed in amount, based upon any sympathy, bias, or prejudice you may feel toward any party in the case.

[If evidence of "other acts" or harm against other parties has been allowed, add the following: Some of the evidence you have heard concerned conduct by the defendant that was not the proximate cause of the damages claimed by the plaintiff in this case. Although you may consider this evidence for any bearing upon the defendant's state of mind in causing damages claimed by the plaintiff in this case, you are not to punish the defendant for conduct relating only to parties other than the plaintiff.]

[If evidence of financial worth has been allowed, add the following: You have heard evidence of the defendant's financial condition. You are not to consider the defendants' financial condition in deciding whether to award punitive damages, but you may consider it in fixing the amount of punitive damages to the extent that the actual [or nominal] damages are insufficient to justly punish the defendant for its behavior or dissuade the defendant or others from acting the same way in future, similar situations.]

COMMENT

See State Farm Mut. Auto. Ins. Co. v. Campbell, 538 U.S. 408 (2003); *Cooper Indus., Inc. v. Leatherman Tool Group, Inc.*, 121 S. Ct. 1678 (2001); *BMW of N. Am., Inc. v. Gore*, 116 S. Ct. 1589 (1996); *Jannotta v. Subway Sandwich Shops, Inc.*, 125 F.3d 503 (7th Cir. 1997); *Fed. Deposit Ins. Corp. v. W.R. Grace & Co.*, 877 F.2d 614 (7th Cir. 1989), *cert. denied*, 110 S. Ct. 1524 (1990); *Aldrich v. Thomson McKinnon Sec., Inc.*, 756 F.2d 243 (2d Cir. 1985); Damages—Modern Cases, 40 A.L.R.4th 11 (1985 & Supp. 2002).

A state may not impose damages on a defendant for actions undertaken in other states that do not violate the other states' laws. *BMW*, 116 S. Ct. at 1597 (1996). Similarly, a "defendant's dissimilar acts, independent from the acts upon which liability was premised, may not serve as the basis for punitive damages." *State Farm*, 123 S. Ct. 1523.

A defendant's financial condition as a factor in setting punitive damages is generally accepted. *See, e.g., Miller v. Rukoff-Sexton, Inc.*, 845 F.2d 209 (9th Cir. 1988) (the defendant's net worth was admissible for setting punitive damages); *Hollins v. Powell*, 773 F.2d 191 (8th Cir.) (reducing punitive damage award in light of defendant's limited resources), *cert. denied*, 475 U.S. 1119 (1985); *Rupert v. Sellers*, 368 N.Y.S.2d 904 (N.Y. App. Div. 1975) (in bifurcated trial, evidence of the defendants' net worth should be considered after special verdict). *See generally* Annotation, *Punitive Damages: Relationship to Defendant's Wealth As a Factor in Determining Propriety of Award*, 87 A.L.R.4th 141 (1991 & Supp. 2002). Some states, such as Hawaii, even have statutes making the financial condition of the defendant relevant to the amount of punitive damages awardable. Others, like New York, protect the defendant from possible prejudice at trial through the use of a bifurcated trial procedure. *See Aldrich v. Thomson McKinnon Sec., Inc.*, 589 F. Supp. 683 (S.D.N.Y. 1984). However, the Supreme Court has cautioned that the financial condition of the defendant may not be used to create bias against big businesses or to permit an award that is unrelated to the actual damages. *State Farm*, 123 S. Ct. at 1525 ("the wealth of a defendant cannot justify an otherwise unconstitutional punitive damage award."). Recent commentators have argued that the defendant's financial condition is only relevant in cases involving noneconomically motivated torts. *See, e.g.,* Andrew L. Frey, *No More Blind Man's Bluff on Punitive Damages: A Plea to the Drafters of Pattern Jury Instructions*, 29 Litig. 24 (Summer 2003). In cases where the defendant was motivated by profits, they argue, compensatory damages are sufficient to act as a deterrent. *Id.*

Chapter Three
Injurious Falsehood

Kenneth E. Kraus & Ellen S. Martin*

*   Kenneth E. Kraus is a partner and Ellen S. Martin is counsel at Schopf & Weiss LLP, 312 W. Randolph, Suite 300, Chicago, Illinois 60606, www.sw.com. Mr. Kraus may be reached at (312) 701-9328 or kraus@sw.com. Ms. Martin may be reached at (312) 701-9379 or martin@sw.com.

3.1   Introduction

The model jury charges in this chapter address the conditions for the imposition of liability at common law upon one who makes false statements of fact that disparage the quality of another's good or services. This tort has many names, including "injurious falsehood," "commercial disparagement," "product disparagement," "trade libel," "disparagement of property," and "slander of goods" (*see* Prosser, *Injurious Falsehood: The Basis of Liability*, 59 Colum. L. Rev. 425 (1959)), and is referred to here as "injurious falsehood," the name given in the *Restatement (Second) of Torts* (1976). Injurious falsehood embraces any false statement that causes financial injury. *E.g., Leavitt v. Cole*, 291 F. Supp. 2d 1338 (M.D. Fla. 2003) (injurious falsehood claims stated where clinic falsely reported that physician had retired and one physician accused another of having tax problems).

Injurious falsehood also includes slander of title, in which a defendant can incur liability for making malicious statements about the title to the plaintiff's property resulting in special damages to the plaintiff. *Childers v. Commerce Mortgage Inv.*, 579 N.E.2d 219 (Ohio Ct. App. 1989); *Kensington Dev. Corp. v. Israel*, 407 N.W.2d 269 (Wis. Ct. App. 1987), *aff'd*, 419 N.W.2d 241 (Wis. 1988). *See generally* W. Page Keeton, *Prosser & Keeton on the Law of Torts* § 128 (5th ed. 1984) [hereinafter Keeton]; Prosser, *Restatement (Second) of Torts* § 23A (1976).

A plaintiff must prove publication or communication to a third person of a false derogatory statement of fact concerning its goods or services. *Art Metal-U.S.A., Inc. v. United States*, 753 F.2d 1151 (D.C. Cir. 1985); *System Ops., Inc. v. Scientific Games Dev. Corp.*, 555 F.2d 1131 (3d Cir. 1977); 1 F. Harper & F. James, *Law of Torts* § 6.3 (1956); Note, *The Law of Commercial Disparagement: Business Defamation's Impotent Ally*, 63 Yale L.J. 75, n.58 (1953).

The plaintiff must also show that the defendant's statement was understood to refer to the plaintiff's goods or services and to disparage their quality. *Art Metal-U.S.A., Inc. v. United States*, 753 F.2d 1151 (D.C. Cir. 1985); *Nat'l Ref. Co. v. Benzo Gas Motor Fuel*

Co., 20 F. 2d 763 (8th Cir.), *cert. denied,* 275 U.S. 570 (1927); *Caron Corp. v. R.K.O. Pictures, Inc.,* 28 N.Y.S.2d 1020 (N.Y. App. Div. 1941), *aff'd,* 35 N.Y.S.2d 715 (N.Y. App. Div. 1942), *cert. denied,* 318 U.S. 757 (1943). Whether the injurious statement is capable of a disparaging meaning is a question of law for the court. *Redco Corp. v. CBS, Inc.,* 758 F.2d 970 (3d Cir. 1985), *cert. denied,* 474 U.S. 843 (1985).

In addition, the plaintiff must prove that the statement was made maliciously. *Dale Sys. v. Gen. Teleradio,* 105 F. Supp. 745 (S.D.N.Y. 1952); *Tagart v. Savannah Gas Co.,* 175 S.E. 491 (Ga. 1934); William L. Prosser, *Injurious Falsehood: The Basis of Liability,* 59 Colum. L. Rev. 425 (1959). In some jurisdictions, this element may be satisfied by establishing that the defendant acted with knowledge or reckless disregard of the falsity of the statement (*Art Metal-U.S.A., Inc.,* 753 F.2d at 1155). In other jurisdictions, the plaintiff must establish a specific intent to cause harm to the plaintiff or plaintiff's pecuniary interest. *Williams v. Burns,* 540 F. Supp. 1243 (D. Colo. 1982).

Finally, the plaintiff must prove that the statements were a substantial factor in causing plaintiff's actual monetary loss (special damages). *E.g., Landstrom v. Thorpe,* 189 F.2d 46 (8th Cir.) *cert. denied,* 342 U.S. 819 (1951); *Eversharp, Inc. v. Pal Blade Co.,* 182 F.2d 779 (2d Cir. 1950); *Polygram Records, Inc. v. Superior Court,* 216 Cal. Rptr. 252 (Cal. Ct. App. 1985); *Rite Aid Corp. v. Lake Shore Inv.,* 471 A.2d 735 (Md. 1984); *Julie Research Lab., Inc. v. Gen. Resistance, Inc.,* 25 A.D.2d 634, 268 N.Y.S.2d 187 (N.Y. App. Div. 1966), *aff'd,* 227 N.E.2d 892 (N.Y. 1967); *Restatement (Second) of Torts* § 633 (1976).

Injurious falsehood is not identical to defamation. They have different roots, the former growing out of tortious interference with contract and the latter from damage to reputation. The law generally affords reputational interests greater protection than the merely commercial.[1] However, in practice, the two torts are

---

1. "Who steals my purse steals trash . . . But he that filches from me my good name robs me of that which not enriches him and makes me poor indeed." Shakespeare, *Othello,* Act III, sc. 3.

often conflated and confused by the courts. *See Flotech, Inc. v. E.I. DuPont de Nemours Co.*, 627 F. Supp. 358 (D. Mass.1985), *aff'd*, 814 F.2d 775 (1st Cir. 1987).

Because both torts seek to impose liability for publication of a false statement to third parties, many of the same First Amendment protections may be available to defendants. *Blatty v. New York Times Co.*, 42 Cal. 3d 1033, 1042-43, 232 Cal. Rptr. 542, 728 P.2d 1177 (1986), *cert. denied*, 485 U.S. 934, 99 L. Ed. 2d 268, 108 S. Ct. 1107 (1988) ("Although the limitations that define the First Amendment's zone of protection for the press were established in defamation actions, they are not peculiar to such actions but apply to all claims whose gravamen is the alleged injurious falsehood of a statement. . . . [I]t is immaterial for First Amendment purposes whether the statement in question relates to the plaintiff himself or merely to his property broadly defined."); *Amcor Inv. Corp. v. Cox Ariz. Publ'ns*, 158 Ariz. 566, 764 P.2d 327 (Ariz. Ct. App. 1988) ("[T]here is no basis for distinguishing between libel and disparagement [with] respect [to constitutional protections]."); *Teilhaber Mfg. Co. v. Unarco Materials Storage*, 791 P.2d 1164 (Colo. Ct. App. 1989) *cert. denied*, 803 P.2d 517 (Colo. 1991) ("The constitutional protections afforded a defendant in a defamation action are applicable to a defendant in a product disparagement action."); *Unelko Corp. v. Rooney*, 912 F.2d 1049 (9th Cir. 1990), *cert. denied*, 499 U.S. 961, 113 L. Ed. 2d 650, 111 S. Ct. 1586 (1991) (trade libel claims "are subject to the same First Amendment requirements that govern actions for defamation"); *Quantum Elecs. Corp. v. Consumers Union*, 881 F. Supp. 753 (D.R.I. 1995) ("The . . . actual malice standard applies to both product disparagement claims and defamation claims where the plaintiff is a public figure."); *Suzuki Motor Corp. v. Consumers Union of U.S., Inc.*, 292 F.3d 1192 (9th Cir. 2002), *withdrawn and superseded in part on denial of reh'g en banc*, 330 F.3d 1110 (9th Cir. 2003) (a public figure plaintiff in a product disparagement case must prove by clear and convincing evidence that media defendant published disparaging statements with "actual malice."); *Moldea v. New York Times Co.*, 22 F.3d 310 (D.C. Cir. 1994) ("[A] plaintiff may not use related causes of action to avoid the constitutional requisites of a defamation."). The Supreme Court, however, has yet to decide the issue. *Bose Corp. v. Consumers Union of United States, Inc.*, 466 U.S. 485 (1984) ("We express no view" on whether the actual malice standard applies to product disparagement claim). Also, it is not clear whether the same standards would be applied. *Va. Bd. of Pharm. v. Va. Citizens Consumer Council, Inc.*, 425 U.S. 748 (1976) ("commonsense differences" that exist between commercial messages and other types of protected expression justify different levels of protection).

The generally accepted rules regarding privilege to publish defamatory matter apply to the publication of injurious falsehood. *See, e.g., General Elec. v. Sargent & Lundy*, 916 F.2d 1119 (6th Cir. 1990), *appeal after remand*, 954 F.2d 724 (6th Cir. 1992); *B.C. Morton Int'l Corp. v. FDIC*, 199 F. Supp. 702 (D. Mass. 1961); *Restatement (Second) of Torts* §§ 646A, 649 (1976); Keeton, *supra* § 128 at 924.

Whether the alleged circumstances would make the statement privileged is a question of law for the court. *General Elec. Co.*, 916 F.2d at 1119; *Restatement (Second) of Torts* § 652. The existence of the circumstances on which the privilege is based and the determination, in the case of a conditional privilege, whether it has been abused are, however, questions of fact for the jury. *General Elec. Co.*, 916 F.2d at 1119. The defendant bears the burden of proving the facts establishing the existence of an absolute or conditional privilege. *Restatement (Second) of Torts* § 651B.

A plaintiff may then refute a conditional privilege by showing actual malice. *Salit v. Ruden*, 742 So. 2d 381 (Fla. Dist. Ct. App. 1999); *Olivieri v. McDonald's Corp.*, 678 F. Supp. 996 (E.D.N.Y. 1988). Most courts hold that actual malice is established by proof that the person making the statement knew it was false, that it was made with a deliberate desire to do another person harm, or was made recklessly, without regard to the consequences and under circumstances from which a reasonably prudent person should have anticipated that injury to another would follow. *See, e.g., Redco Corp. v. CBS, Inc.*, 758 F.2d 970 (3d Cir. 1985), *cert. denied*, 474 U.S. 843 (1985); *Modern Prods., Inc. v. Schwartz*, 734 F.

Supp. 362 (E.D. Wis. 1990); *Morrison v. Nat'l Broad. Co.*, 266 N.Y.S.2d 406 (N.Y. App. Div. 1965), *rev'd on other grounds*, 227 N.E.2d 572 (N.Y. 1967).

Several model instructions for the tort of injurious falsehood are available. *Alabama Pattern Jury Instructions Civil, Second Edition* § 23.27, Alabama Pattern Jury Instructions Committee-Civil (2004); *Pennsylvania Suggested Standard Civil Jury Instructions, Second Edition* § 13.11, Pennsylvania Bar Institute (2003); *Maryland Civil Pattern Jury Instructions, 4th Edition* § 7.3, Maryland Institute for Continuing Professional Education of Lawyers, Inc. (2003); Wolokoff, Harvey J., *Massachusetts Superior Court Civil Practice Jury Instructions* § 12.7 (2003); *New York Pattern Jury Instructions-Civil* § 3:55, Committee on Pattern Jury Instructions, Association of Supreme Court Justices (2003).

3.2 General Instructions

3.2.1 Elements of Liability

To find liability for injurious falsehood, you must find from a preponderance of the evidence that:

- the defendant published a statement, and the statement was reasonably understood by those who heard it to cast doubt upon the [title/quality] of plaintiff's [identify goods and/or services];

- the statement was false;

- the defendant intended to cause monetary loss or reasonably should have known that such loss would result; and

- the statement was a substantial factor in causing the plaintiff monetary loss.

If you find that the plaintiff has proved these elements by a preponderance of the evidence, then you will consider the questions of damages under instructions to be given.

COMMENT

This charge reflects the traditional standard for establishing liability for injurious falsehood concerning one's goods or services. *Salit v. Ruden*, 742 So. 2d 381 (Fla. Dist. Ct. App. 1999); *Art Metal-U.S.A., Inc. v. United States*, 753 F.2d 1151 (D.C. Cir. 1985); *Bacchus Indus., Inc. v. Arvin Indus., Inc.*, 939 F.2d 887 (10th Cir. 1991); *Williams v. Burns*, 540 F. Supp. 1243 (D. Colo. 1982); *Neville v. Higbie*, 20 P.2d 348 (Cal. Ct. App. 1933); *Teilhaber Mfg. Co. v. Unasco Materials Storage*, 791 P.2d 1164 (Colo. Ct. App. 1989), *cert. denied*, 803 P.2d 517 (Colo. 1991); *Drug Research Corp. v. Curtis Publ'g Co.*, 166 N.E.2d 319 (N.Y. 1957); Keeton, *supra* § 128; Note, *Corporate Defamation and Product Disparagement: Narrowing the Analogy to Personal Defamation*, 75 Colum. L. Rev. 963, 968-72 (1975); Note, *The Law of Commercial Disparagement: Business Defamation's Impotent Ally*, 63 Yale L.J. 65 (1953).

The defendant need not be solely motivated to injure the plaintiff. *Kollenberg v. Ramirez*, 339 N.W. 2d 176 (Mich. Ct. App. 1983).

Note that there will also be liability if the statement is intended to convey a disparaging meaning and is so understood, although reasonable people would not have so understood it. *Restatement (Second) of Torts* § 629, cmt. f (1976). In such a case, the charge should be amended to read "that it was intended to be and was in fact understood to cast doubt."

Some courts require that the defendant know that the statement is false or make it in reckless disregard to its truth or falsity as an element of the tort of injurious falsehood. *Patel v. Soriano*, 848 A.2d 803 (N.J. Super. Ct. App. Div. 2004); *Forbes, Inc. v. Granada Biosciences, Inc.*, 124 S.W.3d 167 (Tex. 2003); *Melaleuca, Inc. v. Clark*, 78 Cal. Rptr. 2d 627 (Cal. Ct. App. 1999) ("We believe that it is clear the Constitution will not permit liability to be imposed for injurious falsehood absent a showing of actual malice."); *New York Pattern Jury Instructions-Civil* § 3:55 (2003). In these jurisdictions, a new paragraph (3) should be added to the charge, "that the defendant knew that the statement was false or acted in reckless disregard to its truth or falsity," and the rest of the charge should be renumbered appropriately.

3.3   Publication

3.3.1   Generally

The plaintiff contends that the defendant published a statement that could reasonably be understood by those who heard it to cast doubt on the quality of the plaintiff's [goods and/or services]. The defendant denies that such a statement was published. If you find that the statement was not published, your verdict will be for the defendant.

COMMENT

Injurious falsehood requires publication. *Art Metal-U.S.A., Inc. v. United States*, 753 F.2d 1151 (D.C. Cir. 1985); Keeton, *supra*, § 128. Note that this charge assumes the defendant is not denying that the statement was made, but is only denying publication. If the making of the statement is denied, then, of course, an additional charge will be required to reflect this issue.

3.3.2   Definition of Publication

Words are published when they are communicated or circulated in any manner to any person other than the [plaintiff, or, if plaintiff is a corporation, the officers of the plaintiff].

[State basis here of claimed publication.] Defendant denies [state disputed facts].

If you find that the plaintiff has not sustained plaintiff's burden of proving that [state disputed facts], your verdict must be for the defendant.

COMMENT

This charge is based on the charge used in *Big O Tire Dealers, Inc. v. Goodyear Tire & Rubber Co.,* 408 F. Supp. 1219 (D. Colo. 1976), *modified on other grounds,* 561 F.2d 1365 (10th Cir. 1977), *cert. dismissed,* 434 U.S. 1052 (1978). *See Gen. Elec. Co. v. Sargent & Lundy,* 916 F.2d 1119 (6th Cir. 1990); *Hawaiian Ins. & Guar. Co., Ltd. v. Blair, Ltd.,* 726 P.2d 1310 (Haw. Ct. App. 1986).

3.4   Disparaging Statement

3.4.1   Theory of Injurious Falsehood

In this action, plaintiff contends that defendant said of plaintiff's [specify property or services involved] that it [set forth statement claimed to be disparaging]. Defendant denies that [he made such statement, that it was understood to be disparaging]. You must first determine [whether defendant made such statement and/or whether such statement was reasonably understood by those who saw/heard it to cast doubt upon the [quality ownership] of the property/services]. If you find that [no statement was made and/or the statement was not reasonably understood to cast such doubt], your verdict will be for defendant.

COMMENT

This charge is based on the one recommended in section 3:55 of *New York Pattern Jury Instructions* (2003). *See also Big O Tire Dealers, Inc. v. Goodyear Tire & Rubber Co.*, 408 F. Supp. 1219 (D. Colo. 1976), *modified on other grounds*, 561 F.2d 1365 (10th Cir. 1977) *dismissed*, 434 U.S. 1052 (1978); *Art Metal-U.S.A., Inc. v. United States*, 753 F.2d 1151 (D.C. Cir. 1985).

Whether an allegedly disparaging statement refers to the plaintiff's goods or services or is understood to cast doubt upon the quantity or the quality of the plaintiff's goods or services are questions to be resolved by the jury. *See, e.g., Nat'l Ref. Co. v. Benzo Gas Motor Fuel Co.*, 20 F.2d 763 (8th Cir.), *cert. denied*, 275 U.S. 570 (1927); *Caron Corp. v. R.K.O. Pictures, Inc.*, 28 N.Y.S. 2d 1020 (N.Y. App. Div. 1941), *aff'd*, 35 N.Y.S.2d 715 (N.Y. App. Div. 1942), *cert. denied*, 318 U.S. 757 (1943).

Also note that section 629, cmt. f of the *Restatement (Second) of Torts* (1976) provides authority for the argument that liability will be found if the statement is intended to convey a disparaging meaning and is so understood, although reasonable people would not have so understood it. *See Kollenberg v. Ramirez*, 339 N.W.2d 176 (Mich. Ct. App. 1983).

3.4.2 Reference to Plaintiff

The statement does not mention the plaintiff's [goods and/or services] by name, but the plaintiff contends that it was reasonably understood by those who [heard or read] the statement from [set forth references in the statement and extrinsic facts in the case that the plaintiff contends relate the statement to plaintiff] that the statement referred to plaintiff's [goods and/or services]. If you find that those who [heard or read] the statement reasonably understood that it referred to the plaintiff's [goods and/or services], based on the content of the statement and from facts about the plaintiff's [goods and/or services] known to such people, then you will consider [state next disputed issue in the action].

COMMENT

This charge is based on the one recommended in section 3.23 of New York Pattern Jury Instructions (1968). Although the charge is for use in a defamation cause of action, the charge is equally applicable to injurious falsehood actions. The authorities referenced in the comment to section 3.4.1 and *Blatty v. New York Times Co.*, 728 P.2d 1177 (Cal. 1986), *cert. denied*, 485 U.S. 934 (1988) (omission of plaintiff's book from best-seller list not actionable as injurious falsehood because no statement was made regarding the plaintiff) also support this charge.

3.4.3 Disparaging Quality

The plaintiff contends that the defendant's statement was reasonably understood by those who [heard or read] it to cast doubt upon the quality of its [goods and/or services] in that [set forth plaintiff's argument on this point]. If you find that such meaning could reasonably be attached to it, you will then consider [set forth next disputed issue in the action].

COMMENT

This charge is based upon *Denis v. R.J. Reynolds Tobacco Co.*, 107 N.Y.S.2d 877 (N.Y. App. Div. 1951), *aff'd*, 106 N.E.2d 64 (N.Y. 1952) and *Restatement (Second) of Torts* § 629 cmt. (f) (1976). As noted in section 3.2.2, above, if the statement is intended to convey a disparaging meaning and is in fact so understood, although reasonable people would not have so understood it, the suggested charge in section 3.2.2 should be used.

3.4.4   Plain Meaning

In determining whether the statement was reasonably understood to [insert "refer to the plaintiff's goods and/or services"
or "cast doubt on the quality of the plaintiff's goods and/or services," depending on the allegation], you should consider the
plain and natural meaning of the words used in the plain and
popular sense in which the public would understand them. You
should also consider the words used in their complete context
and not dwell upon isolated parts of phrases. Thus, you must
interpret the words used in connection with and as a related
part of the complete communication and give them such meaning as would naturally be given by persons of ordinary understanding and intelligence.

COMMENT

This charge is one that was used in *Big O Tire Dealers v. Goodyear
Tire & Rubber Co.*, 408 F. Supp. 1219 (D. Colo. 1976), *modified on
other grounds*, 561 F.2d 1365 (10th Cir. 1977), *cert. dismissed*, 434
U.S. 1052 (1978). *See Flotech, Inc. v. E.I. DuPont de Nemours Co.*,
627 F. Supp. 358 (D. Mass.1985), *aff'd on other grounds*, 814 F.2d
775 (1st Cir. 1987).

3.5   Falsity

3.5.1   Generally

If you find that the statement made by the defendant was reasonably understood by those who read it to cast doubt on the quality of the plaintiff's [goods and/or services], you must then determine whether the statement was false. If you find that it was not, your verdict will be for the defendant. If you find that it was false, you will then consider whether the statement was made maliciously.

COMMENT

In injurious falsehood cases, the burden is upon the plaintiff to prove the statement is false, rather than upon the defendant to establish truth as a defense. *Systems Ops., Inc. v. Scientific Games Dev. Corp.*, 555 F.2d 1131, 1142 (3d Cir. 1977) (following "the unanimous view of the other jurisdictions that the plaintiff in a product disparagement action must bear the burden of proving the falsity of the disparaging communications"); *Zerpol Corp. v. DMP Corp.*, 561 F. Supp. 404 (E.D. Pa. 1983); *Aldabbagh v. Arizona Dep't of Liquor Licenses & Control*, 783 P.2d 1207 (Ariz. Ct. App. 1989); *Hurlbut v. Gulf Atl. Life Ins. Co.*, 749 S.W.2d 762 (Tex. 1987); Keeton, *supra* § 128.

3.5.2   Puffing

A general statement of opinion or of comparison by the defendant stating that [his/her] [goods and/or services] are of better quality than those of the plaintiff, when the statement does not include specific facts relating to the plaintiff's [goods and/or services], is not actionable.

COMMENT

An injurious falsehood is not actionable if it is merely a statement of comparison or opinion. *Skinder-Strauss Assocs. v. MCLE,* 914 F. Supp. 665 (D. Mass. 1995) (trade disparagement does not include a competitor's general claims that its product is superior, because such conduct "is part and parcel of competition"); *Chernick v. Rothstein,* 612 N.Y.S.2d 77 (N.Y. App. Div. 1994) ("personal opinion and rhetorical hyperbole" not actionable); *Brignoli v. Balch Hardy & Scheinman, Inc.,* 645 F. Supp. 1201 (S.D.N.Y. 1986); *Rodco Corp. v. CBS, Inc.,* 758 F.2d 970, 972 (3d Cir. 1985), *cert. denied,* 474 U.S. 843 (1985) ("It is well settled that the use of catchy phrases or hyperbole does not necessarily render statements defamatory that would otherwise be non-actionable.").

However, the expression of opinion implying the existence of a basis in undisclosed fact can be actionable. *Aerosonic v. Trodyne,* 402 F.2d 223 (5th Cir.1968) (exact copy claimed "superior"); *System Ops.,* 555 F.2d at 1131 (lottery tickets "insecure"); *Harris Diamond Co., Inc. v. Army Times Publ'g Co.,* 280 F. Supp. 273 (S.D. N.Y. 1968) ("poor quality").

Some courts include puffing as a conditional privilege. *Picker Int'l, Inc. v. Leavitt,* 865 F. Supp. 951 (D. Mass. 1994).

3.5.3 Determining Falsity

The plaintiff contends that the statement made by the defendant was false because [set forth plaintiff's argument]. You will determine from the evidence presented whether the plaintiff has established what plaintiff claims to be the actual situation, and then compare that with the statement made by the defendant. The motivation of the defendant is unimportant if you find that there is no substantial difference between the statement and the actual situation as determined by you. If you find that there was no substantial difference between the statement and the actual situation as determined by you, your verdict will be for the defendant. If you find that the statement differed in some substantial respect from the actual situation as determined by you, your finding will be for the plaintiff on the question of whether the statement was false.

COMMENT

This charge is based on section 634 of the *Restatement (Second) of Torts* (1976). Truthfulness, and not motivation, is the decisive factor of this instruction. Thus, even if defendant's goal in publishing the statement is to harm the plaintiff, there is no injurious falsehood if the statement is true. *C.R. Bard, Inc. v. Wordtronics Corp.*, 561 A.2d 694 (N.J. Super. Ct. Law Div. 1989).

3.6 Privileges

3.6.1 Absolute Privilege

The defendant claims that the defendant's statement is absolutely privileged. The law recognizes that a person has the right to make a statement, even though the statement is disparaging or maliciously made, when [state basis of the claimed absolute privilege].

In this action, you must determine whether the defendant's statement was made on an absolutely privileged occasion. Defendant claims [state basis of claimed privilege]. Plaintiff denies [state disputed fact or facts]. If you find that the defendant has not sustained its burden of proving [state disputed fact or facts], then the occasion was not privileged and your verdict will be for the plaintiff, provided you find that plaintiff has met the burden of proof on what plaintiff must establish to prove liability. If you find that the defendant has sustained the burden of proving [state disputed fact or facts], your verdict will be for the defendant.

COMMENT

Absolute privilege arises in relatively few situations. For example, statements made in judicial proceedings and statements made preceding a judicial proceeding, if made in contemplation of litigation, are absolutely privileged. *Gen. Elec. Co. v. Sargent & Lundy*, 916 F.2d 1119 (6th Cir. 1990). This charge will rarely be necessary because the existence of an absolute privilege is generally a question of law. *Gen. Elec. Co. v. Sargent & Lundy*, 916 F.2d 1119 (6th Cir. 1990); *Cheatum v. Wehle*, 159 N.E.2d 166 (N.Y. 1959); *Restatement (Second) of Torts* § 52 (1976). Only when there is a question of fact concerning when and where the statement in issue was made will there be a question for the jury. *E.g., Douglas v. Collins*, 196 N.E. 577 (N.Y. 1935); *Restatement (Second) of Torts* § 52.

■ 129

Courts disagree as to whether the filing of a lien is part of a judicial proceeding and entitled to the absolute privilege. *Compare, Frank Pisano & Assocs. v. Taggart,* 29 Cal. App. 3d 1, 105 Cal. Rptr. 414 (Cal. Ct. App. 1972) (lien entitled to absolute privilege); *Donohoe Constr. v. Mount Vernon Assocs.,* 369 S.E.2d 857 (Va. 1988) (same); *Peters Well Drilling Co. v. Hanzula,* 575 A.2d 1375 (N.J. Super. Ct. App. Div.1990) (perfected lien sought to be enforced by suit entitled to absolute privilege) *with Simmons v. Futral,* 586 S.E.2d 732 (Ga. Ct. App. 2003) (lien not entitled to absolute privilege until suit filed); *Jeffrey v. Cathers,* 104 S.W.3d 424 (Mo. Ct. App. 2003) (absolute privilege does not apply to mechanic's lien); *Gregory's Inc. v. Haan,* 545 N.W. 2d 488 (S.D. 1996) (filing of a materialman's lien need not result in a lawsuit, so absolute privilege does not apply); *Kensington Dev. Corp. v. Israel,* 142 Wis. 2d 894, 419 N.W.2d 241 (Wis. 1988) (conditional privilege, rather than an absolute privilege, applied to statements in a *lis pendens* notice).

3.6.2   Conditional Privilege

A statement concerning another's [goods and/or services] made by one who [state basis of claim of conditional privilege] is privileged if [state elements of privilege]. Even if a privileged statement is in fact false and disparages the plaintiff's [goods and/or services], the person making the statements may not be held liable unless, in making the statement, [state conditions when conditional privilege will be exceeded].

If you determine that the defendant's statement was privileged, you must then consider whether the plaintiff has established that the statement was maliciously made.

COMMENT

This charge should be used when there is a claim of conditional privilege and the court rules that if the facts claimed are proved, a conditional privilege will exist. Conditional privileges such as discharge of duty to public or duty to others, common interest in subject matter, self-defense and request or provocation by the person injured are available defenses to the tort of injurious falsehood. *Patel v. Soriano*, 848 A.2d 803 (N.J. Super. Ct. App. Div. 2004); *Paint Brush Corp. v. Neu*, 599 N.W.2d 384 (S.D. 1999); *Chernick v. Rothstein*, 612 N.Y.S.2d 77 (N.Y. App. Div. 1994); *Cambridge Title Co. v. Transamerica Title Ins. Co.*, 817 F. Supp. 1263 (D. Md. 1992); *Williams v. Burns*, 540 F. Supp. 1243 (D. Colo. 1982) (duty to others and request of person injured); *Binkewitz v. Allstate Ins. Co.*, 537 A.2d 723 (N.J. Super. Ct. App. Div. 1988) (statement by insurer that appraiser not competent was conditionally privileged because appraisal procedure is quasi-judicial); *cf. Restatement (Second) of Torts* § 651 cmt. e (1976). A showing of actual malice or that the privilege has been exceeded will defeat the affirmative defense of conditional privilege. *Olivieri v. McDonald's Corp.*, 678 F. Supp. 996 (S.D.N.Y. 1988).

There are two special conditional privileges for injurious falsehood. The privilege of a rival claimant to property to disparage another's claim to the property (see *Restatement (Second) of Torts* § 647) is abused by asserting the claim without an honest belief that there is a substantial chance that the claim is sustainable. The privilege of a competitor to claim that his products or other things are superior to those of his rival *(Picker Int'l, Inc. v. Leavitt*, 865 F. Supp. 951 (D. Mass. 1994); *see also Restatement (Second) of Torts* § 649) does not depend upon even an honest belief to this effect. The scope of this privilege can be exceeded when the defendant's statements contain or imply assertions of specific unfavorable facts regarding the competitor's product or services. *Paint Brush*, 599 N.W.2d at 384. *See* section 3.5.2. *supra.* The rules on conditional privilege to publish defamatory matter generally apply to the publication of an injurious falsehood. *Restatement (Second) of Torts* § 646A. A conditional privilege may be exceeded when the statement contains matters beyond that which is necessary to protect the interest claimed or when the statement is published more widely than necessary. *Dairy Stores v. Sentinel Publ'g*, 516 A.2d 220 (N.J. 1986); *Am. Pet Motels v. Chicago Veterinary Med. Assocs.*, 435 N.E.2d 1297 (Ill. Ct. App. 1982), *abrogated on other grounds; Kuwik v. Starmark*, 619 N.E.2d 129 (Ill. 1993).

3.6.3 Malice

If you find that the statement was subject to a conditional privilege, you must consider whether it was made with malice. In determining whether the statement was made with malice, you may consider [set forth factors for which there is evidence, such as the language in which the statement was cast; whether at the time the defendant made the statement defendant knew that the statement was false or believed that it was true; whether it was recklessly made with intent to interfere; and all of the other facts and circumstances surrounding the making of the statement].

The burden of proving malice by clear and convincing evidence is upon the plaintiff. [Use as much of the remainder of this paragraph as the evidence in the case warrants and depending upon whether your jurisdiction requires knowing falsity, reckless disregard or ill will.] A false statement is made maliciously if the person making it knows that the statement is false. A false statement is made maliciously even though the person making it did not know that it was false if (1) it is made with intent to interfere with another person's interest or a deliberate desire to do another person harm, and/or (2) it is made recklessly, without regard to the consequences, and under circumstances from which the defendant as a reasonably prudent person would have anticipated that injury to another would follow. If you find [that the defendant had serious doubts about the truth of the statement and/or that the statement was made in order to injure the plaintiff], you will conclude that it was made maliciously.

If you find that the statement was conditionally privileged but was made with malice, you should find the privilege does not apply.

COMMENT

This charge is based on section 3.55 of New York Pattern Jury Instructions (2003). It reflects, in part, the accepted view concerning how malice may be established. *See, e.g., Melaleuca, Inc. v. Clark*, 78 Cal. Rptr. 2d 627 (Cal. Ct. App. 1999) (instruction that jury could find malice if defendant "must have had" serious doubts about the truth of the statement was in error because malice requires subjective recklessness or doubt); *Morrison v. Nat'l Broad. Co.*, 266 N.Y.S.2d 406 (N.Y. App. Div. 1965), *rev'd on other grounds*, 227 N.E.2d 572 (N.Y. 1967); *Restatement (Second) of Torts* § 623A (1976); *Art Metal-U.S.A., Inc. v. United States*, 753 F.2d 1151 (D.C. Cir. 1985); *Modern Prods., Inc. v. Schwartz*, 734 F. Supp. 362 (E.D. Wis. 1990); *L.L. Bean, Inc. v. Drake Publishers, Inc.*, 625 F. Supp. 1531 (D. Me. 1986), *rev'd on other grounds*, 811 F.2d 26 (1st Cir.), *appeal dismissed and cert. denied*, 483 U.S. 1013 (1987).

Commonly, malice is defined by the "actual malice" standard enunciated in *New York Times Co. v. Sullivan*, 376 U.S. 254 (1964): that the defendant made the statement with knowledge that it was false or with reckless disregard of whether it was false or not. In fact, according to the *Restatement (Second) of Torts* commentators, the Supreme Court borrowed the *New York Times* standard from the scienter requirement governing trade libel and product disparagement. (*Restatement (Second)* § 623A, cmt. d; *see, e.g., Melaleuca, Inc. v. Clark*, 78 Cal. Rptr. 2d 627 (Cal. Ct. App. 1999)).

However, malice in a disparagement action may also mean that the defendant was motivated by either ill will or an intent to harm even without knowing falsity or reckless disregard for the truth or falsity. *Williams v. Burns*, 540 F. Supp. 1243, 1248 n.3 (D. Colo. 1982). It remains to be seen (and is beyond the scope of this chapter) whether an injurious falsehood claim alleging only intent to interfere with another person's interest or deliberate desire to do another person harm, rather than the more traditional knowingly false or in reckless disregard of truth or falsity, will survive constitutional scrutiny. *Restatement (Second) of Torts* § 623A cmt. d.

In most situations, both types of malice are required. *Peckham v. Hirschfeld*, 570 A.2d 663 (R.I. 1990) (In a slander of title action, the mere filing of an interest in the land records that is later determined to be false does not show malice. Rather, it must be shown that the claim was false, that the defendant knew it was false when the defendant filed it, and/or that defendant filed it intending to harm the plaintiff). Malice is an issue of fact that must be proved by clear and convincing evidence. *Patel v. Soriano*, 848 A2d 803 (N.J. Super. Ct. App. Div. 2004). For a discussion of problems in proving malice, see Note, *The Law of Commercial Disparagement: Business Defamation's Impotent Ally*, 63 Yale L.J. 65, 78-82 (1953.)

3.7 Special Damages

3.7.1 Generally

If you found that the statement was false [and, if applicable, not protected by a conditional privilege, or conditionally privileged but malicious], you will next consider whether the statement was a substantial factor in causing monetary loss to plaintiff.

COMMENT

This charge reflects the essential element of special damages, which plaintiff must prove as an essential part of plaintiff's cause of action. See sections 3.1, 3.2.3, *supra. See also, e.g., Salit v. Ruden*, 742 So. 2d 381 (Fla. Dist. Ct. App. 1999); *Golden Palace, Inc. v. Nat'l Broad. Co., Inc.*, 386 F. Supp. 107 (D.D.C. 1974), *aff'd mem.*, 530 F.2d 1094 (1976); *Morrison v. Nat'l Broad. Co.*, 266 N.Y.S.2d 406 (N.Y. App. Div. 1965), *rev'd on other grounds*, 227 N.E.2d 572 (N.Y. 1967); *Penn-Ohio Steel Corp. v. Allis-Chalmers Mfg. Co.*, 184 N.Y.S.2d 58 (N.Y. App. Div. 1959).

3.7.2 Monetary Loss

The plaintiff claims to have suffered monetary loss in the following respects: [set forth plaintiff's claims].

If you find that the plaintiff did not suffer such a loss, your verdict will be for the defendant.

COMMENT

Special damages are essential to a claim of injurious falsehood. *Zerpol Corp. v. DMP Corp.,* 561 F. Supp. 404 (E.D. Pa. 1983); *Polygram Records, Inc. v. Superior Court,* 216 Cal. Rptr. 252 (Cal. Ct. App. 1985); *Falls v. Sporting News Publ'g Co.,* 714 F. Supp. 843 (E.D. Mich. 1989), *on remand from* 834 F.2d 61(6th Cir. 1987), *aff'd,* 899 F.2d 1221 (6th Cir. 1990). Examples of special damages that are recoverable include lost sales (*e.g., Hunt Oil Co. v. Berry,* 86 So. 2d 7 (Miss. 1956), *corrected,* 86 So. 2d 854 (Miss. 1956); *but see Marr v. Putnam,* 246 P.2d 509 (Or. 1952)) and expenses of legal proceedings, as well as other expenses necessary to counteract the publication (*e.g., Maytag Co. v. Meadows Mfg. Co.,* 45 F.2d 299 (7th Cir. 1930), *cert. denied,* 283 U.S. 843 (1931); *Womack v. McDonald,* 121 So. 57 (Ala. 1929); *Dowse v. Doris Trust Co.,* 208 P.2d 956 (Utah 1949); *see Salit v. Ruden,* 742 So. 2d 381 (Fla. Dist. Ct. App. 1999) (shareholder alleging injurious falsehood must plead realized loss rather than just diminution in value)). Damages for emotional distress are not available.

Generally, for plaintiff to recover damages for lost sales, it must show an established business, the amount of sales from a substantial time period preceding the publication, the amount of sales following the publication, facts showing that the decrease was caused by the publication (*see* section 3.7.3), and either the identity of specific lost customers or facts showing that it would not be possible to identify specific customers. *Forum Publ'ns, Inc. v. P.T. Publishers, Inc.,* 700 F. Supp. 236 (E.D. Pa. 1988); *Verizon Directories v. Yellow Book USA, Inc.,* 309 F. Supp 2d 401 (E.D. N.Y. 2004) (persons who ceased to be customers or who refused to purchase must be named); *Charles Atlas, Ltd. v. Time-Life Books,*

Inc., 570 F. Supp. 150 (S.D.N.Y. 1983) (fact that business depended upon mail orders sufficiently explained plaintiff's inability to identify lost customers); *Teilhaber Mfg. Co. v. Unasco Materials Storage,* 791 P.2d 1164 (Colo. Ct. App. 1989), *cert. denied,* 803 P.2d 517 (Colo. 1991) (customers need not be identified where sales made through independent distributors).

Counsel should be cognizant of the fact that, when applicable, the requirement of "special damages" may limit the utility of the action, because documenting the loss of specific customers will often be difficult. As one commentator has observed:

> The result of this requirement is that the more sophisticated the business, the more difficult it is to satisfy the damage proof requirements. As the business increases in size and complexity, and if the plaintiff is a national or regional seller, it becomes more and more difficult for him to compile a list of lost customers. In contrast to the small storekeeper, he often does not note the loss of customers immediately, nor recall their names or their reasons for terminating their business with him.

Edward L. Graf, *Disparaging the Product—Are the Remedies Reliable?* 9 Duq. L. Rev. 163, 176 (1971).

3.7.3   Proximate Cause

If you find that the plaintiff did suffer the claimed losses, you must then determine whether the defendant's statement was the proximate cause of the plaintiff's loss or damage.

In this regard, the defendant's statement will be determined to be the proximate cause of the plaintiff's loss or damage if you find that it was a substantial factor in causing the loss or damage, but it need not be the only factor. The statement is a substantial factor in causing the loss or damage if it had such an effect in producing the loss that reasonable persons would regard it as a cause of the loss or damage, considering any other contributing factors, including whether defendant's conduct created a condition or chain of events that was continuous and active up to the time of the damage to the plaintiff, and the lapse of time between the defendant's conduct and the damage to the plaintiff. A mere possibility that the statement caused the damage is insufficient.

COMMENT

Injurious falsehood is actionable only if it is a substantial factor in causing monetary loss. *E.g.*, *Erick Bowman Remedy Co. v. Jensen Salsbery Lab.*, 17 F.2d 255 (8th Cir. 1926); *Polygram Records, Inc. v. Superior Court*, 216 Cal. Rptr. 252 (Cal. Ct. App. 1985); *Am. Ins. Co. v. Franc*, 111 Ill. App. 382 (Ill. App. Ct. 1903); *Waste Distillation Tech., Inc. v. Blasland & Bouck Eng'rs, P.C.*, 523 N.Y.S.2d 875 (N.Y. App. Div. 1988); *SRW Assocs. v. Bellport Beach Prop. Owners*, 517 N.Y.S.2d 741 (N.Y. App. Div. 1987); *Raeder v. New York Times*, 149 N.E.2d 526 (N.Y. 1957), *aff'd*, 165 N.Y. 2d 619 (N.Y. App. Div. 1957). The charge is based upon these cases and other sources. *See* Bernard S. Meyer, chairman, *New York Pattern Jury Instructions* §§ 3.55, 2.70 (1968); *Restatement (Second) of Torts* § 433 (1965); 1 J. Dooley, *Modern Tort Law* § 8.03 (1977).

For further discussion on establishing causation, *see* Note, *The Law of Commercial Disparagement: Business Defamation's Impotent Ally*, 63 Yale L.J. 65, 88-90 (1953).

3.7.4 Award of Damages

If you find that even though the plaintiff suffered a loss, the statement was not a substantial factor in causing that loss, your verdict will be for the defendant. If you find the statement was a substantial factor in causing the plaintiff pecuniary loss, your verdict will be for the plaintiff in the amount of such monetary loss as you find resulted directly and naturally from the making of the statement.

COMMENT

See section 3.7.3 cmt. In most jurisdictions, an award of only nominal damages will not satisfy the requirement of special damages and, therefore, will result in a verdict for the defendant. *Rite Aid Corp. v. Lake Shore Investors*, 471 A.2d 735 (Md. 1984).

Available damages may include advertising expenses necessary to counteract the disparagement as well as loss of customers. *Charles Atlas, Ltd. v. Time-Life Books, Inc.*, 570 F. Supp. 150 (S.D. N.Y. 1983).

In many situations, the torts of injurious falsehood and defamation overlap; however, although the plaintiff can sue under both theories, plaintiff may recover damages under only one. *Falls v. Sporting News Publ'g Co.*, 834 F.2d 611 (6th Cir. 1987); *aff'd*, 899 F.2d 1221 (6th Cir. 1990).

3.8   Punitive Damages

3.8.1   Decision to Award Punitive Damages

If you find for the plaintiff and against the defendant and you have determined that the defendant must pay damages, then you should consider whether the conduct that led to your decision also subjects the defendant to punitive damages. To award punitive damages, you must find that the defendant's conduct that proximately caused actual [or nominal] damages to the plaintiff was the result of actual malice, wanton conduct, or oppressive conduct, as measured by the instructions I will give you.

COMMENT

This charge represents the modern view of damages. *See, e.g., State Farm Mut. Auto. Ins. Co. v. Campbell*, 538 U.S. 408 (2003); *Rabun v. Kimberly-Clark Corp.*, 678 F.2d 1053 (11th Cir. 1982); *Christman v. Voyer*, 595 P.2d 410 (N.M. Ct. App. 1979); *Wussow v. Commercial Mechanisms, Inc.*, 279 N.W.2d 503 (Wis. Ct. App. 1979); *Restatement (Second) of Torts* § 908 (1979); 45 Am. Jur. 2d *Interference* § 62 (1999 & Supp. 2003). Counsel should note that although punitive damages generally will be awarded upon a showing of malice, wantonness, or oppressiveness, this principle is not universal and may well be affected by statute in a particular jurisdiction.

Most states require that the jury find liability and actual, or at least nominal, damages before punitive damages are allowed. *See* Richard C. Tinney, Annotation, *Showing of Actual Damages to Support Award of Punitive Damages*, 40 A.L.R.4th 11 (1985 & Supp. 2002); 45 Am. Jur. 2d *Interference* § 62 (1999 & Supp. 2003); *Am. Bus. Interiors, Inc. v. Haworth, Inc.*, 798 F.2d 1135 (8th Cir. 1986). *But see Platte v. Whitney Realty Co.*, 538 So. 2d 1358 (Fla. Dist. Ct. App. 1989) (punitive damages recoverable although actual damages could not be proved). For a discussion of the prerequisite of a verdict for actual damages, see the comment to section 3.8.2.

For the requirement of malicious, wanton, or oppressive conduct, see sections 3.8.3, 3.8.4, and 3.8.5.

3.8.2   Nominal Damages

The award of only a nominal sum with respect to the specific losses claimed by the plaintiff will not prevent your awarding punitive damages if you find that the award of punitive damages is justified under these instructions.

COMMENT

In most states the jury must make a finding of liability and actual, or at least nominal, damages before punitive damages are allowed. *See* Richard C. Tinney, Annotation, *Showing of Actual Damages to Support Award of Punitive Damages*, 40 A.L.R.4th 11 (1985 & Supp. 2002); 45 Am. Jur. 2d *Interference* § 62 (1999 & Supp. 2003); *Am. Bus. Interiors, Inc. v. Haworth, Inc.*, 798 F.2d 1135 (8th Cir. 1986). *But see Platte v. Whitney Realty Co.*, 538 So. 2d 1358 (Fla. Dist. Ct. App. 1989) (punitive damages recoverable although actual damages could not be proved).

In most jurisdictions, an award of nominal damages will suffice for this purpose. *See, e.g., Taylor v. Sandoval*, 442 F. Supp. 491 (D. Colo. 1977); *Tennant v. Vazquez*, 389 So. 2d 1183 (Fla. Dist. Ct. App. 1980); *Christman v. Voyer*, 595 P.2d 410 (N.M. Ct. App. 1979). *But see Wussow v. Commercial Mechanisms, Inc.*, 279 N.W.2d 503 (Wis. Ct. App. 1979). *See generally* Richard C. Tinney, Annotation, *Showing of Actual Damages to Support Award of Punitive Damages—Modern Cases*, 40 A.L.R.4th 11 (1985 & Supp. 2002).

3.8.3 Ill Will

You may find the defendant's conduct sufficient to enable you to award punitive damages if you find it to have been prompted or accompanied by personal ill will, spite, or hatred, either toward the plaintiff individually or toward all persons in one or more groups or categories of which the plaintiff is a member.

COMMENT

Generally, courts require proof of facts establishing ill will to justify an award of punitive damages. *See* 45 Am. Jur. 2d *Interference* § 62 (1999 & Supp. 2003); *Norwood Easthill Assocs. v. Norwood Easthill Watch*, 536 A.2d 1317 (N.J. Super. Ct. App. Div. 1988); *Anthony Pools, Inc. v. Charles & David, Inc.*, 797 S.W.2d 666 (Tex. App. 1990); *Bellefonte Underwriters Co., Inc. v. Brown*, 663 S.W.2d 562 (Tex. App. 1984). Even if not required, ill will is always an important factor in an award of punitive damages. *See, e.g., Universal City Studios, Inc. v. Nintendo Co.*, 615 F. Supp. 838 (S.D. N.Y. 1985), *aff'd*, 797 F.2d 70 (2d Cir.), *cert. denied*, 479 U.S. 987 (1986); *Int'l Wood Processors Corp. v. Power Dry, Inc.*, 593 F. Supp. 710 (D.S.C. 1984); *Edward Vantine Studios, Inc. v. Fraternal Composite Serv., Inc.*, 373 N.W.2d 512 (Iowa Ct. App. 1985).

3.8.4 Wanton Conduct

You may also award punitive damages if you find that the defendant's conduct was "wanton"; that is, that the conduct was undertaken in reckless or callous disregard of, or indifference to, the rights of one or more persons, including the plaintiff.

COMMENT

See King v. G.D. Van Wagenen Co., 717 F. Supp. 667 (D. Minn. 1989); *Liston v. Home Ins. Co.,* 659 F. Supp. 276 (S.D. Miss. 1986); *Universal City Studios, Inc. v. Nintendo Co.,* 615 F. Supp. 838 (S.D.N.Y. 1985), *aff'd,* 797 F.2d 70 (2d Cir.), *cert. denied,* 479 U.S. 987 (1986); *Ramona Manor Convalescent Hosp. v. Care Enterprises,* 225 Cal. Rptr. 120 (Cal. Ct. App. 1986).

3.8.5   Oppressive Conduct

You also may award punitive damages if, from all of the evidence, you find that the defendant's conduct was "oppressive"; that is, that the conduct was done in a way or manner that injured, damaged, or otherwise violated the rights of the plaintiff with unnecessary harshness or severity, as by misuse or abuse of authority or power, or by taking advantage of some weakness, disability, or misfortune of the plaintiff.

COMMENT

See Barnes Group, Inc. v. C & C Prod., Inc., 716 F.2d 1023 (4th Cir. 1983); *Rabun v. Kimberly-Clark Corp.*, 678 F.2d 1053 (11th Cir. 1982); *Int'l Wood Processors Corp. v. Power Dry, Inc.*, 593 F. Supp. 710 (D.S.C. 1984), *aff'd*, 792 F.2d 416 (4th Cir. 1986).

3.8.6   Amount of Punitive Damages Award

If you decide that punitive damages are appropriate in this case based upon my prior instructions, you should award the amount of punitive damages that, in your sound judgment, will justly punish the defendant for its behavior and dissuade the defendant and others from acting the same way in future, similar situations.

In fixing the amount of punitive damages, you may consider the following factors:

1. The character of the defendant's act(s);

2. The nature and extent of the harm to the plaintiff that the defendant caused or intended to cause; and

3. The defendant's financial condition.

The amount of any punitive damages should bear a reasonable relationship to the injury, harm, or damage caused by the defendant. You must also keep in mind that the amount of such punitive damages, when awarded, must be fixed with calm discretion and sound reason. Punitive damages must not be awarded, or fixed in amount, based upon any sympathy, bias, or prejudice you may feel toward any party in the case.

[If evidence of "other acts" or harm against other parties has been allowed, add the following: Some of the evidence you have heard concerned conduct by the defendant that was not the proximate cause of the damages claimed by the plaintiff in this case. Although you may consider this evidence for any bearing upon the defendant's state of mind in causing damages claimed by the plaintiff in this case, you are not to punish the defendant for conduct relating only to parties other than the plaintiff.]

[If evidence of the defendant's financial condition has been allowed, add the following: You have heard evidence of the defendant's financial condition. You are not to consider the defendants' financial condition in deciding whether to award punitive damages, but you may consider it in fixing the amount of punitive damages to the extent that the actual [or nominal] damages are insufficient to justly punish the defendant for its behavior or dissuade the defendant or others from acting the same way in future, similar situations.

COMMENT

See State Farm Mut. Auto. Ins. Co. v. Campbell, 538 U.S. 408 (2003); *Cooper Indus., Inc. v. Leatherman Tool Group, Inc.*, 121 S. Ct. 1678 (2001); *BMW of N. Am., Inc. v. Gore*, 116 S. Ct. 1589 (1996); *Jannotta v. Subway Sandwich Shops, Inc.*, 125 F.3d 503 (7th Cir. 1997); *Fed. Deposit Ins. Corp. v. W.R. Grace & Co.*, 877 F.2d 614 (7th Cir. 1989), *cert. denied*, 110 S. Ct. 1524 (1990); *Aldrich v. Thomson McKinnon Sec., Inc.*, 756 F.2d 243 (2d Cir. 1985); *Damages—Modern Cases*, 40 A.L.R.4th 11 (1985 & Supp. 2002).

A state may not impose damages on a defendant for actions undertaken in other states that do not violate the other states' laws. *BMW*, 116 S. Ct. at 1597 (1996). Similarly, a "defendant's dissimilar acts, independent from the acts upon which liability was premised, may not serve as the basis for punitive damages." *State Farm*, 123 S. Ct. 1523.

A defendant's financial condition as a factor in setting punitive damages is generally accepted. *See, e.g., Hollins v. Powell*, 773 F.2d 191 (8th Cir.) (reducing punitive damage award in light of defendant's limited resources), *cert. denied*, 475 U.S. 1119 (1985); *Miller v. Rukoff-Sexton, Inc.*, 845 F.2d 209 (9th Cir. 1988) (the defendant's net worth was admissible for setting punitive damages); *Rupert v. Sellers*, 368 N.Y.S.2d 904 (N.Y. App. Div. 1975) (in bifurcated trial, evidence of the defendants' net worth should be considered after special verdict). *See generally* Annotation, *Punitive Damages: Relationship to Defendant's Wealth As a Factor in Determining Propriety of Award*, 87 A.L.R.4th 141 (1991 & Supp. 2002). Some states, such as Hawaii, even have statutes making the financial condition of the defendant relevant to the amount of punitive damages awardable. Others, like New York, protect the defendant from possible prejudice at trial through the use of a bifurcated trial procedure. *See Aldrich v. Thomson McKinnon Sec., Inc.*, 589 F. Supp. 683 (S.D.N.Y. 1984). However, the Supreme Court has cautioned that the financial condition of the defendant may not be used to create bias against big businesses or to permit an award that is unrelated to the actual damages. *State Farm*, 123 S. Ct. at 1525 ("[T]he wealth of a defendant cannot justify an otherwise unconstitutional punitive damage award."). Recent commentators have argued that the defendant's financial condition is only relevant in cases involving non-economically motivated torts. *See, e.g.,* Andrew L. Frey, *No More Blind Man's Bluff on Punitive Damages: A Plea to the Drafters of Pattern Jury Instructions*, 29 Litig. 24 (Summer 2003). In cases where the defendant was motivated by profits, they argue, compensatory damages are sufficient to act as a deterrent. *Id.*

Chapter Four
Confusion of Source

Merrick L. Gross and Jason Kellogg*

---

* Merrick L. Gross is a shareholder and Jason Kellogg is an associate at Akerman Senterfitt, 1 S.E. 3rd Avenue, 28th Floor, Miami, FL 33131. Mr. Gross may be reached at (305) 982-5638 or merrick.gross@akerman.com. Mr. Kellogg may be reached at (305) 374-5600 or jason.kellogg@akerman.com.

4.1   Introduction

The model jury charges in this section pertain to the conditions of liability at common law for one who attempts to sell one's goods or services as the goods or services of another. Although no uniform terminology has been generally accepted, the courts are in agreement that relief may be predicated upon theories commonly known as trademark infringement, trade name infringement, and unfair competition. *See* 1 J. McCarthy, *Trademarks & Unfair Competition* § 4.1 (4th ed. 1996); *Developments in the Law— Competitive Torts*, 77 Harv. L. Rev. 888, 908-09 (1964).

The touchstone of liability for trademark and trade name infringement and for unfair competition is the likelihood of customer confusion about the source of products or services. Some modern courts, however, have drawn a distinction between "trademark" (or trade name) law and "unfair competition" law by stating that the former focuses on the narrow question of the use of a word, device, or symbol to distinguish one's goods, services, or business, while the latter concerns the broader issue of the total effect of a product and package on the consumer. As one court has observed: "The essential element of a trademark [or trade name] is the exclusive right of its owner to use a word or device to distinguish [the owner's] product [or business]. On the other hand, a claim of unfair competition considers the total physical image given by the product and its name together. Thus, unfair competition exists if the total impression of package, size, shape, color, design and name upon the consumer will lead the consumer to confuse the origin of the product." *Jean Patou, Inc. v. Jacqueline Cochran, Inc.*, 201 F. Supp. 861 (S.D.N.Y. 1962), *aff'd*, 312 F.2d 125 (2d Cir. 1963); 1 J. McCarthy, *Trademarks & Unfair Competition* § 2.02 at 2-13 (3d ed. 1992); *see also Corning Glass Works v. Jeannette Glass Co.*, 308 F. Supp. 1321 (S.D.N.Y.), *aff'd*, 432 F.2d 784 (2d Cir. 1970). Accordingly, counsel will have to make an initial decision as to whether to seek relief for trademark and/or trade name infringement, for unfair competition, or both.

4.1.1 Trademark Infringement

The term "trademark" includes any word, name, symbol, device, or any combination thereof adopted and used by a manufacturer or merchant to identify its goods and distinguish them from those manufactured or sold by others. This definition originally appeared in the Lanham Act of 1946, as codified in 15 U.S.C. section 1127, and has been widely cited in cases involving common law claims. *See, e.g., New England Butt Co. v. Int'l Trade Comm'n*, 756 F.2d 874 (D.C. Cir. 1985). In the Tradework Law Revision Act of 1988, the definition of trademark contained in 15 U.S.C. section 1127 was expanded to include "any word, name, symbol, or device, or any combination thereof (1) used by a person, or (2) which a person has a bona fide intention to use in commerce and applies to register on the principal register established by this chapter, to identify and distinguish his or her goods, including a unique product, from those manufactured or sold by others and to indicate the source of the goods, even if that source is unknown." 15 U.S.C. § 1127 (Supp. 2002).

This new definition reflects an overall revision in the Lanham Act. Under the 1988 amendments, applications for tradework registration can be based on a bona fide intent to use a mark in interstate commerce in the future, as well as an actual use of a mark before application. *See generally* 1 J. Gilson, *Tradework Protection and Practice* § 1.04.4 (2002).

In practice, trademarks, which identify and distinguish tangible goods, should be differentiated from service marks, which identify and distinguish services. Service mark infringement is, however, governed by the same principles as trademark infringement. *See, e.g., Nat'l Football League Props., Inc. v. New Jersey Giants, Inc.*, 637 F. Supp. 507 (D.N.J. 1986); *see also Newport Elecs., Inc. v. Newport Corp.*, 157 F. Supp. 2d 202 (D. Conn. 2001). Therefore, for the purposes of these suggested instructions and charges, the word "trademark" will be used generically to refer to both trademarks and service marks. Counsel is advised to consult more specialized treatises for a thorough discussion of service marks. The terminological distinction between trademarks and service marks originated by statute in 1946 with the Lanham Act, 15 U.S.C. § 1127. Before that enactment, goods and services both fell within the rubric of "trademark" law.

In determining what can be protected as a trademark, it is generally recognized that a trademark at common law may be a word, symbol, device, letter, numeral, or any combination of them in any form or arrangement. *See generally* 1 J. McCarthy, *Trademarks & Unfair Competition*, ch. 7 (4th ed. 1996). *See also* Annotation, *Letters, Initials, or Numerals as Common-Law Trademarks*, 56 A.L.R. Fed. 232 (1982). Thus, a word such as "Ivory" may be a trademark; so may an individual letter, a group of letters, numbers, combinations of letters and numbers, abbreviations and nicknames, slogans, the title of a newspaper column, designs, or color configurations. *See, e.g., Estee Lauder, Inc. v. The Gap, Inc.*, 108 F.3d 1503 (2d Cir. 1997) ("100%"); *Shakespeare Co. v. Silstar Corp. of Am.*, 9 F.3d 1091 (4th Cir. 1993) (color configuration of fishing rod); *Ideal Toy Corp. v. Plawner Toy Mfg. Corp.*, 685 F.2d 78 (3d Cir. 1982) (color of cube puzzles); *Elec. Communications, Inc. v. Elec. Components for Ind. Co.*, 443 F.2d 487 (8th Cir.), *cert. denied*, 404 U.S. 833 (1971) (letters "ECI"); *Tel. Enter. Network, Inc. v. Entm't Network, Inc.*, 630 F. Supp. 244 (D.N.J. 1986) (number "Ten"); *Application of Kopy Kat, Inc.*, 498 F.2d 1379 (C.C.P.A. 1974) ("We Print-It In A Min-It"); *Southland Corp. v. Schubert*, 297 F. Supp. 477 (C.D. Cal. 1968) ("7-Eleven"); *Coca-Cola Co. v. Pace*, 283 F. Supp. 291 (W.D. Ky. 1968) ("Coke"); *Singer Mfg. Co. v. Singer Upholstery & Sewing Co.*, 130 F. Supp. 205 (W.D. Pa. 1955) (the letter "S"); *Anheuser-Busch, Inc. v. Power City Brewery, Inc.*, 28 F. Supp. 740 (W.D.N.Y. 1939) ("Bud"); *Cytanovich Reading Ctr. v. Reading Game*, 208 Cal. Rptr. 412 (Cal. Ct. App. 1984) (alphanumeric telephone number letters). Even the color pink has been held, in certain circumstances, to be entitled to protection as a trademark. *See In re Owens-Corning Fiberglass Corp.*, 774 F.2d 1116 (D.C. Cir. 1985). Furthermore, the shapes of packages and containers and the shapes of products may themselves constitute trademarks. *See generally* 1 J.

McCarthy, *Trademarks & Unfair Competition* § 7:53 (4th ed. 1996); *see also* Gary Schumann, *Trademark Protection of Container and Package Configurations—A Primer,* 59 Chi.-Kent L. Rev. 779 (1983).

A product or service may bear more than one protectable trademark. *See, e.g., In re Polar Music Int'l A.B.,* 714 F.2d 1567 (Fed. Cir. 1983); *Fleischmann Distilling Corp. v. Maier Brewing Co.,* 314 F.2d 149 (9th Cir.), *cert. denied,* 374 U.S. 830 (1963). There is a limit, however, on the trademark significance of each word, number, picture, slogan, and so on, that appears on a product; that is, not everything that appears on a label can be said to be, by itself, of trademark significance. *See generally* 1 J. McCarthy, *Trademarks & Unfair Competition* § 7:1 (4th ed. 1996).

Not all items or symbols qualify for legal protection as trademarks. Only those items or symbols that are used by a person in a manner that identifies that person's own goods or services and distinguishes them from those of others will be protected. *See* 1 J. Gilson, *Trademark Protection & Practice* § 2.01 (2002). The reason for this general rule is that unless the words or devices identify and distinguish the goods, the first user of the mark cannot be injured by misappropriation.

If a symbol is inherently distinctive, it is entitled to legal protection as a trademark. In those cases in which a symbol is not inherently distinctive, it may nevertheless be possible to show that the symbol has acquired a "secondary meaning," according to which the symbol may by usage develop a special, secondary, or trade meaning distinguishing such goods or services in a way that merits legal protection. *See* Annotation, *Doctrine of Secondary Meaning of the Law of Trademarks and Unfair Competition,* 150 A.L.R. 1067 (1944); *see also Harp v. Appliance Mart, Inc.,* 827 P.2d 1209 (Kan. Ct. App. 1992). When the right to protection of a word or symbol is founded on the doctrine of secondary meaning, the geographical extent of such protection will generally be limited to that area where the symbol is used or understood in its secondary sense. *See, e.g., Natural Footwear, Ltd. v. Hart Schaffner & Marx,* 760 F.2d 1383 (3d Cir.), *cert. denied,* 474 U.S. 920 (1985);

Annotation, *Unfair Competition: Geographical Extent of Protection of Word or Symbol under Doctrine of Secondary Meaning,* 41 A.L.R.3d 434 (1972).

4.1.2 Trade Name Infringement

A trade name is a word, name, symbol, device, or any combination thereof in any form or arrangement used to identify one's business, vocation, or occupation, and to distinguish it from the business, vocation, or occupation of others. *See, e.g., AutoZone, Inc. v. Tandy Corp.*, 174 F. Supp. 2d 718 (D. Tenn. 2001). A trade name may be a personal name, corporate name, or fictitious name, and it may be dominated by words or terms that are merely descriptive of the goods produced or sold, or by a geographical name identifying the location of the business. *See generally* 1 J. Gilson, *Trademark Protection and Practice* § 2:15 (1997); 1 J. McCarthy, *Trademarks & Unfair Competition* § 9.1 (4th ed. 1996).

4.1.3   Unfair Competition

An unfair competition claim may be premised on, but is not limited to, the following:

1. The simulation of advertising methods: *e.g., Echo Travel, Inc. v. Travel Assocs., Inc.,* 674 F. Supp. 656 (E.D. Wis. 1987), *aff'd,* 870 F.2d 1264 (7th Cir. 1989); *B.D. Communications, Inc. v. Dial Media, Inc.,* 429 F. Supp. 1011 (S.D.N.Y 1977); Annotation, *Rights and Remedies with Respect to Another's Use of a Deceptively Similar Advertising Slogan,* 2 A.L.R.3d 748 (1965);

2. Deceptive comparative advertising practice: *e.g., Johnson & Johnson Merck v. Smithkline Beecham,* 960 F.2d 294 (2d Cir. 1992); *Mobius Mgmt. Sys., Inc. v. Fourth Dimension Software, Inc.,* 880 F. Supp. 1005 (S.D.N.Y. 1994); *W.L. Gore & Assocs., Inc. v. Totes, Inc.,* 788 F. Supp. 800 (D. Del. 1992), *amended,* 1992 U.S. Dist. LEXIS 8055 (D. Del. 1992); *Alpo Petfoods, Inc. v. Ralston Purina Co.,* 720 F. Supp. 194 (D.D.C. 1989), *aff'd in part, vacated in part,* 913 F.2d 958 (D.C. Cir. 1990); *U-Haul Int'l, Inc. v. Jartran, Inc.,* 601 F. Supp. 1140 (D. Ariz. 1984), *aff'd in part, modified in part, rev'd in part,* 793 F.2d 1034 (9th Cir. 1986); *cf. Harper House, Inc. v. Thomas Nelson, Inc.,* 5 F.3d 536 (9th Cir. 1993); Annotation, *Actionable Nature of Advertising Impugning Quality or Worth of Merchandise or Products,* 42 A.L.R.4th 318 (1985);

3. The appearance of business facilities: *e.g., White Tower Sys., Inc. v. White Castle Sys.,* 90 F.2d 67 (6th Cir.), *cert. denied,* 302 U.S. 720 (1937); *Rally's, Inc. v. Int'l Shortstop, Inc.,* 776 F. Supp. 451 (E.D. Ark.), *aff'd,* 985 F.2d 565 (8th Cir. 1990); *Fotomat Corp. v. Photo Drive-Thru, Inc.,* 425 F. Supp. 693 (D.N.J. 1977); *see also Two Pesos, Inc. v. Taco Cabana, Inc.,* 505 U.S. 615 (1992) and "trade dress," *infra. But cf. Demetriades v. Kaufman,* 680 F. Supp. 658 (S.D.N.Y. 1988); Annotation, *Trade Dress Simulation of Cosmetic Products as Unfair Competition,* 86 A.L.R.3d 505 (1978); *Unfair Competition by Imitation in Sign or Design of Business Place,* 86 A.L.R.3d 884 (1978);

4. A product's shape or configuration: *e.g.*, *Chemlawn Serv. Corp. v. GNC Pumps, Inc.*, 690 F. Supp. 1560 (S.D. Tex. 1988); *SunDor Brand, Inc. v. Borden, Inc.*, 657 F. Supp. 86 (M.D. Fla. 1986); *Duo-Tint Bulb & Battery Co. v. Moline Supply Co.*, 360 N.E.2d 798 (Ill. App. Ct. 1977); *cf. Truck Equip. Serv. Co. v. Fruehauf Corp.*, 536 F.2d 1210 (8th Cir.), *cert. denied*, 429 U.S. 861 (1976);

5. The use of similar corporate, business, and professional names: *e.g.*, *Patsy's Brand, Inc. v. I.O.B. Realty, Inc.*, 317 F.3d 309 (2d Cir. 2003); *Century 21 Real Estate Corp. v. Sandlin*, 846 F.2d 1175 (9th Cir. 1988); *Healing the Children, Inc. v. Heal the Children, Inc.*, 786 F. Supp. 1209 (W.D. Pa. 1992); *Dollar Rent A Car Sys., Inc. v. Sand Dollar Car Rentals*, 765 F. Supp. 876 (D.S.C. 1990); *Caesars World, Inc. v. Caesar's Palace*, 490 F. Supp. 818 (D.N.J. 1980); 47 P.O.F.2d, *Wrongful Use of Another's Trademark or Tradename* (1987); Annotation, *Use of "Family Name" by Corporation as Unfair Competition*, 72 A.L.R.3d 8 (1976); Annotation, *Right of Benevolent or Fraternal Society or Organization to Protection Against Use of Same or Similar Name, Insignia, or Ritual by Another Organization*, 76 A.L.R.2d 1396 (1961);

6. "Trade dress," a term that refers to everything the consumer sees when the consumer looks at a packaged product, such as the color or color combinations on the package, the shape or configuration of the package, the wording and the form and placement of wording on the package, and the presence of any decorative indicia on the package: *e.g.*, *Two Pesos, Inc. v. Taco Cabana, Inc.*, 505 U.S. 615 (1992); *Masterfoods USA v. Arcor USA, Inc.*, 230 F. Supp. 2d 302 (W.D.N.Y. 2002); *Speedry Prod., Inc. v. Dri Marks Prod., Inc.*, 271 F.2d 646 (2d Cir. 1959); *Tas-T-Nut Co. v. Variety Nut & Date Co.*, 245 F.2d 3 (6th Cir. 1957); *Storck U.S.A., L.P. v. Farley Candy Co. Inc.*, 785 F. Supp. 730 (N.D. Ill. 1992); *Mr. Gasket Co. v. Travis*, 299 N.E.2d 906 (Ohio Ct. App. 1973). *See generally* 1 J. McCarthy, *Trademarks & Unfair Competition* ch. 8 (4th ed. 1996); 3 P.O.F.2d *Trade Dress (Packaging) Simulation* 577 (1974); and/or

7. The dilution of goodwill of a trademark: *e.g., L.L. Bean, Inc. v. Drake Publishers Inc.*, 811 F.2d 26 (1st Cir.), *cert. denied*, 483 U.S. 1013 (1987); *Chem. Corp. of Am. v. Anheuser-Busch, Inc.*, 306 F.2d 433 (5th Cir. 1962), *cert. denied*, 372 U.S. 965 (1963); *Frances Denney Inc. v. New Process Co.*, 670 F. Supp. 661 (W.D. Va. 1985); *cf. E&J Gallo Winery v. Consorizo del Gallo Nero*, 782 F. Supp. 457 (N.D. Cal. 1991). The existence of a common law remedy for dilution, however, is controversial. *See Int'l Order of Job's Daughters v. Lindburgh & Co.*, 633 F.2d 912 (9th Cir. 1980), *cert. denied*, 452 U.S. 941 (1981).

This section does not address all torts that may be considered as falling under the category of unfair competition. For example, this section does not encompass "palming off"—that is, when there is proof that one subjectively and knowingly intended to confuse buyers. The most familiar example of "palming off" is when a seller knowingly substitutes product X in response to an order for product Y (*see* 4 J. McCarthy, *Trademarks & Unfair Competition* § 25:3 (4th ed. 1996)), as classically illustrated in the Coca-Cola cases when a customer at a restaurant, having asked for a "Coke" or "Coca-Cola," is served another cola beverage. *See, e.g., Coca-Cola Co. v. Dorris*, 311 F. Supp. 287 (E.D. Ark. 1970). In effect, "palming off" is simply a more direct and flagrant way of confusing purchasers about the source of the product or service. *See, e.g., Worthington Foods, Inc. v. Kellogg Co.*, 732 F. Supp. 1417 (S.D. Ohio 1990); *Pezon et Michel v. E. R. Hewin Assocs., Inc.*, 270 F. Supp. 423 (S.D.N.Y. 1967).

4.2 General Instructions: Trademark Infringement

4.2.1 Theory of Trademark Infringement

In this case, the plaintiff, [name], seeks to recover money damages from the defendant, [name], for what the plaintiff claims to be a trademark infringement in the use of [describe symbol] in connection with the sale of [identify goods and/or services]. The legal principles discussed in these instructions regarding the law of trademark infringement have resulted from attempts to balance the following conflicting policy objectives:

1. There is a need to protect the public from being misled about the nature and source of the goods and services they buy;

2. There is a need to protect the property rights of a business to identify itself and its goods and services to the public;

3. There is a need to try to achieve these goals without injury to the free market economic system, which encourages fair competition among those providing goods and services. Fair competition is encouraged, but unfair competition is destructive of the competitive process and is illegal.

Because of the conflicting policy objectives involved in cases of this type, each such case must be decided largely on its specific facts, and you, the jury, are the judge of the facts.

COMMENT

This charge is based upon the one given by Judge Richard P. Matsch in *Big O Tire Dealers, Inc. v. Goodyear Tire & Rubber Co.*, 408 F. Supp. 1219 (D. Colo. 1976), *modified on other grounds*, 561 F.2d 1365 (10th Cir. 1977), *cert. dismissed*, 434 U.S. 1052 (1978). This charge informs the jury of the competing interests underlying trademark infringement litigation. *See Scott Paper Co. v. Scott's Liquid Gold, Inc.*, 589 F.2d 1225 (3d Cir. 1978), *superseded on other grounds; Shire US Inc. v. Barr Labs., Inc.*, 329 F.3d 348 (3d Cir. 2003); *Holiday Inns, Inc. v. Trump*, 617 F. Supp. 1443 (D.N.J. 1985).

4.2.2   Definition of Trademark

The term "trademark" includes any word, name, symbol, device, or any combination thereof adopted and used by a manufacturer or merchant to identify and distinguish its goods [or services], including a unique product, from those manufactured [or sold] by others and to indicate the source of the goods [or services], even if that source is unknown.

The main function of a trademark is to identify and distinguish goods or services as a product of a particular manufacturer or merchant and to protect its goodwill against the sale of another's product or service as its own.

A trademark is also a merchandising symbol that helps a prospective purchaser to select what such purchaser wants. A trademark signifies that all goods bearing that trademark come from a single source and that all goods bearing the trademark are of an equal level of quality. There is, therefore, a public interest in avoiding confusion in the use of trademarks.

When a manufacturer or merchant has established a trademark right by use of, or in connection with, a product or service before anyone else, the right to use it becomes an exclusive right, and the trademark is property of the manufacturer or merchant. No other person can then use the same or similar [symbol] in any manner that makes confusion likely in the consumer's mind regarding the source or origin of those goods [or services].

COMMENT

This charge is also based on the one given by Judge Matsch in *Big O Tire Dealers, Inc. v. Goodyear Tire & Rubber Co.*, 408 F. Supp. 1219 (D. Colo. 1976), *modified on other grounds,* 561 F.2d 1365 (10th Cir. 1977), *cert. dismissed,* 434 U.S. 1052 (1978). Its use is recommended to alert the jury that a wide variety of items may function as trademarks, and that trademarks are not limited to words. The jury should, however, be instructed that a trademark is not a monopoly; rather, its legal relevance is showing the source, identity, sponsorship, or origin of a product. *See Calvin Klein*

Cosmetics Corp. v. Lennox Lab., 815 F.2d 500 (8th Cir. 1987); *see also Citrus Group Inc. v. Cadbury Beverages, Inc.*, 781 F. Supp. 386 (D. Md. 1991) (to be a trademark, words must be indicative of source of origin; not infringement to use words in their ordinary meanings).

The use of this charge also alerts the jury to the functions of a trademark and the legal effect of establishing a trademark. *See Scandia Down Corp. v. Euroquilt, Inc.*, 772 F.2d 1423 (7th Cir. 1985), *cert. denied*, 475 U.S. 11471 (1986); *Processed Plastic Co. v. Warner Communications, Inc.*, 675 F.2d 852 (7th Cir. 1982); *Kentucky Fried Chicken Corp. v. Diversified Packaging Corp.*, 549 F.2d 368 (5th Cir. 1977); *Turner v. HMH Publ'g Co.*, 380 F.2d 224 (5th Cir.), *cert. denied*, 389 U.S. 1006 (1967); *Fleischmann Distilling Corp. v. Maier Brewing Co.*, 314 F.2d 149 (9th Cir.), *cert. denied*, 374 U.S. 830 (1963); Julius R. Lunsford, *Trademarks: Prestige, Practice and Protection*, 4 Ga. L. Rev. 322, 324 (1970); Ralph S. Brown, *Advertising and the Public Interest*, 57 Yale L J 1165, 1185 (1948). *See generally* 3 R. Callman, *Unfair Competition, Trademarks & Monopolies* § 17.01 (4th ed. 1983).

4.2.3   Elements of Liability

To find liability for trademark infringement, you, the jury, must find from a preponderance of the evidence that

1. the plaintiff has established its [describe symbol] as a trademark for plaintiff's [identify product or service]; and

2. the plaintiff had established [name or symbol] as a trademark before the defendant began to market defendant's [identify product or service] in the area where plaintiff sells its [identify product or service]; and

3. the defendant used [describe symbol] in a manner likely to cause confusion about the source of the [identify product or service] among a significant number of persons using ordinary care and prudence in the purchase of [identify product or service].

If you find by a preponderance of the evidence that the plaintiff has proved these elements, then and only then may you find the defendant liable of trademark infringement. You will then consider the question of damages under separate instructions.

COMMENT

This charge reflects the traditional standard for establishing liability for trademark infringement. *See, e.g., Big O Tire Dealers, Inc. v. Goodyear Tire & Rubber Co.,* 408 F. Supp. 1219 (D. Colo. 1976), *modified on other grounds,* 561 F.2d 1365 (10th Cir. 1977), *cert. dismissed,* 434 U.S. 1052 (1978); *see also Bass Buster, Inc. v. Gapen Mfg. Co.,* 420 F. Supp. 144 (W.D. Mo. 1976).

The jury may find liability without also concluding that the defendant intended to deceive the public (*see, e.g., Emerson Elec. Co. v. Emerson Quiet Kool Corp.,* 577 F. Supp. 668 (E.D. Mo. 1983)), and damages may be awarded without a finding that the defendant acted with a wrongful intent. *See generally* 5 J. McCarthy, *Trademarks & Unfair Competition* § 30:78 (4th ed. 1996). However, an accounting of the defendant's profits requires proof of a wrongful intent. *Nalpac, Ltd. v. Corning Glass Works,* 784 F.2d 752,

5 J. McCarthy, *Trademarks & Unfair Competition* § 30:64 (4th ed. 1996).

4.2.4   Jury's Reliance on Improper Fact

The fact that the defendant used a [describe symbol] that is similar (or even identical in some respects) to plaintiff's [describe symbol], and that the purchasing public is likely to be confused as a result, does not, in and of itself, constitute trademark infringement. To establish its claim against the defendant, the plaintiff must prove by a preponderance of the evidence each of the three elements previously set forth for your consideration. Only then may you find for the plaintiff.

COMMENT

This charge follows from the authority cited in the comment to section 4.2.3. Its use is recommended to reinforce the fact that liability for trademark infringement will be established only upon a finding that all three elements have been proved.

4.3 Trademark Infringement: Proof of Identifying Function

4.3.1 Generally

In this case, the plaintiff claims that plaintiff has established [describe symbol] as a trademark for the [goods or services—choose one] that are [sold or produced—choose one] by [him/her].

In determining whether the plaintiff has established [describe symbol] as a trademark, the first question for you, the jury, to decide is whether the public recognizes the plaintiff's [describe symbol] in connection with the sale of plaintiff's [identify product or service] as identifying plaintiff's [identify product or service] and distinguishing it from those of others. To determine whether the plaintiff has proved this, you must consider whether the evidence shows that the plaintiff's [describe symbol] is inherently distinctive or that, even if not inherently distinctive, the [describe symbol] has become distinctive through the acqui sition of what the law calls "secondary meaning." If the trademark is inherently distinctive, then no determination regarding "secondary meaning" need be made.

COMMENT

This charge describes the proof necessary to establish the requisite identifying function. An identifying work is distinctive if either it is inherently distinctive or it has become distinctive through the acquisition of secondary meaning. *Two Pesos, Inc. v. Taco Cabana, Inc.*, 505 U.S. 615 (1992); *see also Secular Orgs. for Sobriety, Inc. v. Ullrich*, 213 F.3d 1125 (9th Cir. 2000); 1 J. McCarthy, *Trademarks & Unfair Competition* ch. 11 (4th ed. 1996).

It is possible that a court may consider the issue of whether a symbol is inherently distinctive as a question of law. These charges should not be interpreted as resolving this issue. On the other hand, whether a symbol has acquired secondary meaning is a question of fact for the jury. *See, e.g., Japan Telecom, Inc. v. Japan Telecom Am. Inc.*, 287 F.3d 886 (9th Cir. 2002); *Suo-Wizard*

Mfg., Inc. v. Eisemann Prod. Co., 791 F.2d 423 (5th Cir. 1986); *Transgo, Inc. v. Ajac Transmissions Parts Corp.*, 768 F.2d 1001 (9th Cir. 1985); *Zatarains, Inc. v. Oak Grove Smokehouse, Inc.*, 698 F.2d 786 (5th Cir. 1983); *Volkswagenwerk Aktiengesellschaft v. Rickard*, 492 F.2d 474 (5th Cir. 1974). *But see Resorts of Pinehurst, Inc. v. Pinehurst Nat'l Corp.*, 148 F.3d 417 (4th Cir. 1998) (issue of likelihood of confusion is a question of fact, but summary judgment may be appropriate); *Marker Int'l v. De Bruler*, 844 F.2d 763 (10th Cir. 1988) (issue of whether trademark has acquired secondary meaning is issue of fact, but when underlying facts not in dispute, question of secondary meaning appropriate for resolution by summary judgment).

4.3.2   Word(s) as Trademark: Strong versus Weak Marks

The plaintiff asserts that the word(s) [insert word(s)] is a trademark for plaintiff's [identify goods or services]. In trademark usage, words can be classified along a continuum from those that are inherently distinctive to those that are not distinctive at all, or generic.

A "coined" word is an artificial word that has no language meaning except as a trademark. A coined word bears no relationship to the product or service with which it is associated. "EXXON," for example, is a coined word used by an oil company.

A "fanciful" word is like a coined word, in that it is invented for the sole purpose of functioning as a trademark. A fanciful word bears no relationship to the product or service with which it is associated. A fanciful word differs from a coined word only in that it may bear a relationship to another word or it may be an obsolete word. "Fab," for example, is a shortened version of the word "fabulous" and is a fanciful word used for detergent.

An "arbitrary" word is one that is commonly used, but when used with the goods in issue neither suggests nor describes any ingredient, quality, or characteristic of those goods, but is used only in an arbitrary capacity. An arbitrary word bears no relationship to the product or service with which it is associated. "Wild Turkey" for whiskey is an example of arbitrary wording.

A "suggestive" word is one that suggests, rather than describes, a characteristic or quality of a product or service. "Stronghold" for threaded nails is, for example, suggestive of their superior holding power.

A merely "descriptive" word is one that identifies or describes a characteristic or quality of a product, such as its intended use, its ingredients, or its desirable features. "Tender Vittles" for cat food is descriptive.

A merely "geographically descriptive" word is one used to indicate the location or origin of goods and services. "California Apparel" as applied to clothing produced in California is geographically descriptive. "North Pole" as applied to bananas would, however, be an arbitrary use of geographical wording because it bears no relationship to the product.

A word is merely a "personal name" (surname or first name) if its ordinary significance is that of a personal name. "Gallo" applied to wine is a personal name. "King's" as applied to cologne would, however, be an arbitrary use of a personal name.

A "generic" word is one that is the common name for the product. "Butter" is the common generic name for butter. There can be no trademark rights in a generic term. Generic words remain in the public domain as a part of our language.

The right to protection of a trademark comes from its utility in identifying a specific product.

We speak of strong and weak marks in terms of the amount of use necessary to create protected rights. A strong mark is one that symbolizes or signifies a single source or origin. Weak marks are those that do not symbolize or signify a single source or origin. Coined, fanciful, arbitrary, and suggestive words are strong marks. Words that are merely descriptive are weak marks.

Weak marks do not obtain protection solely from their use as a trademark. Weak marks must first acquire distinctiveness from the effect of the owner's efforts in the marketplace. This is what is called the development of secondary meaning. For example, a merely descriptive term used as a trademark must have been so used that its primary significance in the minds of the consuming public is not the product itself but the identification of it with a single source. This does not mean that the consuming public must know the identity of that single source in the sense that the consumer knows the corporate name of the [producer or seller—choose one]. All that is necessary is that the ordinary consumer associates the symbol with a single source, regardless of whether the buyer knows who or what that source is. Once secondary meaning has been established for a mark, that mark is entitled to protection as a trademark.

COMMENT

This charge is suggested for use when the plaintiff asserts that a word or words are the trademark, in contrast to those situations that involve nonword symbols. The language is generally based upon the charge in *Big O Tire Dealers, Inc. v. Goodyear Tire & Rubber Co.*, 408 F. Supp. 1219 (D. Colo. 1976), *modified on other grounds,* 561 F.2d 1365 (10th Cir. 1977), *cert. dismissed,* 434 U.S. 1052 (1978). *See generally* 2 J. McCarthy, *Trademarks & Unfair Competition* ch. 11 (4th ed. 1996); 1 J. Gilson, *Trademark Protection & Practice* ch. 2 (2002); George K. Chamberlain, Annotation, *When Does Product Mark Become Generic Term or "Common Descriptive Name" So As to Warrant Cancellation of Registration of Mark, Pursuant to § 14 of Lanham Act (15 U.S.C.S. § 1064),* 55 A.L.R. Fed. 241 (1981) (when product mark becomes generic term or common descriptive name so as to warrant cancellation of registration of mark).

In some instances, it may be preferable to limit the categories of words included in the previous charge, as not all categories may be necessary or relevant in all circumstances. *See Two Pesos, Inc. v. Taco Cabana, Inc.*, 505 U.S. 615 (1992); *Branoff-Perlstein Assocs. v. Sklar,* 967 F.2d 852 (3d Cir. 1992); *Bernard v. Commerce Drug Co.,* 964 F.2d 1338 (2d Cir. 1992) (citing *Abercrombie & Fitch Co. v. Hunting World, Inc.,* 537 F.2d 4 (2d Cir. 1976)); *Perini Corp. v. Perini Constr., Inc.,* 915 F.2d 121 (4th Cir. 1990); *Union Nat'l Bank of Tex., Laredo, Tex. v. Union Nat'l Bank of Tex., Austin, Tex.,* 909 F.2d 839, 844 (5th Cir. 1990); *Wiley v. Am. Greetings Corp.,* 762 F.2d 139 (1st Cir. 1985). When applicable, it is appropriate to weigh the interest a person has in doing business in his or her own name. *See S.C. Johnson & Son, Inc. v. Johnson,* 175 F.2d 176 (2d Cir.), *cert. denied,* 338 U.S. 860 (1949).

4.3.3 Word(s) as Trademark: Secondary Meaning— Permissible Considerations

The mere fact that the plaintiff is using the [describe symbol], or that the plaintiff began using it before the defendant, does not establish or create secondary meaning.

Similarly, the mere fact that you might consider plaintiff's [describe symbol] to be unique is not enough to establish secondary meaning. Additionally, the mere fact that a product is popular is not itself sufficient to show secondary meaning.

There is no particular length of time within which secondary meaning is established. The question for you to determine is whether secondary meaning has been established, not in how long or short a time this was done.

COMMENT

This charge is suggested for use when the issue at trial is whether plaintiff's symbol is arbitrary, fanciful, or suggestive on the one hand, or descriptive, geographically descriptive, a personal name, or generic on the other hand. It is based upon the jury charge in *Big O Tire Dealers, Inc. v. Goodyear Tire & Rubber Co.*, 408 F. Supp. 1219 (D. Colo. 1976), *modified on other grounds*, 561 F.2d 1365 (10th Cir. 1977), *cert. dismissed*, 434 U.S. 1052 (1978), and the charges used in *Gordon v. Warner Brothers Pictures, Inc.*, 74 Cal. Rptr. 499 (Cal. Ct. App. 1969). *See WLWC Ctrs., Inc. v. Winners Corp.*, 563 F. Supp. 717 (M.D. Tenn. 1983) (popularity in sales alone cannot establish secondary meaning); *see also* 2 J. McCarthy, *Trademarks & Unfair Competition* ch. 15 (4th ed. 1996); 1 J. Gilson, *Trademark Protection & Practice* ch. 2.09 (2002); Annotation, *Application of Secondary Meaning Test in Action for Trademark Infringement*, 86 A.L.R. Fed. 489 (1988).

Depending upon the specific facts of the case, counsel may expand upon what is descriptive, generic, and so forth, and why the symbol at issue does or does not fall within such a category, using the evidence introduced at trial. The law relating to whether a trademark is generic or descriptive is developing, and there are differences among jurisdictions.

Counsel should consider the point raised in the comment to section 4.3.1 that the issue of whether the symbol is inherently distinctive may be one of law for the court to decide.

4.3.4 Word(s) as Trademark: Dispute between Arbitrary, Fanciful, or Suggestive Word(s), and Descriptive, Generic, Geographically Descriptive, or Personal Name Word(s)

Plaintiff claims that [describe symbol] is inherently distinctive because it is a [coined, fanciful, arbitrary, and/or suggestive—choose one or more adjectives as applicable] word(s).

Defendant, however, contends that plaintiff has not established [describe symbol] as a trademark because it constitutes a word(s) that is [insert "merely descriptive of a quality or characteristic of plaintiff's goods and/or services," "geographically descriptive of the origin of plaintiff's goods and/or services," "merely a personal name," and/or "a generic name for plaintiff's goods and/or services"—choose one or more phrases as appropriate].

This is a question for you, the jury, to decide. Is the [describe symbol] a [coined, fanciful, arbitrary, and/or suggestive—choose one or more adjectives as applicable] word(s), or ["merely descriptive," "merely geographically descriptive," "merely a personal name," and/or "generic"—choose one or more phrases as applicable] in accordance with what I have just charged you?

If your answer to that question is that the [describe symbol] is inherently distinctive, you will then consider whether the quantity and quality of the plaintiff's use of [describe symbol] has established plaintiff's priority so as to earn legal protection of the [describe symbol] as a trademark.

On the other hand, if you decide that the plaintiff's [describe symbol] is [insert "merely descriptive," "merely geographically descriptive," "merely a personal name," and/or "generic"—choose one or more phrases as applicable] as applied to plaintiff's goods and/or services, then you will consider whether the evidence shows that plaintiff's [describe symbol] has developed secondary meaning.

COMMENT

This text clarifies and defines the differences between "descriptive" and "generic" words, and "arbitrary" and "suggestive" words.

4.3.5 Word(s) as Trademark: Secondary Meaning Defined

By the term "secondary meaning," the law means that a symbol has been so used that its primary significance in the minds of the consuming public is not the [product or service—choose one] itself but the identification of such [product or service] with a single source. This does not mean that the consuming public must know the exact identity of that single source in the sense that it knows the corporate name of the [producer or seller—choose one]. All that is necessary to establish secondary meaning is that the ordinary consumer associates the [product or service] with a single source, regardless of whether the consumer knows who or what that source is.

You must find, therefore, from a preponderance of the evidence, that a significant number of the consuming public associates the [describe symbol] involved in this case with a single source. It is for you to decide how many constitute a significant number, keeping in mind that the plaintiff need not prove that all or even a majority of the consuming public understands this secondary meaning.

In determining whether the plaintiff's [describe symbol] has attained secondary meaning, it is appropriate for you to consider the evidence (if any) relating to:

1. the length and manner of its use;

2. the nature and extent of advertising and promotion;

3. sales volume;

4. other efforts made by the plaintiff to promote the connection in the consuming public's mind between the [symbol] and the plaintiff;

5. properly designed and conducted consumer surveys;

6. the testimony of consumers relating to the identity of source or the origin of the [describe symbol] in the minds of the consuming public; and

7. copying by others.

COMMENT

This text includes a composite of the factors that may be considered in determining whether secondary meaning has been established as set forth by various courts. Counsel is advised to refer to the law of the appropriate jurisdiction, as various courts have delineated different sets of factors. *See, e.g., Laureyssens v. Idea Group, Inc.*, 964 F.2d 131 (2d Cir. 1992); *Faberge, Inc. v. Saxony Prods., Inc.*, 605 F.2d 426 (9th Cir. 1979); *see also Empi, Inc. v. Iomed, Inc.*, 923 F. Supp. 1159 (D. Minn. 1996); *Essie Cosmetics, Ltd. v. Dae Do Int'l Ltd.*, 808 F. Supp. 952 (E.D.N.Y. 1992); *Sprinklets Water Ctr., Inc. v. McKesson Corp.*, 806 F. Supp. 656 (E.D. Mich. 1992); *Spraying Sys. Co. v. Delavan, Inc.*, 762 F. Supp. 772 (N.D. Ill. 1991), *Ginger Group, Ltd. v. Beatrice Cos., Inc.*, 678 F. Supp. 555 (E.D. Pa. 1988); *Shen Mfg. Co., Inc. v. Suncrest Mills, Inc.*, 673 F. Supp. 1199 (S.D.N.Y. 1987); *Southwestern Bell Tel. Co. v. Nationwide Indep. Directory Serv., Inc.*, 371 F. Supp. 900 (W.D. Ark. 1974); *Filter Dynamics Int'l, Inc. v. Astron Battery, Inc.*, 311 N.E.2d 386 (Ill. App. Ct. 1974); *Gordon v. Warner Bros. Pictures, Inc.*, 74 Cal. Rptr. 499 (Cal. Ct. App. 1969). *See generally* 1 J. Gilson, *Trademark Protection & Practice* § 2.09 (2002); 3 R. Callman, *Unfair Competition, Trademarks & Monopolies* § 18.01 (4th ed. 1992).

Several opinions issued by the U.S. District Court for the Southern District of New York have concluded that when "incipient secondary meaning" or "secondary meaning in the making" is shown, a court may dispense with most, if not all, of the normal secondary meaning proof requirements. *See, e.g., Mets Kane Imports, Ltd. v. Federated Dep't Stores, Inc.*, 625 F. Supp. 313 (S.D.N.Y. 1985), *aff'd sub nom.* 800 F.2d 1128 (2d Cir. 1986); *West & Co., Inc. v. Arica Inst., Inc.*, 194 U.S.P.Q. 32 (S.D.N.Y. 1976), *aff'd*, 557 F.2d 338 (2d Cir. 1977); *Nat'l Lampoon, Inc. v. Am. Broad. Cos.*, 376 F.

Supp. 733 (S.D.N.Y.), *aff'd,* 497 F.2d 1343 (2d Cir. 1974*). But see Cicena Ltd. v. Columbia Telecomms. Group,* 900 F.2d 1546 (Fed. Cir. 1990) (criticizing "secondary meaning in the making" doctrine). *See generally* 3 R. Callman, *Unfair Competition, Trademarks & Monopolies* § 77.3 at 356 (3d ed. 1971).

Some courts also have held that evidence of deliberate copying establishes a prima facie case of secondary meaning, with the defendant bearing the ultimate burden of proof once deliberate copying is shown. *M. Kramer Mfg. Co., Inc. v. Andrews,* 783 F.2d 421 (4th Cir. 1986); *see also Two Pesos, Inc. v. Taco Cabana, Inc.,* 505 U.S. 615 (1992) (inherently distinctive trade dress held protectable from infringement without proof of secondary meaning); *Ideal Toy Mfg. Corp. v. Plawner Toy Mfg. Corp.,* 685 F.2d 78 (3d Cir. 1982) (admission of copying persuasive evidence of secondary meaning); *Libbey Glass, Inc. v. Oneida Ltd.,* 61 F. Supp. 70 (N.D. Ohio 1999); *Maryland Stadium Auth. v. Becker,* 806 F. Supp. 1236 (D. Md. 1992) ("Intentional copying of a mark . . . raises a presumption of secondary meaning."); *Am. Greetings Corp. v. Dan-Dee Imports, Inc.,* 619 F. Supp. 1204 (D.N.J. 1985) (court's finding that plaintiff in fact copied design persuasive evidence of secondary meaning). *But see Fuddruckers, Inc. v. Doc's B.R. Others, Inc.,* 826 F.2d 837 (9th Cir. 1987) (burden not shifted). This view has been criticized. *See Mr. Gasket Co. v. Travis,* 299 N.E.2d 906 (Ohio Ct. App. 1973); *Developments in the Law—Competitive Torts,* 77 Harv. L. Rev. 888, 916 (1963).

4.3.6 Nonword Symbols as Trademarks

In this case, the plaintiff claims that plaintiff has established [describe nonword symbol] as a trademark for the [goods or services—choose one] that are [sold or produced—choose one] by [him/her]. Not only words constitute valid and protectable trademarks. The term trademark includes any word, name, symbol, device, or combination thereof adopted and used by a manufacturer or merchant to identify and distinguish its goods or services, including a unique product, from those manufactured or sold by others.

In determining whether the plaintiff has established [describe nonword symbol] as a trademark, the first question for you, the jury, to decide is whether the public recognizes plaintiff's [describe nonword symbol] in connection with the sale of plaintiff's [identify product or service] as identifying plaintiff's [identify product or service] and distinguishing plaintiff's [describe goods and services] from those of others. To determine whether plaintiff has proved this, you must consider whether the evidence shows that the plaintiff's [describe nonword symbol] is inherently distinctive or, even if it is not inherently distinctive, the [describe nonword symbol] has become distinctive through the acquisition of what the law calls "secondary meaning."

COMMENT

Word symbols as well as nonword symbols, such as letters, numbers, product and container shapes, designs, and pictures, may be regarded as being inherently distinctive in an appropriate case. *See generally* 1 J. McCarthy, *Trademarks & Unfair Competition* § 7:25 (4th ed. 1996); Richard P. Shafer, Annotation, *Letters, Initials, or Numerals as Commonlaw Trademarks*, 56 A.L.R. Fed. 232 (1992). Some symbols ordinarily require proof of secondary meaning, however. These include ordinary geometric shapes, descriptive symbols, geographically descriptive symbols, personal name symbols, and noninherently distinctive designs and product and container shapes. *See, e.g., Brooks Shoe Mfg. Co. v. Suave Shoe Corp.*, 716 F.2d 854 (11th Cir. 1983) ("V" design on side of shoe not distinctive);

Application of David Crystal, Inc., 296 F.2d 771, 773 (C.C.P.A. 1961) (stripes on top of men's socks not inherently distinctive). *See generally* 1 J. McCarthy, *Trademarks & Unfair Competition* § 7:25 (4th ed. 1996).

Section 43(a) of the Lanham Trademark Act, 15 U.S.C. § 1125(a), has also been interpreted to provide a cause of action for trade dress infringement. *See e.g., Am. Greetings Corp. v. Dan-Dee Imports, Inc.*, 807 F.2d 1136 (3d Cir. 1986); *Allfast Fastening Sys. v. Briles Rivet Corp.*, 16 F. Supp. 2d 1154 (C.D. Cal. 1998). For the purposes of an infringement action, "trade dress" is defined as the total image of a product and may include features such as size, shape, color or color combinations, textures, graphics, or particular sales techniques. *Epic Metals Corp. v. Souliere*, 99 F.3d 1034 (11th Cir. 1996); *Mana Prods., Inc. v. Columbia Cosmetics Mfg., Inc.*, 65 F.3d 1063 (2d Cir. 1995); *Vision Sports, Inc. v. Melville Corp.*, 888 F.2d 609 (8th Cir. 1988). Secondary meaning is a required element of a cause of action for trade dress infringement. *Am. Greetings Corp.*, 807 F.2d at 1141; *Bauer Lamp Co., Inc. v. Schaffer*, 941 F.2d 1165 (11th Cir. 1991).

The issue of distinctiveness may be one of law for the court to decide. *See* § 4.3[1], cmt., *supra*.

When trademark protection is sought for a design used as a background for a word or other marks, it may be contended that the design is simply a decorative or ornamental feature, and thus has no trademark function. *See, e.g., Team Cent., Inc. v. Xerox Corp.*, 606 F. Supp. 1408 (D. Minn. 1985); *Ventura Travelware, Inc. v. Baltimore Luggage Co.*, 322 N.Y.S.2d 93 (N.Y. App. Div. 1971), *aff'd*, 328 N.Y.S.2d 811 (N.Y. App. Div. 1972). In such a case, it will be necessary to include an additional charge to the jury:

> To be a trademark, the design's principal function must be to identify and distinguish the plaintiff's goods. This function will be present if you find that the design creates a separate impression upon the consuming public. In other words, you must find that the consuming public recognizes the [plaintiff's nonword symbol] as a mark to identify and distinguish the plaintiff's

goods and services when they see the design alone, apart from any other marks used in connection with the [nonword symbol].

4.3.7 Nonword Symbols as Trademarks: Secondary Meaning—Permissible Consideration

The mere fact that the plaintiff is using [describe nonword symbol], or that the plaintiff began using it before the defendant, does not establish or create secondary meaning.

Similarly, the mere fact that you might consider the plaintiff's [describe nonword symbol] to be unique is not enough to establish secondary meaning. Additionally, the mere fact that a product is popular is not itself sufficient to show secondary meaning.

There is no particular length of time within which secondary meaning is established. The question for you to determine is whether secondary meaning has been established, not in how long or short a time this was done.

COMMENT

"Secondary meaning" is the circumstance when a nonword symbol identifies one's goods or services and distinguishes them from those of others. *See* 2 J. McCarthy, *Trademarks & Unfair Competition* ch. 15 (4th ed. 1996); *see also Qualitex Co. v. Jacobson Prods. Co., Inc.*, 514 U.S. 159 (1995). The issue of distinctiveness may be one of law for the court to decide.

This charge concerning secondary meaning is identical to that contained in section 4.3.3 for word symbols.

4.3.8 Nonword Symbols as Trademarks: Dispute between Inherently Distinctive and Noninherently Distinctive Nonword Symbols

Nonword symbols that are fanciful or arbitrary, in contrast to descriptive or generic, are inherently distinctive and can be protected as common law trademarks. For example, nonword symbols that comprise designs that are not commonly used at the time of adoption may be inherently distinctive. Pictures of products that create or present arbitrary or fanciful impressions may also be inherently distinctive. On the other hand, common basic designs such as circles, ovals, triangles, diamonds, or stars are not examples of inherently distinctive symbols.

The plaintiff claims that [describe nonword symbol] is inherently distinctive. The defendant, however, contends that the [describe nonword symbol] is not inherently distinctive. This is a question for you, the jury, to decide in accordance with what I have just read to you.

If you decide that the [describe nonword symbol] is inherently distinctive, you will then consider whether [insert the following in an appropriate case] the [describe nonword symbol] is functional and whether the quantity and quality of the plaintiff's use of the [describe nonword symbol] has established plaintiff's priority so as to have earned legal protection for the [describe nonword symbol] under instructions to be given.

If you decide that plaintiff's [describe nonword symbol] is not inherently distinctive, then you will consider whether the evidence shows that the plaintiff's [describe nonword symbol] has developed secondary meaning.

By the term "secondary meaning," the law means that one's nonword symbol has been so used that its primary significance in the minds of a significant number of the consuming public is not the [product or service—choose one] itself but the identification of it with a single source. This does not mean that the consuming public knows the identity of that single source in the sense that the consumer knows the corporate name of the [producer or seller—choose one]. All that is necessary to establish secondary meaning is that the ordinary consumer associates the nonword symbol with a single source, regardless of whether the buyer knows who or what that source is.

You must find, therefore, from a preponderance of the evidence, that a significant number of the consuming public has associated the [describe nonword symbol] involved in this case with a single source. It is for you to decide how many constitute a significant number, keeping in mind that it is not necessary for the plaintiff to prove that all or even a majority of the consuming public understand this secondary meaning.

In determining whether the plaintiff's [describe nonword symbol] has attained secondary meaning, it is appropriate for you to consider the evidence (if any) relating to:

1. the length and manner of its use;

2. the nature and extent of the plaintiff's advertising and promotion;

3. sales volume;

4. other efforts made by the plaintiff to promote the connection in the consuming public's mind between the [describe nonword symbol] and the plaintiff;

5. properly designed and conducted consumer surveys;

6. the testimony of consumers relating to the identity of source or origin in the minds of the consuming public; and

7. copying by others.

COMMENT

See sections 4.3.1, 4.3.3, 4.3.4, cmts., *supra; see also Wiley v. Am. Greetings Corp.*, 762 F.2d 139 (1st Cir. 1985).

4.3.9　Nonword Symbols as Trademarks: Functional or Nonfunctional

In this case, the defendant claims that the [describe nonword symbol] used by the plaintiff is functional, and that the defendant may therefore also use the [describe nonword symbol].

Under the law of trademark infringement, any feature of goods or services that is functional cannot be legally protected. That is, the use of such a feature cannot constitute trademark infringement. For plaintiff to establish liability in this case, it will therefore be necessary for you to find that the [describe nonword symbol] is nonfunctional.

Design features that are useful or practical or that serve a utilitarian purpose are merely functional and cannot be legally protected. Moreover, if the [describe nonword symbol] functions primarily to beautify a product, then the [describe nonword symbol] must also be considered merely functional. In short, any feature that gives the consumer a substantial reason for purchasing the goods or services because the feature adds to either the utility or the style and attractiveness of the goods or services is functional. For example, a twist-off bottle cap is functional because it adds to the utility of the product. Conversely, a feature that serves only to distinguish the goods or services from other goods and services is nonfunctional. For example, a logo is an arbitrary symbol of source and is nonfunctional.

If you find from the evidence that the plaintiff's [describe nonword symbol] substantially contributes to the usefulness, utility, or practicality of the product, then you must find that the [describe nonword symbol] is functional and that the defendant was free to copy or simulate it.

If you find from the evidence that the plaintiff's [describe nonword symbol] substantially contributes to the general appeal of its product, because of the design of the [describe nonword symbol] itself and not because it indicates a source for the goods the consumer desires to purchase, then you must also find that the [describe nonword symbol] is functional and that the defendant was free to copy or simulate it.

If you find, however, that the plaintiff's [describe nonword symbol] is used to distinguish the product from others, the [describe nonword symbol] is nonfunctional.

COMMENT

The issue of functionality may arise when trademark rights are asserted in nonword symbols, such as designs or container shapes. *See, e.g., Qualitex Co. v. Jacobson Co., Inc.,* 514 U.S. 159 (1995); *Fabrica, Inc. v. El Dorado Corp.,* 697 F.2d 890 (9th Cir. 1983). This charge reflects the generally accepted standard in determining whether such nonword symbols are functional.

The landmark case pertaining to functionality is *Pagliero v. Wallace China Co.,* 198 F.2d 339 (9th Cir. 1952). "Functionality," as defined in *Pagliero,* is a measure of the effect of a design or physical detail in the marketplace. If a design functions in the marketplace (1) by means of aesthetic appeal, (2) by increasing the utility or practicality of a product, or (3) by saving the consumer or producer time or money, then the design may be legally functional. *Fabrica, Inc.,* 697 F.2d at 894; *see also J. C. Penney Co. v. H. D. Lee Mercantile Co.,* 120 F.2d 949 (8th Cir. 1941); *Zippo Mfg. Co. v. Rogers Imps., Inc.,* 216 F. Supp. 670 (S.D.N.Y. 1963). *But see Wallace Int'l Silversmiths, Inc. v. Godinger Silver Art Co., Inc.,* 916 F.2d 76 (2d Cir.) (rejecting *Pagliero* on the grounds that "[b]y allowing the copying of an exact design without any evidence of market foreclosure, the *Pagliero* test discourages both originators and later competitors from developing pleasing designs"), *cert. denied,* 499 U.S. 976 (1991).

It should be noted, however, that some courts may not accept this broad definition of functionality. *See W. T. Rogers Co., Inc. v. Keene,* 778 F.2d 334 (7th Cir. 1985) (attractiveness of design feature does not preclude its being trademarked); *Sicilia di R. Biebow & Co. v. Cox,* 732 F.2d 417 (5th Cir. 1984). *But see Unital, Ltd. v.*

Sleepco Mfg., Ltd., 627 F. Supp. 285 (W.D. Wash. 1985) (if eye appeal is essential, then purely aesthetic design is functional). Specifically, there is a conflict about whether aesthetic features of a product may be termed functional. For a fuller discussion, see Bradford J. Duft, *"Aesthetic" Functionality*, 73 Trade. Rep. 151 (1983); *see also* section 4.9.2, cmt., *infra*.

In *Inwood Labs., Inc. v. Ives Labs., Inc.*, 456 U.S. 844, 850 n.10 (1982), the Supreme Court held that a product feature is functional if it is essential to the product's use or if it affects the cost or quality of the article. Case law also defines nonfunctionality in terms of the dispensability of a feature (*e.g., W. T. Rogers Co., Inc. v. Keene*, 778 F.2d 334 (7th Cir. 1985)), and/or whether a given feature is essential to effective competition. *E.g., Eppendorfer-Netheler-Hinz GMBH v. Ritter GMBH*, 289 F.3d 351 (5th Cir. 2002); *Essie Cosmetics Ltd. v. Dae Do Int'l, Ltd.*, 808 F. Supp. 952 (E.D.N.Y. 1992); *New England Butt Co. v. Int'l Trade Comm'n*, 756 F.2d 874 (D.C. Cir. 1985); *see also U.S. Golf Ass'n v. St. Andrews Sys.*, 749 F.2d 1028 (3d Cir. 1984) (asserting that functionality depends on "whether a particular feature of a product or service is substantially related to its value *as a product or service*, i.e., if the feature is part of the 'function' served, or whether the primary value of a particular feature is the identification of the provider"). It is important to frame this charge in accordance with the current view of the appropriate jurisdiction.

The United States Supreme Court has interpreted federal patent law as preempting state law insofar as the latter restricts the ability of a competitor to copy the functional features of a competitor's unpatented product. *Sears, Roebuck & Co. v. Stiffel Co.*, 376 U.S. 225 (1964); *Compco Corp. v. Day Brite Lighting, Inc.*, 376 U.S. 234 (1964); *Sunbeam Corp. v. Equity Indus. Corp.*, 635 F. Supp. 625 (E.D. Va. 1986). *But see Towle Mfg. Co. v. Godinger Silver Art Co. Ltd.*, 612 F. Supp. 986 (S.D.N.Y. 1985) (statute still permits states to afford common law remedies to limited degree); 1 J. McCarthy, *Trademarks & Unfair Competition* § 8:7 (3d ed. 1992) ("Since the shape of a container or package may be an essential element of similarity in simulation of trade dress, and has always been so considered, it can be argued that there is no federal preemption of unfair competition protection, even though the shape is not protected by a design patent.").

Finally, it is important to note that courts may construe functionality as a question of law or as a mixed question of fact and law. *See Unital, Ltd. v. Sleepco Mfg., Ltd.,* 627 F. Supp. 285 (W.D. Wash. 1985).

4.4 Trademark Infringement: Acquisition and Priority of Trademark Rights

4.4.1 Generally

If you find that the public recognizes the plaintiff's [describe symbol] as identifying plaintiff's [identify product or service] and distinguishing it from those of others, you must then find that plaintiff had used the [describe symbol] as a trademark before the defendant began to market its [identify product or service] in the area where the plaintiff sells its [identify product or service].

COMMENT

See section 4.2.3, cmt., *supra.* This charge is important when the plaintiff and defendant both assert that they are the "owner" of the trademark in litigation

4.4.2   Priority of Use: Inherently Distinctive Trademarks

If you find that the plaintiff's [describe symbol] is inherently distinctive, then you must consider whether the evidence shows that the plaintiff used [describe symbol] as a trademark for plaintiff's [identify product or service] before the defendant began to use the [describe symbol]. That is, the plaintiff must have attached the symbol to plaintiff's [identify product or service] or its label or container before the defendant made such use of the [describe symbol].

You must also determine whether the evidence shows that the plaintiff's use of the [describe symbol] as a trademark for its [identify product or service] was continuous. That is, the plaintiff's use of the [describe symbol] must not have constituted merely a token use of the [describe symbol]. Token use is sporadic, casual, or transitory use that is not part of an ongoing program to exploit the trademark commercially. The number of sales does not conclusively establish continuous use, but there must be a bona fide attempt to establish a trade or a market in the product.

The date that the party conceived the idea of the symbol does not constitute use.

COMMENT

This charge reflects the traditional view that trademark rights are obtained by the party who first makes an actual, bona fide use of the trademark in a going business. *See, e.g., Blue Bell, Inc. v. Farah Mfg. Co.,* 508 F.2d 1260 (5th Cir. 1975); *Blisscraft of Hollywood v. United Plastics Co.,* 294 F.2d 694 (2d Cir. 1961); *Rolley v. Younghusband,* 204 F.2d 209 (9th Cir. 1953); *In re* Impact Distribs., Inc., 260 B.R. 48 (Bankr. S.D. Fla. 2001); *Bell v. Streetwise Records, Ltd.,* 640 F. Supp. 575 (D. Mass. 1986); *see generally* 3 J. McCarthy, *Trademarks & Unfair Competition* ch. 16 (4th ed. 1996); 1 J. Gilson, *Trademark Protection & Practice* § 3.03 (2002).

4.4.3 Priority of Use: Secondary Meaning Trademarks

If you find that the plaintiff's [describe symbol] is not inherently distinctive, but that the plaintiff has established secondary meaning in it, you must then consider whether the plaintiff can prove, by a preponderance of the evidence, that plaintiff's [describe symbol] possessed secondary meaning before the defendant first began use of [describe symbol].

COMMENT

This charge reflects the well-established rule that for secondary meaning marks—unlike inherently distinctive marks—the issue of priority is resolved in favor of the party who first uses the mark with secondary meaning. The senior user must prove the existence of secondary meaning in its mark at the time and place that the junior user first began use of that mark. *See Scott Paper Co. v. Scott's Liquid Gold, Inc.*, 589 F.2d 1225 (3d Cir. 1978); *Carter Wallace, Inc. v. Procter & Gamble Co.*, 434 F.2d 794 (9th Cir. 1970); *Indus., Inc. v. Stone Age Entm't, Inc.*, 12 F. Supp. 2d 796 (N.D. Ill. 1998); 3 J. McCarthy, *Trademarks & Unfair Competition* § 16:34 (4th ed. 1996).

4.4.4 Failure to Establish Priority

If you determine that the plaintiff has not established that plaintiff used [describe symbol] before the defendant's use of [describe symbol], then you must find for the defendant, as there can be no trademark infringement.

COMMENT

This charge follows from the law discussed in the three previous sections. *See, e.g., Scott Paper Co. v. Scott's Liquid Gold, Inc.,* 589 F.2d 1225 (3d Cir. 1978); *Ball v. United Artists Corp.,* 214 N.Y.S.2d 219 (N.Y. App. Div. 1961).

4.5 Trademark Infringement: Likelihood of Confusion

4.5.1 Generally

If you decide that the plaintiff established [describe symbol] as a trademark for plaintiff's [identify product or service] before the defendant did, then you must consider whether the defendant used [describe symbol] in a manner likely to cause confusion regarding the source of [identify product or service] among consumers using ordinary care and prudence in the purchase of [identify product or service].

In other words, you must find that ordinary purchasers, buying under the usual conditions and exercising ordinary care, would be likely to purchase the defendant's [identify product or service] in the belief that it was [produced or provided—choose one] by the plaintiff.

It is unnecessary that the evidence show that any specific person has been confused or misled. It is enough if you find that the consequences of the sale of the [describe symbol] complained of in all reasonable probability would be to confuse the public regarding the source, sponsorship, approval, or affiliation of the [identify product or service].

The fact that the [identify product or service] could be distinguished by careful or discriminating purchasers is not enough to lead you to conclude that there is no likelihood of confusion.

COMMENT

This charge reflects the traditional standard of likelihood of confusion. *See, e.g., Plus Prods. v. Plus Discount Foods Inc.*, 722 F.2d 999 (2d Cir. 1983); *Union Carbide Corp. v. Ever-Ready, Inc.*, 531 F.2d 366 (7th Cir.), *cert. denied*, 429 U.S. 830 (1976); *Omega Importing Corp. v. Petri-Kine Camera Co.*, 451 F.2d 1190 (2d Cir. 1971); *Seven-Up Co. v. Cheer Up Sales Co.*, 148 F.2d 909 (8th Cir.), *cert. denied*, 326 U.S. 727 (1945); *Softman Prods. Co., LLC v. Adobe Sys., Inc.*, 171 F.2d 1075 (C.D. Cal. 2001); *Thomas J. Lipton, Inc. v. Borden*,

Inc., 340 N.Y.S.2d 328 (N.Y. App. Div. 1972); 3 J. McCarthy, *Trademarks & Unfair Competition* ch. 23 (4th ed. 1996); 2 J. Gilson, *Trademark Protection & Practice* ch. 5 (2002).

The charge is generally based upon the ones used in *El Rancho, Inc. v. First Nat'l Bank of Nevada*, 406 F.2d 1205 (9th Cir. 1968), *cert. denied sub nom. Gerber v. First Nat'l Bank of Nev.*, 396 U.S. 875 (1969), and *Big O Tire Dealers, Inc. v. Goodyear Tire & Rubber Co.*, 408 F. Supp. 1219 (D. Colo. 1976), *modified on other grounds*, 561 F.2d 1365 (10th Cir. 1977), *cert. dismissed*, 434 U.S. 1052 (1978).

4.5.2　Factors for the Jury's Consideration

In determining whether there is or will be a likelihood of confusion caused by use of [describe symbol] by both plaintiff and defendant in connection with [identify product or service], you may draw on your common experience as citizens of the community. Likelihood of confusion is also determined by evaluating the following factors:

1. The degree of similarity between the original [describe symbol] and the allegedly infringing [describe symbol];

2. The manner and method in which the plaintiff and defendant used the [describe symbol];

3. The strength of the [describe symbol];

4. The price of the goods and other factors indicative of the degree of care and attention likely to be used by consumers when making a purchase;

5. The length of time the defendant has used the [describe symbol] without evidence of actual confusion;

6. The intent of the defendant in adopting the [describe symbol]; that is, whether there was an intent to confuse;

7. Evidence (if any) of instances of actual confusion;

8. Other factors about the [describe symbol] that would tend to reduce any tendency to confuse the purchaser about the source or origin of the [describe product];

9. The extent to which the target of the parties' sales efforts is the same; and

10. Other facts suggesting that the consuming public might expect the first user to manufacture a product in the defendant's market.

No one factor or consideration is conclusive, but each aspect should be weighed in light of the total evidence presented at the trial.

In light of these considerations and your common experience, you must determine if ordinary consumers, neither overly careless nor overly careful, would be confused about the origin, sponsorship, approval, or affiliation of the [identify product or service] upon encountering the [describe symbol] as the respective parties have used it in connection with [identify product or service].

COMMENT

The charge is based upon the one used in *Big O Tire Dealers, Inc. v. Goodyear Tire & Rubber Co.*, 408 F. Supp. 1219 (D. Colo. 1976), *modified on other grounds*, 561 F.2d 1365 (10th Cir. 1977), *cert. dismissed*, 434 U.S. 1052 (1978), and the charge in *Control Components, Inc. v. Valtek, Inc.*, 609 F.2d 763 (5th Cir.), *cert. denied*, 449 U.S. 1022 (1980).

The charge includes a composite of the factors, as set forth by various courts, that may be weighed in determining whether there is a likelihood of confusion. *See generally* 3 J. McCarthy, *Trademarks & Unfair Competition* ch. 23 (4th ed. 1996); 2 J. Gilson, *Trademark Protection & Practice* ch. 5 (2002). Because various courts have delineated different sets of factors, counsel is advised to refer to the law of the appropriate jurisdiction. *See, e.g., Moore Bus. Forms, Inc. v. Ryu*, 960 F.2d 486 (5th Cir. 1992) (seven factors are type of trademark at issue [that is, strength of trademark], degree of similarity between the two marks, similarity of products, identity of retail outlets and purchasers, identity of advertising media utilized, defendant's intent, and actual confusion); *Mutual of Omaha Ins. Co. v. Novak*, 836 F.2d 397 (8th Cir. 1987) (six factors are strength of trademark, similarity between trademarks, competitive proximity of products, defendant's intent, indications of actual confusion, and degree of care likely to be exercised by potential customers); *Holiday Inns, Inc. v. Trump*, 617 F. Supp. 1443 (D. N.J. 1985) (five factors are strength of mark, degree of similarity, defendant's intent, similarity of products or services involved, and evidence of actual confusion); *Emerson Elec. Co. v. Emerson Quiet Kool Corp.*, 577 F. Supp 668 (E.D. Mo. 1983) (eight factors are similarity of marks, similarity of products, identity of channels of trade, identity of advertising, type of purchasers, evidence of actual confusion, defendant's intent, and strength of mark).

4.6 Trademark Infringement: Damages

4.6.1 Generally

Two kinds of damages can be considered in this case: compensatory damages and punitive damages.

Compensatory damages consist of the plaintiff's direct economic losses and out-of-pocket expenses resulting from the effect of the defendant's conduct on the plaintiff. In other words, if you determine that the defendant is liable to the plaintiff in accordance with the instructions already given to you, the defendant is liable for all damages suffered by the plaintiff that were caused by the defendant's conduct. The question you should attempt to answer is: What is the amount of money required to right the wrong done to the plaintiff by the defendant?

Punitive damages, which I will discuss later, are damages that you may award not as compensation to the plaintiff, but to punish the defendant for its behavior and to dissuade the defendant and others from acting the same way in future, similar situations.

COMMENT

In jurisdictions where punitive damages are allowable in tort cases, they are equally allowable in cases of trademark infringement and unfair competition. *See, e.g., Transgo, Inc. v. Ajac Transmission Parts Corp.*, 768 F.2d 1001 (9th Cir. 1985), *cert. denied*, 474 U.S. 1059 (1986); *Big O Tire Dealers, Inc. v. Goodyear Tire & Rubber Co.*, 408 F. Supp. 1219 (D. Colo. 1976), *modified on other grounds*, 561 F.2d 1365 (10th Cir. 1977), *cert. dismissed*, 434 U.S. 1052 (1978); *Five Platters, Inc. v. Purdie*, 419 F. Supp. 372 (D. Md. 1976); 2 J. McCarthy, *Trademarks & Unfair Competition* §§ 3027, 3029 (3d ed. 1992); Annotation, *Punitive or Exemplary Damages as Recoverable for Trademark Infringement or Unfair Competition*, 47 A.L.R.2d 1117 (1956). Most states restrict the award of punitive damages in tort cases to circumstances in which some level of wrongful intent has been shown. For example, California state law limits the availability of punitive damages to cases "where defendant has been guilty of oppression, fraud or malice." Cal. Civ. Code § 3294 (West 2003). The Ninth Circuit affirmed punitive damages for trademark infringement when defendant acted with "reckless disregard" for plaintiff's rights. *Transgo, Inc. v. Ajac Transmission Parts Corp.*, 768 F.2d 1001 (9th Cir. 1985). New York law will allow punitive damages for unfair competition if the defendant "acted knowingly and with reckless disregard." *Murphy Door Bed Co. v. Interior Sleep Sys., Inc.*, 874 F.2d 95 (2d Cir. 1989). Other jurisdictions place similar intent requirements on the availability of punitive damages. *See, e.g., Charles Jacquin Et Cie, Inc. v. Distileria Serralles, Inc.*, 921 F.2d 467 (3d Cir. 1990) (to support punitive damages, defendant's conduct must be "outrageous," resulting from ill motive or reckless indifference); *see also Bandig, Inc. v. Al Bolser's Tire Stores, Inc.*, 750 F.2d 903 (D.C. Cir. 1984). In at least one state, punitive damages have been limited to an amount that will compensate the plaintiff to the extent of plaintiff's litigation expenses less taxable costs. *Triangle Sheet Metal Works, Inc. v. Silver*, 222 A.2d 220 (Conn. 1966). *But see Chrysler Corp. v. Wolmer*, 499 So. 2d 823 (Fla. 1986).

Counsel should be aware that an award to the plaintiff may be measured by the defendant's profits, the ascertainment of which will be accomplished through an accounting. *GTFM, Inc. v. Solid Clothing, Inc.*, 215 F. Supp. 2d 273 (S.D.N.Y. 2002); *Hamilton-Brown Shoe Co. v. Wolf Bros. & Co.*, 240 U.S. 251 (1916); 2 J. McCarthy, *Trademarks & Unfair Competition* §§ 3025-3026 (3d ed. 1992). In an appropriate case, the plaintiff may be awarded damages in addition to the defendant's profits.

4.6.2   Compensatory Damages

In determining compensatory damages, the difficulty or uncertainty in ascertaining or measuring the precise amount of any damages does not preclude recovery, and the jury should use its best judgment in determining the amount of such damages, if any, based upon the evidence. You may not, however, determine damages by speculation or conjecture.

In determining compensatory damages, you may consider whether the plaintiff suffered any measurable loss to its goodwill.

The goodwill of a company is an intangible business value that reflects the basic human tendency to do business with merchants who offer products of the type and quality the customer desires and expects. Service to the customer, and a willingness to stand behind a warranty and other representations about the quality of the products sold by a merchant, are factors that help establish the goodwill of a business.

The goodwill associated with a particular product or a business may be symbolized in whole or in part by the consuming public's acceptance and recognition of a trademark. The goodwill attached to a product is a part of the overall business value that is the goodwill of the company. It is possible, therefore, that the general goodwill of a company may be damaged by the loss of goodwill to a particular product. Whether this has occurred is a question of fact for you to determine.

If you find that the plaintiff's goodwill has been damaged either by injury to its general business reputation or by damage to a particular product, you may assess such compensatory damages as you may find to be shown by evidence. The measure of the plaintiff's damage is the difference between the value of such goodwill before and after the acts of the defendant. In determining compensatory damages, you may also consider other losses for which the plaintiff may seek recovery.

The fact that the defendant did not actually intend, anticipate, or contemplate that these losses would occur is not a relevant factor to be considered by you.

If you find that the plaintiff is entitled to a verdict in accordance with these instructions, but you do not find that the evidence before you is sufficient to show that the plaintiff has sustained any substantial damages, then you may return a verdict for the plaintiff on one or more of the theories of liability and fix the amount of the compensatory damages in a nominal sum such as one dollar.

COMMENT

Plaintiff's damages are "measured by the tort standard under which the infringer-tortfeasor is liable for all injuries caused to plaintiff by the wrongful act, whether or not actually anticipated or contemplated by the defendant when it performed the acts of infringement." 5 J. McCarthy, *Trademarks & Unfair Competition* § 30:72 (4th ed. 1996).

The above instruction seeks compensatory damages for injury to goodwill. A plaintiff may also recover damages based on lost profits. *Broan Mfg. Co. v. Associated Distrib. Inc.*, 923 F.2d 1232 (6th Cir.) (plaintiff manufacturer entitled to lost profits it claims would have accrued from future sales but for defendant's infringement scheme, provided plaintiff can demonstrate amount of future losses), *reconsideration denied, appeal discussed,* 932 F.2d 1146 (6th Cir. 1991); *see also, e.g., Thompson v. Haynes*, 305 F.3d 1369 (Fed. Cir. 2002); *Blue Ribbon Feed Co. v. Farmers Union Cent. Exch. Inc.*, 731 F.2d 415, 421 (7th Cir. 1984); *Obear-Nester Glass Co. v. United Drug Co.*, 149 F.2d 671 (8th Cir.), *cert. denied,* 326 U.S. 761 (1945). Recoverable damages may include amounts lost due to nullification of plaintiff's advertising expenditures. *W. Des Moines State Bank v. Hawkeye Bancorporation*, 722 F.2d 411 (8th Cir. 1983); *see also Cuisinarts, Inc. v. Robot-Coupe Int'l Corp.*, 580 F. Supp. 634 (S.D.N.Y. 1984) (rebuttal advertising). These losses are simply illustrative and should not be interpreted as excluding other kinds of losses. According to at least one court, the plaintiff is not required to prove the amount of damages with mathematical certainty. *W. Des Moines State Bank v. Hawkeye Bancorporation,* 722 F.2d 411 (8th Cir. 1983). However, to be recoverable, damages for lost profits must be supported by more than mere speculation. *Bundy Corp. v. Teledyne Indus., Inc.* 584 F. Supp. 656 (D. Conn. 1984).

4.6.3   Punitive Damages

4.6.3.a   Decision to Award Punitive Damages

If you find for the plaintiff and against the defendant and you have determined that the defendant must pay damages, then you should consider whether the conduct that led to your decision also subjects the defendant to punitive damages. To award punitive damages, you must find that the defendant's act or omission that proximately caused actual [or nominal] damage to the plaintiff was the result of actual malice, wanton conduct, or oppressive conduct, as measured by the instructions I will give you.

COMMENT

As noted in section 4.6.1, in jurisdictions where punitive damages are allowable, they are also permitted in trademark infringement actions. Because the standard for the award of punitive damages varies from state to state, counsel should insert the appropriate local standard where indicated in the charge.

This charge represents the modern view of damages. *See, e.g., State Farm Mut. Auto. Ins. Co. v. Campbell,* 538 U.S. 408 (2003); *Rabun v. Kimberly-Clark Corp.,* 678 F.2d 1053 (11th Cir. 1982); *Christman v. Voyer,* 595 P.2d 410 (N.M. Ct. App. 1979); *Wussow v. Commercial Mechanisms, Inc.,* 279 N.W.2d 503 (Wis. Ct. App. 1979); *Restatement (Second) of Torts* § 908 (1979); 45 Am. Jur. 2d *Interference* § 62 (1999 & Supp. 2003). The *Restatement* makes clear that under appropriate circumstances, punitive damages may be awarded for the tort of contractual interference. *Restatement (Second) of Torts* § 774A cmt. a (1979). *See generally* Sara L. Johnson, Annotation, *Punitive Damages for Interference with Contract or Business Relationship,* 44 A.L.R.4th 1078 (1986 & Supp. 2002). Counsel should note that although punitive damages generally will be awarded upon a showing of malice, wantonness, or oppressiveness, this principle is not universal and may well be affected by statute in a particular jurisdiction.

Of note, most states require that the jury find liability and actual, or at least nominal, damages before punitive damages are allowed. *See* Richard C. Tinney, Annotation, *Showing of Actual Damages to Support Award of Punitive Damages*, 40 A.L.R.4th 11 (1985 & Supp. 2002); 45 Am. Jur. 2d *Interference* § 62 (1999 & Supp. 2003); *see also Am. Bus. Interiors, Inc. v. Haworth, Inc.*, 798 F.2d 1135 (8th Cir. 1986). *But see Platte v. Whitney Realty Co.*, 538 So. 2d 1358 (Fla. Dist. Ct. App. 1989) (punitive damages recoverable although actual damages could not be proved). For a discussion of the prerequisite of a verdict for actual damages, see the comment to section 4.6.3.b. For the requirement of malicious, wanton, or oppressive conduct, see sections 4.6.3.c, 4.6.3.d, and 4.6.3.e.

4.6.3.b Nominal Damages

The award of only a nominal sum with respect to the specific losses claimed by the plaintiff will not prevent your awarding punitive damages, if you find that the award of punitive damages is justified under these instructions.

COMMENT

In most states the jury must make a finding of liability and actual, or at least nominal, damages before punitive damages are allowed. *See* Richard C. Tinney, Annotation, *Showing of Actual Damages to Support Award of Punitive Damages*, 40 A.L.R.4th 11 (1985 & Supp. 2002); 45 Am. Jur. 2d *Interference* § 62 (1999 & Supp. 2003); *Am. Bus. Interiors, Inc. v. Haworth, Inc.*, 798 F.2d 1135 (8th Cir. 1986). *But see Platte v. Whitney Realty Co.*, 538 So. 2d 1358 (Fla. Dist. Ct. App. 1989) (punitive damages recoverable although actual damages could not be proved).

In most jurisdictions, an award of nominal damages will suffice for this purpose. *E.g., Taylor v. Sandoval*, 442 F. Supp. 491 (D. Colo. 1977); *Tennant v. Vazquez*, 389 So. 2d 1183 (Fla. Dist. Ct. App. 1980); *Christman v. Voyer*, 595 P.2d 410 (N.M. Ct. App. 1979). *But see Wussow v. Commercial Mechanisms, Inc.*, 279 N.W.2d 503 (Wis. Ct. App. 1979). *See generally* Richard C. Tinney, Annotation, *Showing of Actual Damages to Support Award of Punitive Damages—Modern Cases*, 40 A.L.R.4th 11 (1985 & Supp. 2002).

4.6.3.c Actual Malice

You may find the defendant's conduct to have been undertaken with actual "malice" sufficient to enable you to award punitive damages if you find it to have been prompted or accompanied by personal ill will, spite, or hatred, either toward the plaintiff individually or toward all persons in one or more groups or categories of which the plaintiff is a member.

COMMENT

Generally, courts require proof of facts tending to establish actual, as opposed to legal, malice to justify an award of punitive damages. *See* 45 Am. Jur. 2d *Interference* § 62 (1999 & Supp. 2003); *Norwood Easthill Assocs. v. Norwood Easthill Watch*, 536 A.2d 1317 (N.J. Super. Ct. App. Div. 1988); *Anthony Pools, Inc. v. Charles & David, Inc.*, 797 S.W.2d 666 (Tex. App. 1990); *Bellefonte Underwriters Co. v. Brown*, 663 S.W.2d 562 (Tex. App. 1984). Even if not required, actual malice is always an important factor in an award of punitive damages. *See, e.g., Universal City Studios, Inc. v. Nintendo Co.*, 615 F. Supp. 838 (S.D.N.Y. 1985), *aff'd*, 797 F.2d 70 (2d Cir.), *cert. denied*, 479 U.S. 987 (1986); *Int'l Wood Processors Corp. v. Power Dry, Inc.*, 593 F. Supp. 710 (D.S.C. 1984); *Edward Vantine Studios, Inc. v. Fraternal Composite Serv., Inc.*, 373 N.W.2d 512 (Iowa Ct. App. 1985).

4.6.3.d Wanton Conduct

You may also award punitive damages if you find that the defendant's act or failure to act was "wantonly" done; that is, that it was undertaken in reckless or callous disregard of, or indifference to, the rights of one or more persons, including the plaintiff.

COMMENT

See King v. G.D. Van Wagenen Co., 717 F. Supp. 667 (D. Minn. 1989); *Liston v. Home Ins. Co.*, 659 F. Supp. 276 (S.D. Miss. 1986); *Universal City Studios, Inc. v. Nintendo Co.*, 615 F. Supp. 838 (S.D.N.Y. 1985), *aff'd*, 797 F.2d 70 (2d Cir.), *cert. denied*, 479 U.S. 987 (1986); *Ramona Manor Convalescent Hosp. v. Care Enters.*, 225 Cal. Rptr. 120 (Cal. Ct. App. 1986).

4.6.3.e   Oppressive Conduct

You also may award punitive damages if, from all of the evidence, you find that the defendant's act or failure to act was "oppressive"; that is, that it was done in a way or manner that injured, damaged, or otherwise violated the rights of the plaintiff with unnecessary harshness or severity, as by misuse or abuse of authority or power, or by taking advantage of some weakness, disability, or misfortune of the plaintiff.

COMMENT

See Barnes Group, Inc. v. C & C Prod., Inc., 716 F.2d 1023 (4th Cir. 1983); *Rabun v. Kimberly-Clark Corp.*, 678 F.2d 1053 (11th Cir. 1982); *Int'l Wood Processors Corp. v. Power Dry, Inc.*, 593 F. Supp. 710 (D.S.C. 1984), *aff'd*, 792 F.2d 416 (4th Cir. 1986).

4.6.3.f   Amount of Punitive Damages Award

If you decide that punitive damages are appropriate in this case based upon my prior instructions, you should award the amount of punitive damages that, in your sound judgment, will justly punish the defendant for its behavior and dissuade the defendant and others from acting the same way in future, similar situations.

In fixing the amount of punitive damages, you may consider the following factors:

1. The character of the defendant's act(s);

2. The nature and extent of the harm to the plaintiff that the defendant caused or intended to cause; and

3. The defendant's financial condition.

The amount of any punitive damages should bear a reasonable relationship to the injury, harm, or damage caused by the defendant. You must also bear in mind that the amount of such punitive damages, when awarded, must be fixed with calm discretion and sound reason. Punitive damages must not be awarded, or fixed in amount, based upon any sympathy, bias, or prejudice you may feel toward any party in the case.

[If evidence of "other acts" or harm against other parties has been allowed, add the following:] Some of the evidence you have heard concerned conduct by the defendant that was not the proximate cause of the damages claimed by the plaintiff in this case. Although you may consider this evidence for any bearing upon the defendant's state of mind in causing damages claimed by the plaintiff in this case, you are not to punish the defendant for conduct relating only to parties other than the plaintiff.

[If evidence of net worth has been allowed, add the following:] You have heard evidence of the defendant's financial condition. You are not to consider the defendants' financial condition in deciding whether to award punitive damages, but you may consider it to the extent that the actual [or nominal] damages are insufficient to justly punish the defendant for its behavior or dissuade the defendant or others from acting the same way in future, similar situations.

COMMENT

See State Farm Mut. Auto. Ins. Co. v. Campbell, 538 U.S. 408 (2003); *Cooper Indus., Inc. v. Leatherman Tool Group, Inc.,* 121 S. Ct. 1678 (2001); *BMW of N. Am., Inc. v. Gore,* 116 S. Ct. 1589 (1996); *Jannotta v. Subway Sandwich Shops, Inc.,* 125 F.3d 503 (7th Cir. 1997); *Fed. Deposit Ins. Corp. v. W.R. Grace & Co.,* 877 F.2d 614 (7th Cir. 1989), *cert. denied,* 110 S. Ct. 1524 (1990); *Aldrich v. Thomson McKinnon Sec., Inc.,* 756 F.2d 243 (2d Cir. 1985); Damages—Modern Cases, 40 A.L.R.4th 11 (1985 & Supp. 2002).

A state may not impose damages on a defendant for actions undertaken in other states that do not violate the other states' laws. *BMW,* 116 S. Ct at 1597. Similarly, a "defendant's dissimilar acts, independent from the acts upon which liability was premised, may not serve as the basis for punitive damages." *State Farm,* 123 S. Ct. at 1523.

A defendant's financial condition as a factor in setting punitive damages is generally accepted. *See, e.g., Miller v. Rukoff-Sexton, Inc.,* 845 F.2d 209 (9th Cir. 1988) (the defendant's net worth was admissible for setting punitive damages); *Hollins v. Powell,* 773 F.2d 191 (8th Cir.) (reducing punitive damage award in light of defendant's limited resources), *cert. denied,* 475 U.S. 1119 (1985); *Rupert v. Sellers,* 368 N.Y.S.2d 904 (N.Y. App. Div. 1975) (in bifurcated trial, evidence of the defendant's net worth should be considered after special verdict). *See generally* Annotation, *Punitive Damages: Relationship to Defendant's Wealth As a Factor in Determining Propriety of Award,* 87 A.L.R.4th 141 (1991 & Supp. 2002). Some states, such as Hawaii, even have statutes making the financial condition of the defendant relevant to the amount of punitive damages awardable. Others, like New York, protect the defendant from possible prejudice at trial through the use of a bifurcated trial procedure. *See Aldrich v. Thomson McKinnon Sec.,*

Inc., 589 F. Supp. 683 (S.D.N.Y. 1984). However, the Supreme Court has cautioned that the financial condition of the defendant may not be used to create bias against big businesses. *State Farm*, 123 S. Ct. at 1525 ("The wealth of a defendant cannot justify an otherwise unconstitutional punitive damage award."). Recent commentators have argued that the defendant's financial condition is only relevant in cases involving non-economically motivated torts. *See, e.g.,* Andrew L. Frey, *No More Blind Man's Bluff on Punitive Damages: A Plea to the Drafters of Pattern Jury Instructions*, 29 Litig. 24 (Summer 2003). In cases where the defendant was motivated by profits, they argue, compensatory damages are sufficient to act as a deterrent. *Id.*

4.7   General Instruction: Trade Name Infringement

COMMENT

Because trade names are protectable under the same basic principles that govern trademarks (see section 4.1.2), the same charges that are found in the trademark infringement sections can be used in an action involving alleged trade name infringement, substituting "trade name" for "trademark" and "business" for "goods or services."

4.8 General Instruction: Unfair Competition

4.8.1 Theory of Unfair Competition

In this case, the plaintiff, [name], seeks to recover money damages from the defendant, [name], for what the plaintiff claims to be unfair competition in the use of [describe symbol], in connection with the sale of [identify goods and/or service]. The legal principles discussed in these instructions regarding the law of unfair competition have evolved from attempts to balance the following conflicting policy objectives:

1. There is a need to protect the public from being misled about the nature and source of the goods and services they buy;

2. There is a need to protect the property rights of a business to identify itself and its goods and services to the public;

3. There is a need to try to achieve these goals without injury to the free-market economic system, which encourages fair competition among those providing goods and services.

Fair competition is encouraged, but unfair competition is destructive of the competitive process and is illegal.

Because of the conflicting policy objectives involved in cases of this type, each such case must be decided largely on its specific facts, and you, the jury, are the judge of the facts.

COMMENT

This charge is identical to section 4.2.1 for trademark infringement. *See* section 4.2.1, cmt., *supra*.

4.8.2   Elements of Liability

To find liability for unfair competition, you, the jury, must find from a preponderance of the evidence that:

1. that the public recognizes the plaintiff's [describe symbol] in connection with the sale of plaintiff's [identify product or service] as identifying plaintiff's [identify product or service] and distinguishing it from those of others; and

2. that such recognition has occurred before the defendant entered the market in which the plaintiff sells its [identify product or service]; and

3. that the defendant uses [describe symbol] in a manner likely to cause confusion about the source of the [identify product or service] among persons using ordinary care and prudence in the purchase of [identify product or service].

If you find by a preponderance of the evidence that the plaintiff has proved these elements, then and only then may you find the defendant liable for unfair competition. You will then consider the question of damages under separate instructions.

COMMENT

This charge reflects the traditional standard for establishing liability for unfair competition. *See* 5 J. McCarthy, *Trademarks & Unfair Competition* § 30:75 (4th ed. 1996). A jury may find liability without also concluding that the defendant intended to deceive the public. *Id.* Moreover, damages may be awarded without a finding that the defendant acted with a wrongful intent. *Id.* § 30:25[2].

There is a developing aspect of unfair competition jurisprudence that will encompass the situation that occurs when a second manufacturer enters the market before the time a first distributor has established its trade dress in the consumer's mind. It is possible that a successful cause of action based on unfair competition can be sustained under these circumstances, regardless of whether public recognition of the first user's product exists, if the defendant is aware of plaintiff's preexisting product and fails to make defendant's product sufficiently dissimilar. *See, e.g., Thompson v. Tega-Rand Int'l*, 740 F.2d 762 (9th Cir. 1984). *Cf. Dominion Bankshares Corp. v. Devar Holding Co., Inc.*, 690 F. Supp. 338 (E.D. Pa. 1988) (imposing on defendant, who entered market subsequent to plaintiff, an "affirmative duty to choose a [trademark] or a trade name so as to avoid all confusion as to the source of origin of its services").

4.8.3 Jury's Reliance on Improper Fact

The fact that the defendant uses [describe symbol] that is similar (or even identical in some respects) to plaintiff's [describe symbol], and that the purchasing public is likely to be confused as a result, does not in and of itself constitute unfair competition. To establish its claim against the defendant, the plaintiff must prove by a preponderance of the evidence each of the three elements I just mentioned to you. Only then may you find for the plaintiff.

COMMENT

This charge follows from the authority cited in the comment to section 4.8.2. It is recommended to reinforce and remind the jury that liability will be established only upon a finding that all three elements have been proved. Reference is made to the comment to section 4.8.2 regarding the possibility that public recognition of a symbol may not be a necessary element for a cause of action based on unfair competition.

4.9 Unfair Competition: Proof of Identifying Function

4.9.1 Secondary Meaning

The first question for you, the jury, to decide is whether the public recognizes the plaintiff's [describe symbol] in connection with the sale of plaintiff's [identify product or service] as identifying its [product or service] and distinguishing it from those of others. To determine whether the plaintiff has proved this, you must consider whether the evidence shows that the plaintiff's [describe symbol] has developed secondary meaning.

By the term "secondary meaning," the law means that a symbol has been so used that its primary significance in the minds of the consuming public is not the [product or service] itself but the identification of such [product or service] with a single source. This does not mean that the consuming public must know the exact identity of that single source in the sense that it knows the corporate name of the [producer or seller]. All that is necessary to establish secondary meaning is that the ordinary consumer associates the [product or service] with a single source, regardless of whether the consumer knows who or what that source is.

You must find, therefore, from a preponderance of the evidence, that a significant number of the consuming public has associated the [describe symbol] involved in this case with a single source. It is for you to decide how many constitute a significant number, keeping in mind that it is not necessary for the plaintiff to prove that all or even a majority of the consuming public understand this secondary meaning.

In determining whether the plaintiff's [describe symbol] has attained secondary meaning, it is appropriate for you to consider the evidence (if any) relating to:

1. the length and manner of its use;

2. the nature and extent of advertising and promotion;

3. sales volume;

4. other efforts made by the plaintiff in the direction of promoting the connection in the consuming public's mind between the [describe symbol] and the plaintiff;

5. properly designed and conducted consumer surveys; and

6. testimony of consumers relating to the identity of the source or origin of the [describe symbol] in the minds of the consuming public.

The mere fact that plaintiff is using [describe symbol], or that the plaintiff began using it before the defendant, does not establish or create secondary meaning.

Similarly, the mere fact that you might consider the plaintiff's [describe symbol] to be unique is not enough to establish secondary meaning.

There is no particular length of time within which secondary meaning is established. The question for you to determine is whether secondary meaning has been established, not in how long or short a time this was accomplished.

COMMENT

This charge reflects the traditional view of what must initially be established in unfair competition cases. *See, e.g., Walt Disney Prods. v. Air Pirates,* 581 F.2d 751 (9th Cir. 1978), *cert. denied sub nom. O'Neill v. Walt Disney Prods.,* 439 U.S. 1132 (1979); *Tas-T-Nut Co. v. Variety Nut & Date Co.,* 245 F.2d 3 (6th Cir. 1957); *Wembley, Inc. v. Diplomat Tie Co.,* 216 F. Supp. 565 (D. Md. 1963); *Filter Dynamics Int'l Inc. v. Astron Battery, Inc.,* 311 N.E.2d 386 (Ill. App. Ct. 1974). In some cases, however, proof of the identifying function could be established by showing that the item the plaintiff is attempting to protect is inherently distinctive. *Cf. Application of McIlhenny Co.,* 278 F.2d 953, 47 C.C.P.A. 985 (C.C.P.A. 1960). *But see Truck Equip. Serv. Co. v. Fruehauf Corp.,* 536 F.2d 1210 (8th Cir.), *cert. denied,* 429 U.S. 861 (1976). Again, as in section 4.3.1, the caveat is raised that the issue of distinctiveness may be one of law for the court to decide.

This charge also reflects the traditional standard for secondary meaning. *See, e.g.,* 2 J. McCarthy, *Trademarks & Unfair Competition* ch. 15 (4th ed. 1996); Julius R. Lunsford, *The Mechanics of Proof of Secondary Meaning,* 60 Trade. Rep. 263 (1970). It is primarily drawn from the charge used in *Big O Tire Dealers, Inc. v. Goodyear Tire & Rubber Co.,* 408 F. Supp. 1219 (D. Colo. 1976), *modified on other grounds,* 561 F.2d 1365 (10th Cir. 1977), *cert. dismissed,* 434 U.S. 1052 (1978), and the charges used in *Gordon v. Warner Brothers Pictures, Inc.,* 74 Cal. Rptr. 499 (Cal. Ct. App. 1969).

It is also important to note that proof of secondary meaning may not be essential to an action for trade dress infringement. *See, e.g., 20th Century Wear, Inc. v. Sanmark-Stardust, Inc.,* 747 F.2d 81 (2d Cir. 1984), *cert. denied,* 470 U.S. 1052 (1985). Similarly, in *Gemveto Jewelry Co. v. Jeff Cooper, Inc.,* 568 F. Supp. 319 (S.D.N.Y. 1983), the court found that the deliberate use of a competitor's nonfunctional marks or trade dress is actionable without a showing of secondary meaning.

The charge also reflects the traditional types of evidence that are accepted by the courts. *See, e.g., Artus Corp. v. Nordic Co.,* 512 F. Supp. 1184 (W.D. Pa. 1981); 1 J. Gilson, *Trademark Protection & Practice* § 2.09[5] (2002); 4 R. Callmann, *Unfair Competition, Trademarks & Monopolies* ¶ 77.3 at 349 (3d ed. 1969). Although some courts have held that proof of secondary meaning is sufficiently made by the inferences to be drawn from mere copying (*see, e.g., Audio Fidelity, Inc. v. High Fidelity Recordings, Inc.,* 283 F.2d 551 (9th Cir. 1960)), this view has been criticized. *See Mr. Gasket Co. v. Travis,* 299 N.E.2d 906 (Ohio Ct. App. 1973); *Developments in the Law—Competitive Torts,* 77 Harv. L. Rev. 888, 916 (1963).

4.9.2 Functional or Nonfunctional

In this case, the defendant claims that the [describe symbol] used by the plaintiff is functional, and therefore the defendant may also simulate the [describe symbol]. Under the law of unfair competition, items that are functional cannot be legally protected. That is, use of such items cannot constitute unfair competition. For the plaintiff to establish liability in this case, you therefore must find that the [describe symbol] is nonfunctional.

The requirement of nonfunctionality involves an evaluation regarding whether the [describe symbol] at issue has any purpose other than the identification of the product. You must determine whether the [describe symbol] is substantially related to its value as a product or service; that is, if the [describe symbol] is part of the "function" served, or whether the primary value of the [describe symbol] is the identification of the product.

A feature of goods, or of their wrappers or containers, may be functional because it contributes to efficiency or economy in manufacturing them or in handling them through the marketing process. It may also be functional because it contributes to their utility, to their durability, or to the effectiveness or ease with which they serve their function or are handled by users. A feature that adds to the utility or the style and attractiveness of a product may also be functional. A feature that, if omitted, would prevent a seller or manufacturer from competing effectively is functional. A feature is nonfunctional if, when it is omitted, nothing of substantial value in the goods is lost. A feature that merely associates goods with a particular source may be a substantial factor in increasing the marketability of the goods. But if that is the entire significance of the feature, it is nonfunctional because its value then lies only in the demand for goods associated with a particular source.

For example, the ribbed or corrugated design on the top of a construction worker's hard hat may be functional because of the design's ability to strengthen the crown. On the other hand, a Fotomat Film kiosk structure with a steep, yellow, three-tiered roof may not be functional because the distinctive shape of the roof was not dictated by the function it was to serve—that is, to shelter personnel from the elements. That the roof may perform a function does not prevent unfair competition protection. It is only when the design or packaging is primarily functional that it will be deemed functional for purposes of unfair competition.

If you find from the evidence that the plaintiff's [describe symbol] falls within the boundaries of the foregoing definition of functionality, then there can be no unfair competition, and the defendant was free to copy and imitate [describe symbol].

COMMENT

This charge becomes pertinent in those cases when an issue raised is that the item for which protection is claimed is functional. *See, e.g., Bristol-Myers Squibb Co. v. McNeil-P.P.C., Inc.*, 973 F.2d 1033 (2d Cir. 1992); *Merchant & Evans, Inc. v. Roosevelt Bldg. Prods. Co., Inc.*, 963 F.2d 628 (3d Cir. 1992); *In re* Morton-Norwich Prods., Inc., 671 F.2d 1332 (C.C.P.A. 1982). This charge is in part derived from section 742 of the *Restatement of Torts*, which provides a commonly cited definition and explanation of functionality. The *Restatement (Second) of Torts* does not deal with the question of functionality because its drafters felt that this issue had become a separate area of the law. Courts, however, continue to cite to the first *Restatement of Torts*.

The charge reflects the generally accepted view about what is functional. *See* 4 A.R. Callmann, *The Law of Unfair Competition, Trademarks & Monopolies* § 25.29 n.11 (4th ed. 1992); 1 J. McCarthy, *Trademarks & Unfair Competition* § 7.26 (3d ed. 1992); 1 J. Gilson, *Trademark Protection & Practice* § 7.02[7] (1992); Colleen R. Courtade, Annotation, *Application of Functionality Doctrine Under § 43 (a) of Lanham Act* (15 U.S.C.S. § 1125 (a)), 78 A.L.R. Fed. 712 (application of functionality doctrine); *see also In re Morton-Norwich Prods., Inc.*, 671 F.2d 1332 (C.C.P.A. 1982); *Filter Dynamics Int'l, Inc. v. Astron Battery, Inc.*, 311 N.E.2d 386 (Ill. App. Ct. 1974); *Fisher Stores, Inc. v. All Nighter Stove Works, Inc.*, 626 F.2d

193 (1st Cir. 1980). There is, however, some dispute about whether aesthetic features are functional. *See* 1 J. McCarthy, *Trademarks & Unfair Competition* § 7:70 (4th ed. 1996); *see also Gemveto Jewelry Co. v. Jeff Cooper, Inc.*, 613 F. Supp. 1052 (S.D.N.Y. 1985), *vacated on other grounds*, 800 F.2d 256 (Fed. Cir. 1986). At least one court has held that a certain design was nonfunctional as a matter of law. *Artus Corp. v. Nordic Co.*, 512 F. Supp. 1184 (W.D. Pa. 1981).

When substantially all of an overall design otherwise eligible for trademark protection is nonfunctional, as is the fluting of the glass in a Coca-Cola bottle, it should not matter that the shape of an insignificant element of the design is arguably functional. *See Textron, Inc. v. Int'l Trade Comm'n*, 753 F.2d 1019 (D.C. Cir. 1985); 1 J. McCarthy, *Trademarks & Unfair Competition* § 7.31 (3d ed. 1992); *see also* section 4.3.9, cmt., *supra*.

4.10 Unfair Competition: Acquisition and Priority of Rights

4.10.1 Generally

If you find that the plaintiff has established secondary meaning in [describe symbol], you must then consider whether the evidence shows that the plaintiff's [describe symbol] possessed secondary meaning before the defendant first began use of [describe symbol].

If you determine that the plaintiff has not established that plaintiff's [describe symbol] possessed secondary meaning before the defendant's use of [describe symbol], then you must find for the defendant, as there can then be no unfair competition.

COMMENT

When the plaintiff and defendant both assert that they are the "owner" of the item in litigation, the court must determine the priority of each right. This reflects the well-established rule that the requisite secondary meaning be developed before the defendant uses the item. *See, e.g., Artus Corp. v. Nordic Co.,* 512 F. Supp. 1184 (W.D. Pa. 1981); *Marion Lab., Inc. v. Michigan Pharmacal Corp.,* 338 F. Supp. 762 (E.D. Mich. 1972), *aff'd,* 473 F.2d 910 (6th Cir. 1973); 1 J. Gilson, *Trademark Protection & Practice* § 3.03 (2002).

4.11 Unfair Competition: Likelihood of Confusion

4.11.1 Generally

If you find that the [describe symbol] used by the plaintiff possessed secondary meaning before the time that the defendant first began use of [describe symbol], then you must consider whether the defendant used [describe symbol] in a manner likely to cause confusion about the source of [identify product or service] among persons using ordinary care and prudence in the purchase of [identify product or service].

In other words, you must find that ordinary purchasers, buying under the usual conditions and exercising ordinary care, would be likely to purchase the defendant's [identify product or service] in the belief that it was [produced or provided—choose one] by the plaintiff.

It is not necessary that the evidence show that any specific person has been confused or misled. It is enough if you find that the probable consequences of the use of the [describe symbol] complained of in all reasonable probability would be to confuse the public about the source, sponsorship, approval, or affiliation of the [identify product or service].

The fact that the [identify product or service] could be distinguished by careful or discriminating purchasers is not enough to lead you to conclude that there is no likelihood of confusion.

COMMENT

This charge reflects the traditional standard of likelihood of confusion. *See, e.g., Jean Patou, Inc. v. Jacqueline Cochran, Inc.,* 201 F. Supp. 861 (S.D.N.Y.), *aff'd,* 312 F.2d 125 (2d Cir. 1963); *Don Alvarado Co. v. Porganan,* 21 Cal. Rptr. 495 (Cal. Ct. App. 1962); 3 J. McCarthy, *Trademarks & Unfair Competition* ch. 23 (4th ed. 1996). A showing of likelihood of confusion is sometimes not necessary. Some courts have held that when a defendant intentionally copies, the second comer will be presumed to have intended to create a confusingly similar appearance and will be presumed to have succeeded. *Morex S.P.A. v. Design Inst. Am., Inc.*, 779 F.2d 799 (2d Cir. 1985); *Perfect Fit Indus., Inc. v. Acme Quilting Co. Inc.*, 618 F.2d 950 (2d Cir. 1980), *cert. denied*, 459 U.S. 832 (1982).

Some courts, though in a minority, have held that proof of actual confusion is required to obtain a damages remedy. *See 20th Century Wear Inc. v. Sanmark-Stardust, Inc.*, 747 F.2d 81 (2d Cir. 1984), *cert. denied*, 470 U.S. 1052 (1985); *Warner Bros. v. Gay Toys, Inc.*, 658 F.2d 76 (2d Cir. 1981).

4.11.2　Factors for the Jury's Consideration

In determining whether there is or will be a likelihood of confusion caused by the use of [describe symbol] by both plaintiff and defendant in connection with [identify product or service], you may draw on your common experience as citizens of the community. Likelihood of confusion is also determined by evaluating the following factors:

1. The degree of similarity between the original [describe symbol] and the allegedly infringing [describe symbol];

2. The manner and method in which the plaintiff and defendant used the [describe symbol];

3. The strength of the [describe symbol];

4. The price of the goods and other factors indicative of the degree of care and attention likely to be used by consumers when making a purchase;

5. The length of time the defendant has used the [describe symbol] without evidence of actual confusion;

6. The intent of the defendant in adopting the [describe symbol]; that is, whether there was an intent to confuse;

7. Evidence (if any) of instances of actual confusion;

8. Other factors about the [describe symbol] that would tend to reduce any tendency to confuse the purchaser about the source or origin of the [describe symbol];

9. The extent to which the target of the parties' sales efforts is the same; and

10. Other facts suggesting that the consuming public might expect the first user to manufacture a product in the defendant's market.

No one factor or consideration is conclusive, but each aspect should be weighed in light of the total evidence presented at the trial.

Similarity of appearance of [describe symbols] is to be determined on the basis of the total effect of the [describe symbols] on the consumer. One cannot avoid liability simply by showing that individual features of the [describe symbols] are dissimilar. Rather, it is the total combination of elements and the similarity of the total, overall impression to the consumer that is to be considered by you.

In light of these considerations and your common experience, you must determine whether ordinary consumers, neither overly careful nor overly careless, would be confused about the origin, sponsorship, approval, or affiliation of the [identify product or service] upon encountering the [describe symbol] as the respective parties have used it in connection with [identify product or service].

COMMENT

This text lists the usual factors considered in determining whether there is a likelihood of confusion. *See* section 4.5.2, *supra; see also Parks v. LaFace Records*, 329 F.3d 437 (6th Cir. 2003); *Scott Paper Co. v. Scott's Liquid Gold, Inc.*, 589 F.2d 1225 (3d Cir. 1978); *Scarves by Vera, Inc. v. Todo Imports, Ltd. (Inc.)*, 554 F.2d 1167 (2d Cir. 1976); *Nat'l Football League Props., Inc. v. New Jersey Giants, Inc.*, 637 F. Supp. 507 (D.N.J. 1986); *Am. Greetings Corp. v. Dan-Dee Imports, Inc.*, 619 F. Supp. 1204, 1222 (D.N.J. 1985); *Caesar's World, Inc. v. Caesar's Palace*, 490 F. Supp. 818 (D.N.J. 1980).

In general, the same factors are considered in cases premised on trademark (or trade name) infringement as in those based on unfair competition. *See, e.g., Am. Footwear Corp. v. Gen. Footwear Co.*, 609 F.2d 655 (2d Cir. 1979), *cert. denied*, 445 U.S. 951 (1980); *Sterling Acceptance Corp. v. Tommar, Inc.*, 227 F. Supp. 2d 454 (D. Md. 2002). Some courts have indicated, however, that in cases involving only unfair competition, the defendant's use of his/her own trademark in connection with an allegedly infringing item may be sufficient to prevent likelihood of confusion. *See, e.g., T & T Mfg. Co. v. A. T. Cross Co.,* 449 F. Supp. 813 (D.R.I.), *aff'd,* 587 F.2d 533 (1st Cir. 1978), *cert. denied,* 441 U.S. 908 (1979); *Ralston Purina Co. v. Thomas J. Lipton, Inc.,* 341 F. Supp. 129 (S.D.N.Y. 1972). In appropriate cases, the charges should be modified accordingly.

4.11.3   Unfair Competition: Damages

[See section 4.6, *supra.*]

Chapter Five
Racketeer Influenced and Corrupt Organizations Act

Jeffrey H. Bergman*

*   Jeffrey H. Bergman is a partner at Sachnoff & Weaver, Ltd., 310 S. Wacker Drive, Chicago, IL 60606, 312-207-1000, jbergman@sachnoff.com.
   This chapter was revised and updated for this fourth edition from materials prepared in the third edition by Edward F. Mannino and Marguerite S. Walsh.

5.1 Introduction

This chapter presents jury instructions for use in cases arising under the Racketeer Influenced and Corrupt Organizations Act (RICO), 18 U.S.C. §§ 1961-68. Although RICO's Statement of Findings and Purpose clearly states that the act was directed primarily toward the problem of the infiltration of legitimate business by organized crime, it is now well settled that RICO reaches far beyond traditional notions of "organized crime." *See, e.g., Sedima, S.P.R.L. v. Imrex Co.,* 473 U.S. 479 (1985); *H.J., Inc. v. Northwestern Bell Tel. Co.,* 492 U.S. 229 (1989). These instructions are designed to address the "heart" of the RICO elements as they may apply in business tort litigation; in an actual trial, as with any case, the instructions should be tailored to address the factual context of the particular case.

Although section 1962 of RICO, in four separate subsections, declares it unlawful for any person to engage in any one of four categories of activities, it is the third subsection—section 1962(c)—under which virtually all business-related RICO cases have been brought. Subsection (c) prohibits the "(1) conduct (2) of an enterprise (3) through a pattern (4) of racketeering activity," terms that are discussed more fully below and in the instructions that follow. *Sedima S.P.R.L. v. Imrex Co.,* 473 U.S. 479 (1985). Subsection (d), which makes it unlawful to conspire to violate any of the other subsections of section 1962, is also employed, although to a lesser extent, in business RICO cases.

The three elements of section 1962(c) that have most lent themselves to varying interpretations by courts are the "pattern," "conduct," and "enterprise" requirements. The pattern controversy has largely been settled by the Supreme Court's decision in *H.J., Inc. v. Northwestern Bell Tel. Co.,* 492 U.S. 229 (1989), upon which the instruction in section 5.11.1 is based. Similarly, questions about the proper interpretation of the conduct requirement have been resolved by the Supreme Court's decision in *Reves v. Ernst & Young,* 507 U.S. 170 (1993). The instructions in sections 5.8.1 and 5.8.2 are based upon that decision.

The enterprise requirement has raised two important issues under section 1962(c). The first issue is whether the person and enterprise must be separate and distinct. In 2001, the Supreme Court confirmed that they must be, and that only the person can be held liable for damages under section 1962(c). *See* § 5.7.1, cmt., *infra.* The second issue focuses on the proper use and structural requirements of association-in-fact enterprises, principally whether the person may be part of such an enterprise and still liable for damages. This issue has created at least semantic conflicts among the courts that have considered it. *See* § 5.7.2, cmt., *infra.*

Once a RICO violation has been established, section 1964(c) mandates an award of treble damages, attorneys' fees, and costs to a person whose business or property has been injured by reason of the RICO violation. With the Supreme Court's rejection in *Sedima* of the concept of a special "racketeering injury" as a condition of relief, and the Court's subsequent decision in *Holmes v. Securities Investor Protection Corp.*, 503 U.S. 258 (1992), requiring some direct relation between the injury asserted and the injurious conduct alleged, the "by reason of" language has taken on enhanced importance as a traditional proximate-cause screening device. This requirement is discussed in § 5.14.2, *infra.*

It is important to remember that many substantive elements of section 1962(c) claims may be appropriate for resolution by motions for summary judgment or directed verdict and should not reach the jury. These include both some of the elements covered in the instructions that follow (such as association-in-fact enterprises [§ 5.7.2], interstate commerce [§ 5.7.3], and pattern of racketeering activity [§ 5.11.1]), and additional elements that are not covered in these instructions because they are appropriate for resolution by the court as a matter of law. These latter elements include standing (*see* Gregory P. Joseph, *Civil RICO: A Definitive Guide* (2d ed.) 27-28 (1999) (hereinafter Joseph, *Civil RICO)*; Edward F. Mannino, *Lender Liability and Banking Litigation* § 4.03.5.c (1989-2002) (hereinafter Mannino, *Lender Liability)*), the existence of any compensable injury (*see* Joseph, *Civil*

RICO; Mannino, *Lender Liability*), and vicarious liability of the "enterprise" (*see generally* Edward F. Mannino, *Lender Liability and Banking Litigation* § 4.03.2.b.iii (1989-2002)). Note that vicarious liability may be appropriate in cases filed under section 1962(a) or (b). *See generally* Joseph, *Civil RICO*. Given the number of cases decided on these and other key RICO elements, it is essential to review and update the applicable case law regularly to assure the continued accuracy of these instructions. Also, so-called state "baby RICO" statutes should be consulted for possible additional claims and relief that may be available in a particular jurisdiction, including extraordinary equitable remedies and prejudgment relief.

These and other legal issues covered in these instructions are discussed in length in Joseph, *Civil RICO*, Mannino, *Lender Liability*, and *Business Torts Litigation* (ABA 1992)

5.2   General Instruction

The plaintiff claims that the defendant has violated the Racketeer Influenced and Corrupt Organizations Act, commonly referred to by the abbreviation RICO.

5.3   No Organized Crime Requirement

Although the RICO statute uses the terms "racketeering" and "corrupt organizations," the statute does not require you to determine whether the defendant is a "racketeer" in the everyday sense of the word, or whether it is associated with "organized crime" in the everyday sense of the word.

COMMENT

This instruction is obviously favorable to the plaintiff and should be requested as part of a RICO plaintiff's charge. See the "Requested Defense Instructions" in *United States v. Scotto*, 641 F.2d 47 (2d Cir. 1980), *cert. denied*, 452 U.S. 961 (1981).

5.4 "Preponderance" Standard Applies

Although the RICO statute refers to the term "racketeering activity," I instruct you that this is a civil case, not a criminal case, and that the plaintiff's RICO allegations do not need to be proved beyond a reasonable doubt, but only by a preponderance of the evidence.

COMMENT

This instruction is supported by *Sedima, S.P.R.L. v. Imrex Co., Inc.*, 473 U.S. 479 (1985) (dictum). *See also Grogan v. Garner*, 498 U.S. 279 (1991). Many circuit courts have expressly held that the preponderance standard governs civil RICO actions. *See, e.g., Matter of EDC, Inc.*, 930 F.2d 1275, 1280 (7th Cir. 1991); *Wilcox v. First Interstate Bank*, 815 F.2d 522 (9th Cir. 1987); *see also*, Joseph, *Civil RICO* at 171.

5.5 General Elements of Section 1962(c)

Section 1962(c) of RICO prohibits the conduct of an enterprise through a pattern of racketeering activity. To prove liability under section 1962(c), the plaintiff must establish each of the following elements by a preponderance of the evidence:

First, that the defendant was a person employed by or associated with an enterprise;

Second, that the enterprise was engaged in, or its activities affected, interstate commerce;

Third, that the defendant conducted or participated, directly or indirectly, in the conduct of that enterprise's affairs; and

Fourth, that the defendant's conduct of, or participation in, the enterprise's affairs was through a pattern of racketeering activity.

To recover damages from the defendant, the plaintiff must further prove that the defendant's acts proximately caused injury to plaintiff's business or property.

Some of these elements are matters for the court to decide, while others are for you the jury to decide. I will instruct you about those matters that are for you to decide.

COMMENT

This instruction tracks the statutory language of 18 U.S.C. §§ 1962(c) and 1964(c). Because the vast majority of RICO cases involving businesses are brought under section 1962(c) (as well as section 1962(d), the conspiracy subpart), this general instruction should be requested in most cases. Note that the Fifth Circuit's Pattern Jury Instructions specify that the defendant's participation in or conduct of the affairs of the enterprise and the participation or conduct through a pattern of racketeering activity must be "knowing and willful." *Fifth Circuit Pattern Jury Instructions,* § 8.1 (1999).

5.6 Person

Before I further explain the elements of a RICO violation, I need to define for you some of the terms used in the RICO statute. The first is the term "person." A person includes any individual or entity capable of holding a legal or beneficial interest in property. [I instruct you that the plaintiff and the defendant are both legal entities capable of holding a legal or beneficial interest in property and are therefore persons under the RICO statute.]

COMMENT

This instruction tracks the statutory language of 18 U.S.C. § 1961(3). Because it would be a rare case when the existence of a "person" would be disputed, the bracketed material will usually be appropriate to include in the instruction.

Two areas pose questions regarding the existence of a RICO "person." First, unincorporated associations may not qualify as persons under section 1961(3) unless the applicable law permits them to hold an interest in property. *See* Joseph, *Civil RICO* at 29 (citing *Fleischhauer v. Feltner,* 879 F.2d 1290, 1298-99 (6th Cir.), *cert. denied,* 493 U.S. 1074 (1989) and *Jund v. Town of Hempstead,* 941 F.2d 1271 (2d Cir. 1991)). Second, some courts have also held that the United States is not a person authorized to sue under section 1964(c). *See United States v. Bonnano Organized Crime Family,* 879 F.2d 20 (2d Cir. 1989).

5.7　Enterprise

5.7.1　General Instruction

The next term I must define for you is "enterprise." An enterprise includes any individual, partnership, corporation, association, or other legal entity, and any union or group of individuals associated in fact although not a legal entity.

I instruct you that for purposes of the RICO statute in this case the "person" and the "enterprise" cannot be the same, but must be separate and legally distinct.

COMMENT

The first paragraph of this instruction tracks the statutory language of 18 U.S.C. § 1961(4).

In *Cedrick Kushner Promotions, Ltd. v. King*, 533 U.S. 158 (2001), the Supreme Court approved the proposition (which all the circuits had previously adopted) that the person and enterprise must be different to establish liability under section 1962(c). The Court stressed, however, that where the alleged "person" was the sole shareholder and an employee of a corporation that was the alleged "enterprise," "the statute requires no more than the formal legal distinction between 'person' and 'enterprise,'" and so the "distinctness" test had been met. *See generally* Mannino, *Lender Liability* at § 4.03.2.b; Joseph, *Civil RICO* at 50-55.

The requirement that the person and enterprise be different entities applies under section 1962(c), but not under sections 1962(a) and (b). *See, e.g., Busby v. Crown Supply, Inc.*, 896 F.2d 833 (4th Cir. 1990) (en banc); *Haroco, Inc. v. Am. Nat'l Bank & Trust Co.*, 747 F.2d 384 (7th Cir. 1984), *aff'd on other grounds*, 473 U.S. 606 (1985).

5.7.2   Association-in-Fact

In this case the plaintiff asserts that the enterprise is an informal, de facto association rather than a structured organization, and that the enterprise is composed of [describe components of alleged association-in-fact]. I instruct you that such an association-in-fact can be considered an enterprise, provided that it (1) is ongoing, (2) functions as a continuing unit, (3) has some type of organization, whether formal or informal, (4) has a common or shared purpose, and (5) constitutes an entity separate and apart from the pattern of racketeering activity in which it is alleged to have engaged.

COMMENT

Courts have offered various formulations regarding when an association-in-fact can satisfy the enterprise requirement. *See, e.g., United States v. Turkette*, 452 U.S. 576 (1981); *Calcasieu Marine Nat'l Bank v. Grant*, 943 F.2d 1453 (5th Cir. 1991); *Atlas Pile Driving Co. v. DiCon Fin. Co.*, 886 F.2d 986 (8th Cir. 1989); *Town of Kearny v. Hudson Meadows Urban Renewal Corp.*, 829 F.2d 1263 (3d Cir. 1987); *Atkinson v. Anadarko Bank & Trust Co.*, 808 F.2d 438 (5th Cir.), *cert. denied*, 483 U.S. 1032 (1987); *Shaffer v. Williams*, 794 F.2d 1030 (5th Cir. 1986); *Miller Hydro Group v. Popovitch*, 793 F. Supp. 24 (D. Me. 1992). *See generally* Joseph, *Civil RICO* at 53-56, 59-62.

Many courts have also imposed the requirement that an association-in-fact have an "ascertainable structure." *See, e.g., Atlas Pile Driving Co. v. DiCon Fin. Co.*, 886 F.2d 986, 995-96 (8th Cir. 1989). *See generally* Mannino, *Lender Liability* at § 4.03.2.b; Joseph, *Civil RICO* at 68-71.

5.7.3   Interstate Commerce

I have previously instructed you that the enterprise must be one that was engaged in, or whose activities affected, interstate commerce. This requirement is satisfied if you determine that the activities of the enterprise itself, or the defendant's conduct with respect to the enterprise, had even a slight or minimal impact on commerce between separate states or between one or more states and foreign countries.

COMMENT

This instruction is supported by *Jund v. Town of Hempstead*, 941 F.2d 1271 (2d Cir. 1991); *Rose v. Bartle*, 871 F.2d 331 (3d Cir. 1989); and *United States v. Robinson*, 763 F.2d 778, 781 (6th Cir. 1985). *But see Musick v. Burke*, 913 F.2d 1390 (9th Cir. 1990) (as matter of practical economics, a local catering service that allegedly drew $500,000 per year in products from interstate commerce did not satisfy requirement). *See generally* Joseph, *Civil RICO* at 96-97. This issue should rarely go to the jury, and typically will be appropriate for determination by the trial court as a matter of law.

5.8   Conduct

5.8.1   Insiders

Among the other elements the plaintiff must prove to establish RICO liability on the part of the defendant are that the defendant was employed by or associated with the enterprise and conducted or participated in the conduct of the affairs of the enterprise through a pattern of racketeering activity. In this regard, you must find that the defendant participated in the operation or management of the enterprise itself, and was involved in the alleged unlawful activities.

To participate in the operation or management of an enterprise, a defendant must have had some part in directing the enterprise's affairs. A defendant need not be a member of upper management to satisfy this requirement, but may be a lower-rung participant in the enterprise who is acting under the direction of upper management.

COMMENT

This instruction should be employed when the defendant holds some formal position with the enterprise, such as officer, director, partner, principal, or employee. The language in the second paragraph of this instruction is based upon the language of the majority opinion in *Reves v. Ernst & Young*, 507 U.S. 170 (1993).

The *Reves* decision resolved a conflict among the circuits on the proper interpretation of section 1962(c). Some courts had followed variations of the operation or management standard adopted in *Reves*, while others had employed a more liberal standard under which performing activities necessary or helpful to the operation of the enterprise was sufficient. *See generally*, Mannino, *Lender Liability* at § 4.03.4; Joseph, *Civil RICO* at 57-61.

5.8.2   Outsiders

Among the other elements the plaintiff must prove to establish RICO liability on the part of the defendant are that the defendant was employed by or associated with the enterprise and conducted or participated in the conduct of the affairs of the enterprise through a pattern of racketeering activity. In this regard, you must find that the defendant participated in the operation or management of the enterprise itself, and was involved in the alleged unlawful activities.

To participate in the operation or management of an enterprise, a defendant must have had some part in directing the enterprise's affairs. This does not require that the defendant hold a formal position in the enterprise. Even an outsider may participate in the operation or management of an enterprise if the outsider is associated with the enterprise and participates in the conduct of its affairs. An example of such association and participation would be if the outsider exerted control over the enterprise through bribery.

COMMENT

This instruction should be employed when the defendant does not hold any formal position with the enterprise but rather is an outsider, such as an outside auditor, outside counsel, a lender, or some other third party. The language in the second paragraph of this instruction is based upon the language of the majority opinion in *Reves v. Ernst & Young,* 507 U.S. 170 (1993).

Courts applying the *Reves* outsider standard have dismissed suits against outside auditors, outside counsel, and lenders, among others. *See, e.g., Univ. of Md. v. Peat, Marwick, Main & Co.,* 996 F.2d 1534 (3d Cir. 1993) (outside auditors); *Nolte v. Pearson,* 994 F.2d 1311 (8th Cir. 1993) (outside counsel); *Info. Exch. Sys., Inc. v. First Bank Nat'l Ass'n,* 994 F.2d 478 (8th Cir. 1993) (lender).

Given the restrictive reach of section 1962(c) when outsider parties are involved, such parties are more likely to be named as defendants on a conspiracy theory rather than under section 1962(c). *See* § 5.13, *infra.*

5.9   Racketeering Activity

The next term I will define for you is the term "racketeering activity." Racketeering activity includes any act or threat that is chargeable under certain state criminal laws, or an act that is indictable as a violation of certain federal statutes. Here the plaintiff contends that defendant engaged in [describe the RICO violations that are alleged].

COMMENT

Section 1961(1) sets forth a long list of predicate acts that are helpfully categorized in Sheehy, *RICO Forfeitures: The Development of* In Personam *Forfeitures as a Sanction in Federal Criminal Cases, in Civil RICO* 101, 176-80 (Pa. Bar Inst. 1990). *See also* Joseph, *Civil RICO* at 79-102.

The most commonly charged RICO predicate act is mail fraud. The elements of proof necessary to establish a mail fraud violation are set forth in § 5.10, *infra*.

5.10 Mail Fraud

5.10.1 General Elements of Mail Fraud

The plaintiff has charged the defendant with mail fraud as a predicate act under RICO. Under 18 U.S.C. § 1341, a person who has devised or intended to devise a scheme or artifice to defraud, or to obtain money or property by means of false or fraudulent pretenses, representations, or promises, and who uses the mails to execute or attempt to execute the scheme or artifice to defraud, has committed mail fraud.

To state a violation of the mail fraud statute, plaintiff must establish each of the following elements:

1. The existence of a scheme or artifice to defraud;

2. Participation by the defendant in that scheme or artifice to defraud;

3. Specific intent to defraud on the part of the defendant;

4. Deception of the plaintiff as a result of the scheme or artifice to defraud; and

5 The use of the United States mails in furtherance of the scheme or artifice to defraud.

COMMENT

See, e.g., United States v. Burks, 867 F.2d 795 (3d Cir. 1989); *In re Phillips Petroleum Sec. Litig.,* 881 F.2d 1236 (3d Cir. 1989); *Lavery v. Kearns,* 792 F. Supp. 847 (D. Me. 1992). *See also* Joseph, *Civil RICO, supra* at 66; 3 Devitt, Blackmar & Wolff, *Federal Jury Practice and Instructions: Civil,* § 100.06 (4th ed. 1987); *Ninth Circuit Manual of Model Criminal Jury Instructions,* § 8.101(2003).

It should be noted that the requirements of the wire fraud statute, 18 U.S.C. § 1343, are essentially similar, so that this instruction may be adapted by substituting "telephone lines" (or "wires") for "mails" in item (5), when wire fraud is charged. *See United States v. Computer Sciences Corp.,* 689 F.2d 1181 (4th Cir. 1982), *cert. denied,* 459 U.S. 1105 (1983).

5.10.2   Scheme or Artifice and Specific Intent

I will now explain to you the terms "scheme or artifice" and "specific intent." To employ a scheme or artifice to defraud means to use material misrepresentations, material omissions, or other dishonest means that are reasonably calculated to deceive persons of ordinary prudence and intelligence. It is necessary that the defendant have a specific intent to defraud, which may be established by proof that the defendant made material misrepresentations of fact with knowledge of their falsity or with reckless disregard for their truth, or that the defendant knowingly or recklessly omitted to state material facts.

COMMENT

In *Neder v. United States*, 527 U.S. 1 (1999), the Supreme Court decided that materiality is an element of the "scheme or artifice" requirement under the federal mail, wire, and bank fraud statutes. For other cases addressing the "scheme or artifice" requirement, see *Pereira v. United States*, 347 U.S. 1 (1954); *Associates in Adolescent Psychiatry, S.C. v. Home Life Insurance Co.*, 941 F.2d 561 (7th Cir. 1991); *Walters v. First Nat'l Bank*, 855 F.2d 267 (6th Cir. 1988), *cert. denied*, 489 U.S. 1067 (1989); *Lavery v. Kearns*, 792 F. Supp. 847 (D. Me. 1992); *Zee-Bar, Inc.-N.H. v. Kaplan*, 792 F. Supp. 895 (D.N.H. 1992). *See also* Joseph, *Civil RICO* at 83; 3 Devitt, Blackmar & Wolff, *Federal Jury Practice and Instructions: Civil*, § 100.07 (4th ed. 1987); *Ninth Circuit Manual of Model Criminal Jury Instructions*, § 8.101 (2003).

For cases addressing the "specific intent" requirement, *see Landry v. Air Line Pilots Ass'n*, 901 F.2d 404 (5th Cir.), *cert. denied*, 498 U.S. 895 (1990); *Atlas Pile Driving Co. v. DiCon Financial Co.*, 886 F.2d 986 (8th Cir. 1989); *Lavery v. Kearns*, 792 F. Supp. 847 (D. Me. 1992). *See also* Joseph, *Civil RICO* at 84.

5.10.3 Mailing May Be Incidental

The alleged scheme or artifice to defraud need not contemplate the use of the mails as an essential element. It is sufficient if the mailing is incidental to an essential part of the scheme, as long as the mailing contributes to the completion of the scheme or artifice to defraud the plaintiff.

COMMENT

Although this instruction, which is generally favorable to a RICO plaintiff, emphasizes that the mailing in question need not be an essential element of the scheme, it nonetheless recognizes that the mailing must be related to the execution or completion of the scheme. Thus, fraudulent mailings that do not have the effect of deceiving the plaintiff are generally insufficient, even if they have the effect of deceiving third parties. *See, e.g., McEvoy Travel Bureau, Inc. v. Heritage Travel, Inc.,* 904 F.2d 786 (1st Cir.), *cert. denied,* 498 U.S. 992 (1991); *United States v. Shelton,* 848 F.2d 1485 (10th Cir. 1988) *But see Shaw v. Rolex Watch USA, Inc.,* 726 F. Supp. 969 (S.D.N.Y. 1989). *See generally* Joseph, *Civil RICO* at 82; 3 Devitt, Blackmar & Wolff, *Federal Jury Practice and Instructions: Civil,* § 100.08 (4th ed. 1987).

Similarly, if the mailings are undertaken after the completion or fruition of the fraudulent scheme, they are generally insufficient to support a claim of mail fraud. *See, e.g., Dennis v. Gen. Imaging, Inc.,* 918 F.2d 496 (5th Cir. 1990).

5.10.4 Good Faith Belief in Truth

Even if you find that the defendant misstated or omitted to state certain facts, I instruct you that if the defendant believed in good faith that the statements made were true at the time of mailing, then there is no mail fraud.

COMMENT

This instruction, which is favorable to a RICO defendant, simply expands upon the "specific intent" requirement discussed in § 5.10.2, *supra*. *See generally* Joseph, *Civil RICO* at 84; 3 Devitt, Blackmar & Wolff, *Federal Jury Practice and Instructions: Civil*, § 100.08 (4th ed. 1987); *Fifth Circuit Civil Pattern Jury Instructions*, § 8.1 (1999).

5.11   Pattern of Racketeering Activity

5.11.1   Definition

Now I will define the term "pattern of racketeering activity." A pattern of racketeering activity requires at least two acts of racketeering activity within ten years of each other [one of which must have occurred after October 15, 1970]. Those acts must be *related* to each other and must also amount to, or pose a threat of, *continuing criminal activity*. [Here describe the alleged pattern of racketeering activity.]

In determining whether these alleged acts, if proved, constituted a pattern of racketeering activity, you should consider the following factors.

First, acts are "related" within the meaning of RICO if they embrace criminal acts that have the same or similar purposes, results, participants, victims, or methods of commission. Acts may also be related for purposes of RICO liability if they otherwise are interrelated by distinguishing characteristics and are not isolated events.

Second, acts may be found to amount to, or pose a threat of, "continuing criminal activity" in two general ways. If the activity has ended, this requirement is satisfied if you find that the defendant committed a series of related unlawful acts extending over a substantial period of time and involving long-term criminal conduct. Unlawful acts extending over a few weeks or months and threatening no future criminal activity do not satisfy this requirement. [Ordinarily, a period of at least twelve months is required to establish sufficient continuity.]

A second way for the plaintiff to satisfy this requirement is by showing either that the unlawful activity is part of the enterprise's regular way of doing business, or that the related unlawful acts themselves involve a distinct threat of long-term racketeering activity. For example, a threat of long-term racketeering activity would be established in a case in which a hoodlum attempted to sell "insurance" to neighborhood storekeepers to cover them against breakage of their windows, telling his victims that the hoodlum would be reappearing each month to collect the "premium" that would continue their "coverage."

[In determining whether plaintiff has proved the existence of a pattern of racketeering activity in this case, you may also consider the following factors:

1. the number, type, and variety of the alleged unlawful acts;

2. the duration or time span of the alleged unlawful acts;

3. the number of perpetrators;

4. the number of victims;

5. the number and separateness of "transactions," "schemes," or "episodes" involving unlawful conduct; and

6. the presence of distinct injuries.]

COMMENT

The second sentence of this instruction tracks the language of 18 U.S.C. § 1961(5). The bracketed material in that sentence can be omitted in most cases. The remainder of the first paragraph, and all of the second through fifth paragraphs, with the exception of the bracketed material at the end of the fourth paragraph, are based on the language of the majority opinion in *H.J., Inc. v. Northwestern Bell Tel. Co.*, 492 U.S. 229, 236-39 (1989).

The bracketed material in the fourth paragraph, suggesting a litmus test of a twelve-month minimum period, finds considerable support in the circuit and district court opinions postdating the *H.J., Inc.* case. *See, e.g., Feinstein v. RTC*, 942 F.2d 34 (1st Cir. 1991); *Kehr Packages, Inc. v. Fidelcor, Inc.*, 926 F.2d 1406 (3d Cir.), *cert. denied*, 501 U.S. 1222 (1991); *Johnston v. Wilbourn*, 760 F. Supp. 578 (S.D. Miss. 1991) (collecting cases). Some circuits, on the other hand, have expressly declined to impose a one-year "bright line" rule. *See, e.g., Allwaste, Inc. v. Hinson*, 65 F.3d 1523 (9th Cir. 1995). This point is discussed further, and additional cases cited, in

Mannino, *Lender Liability*, § 4.03.3.d, and in Joseph, *Civil Rico at* 109-10.

The bracketed material in the sixth and final paragraph of this proposed instruction incorporates elements from those circuit court opinions that followed the so-called "multifactor" test before the *H.J., Inc.* case. Although some circuits have concluded that the test is inconsistent with *H.J.* (*see, e.g., Fleet Credit Corp. v. Sion*, 893 F.2d 441 (1st Cir. 1990)), others still follow it. *See, e.g., Columbia Natural Resources, Inc. v. Tatum*, 58 F.3d 1101 (6th Cir. 1995, *cert. denied*, 516 U.S. 1158 (1996); *Banks v. Wolk*, 918 F.2d 418 (3d Cir. 1990); *U.S. Textiles, Inc. v. Anheuser-Busch Cos., Inc.*, 911 F.2d 1261 (7th Cir. 1990). This point is discussed further, and additional cases cited, in Joseph, *Civil RICO*, at 115-18.

The existence of a pattern of racketeering activity may be a question of law in some cases. As noted above, when a closed-end scheme lasts less than twelve months and threatens no future harm, or affects only a single victim, courts have increasingly held that no pattern exists as a matter of law.

5.11.2 Additional Instruction for Mail Fraud

In this case, plaintiff contends that defendant violated RICO by committing acts of mail fraud that constituted a pattern of racketeering activity. I instruct you that in determining whether a pattern of racketeering activity has been proved, you may consider only defendant's deceptive or fraudulent activity; you may not consider innocent mailings even though they may have continued for a substantial period of time.

COMMENT

This instruction is based upon *Kehr Packages, Inc. v. Fidelcor, Inc.,* 926 F.2d 1406 (3d Cir.), *cert. denied,* 501 U.S. 1222 (1991). *Accord, Feinstein v. RTC,* 942 F.2d 34 (1st Cir. 1991); *Delta Pride Catfish, Inc. v. Marine Midland Bus. Loans, Inc.,* 767 F. Supp. 951 (E.D. Ark. 1991).

This instruction should be coordinated with those on mail fraud to avoid confusion between the pattern element, for which innocent mailings cannot be considered, and the elements of a mail fraud violation, for which the mailings may be incidental as long as they contribute to completion of the fraudulent scheme. *See* § 5.10.3, *supra.*

5.12 General Elements of Section 1962(d)

The plaintiff also claims that the defendant violated section 1962(d). Section 1962(d) states that it is unlawful for any person to conspire to violate any of the other subsections of section 1962. The plaintiff alleges that the defendant conspired with others to violate section 1962 [insert applicable subsection], the section that I have just described to you.

For the plaintiff to prove a violation of section 1962(d), the RICO conspiracy claim, the plaintiff must establish each of the following:

1. that the defendant conspired with others to violate section 1962 [insert applicable subsection];

2. that the defendant knowingly agreed with others to become part of the alleged conspiracy;

3 that the defendant agreed to commit, or to aid and abet another to commit, overt acts in furtherance of the alleged conspiracy, even if those acts were not unlawful acts under RICO, and knew that those acts were part of a pattern of racketeering activity; and

4. that the plaintiff suffered an injury caused by an act that is a "racketeering activity" as I have defined that term.

COMMENT

The RICO conspiracy subsection requires *an agreement to commit* unlawful activity, not simply the commission of such activity. *See, e.g., United States v. Pepe,* 747 F.2d 632 (11th Cir. 1984); *United States v. Taruglio,* 731 F.2d 1123 (4th Cir.), *cert. denied,* 469 U.S. 862 (1984); *United States v. Brooklier,* 685 F.2d 1208 (9th Cir. 1982), *cert. denied,* 459 U.S. 1206 (1983); *United States v. Winter,* 663 F.2d 1120 (1st Cir. 1981), *cert. denied,* 460 U.S. 1011 (1983). However, an agreement to commit unlawful activity, without more, is not enough; there must also be agreement to join the conspiracy and knowledge that such activity is part of a pattern of racketeering activity under RICO. *See, e.g., Glessner v. Kenny,* 952 F.2d 702, 714 (3d Cir. 1991).

Previously, there was a split among the circuits as to whether, under the RICO conspiracy provision, the defendant must himself commit or agree to commit two or more predicate acts. The Supreme Court resolved this issue in *Salinas v. United States,* 522 U.S. 52 (1997), holding that such an agreement is not required. Also, the Supreme Court in *Beck v. Prupis,* 529 U.S. 494 (2000), resolved a split among the circuits by ruling that to state a conspiracy claim under RICO, the plaintiff must allege injury caused by an act that is either a predicate act or otherwise "independently wrongful under RICO." Significantly, the Court stated that "under our interpretation, a plaintiff could, through a Section 1964(c) suit for violation of Section 1962(d), sue co-conspirators who might not themselves have violated one of the substantive provisions of Section 1962." The Court declined to decide the issue of whether a plaintiff alleging a RICO conspiracy must allege an actionable violation under sections 1962(a)-(c), or whether it is sufficient to allege an agreement to complete a substantive violation and the commission of at least one act of racketeering that caused the plaintiff injury. (*See,* 522 U.S. at n. 10.) *See also* Joseph, *Civil RICO* at 49-50; Mannino, *Lender Liability* at § 4.01[3][d].

Conspiracy liability under section 1962(d) is different from liability for aiding and abetting a violation of any of the other subsections of section 1962. Prior to 1994, several courts held that a defendant could be liable for aiding and abetting such a violation. However, in 1994 the Supreme Court held in *Central Bank v. First Interstate Bank,* 114 S. Ct. 1439 (1994) that a private plaintiff may not maintain an aiding and abetting suit under section 10(b) of the Securities Exchange Act of 1934. Since the *Central Bank* decision, a large majority of courts that have considered the issue have held that as a result of that opinion there is no longer liability for aiding and abetting a violation of RICO, either. *See Pa. Ass'n of Edwards Heirs v. Rightenour,* 235 F.3d 839 (3d Cir. 2000); *In re Mastercard Int'l Internet Gambling Litig.,* 132

F. Supp. 2d 468 (E.D. La. 2001) (collecting cases), *aff'd*, 313 F.3d 257 (5th Cir. 2002); *see also* Joseph, *Civil RICO* at 135.

In the majority opinion in *Reves*, the Supreme Court noted that section 1962(c) participation liability required more than aiding and abetting liability, which the Court characterized as "a term of breadth indeed, for 'aid and abet' 'comprehends all assistance rendered by words, acts, encouragement, support, or presence.' " *Reves v. Ernst & Young*, 507 U.S. at 178 (1993) (quoting *Blacks Law Dictionary*). As a result of the elimination of aider and abetter liability, claims against enterprise outsiders are more likely to be brought under section 1962(d). *See* § 5.8.2 cmt., *supra*.

5.13 Conspiracy, Predicate Acts, Multiple Defendants

As you know, there are [number of] defendants in this lawsuit, each of whom is being charged with conspiring to violate RICO. I instruct you that to impose liability upon a defendant for conspiring to violate RICO, you need not find that the defendant agreed to commit at least two predicate acts itself. It is sufficient if a particular defendant agreed that some member of the enterprise would commit the predicate acts.

COMMENT

This instruction should be requested by a RICO plaintiff in cases involving multiple defendants or alleged wrongdoers. *See United States v. Neapolitan*, 791 F.2d 489 (7th Cir.), *cert. denied*, 479 U.S. 939 (1986); *United States v. Tille*, 729 F.2d 615 (9th Cir.), *cert. denied*, 469 U.S. 819 (1984); *Airlines Reporting Corp. v. Barry*, 666 F. Supp. 1311 (D. Minn. 1987). *See also* Joseph, *Civil RICO* at 126.

5.14 Injury and Proximate Cause

5.14.1 Injury

If you find that the defendant violated [insert applicable subsection], then the plaintiff must next prove that it was injured in its business or property by reason of the defendant's violation of [insert applicable subsection].

For the plaintiff to prevail on its RICO claim, you must find that the plaintiff suffered an injury to its business or property and that this injury was proximately caused by reason of the defendant's violation of RICO. I will explain this proximate cause requirement to you in more detail in the next instruction, but I will first describe for you the types of damages that are and are not recoverable under RICO. Damages that are recoverable include, for example, the payment of money, lost profits, and overcharges. They do not include, for example, claims for personal injury or mental anguish. However, before any damages are recoverable at all, the plaintiff must prove that such damages were proximately caused by the defendant's RICO violation, as I will now explain to you.

COMMENT

This instruction focuses upon the types of damages recoverable in RICO cases, while the instruction in § 5.14[2] discusses the proximate cause requirement. Many cases discuss the types of damages recoverable under RICO. *See, e.g., Advanced Bus. Sys., Inc. v. Philips Info. Sys. Co.*, 750 F. Supp. 774 (E.D. La. 1990) (lost profits recoverable if proximate cause requirement satisfied); *Sound Video Unlimited, Inc. v. Video Shack, Inc.*, 700 F. Supp. 127 (S.D.N.Y. 1988) (same holding); *Rodonich v. House Wreckers Union*, 627 F. Supp. 176 (S.D.N.Y. 1985) (lost wages recoverable); *Brandenberg v. Seidel*, 859 F.2d 1179 (4th Cir. 1988) (lost interest income recoverable); *Haroco, Inc. v. Am. Nat'l Bank & Trust Co.*, 747 F.2d 384 (7th Cir. 1984) (excessive interest charges recoverable), *aff'd on other grounds*, 473 U.S. 606 (1985); *Genty v. Resolution Trust Corp.*, 937 F.2d 899 (3d Cir. 1991) (physical and emotional injuries not compensable under RICO); *Moore v. Eli Lilly & Co.*, 626 F. Supp. 365 (D. Mass. 1986) (same holding; loss of consortium not compensable under RICO); *Drake v. B.F. Goodrich Co.*, 782 F.2d 638 (6th Cir. 1986) (wrongful death not compensable under RICO); *Bast v. A.H. Robins Co.*, 616 F. Supp. 333 (E.D. Wis. 1985) (illness and injury based on products liability claim not compensable); *Zimmerman v. HBO Affiliate Group*, 834 F.2d 1163 (3d Cir. 1987) (damage to reputation and mental anguish not compensable under RICO). *Compare Hunt v. Weatherbee*, 626 F. Supp. 1097 (D. Mass. 1986) (claims for discrimination and sexual harassment compensable under RICO, at least when plaintiff forced from job and prevented from pursuing similar work in future). *See also* Joseph, *Civil RICO* at 140-43; Mannino, *Lender Liability* at § 4.03[5].

5.14.2　Proximate Cause

Now I will explain the concept of proximate cause as it applies to RICO. For you to find that defendant's violation of RICO proximately caused injury to plaintiff's business or property, plaintiff must establish a direct relationship between the injury asserted and the injurious conduct alleged. In other words, plaintiff must prove that defendant's conduct was a substantial factor in the sequence of responsible causation, and that plaintiff's injury was reasonably foreseeable or anticipated as a natural consequence of such conduct. It is not enough that the defendant has committed a RICO violation and that the plaintiff has suffered some injury; rather, there must be a direct and proximate link between the two.

A determination of proximate cause depends on the facts of each case. For example, if a defendant engages in a scheme to defraud a plaintiff who is in the construction business by submitting and collecting inflated invoices, and the plaintiff goes out of business—not because of defendant's conduct but rather because of an economic recession affecting the construction industry—then there would be no proximate cause under RICO for the destruction of the business. On the other hand, if it were shown that plaintiff's loss of the business was the reasonably foreseeable and natural consequence of defendant's scheme of submitting and collecting inflated invoices, then the RICO proximate cause requirement would be met.

COMMENT

The foregoing instruction is derived from the Supreme Court's decision in *Holmes v. Securities Investor Protection Corp.*, 503 U.S. 258 (1992), in which the Supreme Court held that a RICO plaintiff had to establish a direct causal connection between the injury alleged and the conduct in question. In *Holmes,* the Ninth Circuit reversed the lower court's entry of summary judgment in favor of a broker-dealer on standing grounds. The Ninth Circuit held that in liquidation proceedings, the Securities Investor Protection Corporation (SIPC) had standing to pursue claims under section 1964(c) on the basis that it had been required to advance funds to certain customers of its member broker-dealers in reimbursement of defendants' allegedly fraudulent stock manipulation scheme. The Supreme Court reversed the Ninth Circuit's decision and rejected a "but for" analysis in favor of a more stringent "direct relation" requirement between the alleged injury and the conduct in question. The Court concluded that the harm suffered as a result of the fraudulent scheme was actually to the member broker-dealers who were then unable to pay customers' claims, thus requiring the SIPC to step in and reimburse those customers. Such harm, the Court determined, was too remote from the alleged violation to fulfill the proximate cause requirement. The "responsible causation" language is found in *Hecht v. Commerce Clearing House, Inc.*, 879 F.2d 21 (2d Cir. 1990). *See also* Joseph, *Civil RICO* at 35-38; Mannino, *Lender Liability* at § 4.03[5][b].

Chapter Six
Fraud, Misrepresentation, Nondisclosure, and Concealment

Daniel C. Johnson and Adam S. Tanenbaum *

---

* Daniel C. Johnson is a shareholder and Adam S. Tanenbaum is an associate at Carlton Fields, P.A., CNL Center at City Commons, 450 S. Orange Avenue, Suite 500, Orlando, FL 32801. Mr. Johnson may be reached at djohnson@carltonfields.com. Mr. Tanenbaum may be reached at atanenbaum@carltonfields.com.

6.1   Introduction

The model jury instructions contained in this chapter address the liability and damage aspects of the common law torts of fraudulent misrepresentation, negligent misrepresentation, fraudulent concealment, and fraudulent nondisclosure. No attempt has been made to survey the statutory liability for causes of action similar to these common law torts, because these instructions are meant to have the broadest possible application.

Moreover, the model instructions closely follow the *Restatement (Second) of Torts* (1977), and they do so for three reasons. First, not every tort contained in this chapter is recognized by every jurisdiction. Second, not all jurisdictions distinguish between and among the torts contained in this chapter. For example, see the comment to the instruction in section 6.2.3, *infra*, which notes how some jurisdictions allow a cause of action for fraudulent misrepresentation to be predicated upon the communication of what effectively would be a negligent representation. Third, due to their common law development, the precise jury charges for each element may vary slightly from jurisdiction to jurisdiction. The model instructions follow the *Restatement* to give the practitioner a thorough understanding of the general state of the law. Important distinctions and clarifications are in the comments that follow the various instructions.

6.2 Fraudulent Misrepresentation

6.2.1 Elements of Liability

In this case, for the plaintiff to recover money damages against the defendant for fraudulent misrepresentation, the plaintiff must prove by a preponderance of the evidence all of the following:

(a) that the defendant made a fraudulent misrepresentation;

(b) that the misrepresentation was made with the purpose or expectation of inducing the plaintiff to act or refrain from action in reliance upon the misrepresentation; and

(c) that the plaintiff's justifiable reliance on the misrepresentation caused his or her injury.

COMMENT

This instruction is modeled on section 525 of the *Restatement (Second) of Torts* (1977). *Cf. Swinson v. Lords Landing Vill. Condo.*, 758 A.2d 1008 (Md. 2000); *Fleming Companies v. GAB Bus. Servs., Inc.*, 103 F. Supp. 2d 1271 (D. Kan. 2000); *Knight v. E.F. Hutton and Co., Inc.*, 750 F. Supp. 1109 (M.D. Fla. 1990); *Arbour v. Hazelton*, 534 A.2d 1303 (Me. 1987); *Southwestern Indem. Co. v. Cimarron Ins. Co.*, 334 S.W.2d 831 (Tex. App. 1960); *Pinney & Topliff v. Chrysler Corp.*, 176 F. Supp. 801 (S.D. Cal. 1959); 37 Am. Jur. 2d *Fraud and Deceit* § 26 (2001).

6.2.2   When Statement Is Misrepresentation

The defendant has made a misrepresentation if he or she asserted, by words or conduct, the existence of a fact that did not exist at the time the defendant made the assertion. The misrepresentation could be based on written or oral assertions, and it could be expressed or implied.

COMMENT

This instruction makes two critical points. First, a representation must have a false aspect to it when uttered in order to be actionable. Second, the misrepresentation need only have been communicated in some way to the plaintiff, whether orally or in writing, directly or by indirect means. *Cf. Restatement (Second) of Torts* § 525 cmt. b (1977); 37 Am. Jur. 2d *Fraud and Deceit* §§ 7, 38, 56, 57, 104 (2001); *Hennig v. Ahearn*, 601 N.W.2d 14 (Wisc. Ct. App. 1999); *Aetna Cas. & Sur. Co. v. Leahey Constr. Co.*, 22 F. Supp. 2d 695 (N.D. Ohio 1998); *Farm Bureau Policy Holders & Members v. Farm Bureau Mut. Ins. Co. of Ark., Inc.*, 984 S.W.2d 6 (Ark. 1998); *Prestwood v. City of Andalusia*, 709 So. 2d 1173 (Ala. 1997).

6.2.3 Conditions Under Which Misrepresentation Is Fraudulent

A misrepresentation is fraudulent in any of the following situations if, at the time the misrepresentation was made:

(a) the defendant knew or believed the matter was not as the defendant represented it to be;

(b) the defendant did not have the confidence in the accuracy of the representation that the defendant stated or implied; or

(c) the defendant knew he or she did not have the basis for the representation that the defendant stated or implied.

COMMENT

This instruction is modeled on section 526 of the *Restatement (Second) of Torts* (1977). *Cf. Froelich v. Erickson*, 96 F. Supp. 2d 507 (D. Md. 2000); *Wilkinson v. Shoney's, Inc.*, 4 P.3d 1149 (Kan. 2000); *Palmacci v.* Umpierrez, 121 F.3d 781 (1st Cir. 1997); *Young v. Johnson*, 538 So. 2d 1387 (Fla. Dist. Ct. App. 1989); *Lambert v. Smith*, 201 A.2d 491 (Md. App. 1964); *Wishnick v. Frye*, 245 P.2d 532 (Cal. App. 1952); *Dundee Land Co. v. Simmons*, 49 S.E.2d 488 (Ga. 1948); 37 Am. Jur. 2d *Fraud and Deceit* §§ 56, 116 (2001).

The critical question of fact is often whether the defendant had knowledge of the truth or falsity of his or her representation when it was communicated. Some jurisdictions allow recovery if the defendant should have known of the falsity of the representation under the circumstances, even though the defendant had no such actual knowledge. These jurisdictions allow a plaintiff to pursue an action for fraudulent misrepresentation for what is, in effect, negligent misrepresentation. *Compare* 37 Am. Jur. 2d *Fraud and* Deceit § 116; *Equitable Life Ins. Co. of Iowa v. Halsey, Stuart & Co.*, 312 U.S. 410 (1941); *Burgess v. Premier Corp.*, 727 F.2d 826 (9th Cir. 1984); *and Cameron v. Outdoor Resorts of Am., Inc.*, 611 F.2d 105 (5th Cir. 1980) *with Look v. Little Caesar Enter., Inc.*, 972 F. Supp. 400 (E.D. Mich. 1997), *aff'd*, 210 F.3d 653 (6th

Cir. 2000); *Cordial v. Ernst & Young*, 483 S.E.2d 248 (W. Va. 1996); *Damon v. Sun Co.*, 87 F.3d 1467 (1st Cir. 1996); *and Kroniger v. Anast*, 116 N.W.2d 863 (Mich. 1962).

6.3 Types of Misrepresentation

6.3.1 Ambiguous Representation

A representation is fraudulent (a) if the defendant knew it to be capable of two interpretations, one of which he or she knew to be false and the other true, and (b) if the misrepresentation was made

(i) with the intention that it be understood in the false sense; or

(ii) without any belief or expectation about how it would be understood; or

(iii) with reckless indifference regarding how it would be understood.

COMMENT

This instruction is modeled on section 527 of the *Restatement (Second) of Torts* (1977). *Cf. In re Chivers*, 275 B.R. 606 (Bankr. D. Utah 2002); *Anderson v. Pine South Capital, LLC*, 177 F. Supp. 2d 591 (W.D. Ky. 2001); *John R. Cowley & Bros., Inc. v. Brown*, 569 So.2d 375 (Ala. 1990); *Berger v. Sec. Pac. Info. Sys.*, 795 P.2d 1380 (Colo. App. 1990); *Thiele v. Davidson*, 440 F. Supp. 585 (M.D. Fla. 1977).

Note that subsection 6.3.1.b.3, *infra*, ("reckless indifference") addresses a type of conduct different from what is addressed by the tort for negligent misrepresentation. Reckless indifference means that the defendant made the representation without any knowledge of the truth, or that the defendant *knew* that he or she had no factual basis for making the representation when it was made. *See Livingston Livestock Exch., Inc. v. Hull State Bank*, 14 S.W.3d 849 (Tex. App. 2000); *Ausley v. Bishop*, 515 S.E.2d 72 (N.C. 1999); *Foiles v. Midwest Street Rod Ass'n of Omaha, Inc.*, 578 N.W.2d 418 (Neb. 1998); 37 Am. Jur. 2d *Fraud and Deceit* § 120 (2001). As discussed in the following instruction, negligence refers to a failure to exercise reasonable care in otherwise obtaining or communicating what was thought at the time by the defendant to be truthful information, but was in fact false, or at the very least, inaccurate.

6.3.2   Negligent Misrepresentation

A misrepresentation cannot be fraudulent if the defendant believed the statement to be a truthful one when it was made, but, because of a failure to exercise reasonable care, the defendant's statement actually was false. Such a statement can be a negligent misrepresentation, but it cannot be a fraudulent misrepresentation.

COMMENT

This instruction is modeled on section 528 of the *Restatement (Second) of Torts* (1977). *Cf. Fleming Companies, Inc. v. GAB Bus. Servs., Inc.*, 103 F. Supp. 2d 1271 (D. Kan. 2000); *Jacobs Mfg. Co. v. Sam Brown Co.*, 792 F. Supp. 1520 (W.D. Mo. 1992), *aff'd in part and rev'd in part*, 19 F.3d 1259 (8th Cir. 1994); 37 Am. Jur. 2d *Fraud and Deceit* § 128 (2001). See, however, the comment to section 6.2.3, *supra*.

6.3.3   Incomplete Representation Becoming Misleading

A representation that was technically accurate but that the defendant knew or believed was materially misleading because of a failure to state additional or qualifying matter is a fraudulent misrepresentation.

COMMENT

This instruction is modeled on section 529 of the *Restatement (Second) of Torts* (1977). *Cf. In re Chivers*, 275 B.R. 606 (Bankr. D. Utah 2002); *United Parcel Serv. Co. v. Rickert*, 996 S.W.2d 464 (Ky. 1999); *Amtruck Factors v. Int'l Forest Prods.*, 795 P.2d 742 (Wash. Ct. App. 1990); *V.S.H. Realty, Inc. v. Texaco, Inc.*, 757 F.2d 411 (1st Cir. 1985); *Jacobs v. Freeman*, 163 Cal. Rptr. 680 (Cal. Ct. App. 1980); 37 Am. Jur. 2d *Fraud and Deceit* § 105 (2001).

6.3.4 Misrepresentation of Defendant's Intention

A misrepresentation of the defendant's own intention to do or not to do a particular thing is fraudulent if the representation was made when the defendant had no intention to perform it, or a positive intention not to perform it.

COMMENT

This instruction is modeled on section 530 of the *Restatement (Second) of Torts* (1977). *Cf. Wharf (Holdings) Ltd. v. United Int'l Holdings, Inc.*, 532 U.S. 588 (2001); *In re Mercer*, 246 F.3d 391 (5th Cir. 2001); *Fowler v. SmithKline Beecham Clinical Labs., Inc.*, 225 F.3d 1013 (8th Cir. 2000); *Couldock & Bohan, Inc. v. Societe Generale Sec. Corp.*, 93 F. Supp. 2d 220 (D. Conn. 2000); *U.S. v. Schwab*, 88 F. Supp. 2d 1275 (D. Wyo. 2000); *Consolidation Serv., Inc. v. KeyBank Nat'l Ass'n*, 185 F.3d 817 (7th Cir. 1999); *In re Reynolds*, 221 B.R. 828 (Bankr. N.D. Ala. 1998); *In re Scocozzo*, 220 B.R. 850 (Bankr. M.D. Pa. 1998); *McEvoy Travel Bureau, Inc. v. Norton Co.*, 563 N.E.2d 188 (Mass. 1990); 37 Am. Jur. 2d *Fraud and Deceit* § 90 (2001).

The intention not to perform must exist when the promise is made. Contrariwise, where a promise had been made in good faith originally, there could be no fraud if the defendant simply changed his or her mind later and refused to perform. 37 Am. Jur. 2d *Fraud and Deceit* § 92 (2001); *cf. Zhang v. Mass. Institute of Tech.*, 708 N.E.2d 128 (Mass. App. 1999).

6.3.5 Misrepresentation of a Third Person's Intention

A misrepresentation by the defendant regarding the intention of a third person is fraudulent in any of the following circumstances:

(a) the defendant knew or believed the matter was not as the defendant represented it to be;

(b) the defendant did not have confidence in the accuracy of the representation at the time it was made; or

(c) the defendant knew he or she did not have a basis for the representation at the time it was made.

COMMENT

This instruction is modeled on section 530 of the *Restatement (Second) of Torts* (1977). *Cf. Denbo v. Badger*, 503 P.2d 384 (Ariz. App. 1972); *United Finance Co. v. Kliks*, 310 P.2d 1103 (Or. 1957); *Cofield v. Griffin*, 78 S.E.2d 131 (N.C. 1953); 37 Am. Jur. 2d *Fraud and Deceit* § 88 (2001).

6.3.6 Representations of Opinions
6.3.6.a General Rule

The plaintiff generally may not recover against the defendant if the defendant made a representation that conveyed only an opinion. A representation conveys only an opinion if it expresses only:

1. the belief of the defendant, without certainty, about the existence of a fact; or

2. the defendant's judgment about quality, value, authenticity, or other matters of judgment.

COMMENT

This instruction is modeled on section 538A of the *Restatement (Second) of Torts* (1977). *Cf. Gentry v. eBay, Inc.*, 121 Cal. Rptr. 2d 703 (Cal. Ct. App. 2002); *Howard Opera House Assocs. v. Urban Outfitters, Inc.*, 166 F. Supp. 2d 917 (D. Vt. 2001); *Lotspeich v. Golden Oil Co.*, 961 P.2d 790 (N.M. Ct. App.1998); *Taggert v. Ford Motor Credit Co.*, 462 N.W.2d 493 (S.D. 1990); *Presidio Enter., Inc. v. Warner Bros. Distrib. Corp.*, 784 F.2d 674 (5th Cir. 1986); *Vaughn v. Gen. Foods Corp.*, 797 F.2d 1403 (7th Cir. 1986); *Cavic v. Grand Bahama Dev. Co., Ltd.*, 701 F.2d 879 (11th Cir. 1983); *Borba v. Thomas*, 138 Cal. Rptr. 565 (Cal. Ct. App. 1977); 37 Am. Jur. 2d *Fraud and Deceit* § 64 (2001).

There are several theories set forth by state courts as to why an opinion ordinarily is not actionable. Some states take the position that an opinion is not a statement of fact. Others assert that an opinion cannot be material. Finally, some state that a plaintiff cannot justifiably rely on an opinion. *Cf. Glen Holly Enter., Inc. v. Tektronix, Inc.*, 100 F. Supp. 2d 1086 (C.D. Cal. 1999); *Yurevich v. Sikorsky Aircraft Div.*, 51 F. Supp. 2d 144 (D. Conn. 1999); *VNA Plus, Inc. v. Apria Healthcare Group, Inc.*, 29 F. Supp. 2d 1253 (D. Kan. 1998); *Perez v. Alcoa Fujikura, Ltd.*, 969 F. Supp. 991 (W.D. Tex. 1997); 37 Am. Jur. 2d *Fraud and Deceit* §§ 62-64, 261 (2001).

6.3.6.b   Representation of Opinion That Implies Basis in Fact

A false representation conveying an opinion is nonetheless actionable as a fraudulent misrepresentation if the representation was as to facts not disclosed and not otherwise known to the plaintiff, and the representation reasonably could have been interpreted by the plaintiff to have implied:

1. that the facts known to the defendant were not incompatible with his or her opinion; or

2. that the defendant knew of facts sufficient to justify the formation of the opinion.

COMMENT

This instruction is modeled on section 539 of the *Restatement (Second) of Torts* (1977) and is an exception to the general rule relating to statements of opinions. An opinion can be actionable if the defendant at the time of making the statement knew of facts incompatible with that opinion or of facts not warranting the opinion. In such an instance, the statement no longer is one simply of opinion, since it implies the existence of a fact. *See Restatement (Second) of Torts* § 539 cmts. a & b (1977); *cf. Grove Holding Corp. v. First Wis. Nat'l Bank of Sheboygan*, 12 F. Supp. 2d 885 (E.D. Wis. 1998); *Arthur D. Little Int'l, Inc. v. Dooyang Corp.*, 928 F. Supp. 1189 (D. Mass. 1996); *McEneaney v. Chestnut Hill Realty Corp.*, 650 N.E.2d 93 (Mass. App. Ct. 1995); *Public Serv. Enter. Group, Inc. v. Philadelphia Elec. Co.*, 722 F. Supp. 184 (D.N.J. 1989); *S. Cal. Dist. Counsel v. Shepherd of Hills Evangelical Lutheran Church*, 144 Cal. Rptr. 46 (Cal. Ct. App. 1976) 279; 37 Am. Jur. 2d *Fraud and Deceit* §§ 69, 122 (2001).

6.3.6.c Opinion of Party With Special Relationship or Position

A false representation conveying an opinion is nonetheless actionable as a fraudulent misrepresentation if the defendant:

1. claimed to have special knowledge of the matter being represented that the plaintiff did not have;

2. stood in a fiduciary or similar relation of trust to the plaintiff;

3. had secured the confidence of the plaintiff; or

4. otherwise had a special reason to expect the plaintiff would rely on the defendant's opinion.

COMMENT

This instruction is modeled on section 542 of the *Restatement (Second) of Torts* (1977) and is an exception to the general rule relating to statements of opinions. This instruction essentially requires that two factors be present to convert a statement of opinion into a fraudulent misrepresentation—a relationship of trust and confidence between plaintiff and defendant, and an intent by the defendant to use that position to imply knowledge of facts (that otherwise do not exist) justifying the opinion. *Cf. Am. Life Ins. Co. v. Parra*, 63 F. Supp. 2d 480 (D. Del. 1999); *Cunningham v. PFL Life Ins. Co.*, 42 F. Supp. 2d 872 (N.D. Iowa 1999); *Davis v. McDonald's Corp.*, 44 F. Supp. 2d 1251 (N.D. Fla. 1998); *Astor Chauffeured Limousine v. Runnfeldt Inv. Corp.*, 910 F.2d 1540 (7th Cir. 1990); *Koagel v. Ryan Homes, Inc.*, 562 N.Y.S.2d 312 (N.Y. App. Div. 1990); *Kociemba v. G.D. Searle Co.*, 707 F. Supp. 1517 (D. Minn. 1989); *Hall v. Edge*, 782 P.2d 122 (Okla. 1989); *Walters v. First Fed. S&L Ass'n*, 641 P.2d 235 (Ariz. 1982); 37 Am. Jur. 2d *Fraud and Deceit* §§ 71-73 (2001).

6.3.6.d Opinion of Apparently Disinterested Person

A representation conveying an opinion is nonetheless actionable as a fraudulent misrepresentation if the defendant, while appearing to be a disinterested third party, conveyed an opinion contrary to the opinion actually held by the defendant with the intent to deceive the plaintiff.

COMMENT

This instruction is modeled on section 543 of the *Restatement (Second) of Torts* (1977). The instruction converts a statement of opinion into an actionable misrepresentation where the requisite elements of falsity and an intent to deceive are present. *Cf. Leftwich v. Gaines*, 521 S.E.2d 717 (N.C. Ct. App. 1999); *Perez v. Alcoa Fujikura, Ltd.*, 969 F. Supp. 991 (W.D. Tex. 1997); *RKB Enterprises Inc. v. Ernst & Young*, 582 N.Y.S.2d 814 (N.Y. App. Div. 1992); 37 Am. Jur. 2d *Fraud and Deceit* § 74 (2001).

6.4 Requirement of Intention or Expectation of Influencing Conduct

6.4.1 General Rule

For the plaintiff to recover against the defendant, the plaintiff must prove by a preponderance of the evidence that the fraudulent misrepresentation was made with the purpose or expectation of inducing the plaintiff to act or refrain from action in reliance upon the misrepresentation, or with the purpose or expectation that the misrepresentation was made otherwise to influence the plaintiff's decision to act or not act.

COMMENT

This instruction is modeled on section 531 of the *Restatement (Second) of Torts* (1977). *Cf. Ernst & Young, L.L.P. v. Pac. Mut. Life Ins. Co.*, 51 S.W.3d 573 (Tex. 2001); *Lovejoy v. AT&T Corp.*, 111 Cal. Rptr. 2d 711 (Cal. Ct.App. 2001); *In re Mercer*, 246 F.3d 391 (5th Cir. 2001); *Sebago, Inc. v. Beazer East, Inc.*, 18 F. Supp. 2d 70 (D. Mass. 1998); *Shapiro v. Sutherland*, 76 Cal. Rptr. 2d 101 (Cal. Ct. App. 1998); *Sherban v. Richardson*, 445 So.2d 1147 (Fla. Dist. Ct. App. 1984); *Hoffman v. Ryan*, 422 N.Y.S.2d 288 (N.Y. Civ. Ct. 1979); *Clark v. Haggard*, 109 A.2d 358 (Conn. 1954); 37 Am. Jur. 2d *Fraud and Deceit* § 108 (2001). This section essentially deals with the "scienter" aspect of fraudulent misrepresentation. In other words, for a misrepresentation to be actionable in fraud, there must be an intent on the part of the defendant to deceive a specific person or class of persons into making a decision to act or not act in manner different than they would have had that person known the truth.

6.4.2 Misrepresentation to More Than One Person

The plaintiff may establish that the defendant intended or expected to influence the plaintiff's conduct by proving by a preponderance of the evidence that the defendant made the fraudulent misrepresentation with the intent or expectation that anyone in a group or class of persons of which plaintiff was a member would be induced to rely on the misrepresentation in deciding to act or not act.

COMMENT

This instruction is modeled on section 534 of the *Restatement (Second) of Torts* (1977) and represents a modification of the general rule set forth in § 6.4.1, *supra*, to address the special circumstances surrounding the publication of a misrepresentation to more than one person. *Cf. Berkowitz v. Baron*, 428 F. Supp. 1190 (S.D.N.Y. 1977); *Gulf Oil Corp. of Penn. v. Newton*, 31 A.2d 462 (Conn. 1943); *Holloway v. Forsyth*, 115 N.E. 183 (Mass. 1917); 37 Am. Jur. 2d *Fraud and Deceit* § 111 (2001). Naturally, an intent to deceive the plaintiff specifically may not be necessary provided that the plaintiff falls within the class of persons for whom the defendant's misrepresentation was intended.

6.4.3 Representation Made to Third Person

The plaintiff may establish that the defendant intended or expected to influence the plaintiff's conduct by proving by a preponderance of the evidence that:

(a) a fraudulent misrepresentation was made by the defendant to a third person; and

(b) the defendant intended or had reason to expect that (i) the misrepresentation's terms would be repeated or its substance communicated to the plaintiff; and (ii) the representation would influence the plaintiff's conduct in the transaction or type of transaction involved in this suit.

COMMENT

This instruction is modeled on section 533 of the *Restatement (Second) of Torts* (1977) and represents a modification of the general rule set forth in § 6.4.1, *supra*, to address the special circumstances surrounding the publication of the misrepresentation to third persons. *Cf. Ernst & Young, L.L.P. v. Pac. Mut. Life Ins. Co.*, 51 S.W.3d 573 (Tex. 2001); *Kaufman v. i-Stat Corp.*, 754 A.2d 1188 (N.J. 2000); *Gawara v. U.S. Brass Corp.*, 74 Cal. Rptr. 2d 468 (Cal. Ct. App. 1998); *Colonial Bank v. Ridley & Schweigert*, 551 So. 2d 390 (Ala. 1990); *Joseph v. Norman LaPorte Realty, Inc.*, 508 So. 2d 496 (Fla. Dist. Ct. App. 1987); *Epperson v. Roloff*, 719 P.2d 799 (Nev. 1986); *Credit Alliance Corp. v. Arthur Anderson & Co.*, 483 N.E.2d 110 (N.Y. 1985); *Varwig v. Anderson-Bethel Porsche-Audi, Inc.*, 141 Cal. Rptr. 539 (Cal. Ct. App. 1977); *Metric Inv., Inc. v. Patterson*, 244 A.2d 311 (N.J. Super. Ct. App. Div. 1968); 37 Am. Jur. 2d *Fraud and Deceit* §§ 109, 240 (2001). Essentially, it must be shown that the defendant intended or had reason to expect that his or her representation to a third party would be repeated and relied upon by the plaintiff. This makes sense, since otherwise the plaintiff would not have had a right to rely on the representation in the first place.

6.4.4 Misrepresentation Incorporated in Document or Other Thing

The plaintiff may establish that the defendant intended or expected to influence the plaintiff's conduct by proving by a preponderance of the evidence that the defendant included the fraudulent misrepresentation in an article of commerce, formal documentary proof of title, negotiable instrument, or similar commercial document that was received by the plaintiff.

COMMENT

This instruction is modeled on section 532 of the *Restatement (Second) of Torts* (1977). *Cf. Sempione v. Provident Bank of Md.*, 75 F.3d 951 (4th Cir. 1996); *Herskowitz v. Nutri-System*, 857 F.2d 179 (3rd Cir. 1988); *Woodward v. Dietrich*, 548 A.2d 301 (Pa. Super. Ct. 1988); *United States v. Puerto*, 730 F.2d 627 (11th Cir. 1984). This instruction applies where the document or article containing the misrepresentation is of the type that ordinarily would pass into the hands of someone other than the one who immediately receives it from the defendant, such that the misrepresentation likely would influence the third person's (i.e., a later recipient's) conduct. *See Restatement (Second) of Torts* § 532 cmt. c (1977).

6.4.5 Continuing Misrepresentation

The plaintiff may establish that the defendant intended or expected to influence the plaintiff's conduct in a transaction by proving by a preponderance of the evidence that the defendant knew that the plaintiff, when acting in that transaction, was relying on a fraudulent misrepresentation made by the defendant to the plaintiff with respect to an earlier transaction, yet the defendant failed to disclose to the plaintiff the falsity of the original misstatement.

COMMENT

This instruction is modeled on section 535 of the *Restatement (Second) of Torts* (1977) and represents a modification of the general rule set forth in § 6.4.1, *supra*, to address the special circumstances when the defendant knows the plaintiff is relying on an earlier fraudulent misrepresentation made by defendant to plaintiff, and the defendant enters into a second transaction without disclosing the falsity of the earlier misrepresentation. The defendant in this instance is subject to liability for fraudulent misrepresentation as though he or she had not repeated the original misrepresentation for the purpose of influencing the plaintiff's conduct in the later transaction. *Cf. Tom's Quality Millwork, Inc. v. Delle Vedove USA*, 10 F. Supp. 2d 1042 (E.D. Wis. 1998); *Sedco Int'l S.A. v. Cory*, 683 F.2d 1201 (8th Cir. 1982); *Guastella v. Wardell*, 198 So. 2d 227 (Miss. 1967); *Shogyo Int'l Corp. v. First Nat'l Bank of Clarksdale*, 475 So. 2d 425 (Miss. 1985); 37 Am. Jur. 2d *Fraud and Deceit* § 241 (2001).

6.4.6 Liability for Misrepresentation Based upon Information Required by Statute

The plaintiff may establish that the defendant intended or expected to influence the plaintiff's conduct by proving by a preponderance of the evidence that the defendant made a fraudulent misrepresentation in information required by statute to be furnished, filed, recorded, or published for the protection of a particular class of persons, of which the plaintiff was one.

COMMENT

This instruction is modeled on section 536 of the *Restatement (Second) of Torts* (1977). It should be noted, though, that the defendant still could be liable for a fraudulent misrepresentation contained in a public filing, even if not required by statute, if the defendant had referred the plaintiff to the filing in response to the plaintiff's inquiry for information. *Cf. Wysong and Miles Co. v. Employers of Wausau*, 4 F. Supp. 2d 421 (M.D.N.C. 1998), *Hundy v. Beck*, 581 P.2d 68 (Or. 1978); *Woodward v. Dietrich*, 548 A.2d 301 (Pa. Super. Ct. 1988); 37 Am. Jur. 2d *Fraud and Deceit* § 112 (2001).

6.5 Requirement of Plaintiff's Justifiable Reliance on Misrepresentation

6.5.1 General Rule

For the plaintiff to recover against the defendant, the plaintiff must prove by a preponderance of the evidence that the plaintiff acted or refrained from acting in reliance on the defendant's fraudulent misrepresentation, and that the plaintiff's reliance was justifiable.

COMMENT

This instruction is modeled on section 537 of the *Restatement (Second) of Torts* (1977). *Cf. Field v. Mans*, 516 U.S. 59 (1995); *TCA Bldg. Co. v. Entech, Inc.*, 86 S.W.3d 667 (Tex. App. 2002); *Slaymaker v. Westgate State Bank*, 739 P.2d 444 (Kan. 1987); *Hershmann v. Univ. of Toledo*, 519 N.E.2d 871 (Ohio Ct. Cl. 1987); *Galego v. Knudsen*, 578 P.2d 769 (Or. 1978); 37 Am. Jur. 2d *Fraud and Deceit* § 239 (2001).

6.5.2   Reliance on Misrepresentation

The plaintiff relied on the fraudulent misrepresentation if the misrepresentation played a substantial part in the plaintiff's decision to act in one way as opposed to another, to not act where he or she otherwise would have, or to act where he or she otherwise would not have.

COMMENT

This instruction is based on comment b to section 546 of the *Restatement (Second) of Torts* (1977). *See also Restatement (Second)* § 537 cmt. a. It recognizes that there must be a causal connection between the defendant's misrepresentation and a decision by the plaintiff to act or not act in a way that resulted in injury to the plaintiff. *Cf. Bank of Am. v. Jarczyk*, 268 B.R. 17 (W.D.N.Y. 2001); *In re Mercer*, 246 F.3d 391 (5th Cir. 2001); *Sauer v. Xerox Corp.*, 95 F. Supp. 2d 125 (W.D.N.Y 2000); *Najem v. Classic Cadillac Atlanta Corp.*, 527 S.E.2d 259 (Ga. 1999); *Asermely v. Allstate Ins. Co.*, 728 A.2d 461 (R.I. 1999); *Liberty Nat'l Life Ins. Co. v. Allen*, 699 So.2d 138 (Ala. 1997); *Wilson v. Henry*, 340 S.W.2d 449 (Ky. 1960). Without the causal connection of actual reliance, "the fact that [the plaintiff] takes some action that would be consistent with his reliance on it and as a result suffers pecuniary loss, does not impose any liability upon [the defendant]." *Restatement (Second)* § 537 cmt. a. This instruction is similar to that found at section 6.6.2, *infra*, for causation-in-fact.

The instructions in §§ 6.5.1 and 6.5.2 accommodate both the objective and subjective components discussed in the comment to the following instruction, § 6.5.3. That is, reliance need not be objectively reasonable to be justifiable, but even if not objectively reasonable, the reliance still must be understandable in light of the surrounding circumstances.

6.5.3 Reliance Must Be Justifiable

Even if plaintiff relied on the defendant's fraudulent misrepresentation, the plaintiff cannot recover against the defendant unless he or she proves by a preponderance of the evidence that his or her reliance was justifiable. For the plaintiff's reliance to be justifiable, the matter or information conveyed in the fraudulent misrepresentation must have been something that:

(a) a reasonable person would attach importance to in deciding to act or not to act with respect to the transaction in question; or

(b) the defendant knew or had reason to know the plaintiff would regard, or would be likely to regard, as important in deciding to act or not to act with respect to the transaction in question, regardless of whether a reasonable person ordinarily would regard the misrepresentation as important.

COMMENT

This instruction is modeled on section 538 of the *Restatement (Second) of Torts* (1977). *Cf. Field v. Mans*, 516 U.S. 59 (1995); *Chase Manhattan Bank v. Motorola, Inc.*, 184 F. Supp. 2d 384 (S.D.N.Y. 2002); *Koch v. Koch Indus., Inc.*, 203 F.3d 1202 (10th Cir. 2000); *Defendant A v. Idaho State Bar*, 2 P.3d 147 (Idaho 2000); *Voilas v. Gen. Motors Corp.*, 170 F.3d 367 (3d Cir. 1999); *Basic v. Levinson*, 485 U.S. 224 (1988); *Hauben v. Harmon*, 605 F.2d 920 (5th Cir. 1979); *Weitzman v. Stein*, 436 F. Supp. 895 (S.D.N.Y. 1977); 37 Am. Jur. 2d *Fraud and Deceit* §§ 236, 239, 249 (2001).

This instruction works in conjunction with § 6.5.2, *supra*. The practitioner, however, should be cautious about how this instruction is to be used. There are jurisdictions that treat materiality and justifiable reliance as separate elements. *See* 37 Am. Jur. 2d *Fraud and Deceit* §§ 235-236, 239, 249 (2001). The *Restatement (Second)* seems to treat materiality more as a component of justifiable reliance. *See Restatement (Second)* §§ 537-538. The different treatment likely is without moment. No matter the label, there are two aspects to the causal relation between the defendant's misrepresentation and the plaintiff's action—whether the misrepresentation effected plaintiff's action or inaction; and whether it was reasonable for plaintiff to have been affected by the misrepresentation. The instructions here tend toward the *Restatement (Second)*, collapsing materiality into the justifiability component. Section 6.5.3 represents this latter component.

Because § 6.5.3 of these model jury instructions subsumes the materiality component mentioned above, it also takes on both the objective and subjective aspects of the materiality inquiry utilized by various jurisdictions. *Cf. Koch v. Koch Indus., Inc.*, 203 F.3d 1202 (10th Cir. 2000); *Granite Ptrs. L.P. v. Bear, Stearns & Co.*, 58 F. Supp. 2d 228 (S.D.N.Y. 1999); *Carter v. Gugliuzzi*, 716 A.2d 17 (Vt. 1998); *Matter of Phoenix Ltd.*, 198 B.R. 78 (Bankr. D. Del. 1996), *rev'd on other grounds*, 213 B.R. 57 (D. Del. 1997). Subsection 6.5.3.a is an adaptation of the objective aspect; subsection 6.5.3.b is an adaptation of the subjective one. *Cf. 37 Am. Jur. 2d Fraud and Deceit* §§ 235 236 (2001).

Subsection 6.5.3.b recognizes that reliance can be said to be justified under the circumstances, even if not entirely reasonable. This subjective standard allows recovery by a plaintiff who, because of peculiarities, is likely to attach significance to a misrepresentation even though a reasonable person would not attach any importance to the same misrepresentation. To do otherwise would reward a defendant who plays upon the known idiosyncrasies of the plaintiff. *Restatement (Second) of Torts* § 538 cmt. f (1977); *cf. Carter v. Gugliuzzi*, 716 A.2d 17 (Vt. 1998); *see also Restatement (Second)* § 545A (noting nexus between plaintiff's negligence and question of justifiable reliance); 37 Am. Jur. 2d *Fraud and Deceit* § 319 (2001) (same). The practitioner must look at the relevant jurisdiction to determine whether it utilizes the objective or subjective test.

6.5.4 Duty to Investigate

The plaintiff did not have a duty to investigate the truth or falsity of the defendant's representation, and the plaintiff would have been justified to rely on the defendant's fraudulent misrepresentation, even though the plaintiff might have learned the falsity of the representation had the plaintiff investigated it.

-or-

The plaintiff was not justified in relying on the defendant's fraudulent misrepresentation if the defendant proves by a preponderance of the evidence that (a) the plaintiff had facts in his or her possession sufficient to create suspicion of the truthfulness of the representation, thereby warranting further investigation; or (b) the defendant did not make a representation as to facts uniquely within his or her knowledge, and the plaintiff had an equal ability to ascertain the facts contained in the defendant's representation with the exercise of reasonable intelligence and ability.

COMMENT

The first alternative instruction is modeled on section 540 of the *Restatement (Second) of Torts* (1977) and presumes a jurisdiction that does not bar recovery simply for failing to investigate. *Cf. In re House of Drugs, Inc.*, 251 B.R. 206 (Bankr. D.N.J. 2000); *Krock v. Lipsay*, 97 F.3d 640 (2d Cir. 1996); *Besett v. Basnett*, 389 So.2d 995 (Fla. 1980); *Ashburn v. Miller*, 326 P.2d 229 (Cal. Ct. App. 1958); 37 Am. Jur. 2d *Fraud and Deceit* §§ 248, 254 (2001).

The second alternative instruction accounts for jurisdictions that impose a duty to investigate, especially where there had been reason to suspect the statement was false or where the facts were equally ascertainable by both the plaintiff and the defendant. *Cf. Westby v. Gorsuch*, 50 P.3d 284 (Wash. Ct. App. 2002); *Enfield Equip. Co., Inc. v. John Deere Co.*, 64 F. Supp. 2d 483 (D. Md. 1999), *aff'd*, 217 F.3d 838 (4th Cir. 2000); *Schlaifer Nance & Co. v. Estate of Warhol*, 194 F.3d 323 (2d Cir. 1999); *In re Hooks*, 238 B.R. 880 (Bankr. S.D. Ga. 1999); *K-B Trucking Co. v. Riss Int'l Corp.*, 763 F.2d 1148

(10th Cir. 1985); *Mallis v. Bankers Trust Co.*, 615 F.2d 68 (2d Cir. 1980); *Danann Realty Corp. v. Harris*, 157 N.E.2d 597 (N.Y. App. 1959); *Feak v. Marion Steam Shovel Co.*, 84 F.2d 670 (9th Cir. 1936). It is fair to suggest, however, that the second alternative instruction is more consistent with the majority of jurisdictions, which tend to collapse the inquiry into a more generalized question of whether reliance was justified under the circumstances. In other words, even where a plaintiff ordinarily is entitled to rely on a representation without further inquiry, that entitlement can be limited by facts that nonetheless made it unreasonable that the plaintiff blindly had accepted the defendant's representation.

6.5.5 Representation Known to Be or Obviously False

The plaintiff was not justified in relying on the defendant's fraudulent misrepresentation if the defendant proves by a preponderance of the evidence either that the plaintiff knew the defendant's representation was false or that it had been obvious to the plaintiff that the misrepresentation was false.

COMMENT

This instruction is modeled on section 541 of the *Restatement (Second) of Torts* (1977). *Cf. Dewey v. Wentland*, 38 P.3d 402 (Wyo. 2002); *M/I Schottenstein Homes, Inc. v. Azam*, 813 So.2d 91 (Fla. 2002); *Hennig v. Ahearn*, 601 N.W.2d 14 (Wis. App. 1999); *Massachusetts Laborers' Health & Welfare Fund v. Philip Morris, Inc.*, 62 F. Supp. 2d 236 (D. Mass. 1999); *Gross v. Sussex, Inc.*, 630 A.2d 1156 (Md. App. 1993); *Sun Bank, N.A. v. E.F. Hutton & Co., Inc.*, 926 F.2d 1030 (11th Cir. 1991); *Phoenix Canada Oil Co., Ltd. v. Texaco, Inc.*, 749 F. Supp. 525 (S.D.N.Y. 1990); *Grimes v. Liberty Nat'l Life Ins. Co.*, 551 So. 2d 329 (Ala. 1989); *Letellier v. Small*, 400 A.2d 371 (Me. 1979); 37 Am. Jur. 2d *Fraud and Deceit* §§ 239, 248, 253 (2001).

This instruction should be sufficient to foreclose recovery by a plaintiff who, instead of relying on the truth of the defendant's misrepresentation, relies on the expectation of recovery against the defendant in damages for its falsity. *Cf. Restatement (Second)* § 548; *Mass. Laborers Health & Welfare Fund v. Philip Morris, Inc.*, 62 F. Supp. 2d 236 (D. Mass. 1999); *State Farm Mut. Auto Ins. Co. v. Wall*, 222 A.2d 282 (N.J. Super. Ct. App. Div. 1965); 37 Am. Jur. 2d *Fraud and Deceit* § 244 (2001). In this situation, the plaintiff would have known of the falsity of the representation, making any reliance unjustified. *See Andale Equip., Inc. v. Deere & Co.*, 985 F. Supp. 1042 (D. Kan. 1997), *aff'd*, 208 F.3d 225 (10th Cir. 2000).

While this instruction may seem to be at odds with the law in those jurisdictions that do not impose a duty to investigate, as discussed in the comment to § 6.5.4, *supra*, of these model jury instructions, even those jurisdictions typically carve out an exception for instances where the falsity is readily apparent or could be discovered with even a cursory inquiry.

6.5.6 Defendant as Adverse Party Not Preclusive of Recovery

The plaintiff could have justifiably relied on the defendant's fraudulent misrepresentation, and therefore is not precluded from recovery against defendant, even if the plaintiff knew or believed the defendant had an interest adverse to the plaintiff in the underlying transaction.

COMMENT

This instruction is modeled on section 541A of the *Restatement (Second) of Torts* (1977). It essentially precludes a defendant from asserting as a dispositive defense the mere fact that the plaintiff knew of their adverse relationship. Similarly, it reinforces the general principal that a party is entitled to rely on the representation of another in arm's length negotiations. Still, this instruction must be used in the context of the others dealing with plaintiff's duty to investigate. *Cf. Lotspeich v. Golden Oil Co.*, 961 P.2d 790 (N.M. Ct. App. 1998); *Williams v. Collins*, 600 P.2d 1235 (Or. App. 1979).

6.5.7 Statement of Intention

The plaintiff could not have justifiably relied on the defendant's fraudulent misrepresentation of intent if the defendant can show by a preponderance of the evidence that:

a) the plaintiff had reason to believe that the defendant would not carry out the intention; or

b) the plaintiff knew of facts that would have made it impossible for the defendant to follow through on that intention.

COMMENT

This instruction is modeled on section 544 of the *Restatement (Second) of Torts* (1977). *Cf. In re Mercer*, 246 F.3d 391 (5th Cir. 2001); *Bank of Am. v. Jarczyk*, 268 B.R. 17 (W.D.N.Y. 2001); *E&S Facilities, Inc. v. Precision Chipper Corp.*, 565 So. 2d 54 (Ala. 1990); *McEvoy Travel Bureau, Inc. v. Norton Co.*, 563 N.E.2d 188 (Mass. 1990); *Travelodge Int'l, Inc. v. E. Ins., Inc.*, 382 So. 2d 789 (Fla. Dist. Ct. App. 1980); *Floyd v. Morgan*, 9 S.E.2d 717 (Ga. Ct. App. 1940). This instruction must be read in conjunction with § 6.3.4, *supra*, of these model jury instructions. It also must be understood within the context of §§ 6.5.4 and 6.5.5 and applicable law to determine whether a subjective or objective standard of justifiable reliance is more appropriate.

6.5.8   Misrepresentations of Law

6.5.8.a   Including Misrepresentation of Fact

The plaintiff could not have justifiably relied on the defendant's fraudulent misrepresentation regarding a matter of law unless the plaintiff can prove by a preponderance of the evidence that the misrepresentation included, expressly or impliedly, a misrepresentation of fact beyond simply the matter of law represented by the defendant.

COMMENT

This instruction is modeled on section 545(1) of the *Restatement (Second) of Torts* (1977). *Cf. Travis v. Knappenberger*, 204 F.R.D. 652 (D. Or. 2001); *Spolnik v. Guardian Life Ins. Co. of Am.*, 94 F. Supp. 2d 998 (S.D. Ind. 2000); *Bowman v. City of Indianapolis*, 133 F.3d 513 (7th Cir. 1998); *Nelson v. Taff*, 499 N.W.2d 685 (Wis. Ct. App. 1993); *Chino Elec., Inc. v. U.S. Fid. & Guar. Co.*, 578 So.2d 320 (Fla. Dist. Ct. App. 1991); *Pich v. Fitton*, 211 N.W. 964 (Minn. 1927); 37 Am. Jur. 2d *Fraud and Deceit* § 100 (2001).

The instruction demonstrates an exception to the general rule that there can be no justifiable reliance on a fraudulent misrepresentation of a pure matter of law, since ordinarily the law is a matter equally accessible to both plaintiff and defendant. By contrast, a plaintiff ordinarily would be justified in relying on a representation of foreign law, since foreign law is not readily accessible. *Cf. Restatement (Second)* § 545 cmt. e; 37 Am. Jur. 2d *Fraud and Deceit* § 103 (2001). Still, the instruction is consistent with a trend away from artificial distinctions between misrepresentations of law and of fact, since a misrepresentation of law often can be shown to imply facts beyond pure matters of law. *Cf. id.* cmts. a-b & illus. 1-2; *Elliot Megdal & Assocs. v. Hawaii Planning Mill*, 814 F. Supp. 898 (D. Hawaii 1993).

Nevertheless, satisfying this instruction should not be a substitute for satisfying the elements discussed above. In other words, even though the plaintiff can prove that the defendant's misrepresentation included more than just a matter of law, the plaintiff must still prove the underlying elements of a fraudulent misrepresentation claim, including justifiable reliance.

6.5.8.b Opinion About Legal Consequences

The plaintiff could not have justifiably relied on the defendant's fraudulent misrepresentation if the defendant can prove by a preponderance of the evidence that the misrepresentation pertained only to the legal consequences of certain facts.

COMMENT

This instruction is modeled on section 545(2) of the *Restatement (Second) of Torts* (1977). *Cf. Elliot Megdal & Assocs. v. Hawaii Planning Mill*, 814 F. Supp. 898 (D. Haw. 1993); *Nelson v. Taff*, 499 N.W.2d 685 (Wis. Ct. App. 1993); *Lawson v. Cagle*, 504 So.2d 226 (Ala. 1987); *Wochnick v. True*, 356 P.2d 515 (Or. 1960); *see generally* 37 Am. Jur. 2d *Fraud and Deceit* §§ 97-103 (2001). This instruction is consistent with the general rule set forth in § 6.3.6.a of these model jury instructions, *supra*, that pure opinion cannot be actionable as a fraudulent misrepresentation. The exceptions listed in subsections 6.3.6.b to 6.3.6.d in turn would be applicable here.

6.6 Requirement That Fraudulent Misrepresentation Cause Damage

6.6.1 General Rule

For the plaintiff to recover from the defendant, the plaintiff must prove by a preponderance of the evidence:

(a) that the plaintiff suffered some harm or damage as a result of plaintiff's reliance upon the defendant's fraudulent misrepresentation; and

(b) that the defendant's fraudulent misrepresentation was both the cause-in-fact and legal cause of plaintiff's damages.

COMMENT

Cf. Cananwill, Inc. v. EMAR Group, Inc., 250 B.R. 533 (M.D.N.C. 1999); *In re Grant*, 237 B.R. 97 (Bankr. E.D. Va. 1999); *Omega Eng'g, Inc. v. Eastman Kodak Co.*, 30 F. Supp. 2d 226 (D. Conn. 1998); *Sanchez v. Sedco Int'l, S.A. v. Cory*, 683 F.2d 1201 (8th Cir. 1982); 37 Am. Jur. 2d *Fraud and Deceit* §§ 280, 389 (2001).

6.6.2   Causation-in-Fact

The defendant's fraudulent misrepresentation was the cause-in-fact of plaintiff's damages if the plaintiff's reliance on defendant's fraudulent misrepresentation was a substantial factor in determining the course of conduct that resulted in plaintiff's loss.

COMMENT

This instruction is modeled on section 546 of the *Restatement (Second) of Torts* (1977). *Cf. Oliveira v. Amoco Oil Co.*, 776 N.E.2d 151 (Ill. 2002); *Miller v. Pfizer Inc.*, 196 F. Supp. 2d 1095 (D. Kan. 2002); *Southern Union Co. v. Southwest Gas Corp.*, 180 F. Supp. 2d 1021 (D. Ariz. 2002); *In re Mercer*, 246 F.3d 391 (5th Cir. 2001); *Sangster v. Paetkau*, 80 Cal. Rptr. 2d 66 (Cal. Ct. App. 1998); 37 Am. Jur. 2d *Fraud and Deceit* § 389 (2001). If the plaintiff's decision to act or not act had been induced by his or her own investigation and not by a belief in the truth of defendant's representation, then there is no causation. *Restatement (Second) of Torts* § 547 (1977). Of course, if the defendant intentionally had prevented plaintiff's investigation from being effective, then there would be causation. *Id.*

Causation-in-fact is practically synonymous with the element of reliance, addressed at § 6.5.2, *supra. See Oliveira v. Amoco Oil Co.*, 776 N.E.2d 151 (Ill. 2002); *Kirkruff v. Wisegarver*, 697 N.E.2d 406 (Ill. App. Ct. 1998); *Navajo Mfg. Co. v. Camp*, 1995 WL 311792 (Minn. Ct. App. 1995); *but see Stutman v. Chem. Bank*, 709 N.Y.S.2d 892 (N.Y. 2000). The practitioner should be aware that perhaps for this reason, some jurisdictions are abandoning this instruction, relying entirely on the legal cause instruction, § 6.6.3, *infra.*

6.6.3   Legal Causation

The defendant's fraudulent misrepresentation was the legal cause of plaintiff's damages if those damages reasonably could have been expected to result from the plaintiff's reliance on the fraudulent misrepresentation.

COMMENT

This instruction is modeled on section 548A of the *Restatement (Second) of Torts* (1977). *Cf. In re Creta*, 271 B.R. 214 (B.A.P. 1st Cir. 2002); *AUSA Life Ins. Co. v. Ernst & Young*, 206 F.3d 202 (2d Cir. 2000); *City of Chicago v. Mich. Beach Housing Co-op*, 696 N.E.2d 804 (Ill. App. Ct. 1998); *Day v. Avery*, 548 F.2d 1018 (D.C. Cir. 1976); 37 Am. Jur. 2d *Fraud and Deceit* § 391 (2001). This instruction limits recoverable damages to those that were reasonably foreseeable, thereby precluding recovery for remote damages.

6.7 Damages for Fraudulent Misrepresentation

6.7.1 General Rule

If you find that the defendant is liable to the plaintiff for damages caused by a fraudulent misrepresentation, the next issue for your determination is the amount of the plaintiff's damages. Two kinds of damages can be considered in this case. They are compensatory damages and punitive damages.

6.7.2   Compensatory Damages

6.7.2.a   Out-of-Pocket

If you find in favor of the plaintiff in this case, the plaintiff is entitled to recover as damages from the defendant the difference in value between what the plaintiff received in the transaction and what the plaintiff paid or provided to the defendant.

COMMENT

This instruction is modeled on section 549(1)(a) of the *Restatement (Second) of Torts* (1977). *Cf. Coffel v. Stryker Corp.*, 284 F.3d 625 (5th Cir. 2002); *In re Sallee*, 286 F.3d 878 (6th Cir. 2002); *Ambassador Hotel Co. v. Wei-Chuan Inv.*, 189 F.3d 1017 (9th Cir. 1999); *Midwest Home Distrib., Inc. v. Domco Indus. Ltd.*, 585 N.W.2d 735 (Iowa 1998); *Lama Holding Co. v. Smith Barney Inc.*, 668 N.E.2d 1370 (N.Y. 1996); *Martin v. Brown*, 566 So.2d 890 (Fla. Dist. Ct. App. 1990); *Gregg v. U.S. Indus., Inc.*, 887 F.2d 1462 (11th Cir. 1989); *Zimpel v. Trawick*, 679 F. Supp. 1502 (W.D. Ark. 1988); 37 Am. Jur. 2d *Fraud and Deceit* § 387 (2001). This instruction is intended to compensate the plaintiff for what was lost because of the fraud, not for what the plaintiff might have gained.

6.7.2.b   Consequential

The plaintiff is entitled to recover as damages from the defendant other economic losses suffered as a result of the plaintiff's reliance on the defendant's fraudulent misrepresentation.

COMMENT

This instruction is modeled on section 549(1)(b) of the *Restatement (Second) of Torts* (1977). It permits recovery of other, incidental damages suffered by the plaintiff, including damages incurred by passing up other business opportunities. 37 Am. Jur. 2d *Fraud and Deceit* § 387 (2001); *cf. Popp Telcom v. Am. Sharecom, Inc.*, 210 F.3d 928 (8th Cir. 2000); *Schonfeld v. Hilliard*, 218 F.3d 164 (2nd Cir. 2000); *Alexander v. Certified Master Bldr. Corp.*, 43 F. Supp. 2d 1242 (D. Kan. 1999); *W. Cities Broad., Inc. v. Schueller*, 849 P.2d 44 (Colo. 1993).

6.7.2.c Benefit-of-the-Bargain Damages for Business Transaction

In addition to out-of-pocket and consequential damages, the plaintiff [in a business transaction] is entitled to recover damages sufficient to give the plaintiff the benefit of his or her contract or bargain with the defendant, or to put the plaintiff in the same position he or she would have been had the defendant's representation been true. You can only award the plaintiff these damages if he or she has proven them with a reasonable certainty.

COMMENT

This instruction is modeled on section 549(2) of the *Restatement (Second) of Torts* (1977). It permits a plaintiff in a business transaction to recover expectancy damages in addition to reliance damages. *Cf. Coffel v. Stryker Corp.*, 284 F.3d 625 (5th Cir. 2002); *In re Sallee*, 286 F.3d 878 (6th Cir. 2002); *Ambassador Hotel Co. v. Wei-Chuan Inv.*, 189 F.3d 1017 (9th Cir. 1999); *Smith v. Walt Bennett Ford, Inc.*, 864 S.W.2d 817 (Ark. 1993); *Bates v. Allied Mut. Ins. Co.*, 467 N.W.2d 255 (Iowa 1991); *Osofsky v. Zipf*, 645 F.2d 107 (2d Cir. 1981); 37 Am. Jur. 2d *Fraud and Deceit* § 385 (2001).

6.7.3   Punitive Damages

6.7.3.a   Decision to Award Punitive Damages

If you find for the plaintiff and against the defendant and you have determined that the defendant must pay damages, then you should consider whether the conduct that led to your decision also subjects the defendant to punitive damages. To award punitive damages, you must find that the defendant's conduct that proximately caused actual [or nominal] damages to the plaintiff was the result of actual malice, wanton conduct, or oppressive conduct, as measured by the instructions I will give you.

COMMENT

As a general rule, punitive damages may be assessed in fraudulent misrepresentation cases. *See* 37 Am. Jur. 2d *Fraud and Deceit* §§ 395-97 (2001); *cf. Connecticut Gen. Life Ins. Co. v. Jones*, 764 So.2d 677 (Fla. App. 2000); *Ambassador Hotel Co. v. Wei-Chuan Inv.*, 189 F.3d 1017 (9th Cir. 1999); *Jimenez v. Chrysler Corp.*, 74 F. Supp. 2d 548 (D.S.C. 1999); *Ischira v. Willingham*, 135 F.3d 1077 (6th Cir. 1998); *Zimpel v. Trawick*, 679 F. Supp. 1502 (W.D. Ark. 1988); *Nader v. Allegheny Airlines, Inc.*, 445 F. Supp. 168 (D.D.C. 1978). The rules governing the consideration of punitive damages vary depending on the jurisdiction, and these instructions relating to punitive damages must be tailored to correspond to those rules.

This charge represents the modern view of damages. *See, e.g., State Farm Mut. Auto. Ins. Co. v. Campbell*, 538 U.S. 408 (2003); *Rabun v. Kimberly-Clark Corp.*, 678 F.2d 1053 (11th Cir. 1982); *Christman v. Voyer*, 595 P.2d 410 (N.M. App. 1979); *Wussow v. Commercial Mechanisms, Inc.*, 279 N.W.2d 503 (Wis. App. 1979); *Restatement (Second) of Torts* § 908 (1979); 45 Am. Jur. 2d *Interference* § 62 (1999 & Supp. 2003). Counsel should note that although generally punitive damages will be awarded upon a showing of malice, wantonness, or oppressiveness, this principle is not universal and may well be affected by statute in a particular jurisdiction.

Most states require that the jury find liability and actual, or at least nominal, damages before punitive damages are allowed. *See* Richard C. Tinney, Annotation, *Showing of Actual Damages to Support Award of Punitive Damages*, 40 A.L.R. 4th 11 (1985 & Supp. 2002); 45 Am. Jur. 2d *Interference* § 62 (1999 & Supp. 2003); *Am. Bus. Interiors, Inc. v. Haworth, Inc.*, 798 F.2d 1135 (8th Cir. 1986). *But see Platte v. Whitney Realty Co.*, 538 So.2d 1358 (Fla. App. 1989) (punitive damages recoverable although actual damages could not be proved). For a discussion of the prerequisite of a verdict for actual damages, see the comment to § 6.7.3.b, *infra*. For the requirement of malicious, wanton, or oppressive conduct, see §§ 6.7.3.c, 6.7.3.d, and 6.7.3.e.

6.7.3.b Nominal Damages

The award of only a nominal sum with respect to the specific losses claimed by the plaintiff will not prevent your awarding punitive damages if you find that the award of punitive damages is justified under these instructions.

COMMENT

In most states the jury must make a finding of liability and actual, or at least nominal, damages before punitive damages are allowed. *See* Richard C. Tinney, Annotation, *Showing of Actual Damages to Support Award of Punitive Damages*, 40 A.L.R. 4th 11 (1985 & Supp. 2002); 45 Am. Jur. 2d *Interference* § 62 (1999 & Supp. 2003); *Am. Bus. Interiors, Inc. v. Haworth, Inc.*, 798 F.2d 1135 (8th Cir. 1986). *But see Platte v. Whitney Realty Co.*, 538 So.2d 1358 (Fla. App. 1989) (punitive damages recoverable although actual damages could not be proved).

In most jurisdictions, an award of nominal damages will suffice for this purpose. *See, e.g., Taylor v. Sandoval*, 442 F. Supp. 491 (D. Colo. 1977); *Tennant v. Vazquez*, 389 So. 2d 1183 (Fla. App. 1980); *Christman v. Voyer*, 595 P.2d 410 (N.M. App. 1979). *But see Wussow v. Commercial Mechanisms, Inc.*, 279 N.W.2d 503 (Wis. App. 1979). *See generally* Richard C. Tinney, Annotation, *Showing of Actual Damages to Support Award of Punitive Damages—Modern Cases*, 40 A.L.R. 4th 11 (1985 & Supp. 2002).

6.7.3.c Actual Malice

You may find the defendant's conduct to have been undertaken with actual "malice" sufficient to enable you to award punitive damages if you find it to have been prompted or accompanied by personal ill will, spite, or hatred, either toward the plaintiff individually or toward all persons in one or more groups or categories of which the plaintiff is a member.

COMMENT

Generally, courts require proof of facts tending to establish actual, as opposed to legal, malice to justify an award of punitive damages. *See* 45 Am. Jur. 2d *Interference* § 62 (1999 & Supp. 2003); *Norwood Easthill Assocs. v. Norwood Easthill Watch*, 536 A.2d 1317 (N.J. Super. Ct. App. Div. 1988); *Anthony Pools, Inc. v. Charles & David, Inc.*, 797 S.W.2d 666 (Tex. App. 1990); *Bellefonte Underwriters Co., Inc. v. Brown*, 663 S.W.2d 562 (Tex. App. 1984). Even if not required, actual malice is always an important factor in an award of punitive damages. *See, e.g., Universal City Studios, Inc. v. Nintendo Co.*, 615 F. Supp. 838 (S.D.N.Y. 1985), *aff'd*, 797 F.2d 70 (2d Cir.), *cert. denied*, 479 U.S. 987 (1986); *Int'l Wood Processors Corp. v. Power Dry, Inc.*, 593 F. Supp. 710 (D.S.C. 1984); *Edward Vantine Studios, Inc. v. Fraternal Composite Serv., Inc.*, 373 N.W.2d 512 (Iowa App. 1985).

6.7.3.d   Wanton Conduct

You may also award punitive damages if you find that the defendant's conduct was "wanton"—that is, that the conduct was undertaken in reckless or callous disregard of, or indifference to, the rights of one or more persons, including the plaintiff.

COMMENT

See King v. G.D. Van Wagenen Co., 717 F. Supp. 667 (D. Minn. 1989); *Liston v. Home Ins. Co.*, 659 F. Supp. 276 (S.D. Miss. 1986); *Universal City Studios, Inc. v. Nintendo Co.*, 615 F. Supp. 838 (S.D.N.Y. 1985), *aff'd*, 797 F.2d 70 (2d Cir.), *cert. denied*, 479 U.S. 987 (1986); *Ramona Manor Convalescent Hosp. v. Care Enterprises*, 225 Cal. Rptr. 120 (Cal. App. 1986).

6.7.3.e   Oppressive Conduct

You also may award punitive damages if, from all of the evidence, you find that the defendant's conduct was "oppressive"; that is, that the conduct was done in a way or manner that injured, damaged, or otherwise violated the rights of the plaintiff with unnecessary harshness or severity, as by misuse or abuse of authority or power, or by taking advantage of some weakness, disability, or misfortune of the plaintiff.

COMMENT

See Barnes Group, Inc. v. C & C Prod., Inc., 716 F.2d 1023 (4th Cir. 1983); *Rabun v. Kimberly-Clark Corp.,* 678 F.2d 1053 (11th Cir. 1982); *Int'l Wood Processors Corp. v. Power Dry, Inc.,* 593 F. Supp. 710 (D.S.C. 1984), *aff'd,* 792 F.2d 416 (4th Cir. 1986).

6.7.3.f   Amount of Punitive Damages Award

If you decide that punitive damages are appropriate in this case based upon my prior instructions, you should award the amount of punitive damages that, in your sound judgment, will justly punish the defendant for its behavior and dissuade the defendant and others from acting the same way in future, similar situations.

In fixing the amount of punitive damages, you may consider the following factors:

1. the character of the defendant's act(s);

2. the nature and extent of the harm to the plaintiff that the defendant caused or intended to cause; and

3. the defendant's financial condition.

The amount of any punitive damages should bear a reasonable relationship to the injury, harm, or damage caused by the defendant. You must also keep in mind that the amount of such punitive damages, when awarded, must be fixed with calm discretion and sound reason. Punitive damages must not be awarded, or fixed in amount, based upon any sympathy, bias, or prejudice you may feel toward any party in the case.

[If evidence of "other acts" or harm against other parties has been allowed, add the following: Some of the evidence you have heard concerned conduct by the defendant that was not the proximate cause of the damages claimed by the plaintiff in this case. Although you may consider this evidence for any bearing upon the defendant's state of mind in causing damages claimed by the plaintiff in this case, you are not to punish the defendant for conduct relating only to parties other than the plaintiff.]

[If evidence of the defendant's financial condition has been allowed, add the following: You have heard evidence of the defendant's financial condition. You are not to consider the defendant's financial condition in deciding whether to award punitive damages. You may, however, consider it in fixing the amount of punitive damages to the extent that the actual [or nominal] damages are insufficient to justly punish the defendant for its behavior or dissuade the defendant or others from acting the same way in future, similar situations.]

COMMENT

See State Farm Mut. Auto. Ins. Co. v. Campbell, 538 U.S. 408 (2003); *Cooper Indus., Inc. v. Leatherman Tool Group, Inc.*, 121 S. Ct. 1678 (2001); *BMW of N. Am., Inc. v. Gore*, 116 S. Ct. 1589 (1996); *Jannotta v. Subway Sandwich Shops, Inc.*, 125 F.3d 503 (7th Cir. 1997); *Fed. Deposit Ins. Corp. v. W.R. Grace & Co.*, 877 F.2d 614 (7th Cir. 1989); *Aldrich v. Thomson McKinnon Sec., Inc.*, 756 F.2d 243 (2d Cir. 1985); Damages—Modern Cases, 40 A.L.R. 4th 11 (1985 & Supp. 2002).

A state may not impose damages on a defendant for actions undertaken in other states that do not violate the other states' laws. *BMW*, 116 S. Ct. at 1597 (1996). Similarly, a "defendant's dissimilar acts, independent from the acts upon which liability was premised, may not serve as the basis for punitive damages." *State Farm*, 123 S. Ct. at 1523.

A defendant's financial condition as a factor in setting punitive damages is generally accepted. *See, e.g., Miller v. Rukoff-Sexton, Inc.*, 845 F.2d 209 (9th Cir. 1988) (the defendant's net worth was admissible for setting punitive damages); *Hollins v. Powell*, 773 F.2d 191 (8th Cir. 1985) (reducing punitive damage award in light of defendant's limited resources); *Rupert v. Sellers*, 368 N.Y.S.2d 904 (N.Y. App. Div. 1975) (in bifurcated trial, evidence of the defendants' net worth should be considered after special verdict). *See generally* Annotation, *Punitive Damages: Relationship to Defendant's Wealth As a Factor in Determining Propriety of Award*, 87 A.L.R. 4th 141 (1991 & Supp. 2002). Some states, such as Hawaii, even have statutes making the financial condition of the defendant relevant to the amount of punitive damages awardable. Others, like New York, protect the defendant from possible prejudice at trial through the use of a bifurcated trial procedure. *See Aldrich v. Thomson McKinnon Sec., Inc.*, 589 F. Supp.

683 (S.D.N.Y. 1984). However, the Supreme Court has cautioned that the financial condition of the defendant may not be used to create bias against big businesses or to permit an award that is unrelated to the actual damages. *State Farm*, 123 S. Ct. at 1525 ("the wealth of a defendant cannot justify an otherwise unconstitutional punitive damage award"). Recent commentators have argued that the defendant's financial condition is only relevant in cases involving non-economically motivated torts. *See, e.g.,* Andrew L. Frey, *No More Blind Man's Bluff on Punitive Damages: A Plea to the Drafters of Pattern Jury Instructions*, 29 Litig. 24 (Summer 2003). In cases where the defendant was motivated by profits, they argue, compensatory damages are sufficient to act as a deterrent. *Id.*

6.8   Negligent Misrepresentation

6.8.1   Elements of Liability

In this case, for the plaintiff to recover money damages against the defendant for negligent misrepresentation, the plaintiff must prove by a preponderance of the evidence all of the following:

(a) that the defendant conveyed or supplied information to the plaintiff that the defendant thought was true but in fact was inaccurate or false;

(b) that the defendant conveyed or supplied the information to the plaintiff either in the course of a transaction in which the defendant had a pecuniary interest or in the course of the defendant's business, profession, or employment;

(c) that the defendant failed to exercise reasonable care or competence in obtaining the information or in conveying or supplying that information, and the failure resulted in the information conveyed or supplied to be inaccurate or false;

(d) that the defendant intended or expected that the plaintiff would rely on the information being conveyed or supplied;

(e) that the plaintiff justifiably relied on the inaccurate or false information; and

(f) that the plaintiff suffered damages as a foreseeable result of his or her reliance on the defendant's inaccurate or false information.

COMMENT

This instruction is modeled on section 552 of the *Restatement (Second) of Torts* (1977). *Cf. Reeves v. Alyeska Pipeline Serv. Co.*, 56 P.3d 660 (Alaska 2002); *Hulse v. First Am. Title Co. of Crook Co.*, 33 P.3d 122 (Wyo. 2001); *Wendy Hong Wu v. Dunkin' Donuts, Inc.*, 105 F. Supp. 2d 83 (E.D.N.Y. 2000); *Fleming Companies, Inc. v. GAB Bus. Servs., Inc.*, 103 F. Supp. 2d 1271 (D. Kan. 2000); *Ragsdale v. Mount Sinai Med. Ctr. of Miami*, 770 So.2d 167 (Fla. Dist. Ct. App. 2000);

37 Am. Jur. 2d *Fraud and Deceit* §§ 128-129 (2001). Note that the defendant must be providing information to the plaintiff in connection with some special relationship that gives rise to a duty of care owed by the defendant to the plaintiff.

Generally speaking, for the inaccurate or false information to be actionable, it must be factual, rather than a conveyance of an opinion. The practitioner should review the comments at subsections 6.3.6.a to 6.3.6.d of these model jury instructions, and applicable law of the relevant jurisdiction, to determine what can constitute actionable false information for purposes of a cause of action for negligent misrepresentation. The question of justifiable reliance here involves the same issues of reasonableness raised in a cause of action for fraudulent misrepresentation. Because negligent misrepresentation is essentially a claim of negligence, however, whether it was reasonable for the plaintiff to have relied on the defendant's false information is directly tied to the question of contributory and/or comparative negligence. Jurisdictions differ in their adoption of the contributory and comparative negligence standards, so the practitioner must determine the applicable standard and then determine how that standard affects the justifiable reliance requirement.

6.8.2 Defendant Conveyed or Supplied Information to the Plantiff

6.8.2.a As Part of a Group

The defendant did not convey or supply false information to the plaintiff unless the plaintiff can prove by a preponderance of the evidence that the plaintiff was one of a limited group of persons for whose guidance the defendant supplied the information.

6.8.2.b Directly or Indirectly

The defendant did not convey or supply false information to the plaintiff unless the plaintiff can prove by a preponderance of the evidence that the defendant (1) conveyed or supplied the information directly to the plaintiff or to a limited group of which plaintiff was a member; or (2) conveyed or supplied the information to a third person whom the defendant knew intended to convey or supply that information to the plaintiff or to a limited group of which plaintiff was a member.

COMMENT

This instruction is modeled on section 552 of the *Restatement (Second) of Torts* (1977). *Cf. Hermelink v. Dynamex Operations East, Inc.*, 109 F. Supp. 2d 1299 (D. Kan. 2000); *Cundiff v. Umfleet*, 21 S.W.3d 127 (Mo. Ct. App. 2000); *NorAm Inv. Serv., Inc. v. Stirtz Bernards Boyden Surdel & Larter, P.A.*, 611 N.W.2d 372 (Minn. App. 2000); *Key v. Pierce*, 8 S.W.3d 704 (Tex. App. 1999), 37 Am. Jur. 2d *Fraud and Deceit* §§ 128, 131 (2001). The practitioner should be mindful that some jurisdictions require that information be conveyed directly to the plaintiff to be actionable. *See, e.g., Wendy Hong Wu v. Dunkin' Donuts, Inc.*, 105 F. Supp. 2d 83 (E.D.N.Y. 2000).

This instruction limits the defendant's liability to those to whom he or she intended to provide information. Contrast this with the scope of a defendant's liability for a fraudulent misrepresentation, which would include any person the defendant had reason to believe would act in reliance upon the fraudulent misrepresentation. *See Restatement (Second)* § 552 cmt. a.

6.8.3   Damages

If you find for plaintiff and against defendant, the next issue for your determination is the amount of plaintiff's damages. The plaintiff is entitled to recover as damages from the defendant only: 1) the difference in value between what the plaintiff received in the transaction and what the plaintiff paid or provided to the defendant; and 2) other economic losses suffered as a result of the plaintiff's reliance on the defendant's negligent misrepresentation.

COMMENT

This instruction is modeled on section 552B of the *Restatement (Second) of Torts* (1977). *Cf. BDO Seidman, LLP v. Mindis Acquisition Corp.*, 578 S.E.2d 400 (Ga. 2003); *Zanakis-Pico v. Cutter Dodge, Inc.*, 47 P.3d 1222 (Haw. 2002); *Bower v. Stein Eriksen Lodge Owners Ass'n, Inc.*, 201 F. Supp. 2d 1134 (D. Utah 2002); *Bokma Farms, Inc. v. State*, 14 P.3d 1199 (Mont. 2000). As a general matter, on a negligent misrepresentation claim, a plaintiff is not entitled to an award of damages equivalent to the benefit the plaintiff would have received under his or her contract with the defendant had the representation been true. *See Restatement (Second)* § 552B(2) and cmt. b.

6.9 Fraudulent Concealment

In this case, for the plaintiff to recover money damages against the defendant for fraudulent concealment, the plaintiff must prove by a preponderance of the evidence all of the following:

(a) that the defendant, as a party to a transaction with plaintiff, prevented the plaintiff from learning an existing fact;

(b) that the defendant knew that the fact existed;

(c) that the defendant, in preventing the plaintiff from learning of the existing fact, intended that the plaintiff would rely on the absence of that fact when determining how to engage in the transaction between them;

(d) that the plaintiff justifiably relied on the belief that the concealed fact did not exist, such that had plaintiff known the fact, he or she would have chosen a different course of action with respect to the transaction; and

(e) that, as a result of the plaintiff choosing to act or not act without the fact, the plaintiff has suffered damages.

COMMENT

This instruction is modeled on section 550 of the *Restatement (Second) of Torts* (1977) and 37 Am. Jur. 2d *Fraud and Deceit* § 200 (2001). This instruction should be utilized in the context of the instructions for fraudulent misrepresentation, since concealment essentially can serve as a substitute for an affirmative false representation in a fraudulent misrepresentation action. 37 Am. Jur. 2d *Fraud and Deceit* § 200 (2001). Indeed, a defendant in a fraudulent concealment action faces liability as if he or she had made an affirmative fraudulent statement that the fact did not exist. *Restatement (Second)* § 550; *cf. Martinelli v. Bridgeport Roman Catholic Diocesan Corp.*, 196 F.3d 409 (2d Cir. 1999); *Roadmaster Indus., Inc. v. Columbia Mfg. Co.*, 893 F. Supp. 1162 (D. Mass. 1995); *Pelster v. Ray*, 987 F.2d 514 (8th Cir. 1993); *Ortho Pharm. Corp. v. Sona Distribs., Inc.*, 663 F. Supp. 64 (S.D. Fla. 1987); *Russow v. Bobola*, 277 N.E.2d 769 (Ill. App. Ct. 1972).

A number of jurisdictions require that the concealed fact be material. However, as discussed in § 6.5.3, *supra*, of these model jury instructions, materiality is subsumed into the element requiring that the plaintiff justifiably rely on the belief that the concealed fact did not exist. By definition, the fact would be material if plaintiff would have acted differently had he or she known the fact before entering into a transaction with the defendant. The only remaining question would be whether the plaintiff was reasonable in relying on that belief, a question that would be objective or subjective depending on the jurisdiction.

The practitioner should be careful not to confuse an action for fraudulent concealment with one for fraudulent nondisclosure, discussed at § 6.10, *infra*. Fraudulent concealment does not require that the defendant have a duty to provide the concealed fact to the plaintiff. The defendant need only take steps to keep the plaintiff from discovering a fact that would be considered important in deciding how to go forward with respect to a transaction. Fraudulent nondisclosure does not require affirmative steps by the defendant to keep the plaintiff from discovering a fact. It instead requires that the defendant fail to disclose a fact he or she had a duty to disclose in an effort to deceive the plaintiff.

6.10 Fraudulent Nondisclosure

6.10.1 Elements of Liability

In this case, for the plaintiff to recover money damages against the defendant for fraudulent nondisclosure, the plaintiff must prove by a preponderance of the evidence all of the following:

(a) that before the plaintiff and defendant consummated a transaction, the defendant failed to disclose to the plaintiff an existing fact of which the defendant had knowledge at the time;

(b) that the defendant owed a duty to the plaintiff to disclose the existing fact;

(c) that the defendant, in failing to disclose the existing fact to the plaintiff, intended that the plaintiff would rely on the absence of that fact when determining how to engage in the transaction between them;

d) that the plaintiff justifiably relied on the belief that the nondisclosed fact did not exist, such that had plaintiff known the fact, he or she would have chosen a different course of action with respect to the transaction; and

(e) that, as a result of the plaintiff choosing to act or not act without the fact, the plaintiff has suffered damages.

COMMENT

This instruction is modeled on section 551 of the *Restatement (Second) of Torts* (1977) and 37 Am. Jur. 2d *Fraud and Deceit* § 200 (2001). *Cf. Wells Fargo Bank v. Ariz. Lab., Teamsters and Cement Masons*, 38 P.3d 12 (Ariz. 2002); *Aetna Cas. & Sur. Co. v. Leahey Constr. Co.*, 219 F.3d 519 (6th Cir. 2000); *Peters v. Amoco Oil Co.*, 57 F. Supp. 2d 1268 (M.D. Ala. 1999); *Hennig v. Ahearn*, 601 N.W.2d 14 (Wis. App. 1999); *In re Cifilia*, 124 B.R. 124 (Bankr. M.D. Fla. 1991); *Everman Nat'l Bank v. United States*, 756 F.2d 865 (Fed. Cir. 1985); *Laventhall v. Gen. Dynamics Corp.*, 704 F.2d 407 (8th Cir. 1983).

6.10.2   Duty

The defendant owed a duty to disclose to the plaintiff an existing fact if the plaintiff proves by a preponderance of the evidence one of the following:

(a) that a fiduciary or other relationship of trust existed between the defendant and the plaintiff with respect to the transaction;

(2) that the defendant knew that the existing fact would be necessary to prevent an ambiguous statement by the defendant from being misleading;

(3) that the defendant knew that the existing fact would be necessary to keep the plaintiff from relying on a prior representation by the defendant that has been rendered false or misleading by the existing fact; or

(5) that the plaintiff, because of customs of the trade, reasonably could expect the defendant to disclose an existing fact basic to their transaction were the plaintiff to make a mistake about such a fact.

COMMENT

This instruction is modeled on section 551 of the *Restatement (Second) of Torts* (1977). *Cf. Wells Fargo Bank v. Ariz. Lab., Teamsters and Cement Masons*, 38 P.3d 12 (Ariz. 2002); *Wiseheart v. Zions Bancorp,*, 49 P.3d 1200 (Colo. Ct. App. 2002); *Estate of White v. R.J. Reynolds Tobacco Co.*, 109 F. Supp. 2d 424 (D. Md. 2000); *Kenney v. Healey Ford-Lincoln-Mercury, Inc.*, 730 A.2d 115 (Conn. Ct. App. 1999); *Riggs Nat'l Bank of Washington, D.C. v. Freeman*, 682 F. Supp. 519 (S.D. Fla. 1988); *Wolf v. Brungardt*, 524 P.2d 726 (Kan. 1974); *Dennis v. Thomson*, 43 S.W.2d 18 (Ky. Ct. App. 1931); 37 Am. Jur. 2d *Fraud and Deceit* § 204 (2001).

Chapter Seven
Breach of Fiduciary Duty

Jack N. Sibley, Thomas P. Mitchell*

---

* Jack N. Sibley is a partner and Thomas P. Mitchell is an associate at Hawkins & Parnell, LLP, 4000 SunTrust Plaza, 303 Peachtree Street NE, Atlanta, GA 30308. Mr. Sibley may be reached at (404) 614-7400 or jsibley@hplegal.com. Mr. Mitchell may be reached at (404) 614-7400 or tmitchell@ hplegal.com.

7.1 Introduction

The model jury charges in this chapter are for use in cases involving a breach of fiduciary duties. A cause of action for breach of fiduciary duty, like most commercial torts, requires a showing of duty, breach of duty, causation, and damage.

Fiduciary relationships may arise as a matter of law by statute, contract, conduct, or confidential relationship. To determine whether a fiduciary duty exists, the trial court may need to make a factual inquiry regarding any proof of a confidential relationship. For example, section 23-2-58 of the Georgia Code defines confidential relations in the state of Georgia as follows:

> Any relationship shall be deemed confidential, whether arising from nature, created by law, or resulting from contracts, where one party is so situated as to exercise a controlling influence over the will, conduct, and interest of another or where, from a similar relationship of mutual confidence, the law requires the utmost good faith, such as the relationship between partners, principal and agent, etc. Ga. Code Ann. § 23-2-58 (1982).

Consequently, the factual circumstances of a particular case may indicate that any of a number of fiduciary duties has arisen. These duties include the duty of care, duty of loyalty, duty to account, duty of confidentiality, duty of full disclosure, duty to act fairly, and duty of good faith and fidelity.

The following model jury instructions deal with particular fiduciary duties that have been recognized in a commercial context. The model jury instructions that relate to corporate fiduciary duties may also apply, in certain circumstances, to the other fiduciary relationships.

7.2   Breach of Fiduciary Duty: Elements of Liability

For the plaintiff to prevail on plaintiff's claim for breach of fiduciary, the plaintiff must prove each of the following elements by a preponderance of the evidence:

1. that the defendant owed the plaintiff a fiduciary duty;

2. that the defendant breached the fiduciary duty owed to the plaintiff; and

3. that the defendant's breach of fiduciary duty was the proximate cause of some injury or damage to the plaintiff.

I will go over each of these elements more specifically in the following instructions.

If after you consider all of the evidence you find that plaintiff has proven each of these elements in accordance with the legal requirements as I describe them to you, then your verdict must be for the plaintiff and you will consider the amount of money damages to be awarded to plaintiff, by following the instructions that I will give you relating to damages.

If, on the other hand, you find that plaintiff has not proven one or more of these elements, then your verdict must be for the defendant.

7.3 Existence of Fiduciary Duty

7.3.1 Explanation of Fiduciary Duty

You are instructed that a fiduciary relationship exists between two persons when one of them is under a duty to act for, or to give advice for, the benefit of the other upon matters within the scope of the relation. The duties that arise under such a relationship include the following: duty of care, duty of loyalty, duty to account, duty of confidentiality, duty of full disclosure, duty to act fairly, and duty of good faith and fidelity [use as applicable].

It is for you to determine whether a fiduciary relationship existed between defendant [name] and plaintiff [name] at the time of the alleged misconduct. If you determine that relationship did exist, you must next determine the scope of the fiduciary relationship and whether one or more of the duties listed above arose within the scope of the relationship. If the alleged misconduct was outside of the scope of the relationship, then you must find for the defendant on this claim. If you find the existence of a fiduciary relationship and that the alleged misconduct was within the scope of one of the duties listed above, then you should consider where the defendant breached that duty.

COMMENT

Local rules of procedure, the type of relation between the parties, and the intricacy of the transaction involved determine whether the beneficiary is entitled to redress at law or in equity. Section 874 of the *Restatement (Second) of Torts* (1979) provides a basic discussion of the existence of fiduciary duties and redress of breaches of such duties at law and in equity. *See also Restatement (Second) of Torts* § 2 (1959).

7.3.2   Circumstances Giving Rise to Non-statutory Fiduciary Duties

Fiduciary duties may arise in the context of contractual relationships, such as those between principal and agent or lawyer and client.

A fiduciary duty of a contractual nature may be shown by the conduct of the parties or the existence of a special relationship between the parties. Indications of such a relationship include the following: where one party acts for the benefit of another, where one party has and exercises influence or control over the other party, where one party reposes trust and confidence in another, where one party dominates the other party, where there is inequality between the parties, or where one party is dependent on the other. Further considerations include weakness of age, mental strength, business intelligence, knowledge of the facts involved, or other conditions giving one party an advantage over the other.

In the absence of express contractual terms creating a fiduciary duty, such a duty may be inferred when one or more of the above-listed incidents of conduct is present.

COMMENT

For examples of non-statutory fiduciary relationships created by conduct, see *Anderson v. Reynolds*, 588 F. Supp. 814 (D.C. Nev. 1984) (agreement to handle real estate transaction created fiduciary duty); see *Herzog v. Leighton Holdings (In re Kids Creek Partners, L.P.)*, 212 B.R. 898, 937 (Bankr. N.D. Ill. 1997) (A fiduciary responsibility develops only when the stockholder takes a role in corporate management and acts to dominate, interfere with, or mislead other stockholders in exercising their rights.); *Matter of Vietri Homes, Inc.*, 58 B.R. 663 (Bankr. Del. 1986) (fiduciary confidence); and *Hofstetter v. Fletcher*, 905 F.2d 897 (6th Cir. 1988) (under Ohio law, de facto fiduciary relationship may result from confidential relationship, and existence of such relationship is question of fact to be determined by jury). *See also Riggs Nat'l*

Bank of Washington D.C. v. Freeman, 682 F. Supp. 519 (S.D. Fla. 1988); *Craig v. First Am. Capital Res., Inc.*, 740 F. Supp. 530 (N.D. Ill. 1990); *but see McClure v. Duggan*, 674 F. Supp. 211 (N.D. Tex. 1987); *Marriott Bros. v. Gage*, 704 F. Supp. 731 (N.D. Tex. 1988) ("subjective trust . . . cannot convert what would otherwise be arms-length dealing into a fiduciary relationship"), *aff'd*, 911 F.2d 1105 (5th Cir. 1990).

7.3.3 Partnerships

I am instructing you that the law says partners owe fiduciary duties to their fellow partners and to the partnership itself. All partnership agreements include an agreement for each partner to act in the utmost good faith toward the other partner or partners. This requires that partners deal fairly with each other and with the partnership.

COMMENT

For a discussion of partnership fiduciary duties, *see Allen v. Sanders*, 337 S.E.2d 428 (Ga. Ct. App. 1985); and *Crosby v. Rogers*, 30 S.E.2d 248 (Ga. 1944). *See also* Ga. Code Ann. § 23-2-58 (1982); *Paciaroni v. Crane*, 408 A.2d 946 (Del. Ch., 1979). For additional support *see Latta v. Kilbourn*, 150 U.S. 524 (1893); *Meinhard v. Salmon*, 164 N.E. 545 (N.Y. 1928); *Main v. Merrill, Lynch, Pierce, Fenner & Smith, Inc.*, 136 Cal. Rptr. 378 (Cal. Ct. App. 1977); *Yeomans v. Lysfjord*, 327 P.2d 957 (Cal. Ct. App. 1958).

7.3.4   General Partner, Limited Partners

In a limited partnership, a general partner, having exclusive power and authority to control and manage the partnership, owes the limited partners an even greater fiduciary duty than is normally imposed.

Among other things, general partners have a duty to the limited partners to render true and full information of all things affecting the partnership, and to account to the partnership for any benefit derived by one partner without consent of the other partners, or from any transactions connected with the conduct of the partnership.

COMMENT

For a detailed discussion of the fiduciary duty of a general partner to limited partners, *see Palmer v. Fuqua,* 641 F.2d 1146 (5th Cir. 1981); *Loft v. Lapidus,* 936 F.2d 633 (1st Cir. 1991); *Fleck v. Cablevision VII, Inc.,* 763 F. Supp. 622 (D.D.C. 1991); *S. Atl. Ltd. P'ship of Tenn. v. Riese,* 284 F.3d 518 (4th Cir. 2002); *Petricca Dev. Ltd. P'ship v. Pioneer Dev. Co.,* 214 F.3d 216 (1st Cir. 2000); *Balabanos v. North Am. Inv. Group, Ltd.,* 708 F. Supp. 1488 (N.D. Ill. 1988); and *Dymm v. Cahill,* 730 F. Supp. 1245 (S.D.N.Y. 1990).

7.3.5   Trustee

I am instructing you that the law says a trustee owes fiduciary duties to the beneficiaries of a trust. In this case, the defendant was a trustee of a trust and plaintiff was a beneficiary of that trust. Among the duties owed by a trustee are the duty to administer the trust solely in the interests of the beneficiaries; the duty of full disclosure of material facts by the trustee when dealing on the beneficiary's account; the duty to keep and render clear and accurate accounts of the administration of the trust; and the duty to take reasonable steps to take, keep control of, and preserve the trust property. A trustee must discharge these duties in good faith and with that degree of diligence, care, and skill that ordinarily prudent persons would exercise under similar circumstances in a like position.

COMMENT

For a discussion of corporate trustee duties, *see Smith v. Hawks*, 355 S.E.2d 669 (Ga. Ct. App. 1987). *See also* Ga. Code Ann. § 7-1-310 (1989); *In re Ellis Estate*, 6 A.2d 602 (Del. Super. Ct & Orphans Ct. 1939) (broker's relationship to customer is that of agent, bailee, or trustee); *Himel v. Cont'l Ill. Nat'l Bank & Trust Co. of Chicago*, 596 F.2d 205 (7th Cir. 1979).

7.3.6   Estate Representatives

I am instructing you that upon appointment by the probate court, an estate representative owes fiduciary duties to the heirs of the estate. An estate representative has a fiduciary relationship with the heirs of the estate, and the representative must act fairly and make full disclosure of all actions taken in connection with estate assets. In this case, the defendant was the estate representative for the estate of [name], and owed a fiduciary duty to the plaintiff, a beneficiary.

This fiduciary relationship imposed a duty on the defendant, as estate representative, to discharge defendant's duties in good faith and with that degree of diligence, care, and skill that ordinarily prudent persons would exercise under similar circumstances in like positions.

COMMENT

For a discussion of fiduciary duties of estate representatives, *see In re Harrison*, 335 S.E.2d 564 (Ga. 1985); *Jones v. Harper*, 55 F. Supp. 2d 530 (S.D.W.V. 1999).

7.3.7 Agency

I am instructing you that the law says a fiduciary relationship exists between a principal and an agent. In this case, the defendant was the agent of plaintiff, the principal.

The fiduciary relationship imposes a duty on an agent, within the limits of the agency, to deal fairly and honestly with the principal, and imposes the responsibility on the agent to disclose any conflicts between the principal's interest and the agent's interest that might make the agent act in its own best interest at the expense or to the detriment of the principal.

COMMENT

Agency relationships with their related fiduciary duties can be created by contract, conduct, and confidential relationships. *See, e.g., Clyde Chester Realty Co. v. Stansell,* 259 S.E.2d 639 (Ga. Ct. App. 1979); *Youngblood v. Mock,* 238 S.E.2d 250 (Ga. Ct. App. 1977). *See also European Bakers, Ltd. v. Holman,* 338 S.E.2d 702 (Ga. Ct. App. 1985); *Scott v. Lumpkin,* 264 S.E.2d 514 (Ga. Ct. App. 1980); *L.A. Draper & Son, Inc. v. Wheelabrator-Frye, Inc.,* 813 F.2d 332 (11th Cir. 1987); *Gerdes v. Estate of Cush,* 953 F.2d 201 (5th Cir. 1992); *Apollo Technologies Corp. v. Centrosphere Indus. Corp.,* 805 F. Supp. 1157 (D.N.J. 1992); *Pierce v. Lyman,* 3 Cal. Rptr. 2d 236 (Cal. Ct. App. 1991).

7.3.8   Stockbrokers

I am instructing you that the law says a broker's duty to account to its customer is fiduciary in nature, resulting in an obligation to exercise the utmost good faith. This requirement of good faith demands that the broker make known to its customer all material facts that concern the transactions and subject matter of the broker-customer relationship.

COMMENT

For a full discussion of broker-customer relationships and fiduciary duties, *see Tigner v. Shearson-Lehman Hutton, Inc.*, 411 S.E.2d 800 (Ga. Ct. App. 1991); *Goodrich v. E.F. Hutton Group, Inc.*, 542 A.2d 1200 (Del. Ch. 1988); *Minor v. E.F. Hutton & Co., Inc.*, 409 S.E.2d 262 (Ga. Ct. App. 1991); *E.F. Hutton & Co., Inc. v. Weeks*, 304 S.E.2d 420 (Ga. Ct. App. 1983); *Aldrich v. Thomson McKinnon Securities, Inc.*, 756 F.2d 243 (2d Cir. 1985); and *Bennett v. E.F. Hutton Co., Inc.*, 597 F. Supp. 1547 (D. Ohio 1984).

7.3.9   Lawyer, Client

I am instructing you that the law says a fiduciary relationship exists between a lawyer and the lawyer's client. This relationship imposes a high standard of care and imposes a duty to provide competent legal representation. Such duty demands undivided loyalty and prohibits the lawyer from engaging in conflicts of interest, or misusing in any way a client's confidential information.

COMMENT

For a detailed discussion of the lawyer-client fiduciary duty, *see Maritrans GP, Inc. v. Pepper, Hamilton & Scheetz*, 602 A.2d 1277 (Pa. 1992); and *Mirabito v. Liccardo*, 5 Cal. Rptr. 2d 571 (Cal. Ct. App. 1992).

7.3.10   Lender, Borrower

I am instructing you that the law says a borrower-lender relationship does not create fiduciary duties in the absence of special circumstances. When such parties bargain at arms length, and each is looking out for its own interests, the lender may not be required to act primarily for the benefit of the borrower rather than itself. Such a requirement would convert ordinary day-to-day business transactions into fiduciary relationships when none were intended or anticipated.

However, a fiduciary relationship may be found between a lender and borrower when the lender is in a position to influence the borrower, or when there is a great disparity of bargaining power between the parties, or when a special relationship existed between the parties besides that of debtor-creditor, or when the lender actually assumes an advisory capacity regarding the borrower's business.

It is for you to determine whether any of the above-listed special relationships existed between the defendant [Lender] and the plaintiff [Borrower] in the case before you. You may also consider the facts and circumstances in this case to determine whether a confidential relationship exists between the parties on other terms.

COMMENT

For a detailed analysis of the state of fiduciary duty between lenders and borrowers, *see Idaho First Nat'l Bank v. Bliss Valley Foods, Inc.*, 824 P.2d 841 (Idaho 1991); *Bloomfield v. Neb. State Bank*, 465 N.W.2d 144 (Neb. 1991); *Richards v. Platte Valley Bank*, 866 F.2d 1576 (10th Cir. 1989); and *In re Horne*, 44 B.R. 796 (Bankr. S.D. Fla. 1984).

7.3.11 Majority Shareholder, Minority Shareholder

I am instructing you that the law says majority shareholders have a fiduciary duty to minority shareholders. If the majority shareholders undertake, either directly, or indirectly through the directors, to conduct, manage, or direct the corporation's affairs, they have a duty to do so in good faith, and consistent with the best interests of the corporation.

COMMENT

Crosby v. Beam, 47 Ohio St.3d 105, 548 N.E.2d 217 (Ohio 1989); *Aschinger v. Columbus Showcase Co.*, 934 F.2d 1402 (6th Cir. 1991); *Pro Football Weekly, Inc. v. Gannett Co.*, 988 F.2d 723 (7th Cir. 1993).

7.3.12   Corporate Fiduciary Duties

I am instructing you that the law says corporate officers, directors, and controlling shareholders owe a fiduciary duty to the corporation and non-controlling shareholders. As officers and directors of [corporation], the defendants owed that corporation and its shareholders fiduciary duties. This means that the defendants were required to discharge the duties of their respective positions in good faith and with that degree of diligence, care, loyalty, and skill that ordinarily prudent persons would exercise under similar circumstances in like positions. In this case, the plaintiff alleges that defendants breached their duty of care and duty of loyalty. I shall now give you general instructions on the law concerning the duties of loyalty and care.

COMMENT

It is settled law that corporate officers and directors occupy a fiduciary relationship with the corporation and its shareholders, and are held to the standard of utmost good faith and loyalty. *See* Marshall L. Small, "Transactions in Control and Tender Offers," in 1 *Principles of Corporate Governance: Analysis and Recommendations* pt. IV (A.L.I. 1994); *Corporate Director's Guidebook,* 33 Bus. Law. 1591, 1599-1600 (1978); Dennis J. Block, Michael J. Maimone, and Steven B. Ross, *The Duty of Loyalty and the Evolution of the Scope of Judicial Review,* 59 Brook. L. Rev. 65, 72 (1993); *Jones v. H.F. Ahmanson & Co.,* 460 P.2d 464 (Cal. 1969); *Stephenson v. Drever,* 947 P.2d 1301 (Cal. 1997). *See* (duty of majority shareholder to minority shareholder) *King Mfg. Co. v. Clay,* 118 S.E.2d 581 (Ga. 1961). *See also Quinn v. Cardiovascular Physicians, P.C.,* 326 S.E.2d 460 (Ga. 1985). For a discussion of the duties of care and loyalty and the business opportunity principle, *see Southeast Consultants, Inc. v. McCrary Eng'g Corp.,* 273 S.E.2d 112 (Ga. 1980). *See also* Ga. Code Ann. § 14-2-851 (1997) (corporation may indemnify directors for actions taken in good faith).

7.3.12.a Fiduciary Duty of Loyalty

As officers and directors of [corporation], defendants owed a duty of undivided and unqualified loyalty to [corporation]. The duty of loyalty means essentially that fiduciaries such as the defendants may not put their own personal interests ahead of those of [corporation]—neither in their dealings with [corporation] nor in their dealings with others. Those defendants were required as a result of this duty of loyalty to exercise the utmost good faith in furthering the interests of [corporation] and conserving its property.

COMMENT

Gearhart Indus. v. Smith Int'l, Inc., 741 F.2d 707 (5th Cir. 1984); *Horwitz v. Southwest Forest Indus., Inc.*, 604 F. Supp. 1130 (D. Nev. 1985); *Jones v. H.F. Ahmanson & Co.*, 460 P.2d 464 (Cal. 1969); *FDIC v. Schuchmann*, 235 F.3d 1217, 1223 (10th Cir. 2000); *Jarvis Christian Coll. v. Nat'l Union Fire Ins. Co.*, 197 F.3d 742, 749 (5th Cir. 1999); *GAB Bus. Servs. v. Lindsey & Newsom Claim Servs.*, 83 Cal. App. 4th 409 (Cal. Ct. App. 2000); 3 William M. Fletcher, *Cyclopedia of the Law of Private Corporations* § 838 (rev. perm. ed. 1986).

If appropriate, instruction concerning the disclosure of corporate opportunities may be inserted at the end of this paragraph. Some of the factors to be considered in determining whether a business opportunity is logically related to the corporation's existing or prospective activities are: the relationship of the opportunity to the corporation's business purposes and current activities, whether essential, necessary, or merely desirable to its reasonable needs and aspirations; whether or not the opportunity embraces areas adaptable to the corporation's business and into which it might easily, naturally, or logically expand; the competitive nature of the opportunity; whether or not prospectively harmful or unfair; whether or not the opportunity includes activities as to which the corporation has fundamental knowledge, practical experience, facilities, equipment, personnel, and the ability to pursue; and whether or not the acquisition by the director or officer would defeat plans and purposes of the corporation in carrying on or developing the legitimate business for which it was created. 19 *C.J.S. Corporation* § 513(d) (1990).

7.3.12.b   Duty of Due Care

As officers and directors of [corporation], defendants also had a duty to perform their functions in good faith, in a manner they reasonably believed to be in the best interest of [corporation], and with the care that ordinarily prudent persons would reasonably be expected to exercise in a like position and under similar circumstances. This duty is called the duty of care.

COMMENT

"Although the specific wording of court decisions has varied, they have long required a director or officer to be attentive to the functions and obligations of his position and to make inquiry when the circumstances would alert a reasonable director or officer to the need therefor." Marshall L. Small, "Transactions in Control and Offers," in 1 *Principles of Corporate Governance* pt. IV cmt., § 4.01(a) (1)-(a)(2) (A.L.I. 1994); *see also Briggs v. Spaulding*, 141 U.S. 132 (1891); *Fitzpatrick v. Fed. Deposit Ins. Corp.*, 765 F.2d 569 (6th Cir. 1985). "Sound public policy dictates that directors and officers be given greater protection than courts and commentators using a 'reasonableness' test would afford." Marshall L. Small, "Transactions in Control and Offers," in 1 *Principles of Corporate Governance* pt. IV cmt. f, § 4.01(c) (A.L.I. 1994); *First Nat'l Bank of Lincolnwood v. Keller*, 318 F. Supp. 339 (N.D. Ill. 1970). For a detailed discussion of a corporate fiduciary's duty of good faith, *see Quinn v. Cardiovascular Physicians, P.C.*, 326 S.E.2d 460 (Ga. 1985). *See also Miller v. Miller*, 222 N.W.2d 71 (Minn. 1974) (discussion of business opportunity rule). If appropriate, instruction concerning the failure to pursue a corporate opportunity may be given here. See previous comment regarding corporate opportunity.

7.3.12.c   The Officer's Functions

Plaintiffs and defendants have submitted conflicting evidence concerning the functions of defendants.

An officer's or director's functions are those corporate tasks that the officer or director is responsible for performing.

In this case, to decide whether a defendant has performed the requisite functions in a manner consistent with defendant's duty of care, you must first decide, from the evidence submitted, what functions a particular defendant was responsible for performing.

COMMENT

The issue about whether an officer or director should have been alerted to peculiar circumstances necessarily revolves around the "functions" that typically are ascribed to that officer or director. Marshall L. Small, "Transactions in Control and Tender Offers," in 1 *Principles of Corporate Governance* pt. IV cmt. b, § 4.01(a) (1)-(a)(2) (A.L.I. 1994). *See Hoye v. Meek*, 795 F.2d 893 (10th Cir. 1986) ("[D]irectors and officers are charged with knowledge of those things which it is their duty to know and ignorance is not a basis for escaping liability. Where suspicions are aroused, or should be aroused, it is the director's duty to make necessary inquiries."), *followed by Macklin v. Retirement Plan for Employees of Kan. Gas*, U.S. App. LEXIS 26461 (10th Cir. 1996) ("Though bad faith would undoubtedly constitute a breach of fiduciary duties, good faith alone cannot compensate for the care, skill, prudence and diligence of a reasonably prudent person."); *see also Francis v. United Jersey Bank*, 432 A.2d 814 (N.J. 1981) ("directors are under a continuing obligation to keep informed about the activities of the corporation"); *see also Mulford v. Computer Leasing, Inc.*, 759 A.2d 887 (1999) ("A director cannot protect himself from performance of his legally imposed duties behind a paper shield bearing the motto 'dummy director'.")

7.3.12.d "Under Similar Circumstances" Defined

An officer or director has a duty to perform requisite functions with the care that an ordinarily prudent person would reasonably be expected to exercise in a like position and under similar circumstances.

The phrase "under similar circumstances" recognizes that the nature and extent of the functions and obligations of an officer or director will vary depending upon such factors as the nature of the business, the urgency and magnitude of a problem, and the corporation's size and complexity. In deciding whether defendants have acted with the care that an ordinarily prudent person would reasonably be expected to exercise in a like position, you should take these circumstances into account.

COMMENT

A director or officer, once put on alert, will fail to make a reasonable inquiry if such director or officer does not believe that an adequate inquiry has been made or if the director or officer is unreasonable in believing such officer or director has made all the inquiry that is necessary. Marshall L. Small, "Transactions in Control and Tender Offers," in 1 *Principles of Corporate Governance* pt. IV cmt. b, § 4.01(a)(1)-(a)(2) (A.L.I. 1994); J. F. Rydstrom, Annotation, *Liability of Corporate Directors for Negligence in Permitting Mismanagement or Defalcations by Officers or Employees*, 25 A.L.R. 3d 941 (2001); *see also Briggs v. Spaulding*, 141 U.S. 132 (1891); *McRoberts v. Spaulding*, 32 F.2d 315 (D. Iowa 1929); *Fed. Deposit Ins. Corp. v. Boone*, 361 F. Supp. 133 (W.D. Okla. 1972).

7.3.12.e   "In a Like Position" Defined

For purposes of analyzing the duty of care, the phrase "in a like position" is intended to emphasize that the critical time for the assessment of the performance of an officer or director is the time of the alleged breach of duty. That is, you are to assess an officer's or director's performance as of the time of the alleged act, omission, or failure of oversight. You are not to use the benefit of hindsight in evaluating a director's or officer's performance.

COMMENT

"Among the factors that may have to be taken into account in judging a director's reasonable belief as to what was 'appropriate under the circumstances' are: (i) the importance of the business judgment to be made; (ii) the time available for obtaining information; (iii) the costs related to obtaining information; (iv) the director's confidence in those who explored a matter and those making presentations; and (v) the state of the corporation's business at the time and the nature of competing demands for the board's attention." Marshall L. Small, "Transactions in Control and Tender Offers," in 1 *Principles of Corporate Governance* pt. IV cmt., § 4.01(a) (A.L.I. 1994); *see also Harman v. Willbern*, 374 F. Supp. 1149 (D. Kan. 1974); *McRoberts v. Spaulding*, 32 F.2d 315 (S.D. Iowa 1929); 3A William M. Fletcher, *Cyclopedia of Corporations* § 1030, at 18 (perm. ed. 1975).

7.4 Factors Determining Breach of Fiduciary Duty

7.4.1 The Business Judgment Rule

In determining whether the defendants breached their fiduciary duties as officers and directors of [corporation], the defendants are entitled to a presumption that they acted with sound business judgment. This presumption includes an assumption that the officers and directors acted on an informed basis.

To be entitled to this presumption, the defendants must:

1. not have an undisclosed personal financial interest in the transaction that is the subject of the directors' or officers' business judgment;

2. be informed about the subject of the business judgment to the extent the directors or officers reasonably believe to be appropriate under the circumstances; and

3. reasonably believe that the directors' or officers' business judgment is in the best interest of the corporation.

To prevail in this case, the plaintiffs, who are challenging the conduct of the officers or directors of [corporation], must prove that the officers or directors did not exercise the proper business judgment for one or more of the following reasons: (a) that an officer or director had an undisclosed personal financial interest in the transaction that is the subject of the officer's or director's business judgment, (b) that the officer or director was not informed about the subject of the business judgment to the extent the officer or director reasonably believed to be appropriate under the circumstances, (c) that the officer or director did not rationally believe that such business judgment was in the best interest of the corporation, or (d) that no business judgment was in fact exercised.

COMMENT

Most courts agree that the business judgment rule extends only as far as the reasons that justify its existence, and that it does not apply when the corporate decision lacks a business purpose, involves a conflict of interest, or results from a prolonged failure to exercise oversight or judgment. Marshall L. Small, "Transaction in Control and Tender Offers," in 1 *Principles of Corporate Governance* pt. IV, § 4.01(c) (A.L.I. 1994). *See Joy v. North*, 692 F.2d 880 (2d Cir. 1982), *cert. denied sub nom. Citytrust v. Joy*, 460 U.S. 1051 (1983); *but see Cramer v. Gen. Tel. & Elec. Corp.*, 582 F.2d 259 (3d Cir. 1978) (rationale for business judgment rule is that for corporation to be managed properly and efficiently, directors must be given wide latitude in handling of corporate affairs), *cert. denied*, 439 U.S. 1129 (1979); *Panter v. Marshall Field & Co.*, 646 F.2d 271 (7th Cir. 1981) (argument that directors have improper interest in alleged transactions because they would have to initiate suit against themselves raises no legally cognizable issue under Delaware corporate law), *cert. denied*, 454 U.S. 1092 (1981); *Tabas v. Mullane*, 608 F. Supp. 759 (D.N.J. 1985) (Delaware law); *AC Acquisitions Corp. v. Anderson, Clayton & Co.*, 519 A.2d 103 (Del. 1986). *See also* 1 *Principles of Corporate Governance* pt. IV, § 4.01(d) cmt. f (A.L.I. 1994); *Treadway Cos., Inc. v. Care Corp.*, 638 F.2d 357 (2d Cir. 1980) (under New Jersey law, corporate director possesses same right as other shareholders to deal freely with personally owned shares of stock, provided director acts in good faith); *First Nat'l Bank of Lincolnwood v. Keller*, 318 F. Supp. 339 (N.D. Ill. 1970); S. Samuel Arsht, "The Business Judgment Rule Revisited," 8 Hofstra L. Rev. 93, 130-33 (1979). A majority of states have adopted the Model Business Corporation Act (MBCA). Section 8.30 of the MBCA further defines a corporate director's or officer's duty of care and the business judgment rule.

7.4.2   Sense of Balance and Fairness

The standards set forth in the duty of care should be applied with balance, fairness, and a realistic sense of what may reasonably be expected in given circumstances from a corporation's officers and directors. Your judgment about whether a given officer or director exercised the requisite care when the officer or director is charged with an act, an omission, or a failure of oversight should take into account all relevant circumstances. These may include:

1. whether the problem that allegedly developed because of the claimed act, omission, or failure of oversight was reasonably foreseeable at the time of the alleged act, omission, or failure of oversight;

2. whether the magnitude of the problem that developed was reasonably foreseeable at the time of the alleged act, omission, or failure of oversight;

3. the state of the corporation's business at the time of the alleged act, omission, or failure of oversight;

4. the state of the economy or areas of the economy at the time of the alleged act, omission, or failure of oversight;

5. the policies of regulatory authorities at the time of the alleged act, omission, or failure of oversight;

6. the complexity and scale of the corporation at the time of the alleged act, omission, or failure of oversight;

7. the policies of the board of directors and committees of the board at the time of the alleged act, omission, or failure of oversight;

8. the reliability of, and confidence to be placed in, other directors, officers, employees, experts, and other persons and committees of the board;

9. the precise role the officer or director played within the corporation at the time of the alleged act, omission, or failure of oversight; and

10. other relevant circumstances.

COMMENT

See comment to section, below; cmt.; Marshall L. Small, "Transactions in Control and Tender Offers," in 1 *Principles of Corporate Governance* pt. IV cmt. h, § 4.01(a) (A.L.I. 1994); *McRoberts v. Spaulding*, 32 F.2d 315 (S.D. Iowa 1929).

7.4.3   Custom, Practice, and Procedures

In determining whether an officer or director of a corporation breached the requisite duty of care, it is proper for you to consider the custom, practice, and procedures of similar corporations.

COMMENT

For example, under Oklahoma law, custom and usage of similar banks are properly considered by the trier of fact in determining duties of bank directors. *Fed. Deposit Ins. Corp. v. Boone*, 361 F. Supp. 133 (W.D. Okla. 1972); *see also McRoberts v. Spaulding*, 32 F.2d 315 (S.D. Iowa 1928); *Wheeler v. Aiken County Loan & Sav. Bank*, 75 F. 781 (D.S.C. 1896).

7.4.4 Duty to Supervise

An officer's or director's duty of care to the corporation includes the duty to use reasonable care in supervising other officers and employees over whom the officer or director has supervisory responsibility.

A director or officer is not an insurer of the fidelity and proper conduct of other directors, officers, and employees, and a director or officer is not liable for losses resulting from the wrongful acts or omissions of such persons, provided the director or officer has exercised ordinary care in discharging the director's or officer's own duties by exercising reasonable supervision over such persons and using reasonable care in their appointment.

COMMENT

See Fields v. Sax, 462 N.E.2d 983 (Ill. App. Ct. 1989) (*citing Briggs v. Spaulding*, 141 U.S. 132 (1891)); *Francis v. United Jersey Bank*, 392 A.2d 1233 (N.J. Super. Ct. Law Div. 1978), *aff'd*, 432 A.2d 814 (N.J. 1981); *In re Caremark Int'l Inc. Deriv. Litig.*, 698 A.2d 959 (Del. Ch. 1996); 3A William M. Fletcher, *Cyclopedia of the Law of Private Corporations*, §§ 1066, 1070 (1986).

7.4.5   Reliance on Subordinates and Delegation

Officers and directors are entitled to rely upon the honesty and integrity of their subordinates until something occurs to put them on notice that something is wrong.

It is also not a breach of duty for an officer or director to delegate responsibility to other officers or directors whose general business insight was confirmed by past service or reputation and when there was no reason to suspect them of mismanagement or wrongdoing.

COMMENT

See Harman v. Willbern, 374 F. Supp. 1149 (D. Kan. 1974), *aff'd*, 520 F.2d. 1333 (10th Cir. 1975); *Graham v. Allis-Chalmers Mfg. Co.*, 188 A.2d 125 (Del. 1963); J. F. Rydstrom, Annotation, *Liability of Corporate Directors for Negligence in Permitting Mismanagement or Defalcations by Officers or Employees*, 25 A.L.R. 3d 941 Supp. §§ 8, 12, 22 (2001).

7.4.6 Reliance on Information Prepared by Others

In performing the required functions, an officer or director who acts in good faith and reasonably believes that such reliance is warranted is entitled to rely on information, opinions, reports, and statements (including financial statements and other financial data), as well as decisions, judgments, or performance, prepared, presented, made, or performed by:

1. one or more directors, officers, or employees of the corporation, whom the director or officer reasonably believes merits confidence; or

2. lawyers, public accountants, engineers, appraisers, or other persons whom the director or officer reasonably believes merit confidence.

COMMENT

"A right to rely is authorized by either legislative provisions or by court decisions in almost all jurisdictions." Marshall L. Small, "Transactions in Control and Tender Offers," in 1 *Principles of Corporate Governance* pt. IV cmt., § 4.02 (A.L.I. 1994). *See* O.C.G.A § 14-2-830; *see also Graham v. Allis-Chalmers Mfg. Co.*, 188 A.2d 125 (Del. 1963); *Harman v. Willbern*, 374 F. Supp. 1149 (D. Kan. 1974), *aff'd*, 520 F.2d 1333 (10th Cir. 1975).

7.4.7 Violation of Regulations of Governmental Agencies

A violation of the regulations of a governmental agency does not, in and of itself, make a director or officer liable for any losses sustained by the corporation. Although conduct that violates a regulation may be considered, your decision about whether a defendant breached such duty must be based on all facts and the entire circumstances in the case as you shall find them.

COMMENT

See Lester v. John R. Jurgensen Co., 400 F.2d 393 (6th Cir. 1968) (Ohio law); *FDIC v. Schuchmann*, 235 F.3d 1217, 1224 (10th Cir. 2000) (New Mexico Law); *Restatement (Second) of Torts* § 286 cmt. d, § 288 cmts. b, c (1965). Oftentimes officers and directors are charged with violating a rule or regulation of a governmental agency and the plaintiff argues that such a violation constitutes "negligence per se" and hence a breach of fiduciary duty. This instruction is meant to advise the jury that such conduct alone is not enough to find a breach of fiduciary duty.

7.4.8   Violation of Internal Policies

A violation of the corporation's internal rules and regulations with regard to policy and procedure does not, without more, make a director or officer liable for losses sustained by the corporation. The law imposes liability for lack of diligence in the conduct of the officer's or director's duties; however, it does not make him or her an insurer of the success of all ventures merely because corporate procedures are ignored.

COMMENT

First Nat'l Bank of Lincolnwood v. Keller, 318 F. Supp. 339 (N.D. Ill. 1970) (citing *Hoehn v. Crews*, 144 F.2d 665 (10th Cir. 1944), *aff'd. sub nom. Garber v. Crews*, 324 U.S. 200 (1945)). This instruction is meant to advise the jury that such conduct alone is not enough to find a breach of fiduciary duty. *See also Larimore v. Comptroller of Currency*, 789 F.2d 1244 (7th Cir. 1986); *but see Cache Nat'l Bank v. Hinman*, 626 F. Supp. 1341 (D. Colo. 1986) (directors who fail to investigate acceptance of loans may be held responsible for loss as having committed intentional violation of National Bank Act, 12 U.S.C. § 93).

7.4.9 Concluding Instruction on the Duty of Care

In light of the previous instructions on the duty of care, you should decide whether a defendant, through actions or omissions, breached the duty of care to the corporation. Unless you find that a defendant breached the duty of care, the defendant did not breach such fiduciary duty to the plaintiff and is not liable for any losses that the plaintiff may have suffered.

COMMENT

About 37 states have now enacted duty-of-care statutory provisions. Common law is the source of duty-of-care standards in about 13 states. *In re Caremark Int'l Inc. Deriv. Litig.*, 698 A.2d 959 (Del. Ch. 1996); *Cinerama, Inc. v. Technicolor, Inc.*, 663 A.2d 1156 (Del. 1995) ("The business judgment rule operates as both a procedural guide for litigants and a substantive rule of law."). *See also* J. F. Rydstrom, Annotation, *Liability of Corporate Directors for Negligence in Permitting Mismanagement or Defalcations by Officers or Employees*, 25 A.L.R. 3d 941, Supp. § 18 (2001); *Hanson Trust PLC v. ML SCM Acquisition, Inc.*, 781 F.2d 264 (2d Cir. 1986).

7.5   Causation—Generally

If you find that any defendant breached a fiduciary duty to the plaintiff, you should then decide whether that breach proximately caused any losses claimed by the plaintiff.

I shall now instruct you on the law and burden of proof regarding proximate cause.

COMMENT

Restatement (Second) of Torts §§ 431, 432, 442B (1965); Marshall L. Small, "Transactions in Control and Tender Offers," in 2 *Principles of Corporate Governance* pt. VII, § 7.18 (A.L.I. 1994); *see also Michelsen v. Penney, et al.*, 135 F.2d 409 (2d Cir. 1943) (in suit against bank director for bank loss occasioned by director's negligence in violation of National Bank Act, act presented standard of care required, which was controlling test of negligence and provided for remuneration of those who suffered loss).

7.5.1 Elements of Causation and Burden of Proof

To find a defendant liable for breach of fiduciary duty, the breach must have caused plaintiff some damage. A defendant's breach is the cause of damage only when (1) the plaintiff has sustained or will sustain a loss of some type, (2) the defendant's act or omission was the cause-in-fact of the loss sustained, and (3) the defendant's act or omission was the legal cause of the loss sustained. Plaintiff bears the burden of proving all three of these elements.

COMMENT

See William L. Prosser, *Law of Torts* § 41, at 238 (4th ed. 1971); *Restatement (Second) of Torts* §§ 431, 432, 442B cmt. b; Marshall L. Small, "Transactions in Control and Tender Offers," in 1 *Principles of Corporate Governance* pt. VII cmt. d, § 7.18 (A.L.I. 1994). *See generally* Edward Brodsky & M. Patricia Adamski, *Law of Corporate Officers and Directors*, § 2.13 (1984). *See also Hanson Trust, PLC v. ML SCM Acquisition, Inc.*, 781 F.2d 264 (2d Cir. 1986); Jay P. Moran, *Comment: Business Judgment Rule or Relic?: Cede v. Technicolor and the Continuing Metamorphosis of Director Duty of Care*, 45 Emory L.J. 339 (1996).

7.5.2   Existence of Damage

An act, even if wrongful, may or may not cause an injury and if it causes no injury, there can be no liability. Consequently, plaintiffs must prove that they have suffered or will suffer such injury to recover damages. Otherwise there can be no liability for breach of a fiduciary duty, and you must find for the defendants.

COMMENT

See Marshall L. Small, "Transactions in Control and Tender Offers," in 2 *Principles of Corporate Governance* pt. VII cmts. a-e, § 7.18 (A.L.I. 1994); *see also First Nat'l Bank of Lincolnwood v. Keller,* 318 F. Supp. 339 (N.D. Ill. 1970); *Barnes v. Andrews,* 298 F. 614 (S.D.N.Y. 1924); *Francis v. United Jersey Bank,* 432 A.2d 814 (N.J. 1981); *Kahle v. Mt. Vernon Trust Co.,* 22 N.Y.S.2d 454 (N.Y. Sup. Ct. 1940); Patricia A. McCoy, *Article: A Political Economy of the Business Judgment Rule in Banking: Implications for Corporate Law,* 47 Case W. Res. 1 (1996).

7.5.3   Cause-in-Fact

To prove that a breach of fiduciary duty was the cause-in-fact of the plaintiff's injury, the plaintiff must establish not only that it has suffered some loss, but also that such loss could have been avoided if the defendants had performed their fiduciary duties as required.

You must weigh the evidence presented by both sides and decide whether plaintiffs have met their burden of proving that the loss could have been prevented if the defendants had performed their duties properly. If the defendants could not have prevented the losses, then they are not liable for those losses.

COMMENT

William L. Prosser, *Law of Torts* § 41, at 238 (4th ed. 1971); Marshall L. Small, "Transactions in Control and Tender Offers," in 2 *Principles of Corporate Governance* pt. VII cmt. d, § 7.18 (A.L.I. 1994); *see also Barnes v. Andrews*, 298 F. 614, 617 (D.N.Y. 1924); *Francis v. United Jersey Bank*, 432 A.2d 814 (N.J. 1981); Jacqueline M. Veneziani, *Note & Comment: Causation and Injury in Corporate Control Transactions: Cede & Co. v. Technicolor, Inc.*, 69 Wash. L. Rev. 1167 (1994).

7.5.4   Legal Cause

If you find that plaintiffs have proved the existence of damages and cause-in-fact, then you must decide whether plaintiffs have proved that defendants' acts or omissions were the "legal cause" of plaintiffs' injuries or losses. The issue you must decide under this element is whether the relationship between the defendants' acts or omissions and the losses sustained by plaintiffs is sufficiently close to attribute the losses to the defendants. Plaintiffs must prove two things to show legal cause: (1) that the defendants' acts or omissions were substantial factors in bringing about the loss, and (2) that the likelihood of injury would have been foreseeable to persons in the defendants' positions under similar circumstances.

You must weigh the evidence and decide whether defendants' acts or omissions were substantial factors in bringing about the losses and, if so, whether the losses sustained were reasonably foreseeable to persons in the defendants' positions. If you find that plaintiffs have not proven both elements, there can be no liability for any losses that may have been sustained by plaintiffs, and you must find for the defendants.

COMMENT

Marshall L. Small, "Transactions in Control and Tender Offers," in 2 *Principles of Corporate Governance* pt. VII cmt. d, § 7.18 (A.L.I. 1994); *Restatement (Second) of Torts* §§ 431, 432 (1965); William L. Prosser, *Law of Torts* § 41, at 240 (4th ed. 1971); *see, e.g., E.F. Hutton Mortgage Corp. v. Pappas,* 690 F. Supp. 1465 (D. Md. 1988) (applying Maryland law); *Francis v. United Jersey Bank,* 432 A.2d 814 (N.J. 1981) (applying New Jersey law); Jay P. Moran, *Comment: Business Judgment Rule or Relic?: Cede v. Technicolor and the Continuing Metamorphosis of Director Duty of Care,* 45 Emory L.J. 339 (1996).

7.5.5 "Foreseeable"—Defined

Something is said to be foreseeable when it can be seen or known in advance; in other words, when it is reasonable to anticipate that something is a likely result of an act, omission, or failure of oversight. The law requires you to consider foreseeability because a person is not responsible for a consequence that is merely possible. A person is responsible only for a consequence that is probable according to ordinary and usual experience.

COMMENT

Black's Law Dictionary 332 (abridged 5th ed. 1983); William L. Prosser, *Law of Torts* § 41 (4th ed. 1971).

7.5.6   Unforeseeable Events

Unforeseen and unforeseeable events may include events beyond those attributable to the actions of a person or an entity. These may include:

1. the state of the economy or areas of the economy;

2. changes in a particular industry;

3. disruptions in a business that are attributable to causes outside the control of the defendant; and

4. acts of nature.

COMMENT

See Raines v. Colt Indus., Inc., 757 F. Supp. 819 (E.D. Mich. 1991) (unforeseeable intervening cause breaks chain of causation and constitutes superseding cause that leaves alleged tortfeasor free of liability); *Restatement (Second) of Torts* §§ 440, 442 (1965). *But see T.M. Doyle Teaming Co., Inc. v. Freels*, 735 F. Supp. 777 (N.D. Ill. 1990) (intervening agency not sole proximate cause of injury if circumstances surrounding intervention were such as could reasonably have been expected to occur in ordinary course of events as indicated by common experience).

7.5.7 Plaintiff's Negligence as a Superseding Cause

From the evidence presented, you must decide whether plaintiff's conduct was negligent and, if so, whether that negligence was the immediate cause of any losses. If you so find, then defendants are relieved of liability unless:

1. at the time of the defendants' conduct defendants realized or should have realized that the plaintiff might act as he or she did; or that

2. a reasonable person knowing the situation existing at the time of the conduct of the plaintiff would not have regarded their conduct as highly extraordinary; or that

3. the conduct of the plaintiff was not extraordinarily negligent and was a normal consequence of the situation created by the defendants.

COMMENT

See Restatement (Second) of Torts §§ 442-453 (1977); *E.F. Hutton Mortgage Corp. v. Pappas,* 690 F. Supp. 1465 (D. Md. 1988); *Fed. Deposit Ins. Corp. v. Carter,* 701 F. Supp. 730 (C.D. Cal. 1987); *but see Fed. Deposit Ins. Corp. v. Buker,* 739 F. Supp. 1401 (C.D. Cal. 1990) (criticizing *Carter* and dismissing defendants' affirmative defenses alleging contributory negligence by FDIC).

7.5.8 "Negligence"—Defined

Negligence is the doing of some act that a reasonably prudent person would not do, or the failure to do something that a reasonably prudent person would do, when prompted by considerations that ordinarily regulate the conduct of human affairs. It is, in other words, the failure to use ordinary care, under the circumstances, in the management of one's person or property, or of agencies under one's control.

COMMENT

3 Devitt, Blackmar & Wolff, *Federal Jury Practice and Instructions* § 80.03 (1987); *Fane v. Zimmer, Inc.*, 927 F.2d 124 (2d Cir. 1991) (negligence is conduct that falls below standard of what reasonably prudent person would do under similar circumstances, judged at time of conduct at issue); *see also Needham v. White Lab., Inc.*, 847 F.2d 355 (7th Cir. 1988) (negligence is failure to take level of precautions commensurate with likelihood of magnitude of risk created by defendant's conduct; the greater the benefits of precaution, the more precautions must be taken).

7.5.9 Third Party's Intentionally Tortious Act as a Superseding Cause

The act of a third person in committing an intentional tort or a crime can be a superseding cause that relieves a defendant of liability. This is true even when the defendant's conduct created a situation that afforded the third person an opportunity to commit such a tort or crime, unless the defendant realized or should have realized at the time of such conduct the likelihood that such a situation might be created and that a third person might avail himself or herself of the opportunity to commit such a tort or crime. From the instructions I will now give you on the elements of [crime or intentional tort alleged], you must decide whether any act of a third person relieves defendants of liability.

COMMENT

"For example, a defendant could allege that the fraud of certain borrowers and lead lenders was a superseding cause and thereby relieves the defendant of liability." [AUTHORS - PLEASE AT-TRIBUTE QUOTATION - COULD NOT FIND IN ANY OF FOL-LOWING CITATIONS. - EDS.] This instruction is based on section 448 of the *Restatement (Second) of Torts* (1965). *See Fed. Deposit Ins. Corp. v. Imperial Bank*, 859 F.2d 101 (9th Cir. 1988) (applying California law); *E.F. Hutton Mortgage Corp. v. Pappas*, 690 F. Supp. 1465 (D. Md. 1988).

7.6   Damages—Generally

I will next instruct you on damages. You must not take these instructions as implying my view about which party is entitled to your verdict in this case. Instructions regarding the measure of damages are given for your guidance in the event you find in favor of plaintiffs from a preponderance of evidence in the case in accordance with the other instructions.

COMMENT

Bray v. Safeway Stores, Inc., 392 F. Supp. 851 (N.D. Cal. 1975).

7.6.1   Compensatory Damages

If, under the instructions I have given you, you find that the plaintiff is entitled to a verdict against a defendant or defendants, then you may award the plaintiff damages in an amount that will reasonably compensate him or her for his or her losses, provided you find that such loss was or will be suffered by him or her and was proximately caused by the act or omission upon which you base the defendants' liability.

COMMENT

Marshall L. Small, "Transactions in Control and Tender Offers," in 2 *Principles of Corporate Governance* pt. VII cmts. a-e, § 7.18 (A.L.I. 1994); 3 William M. Fletcher, *Cyclopedia of the Law of Private Corporations* § 838 (1994). *See, e.g., Lincoln Nat'l Life Ins. Co. v. NCR Corp.,* 603 F. Supp. 1393 (N.D. Ind. 1984) (to recover damages, plaintiffs have burden of proving they suffered damages), *aff'd,* 772 F.2d 315 (7th Cir. 1985); *Tom Shaw, Inc. v. Derektor,* 639 F. Supp. 1064 (D.R.I. 1986) (apart from issue of liability, to recover in negligence action plaintiff has burden of proving damages by fair preponderance of the evidence, and damages are not to be presumed).

7.6.2   Reasonable Damages Not Speculative

Damages must be reasonable. If you find that the plaintiff is entitled to a verdict, you may award him or her only the amount of damages necessary to compensate him or her reasonably for any losses caused by the defendants' alleged breach of duty. The plaintiff must prove by a preponderance of the evidence that such losses were sustained as a proximate result of the alleged breach of duty.

You are not permitted to award speculative damages. This means that you may not include any compensation in the verdict for any prospective loss that, although possible, is not reasonably certain to happen in the future. From the evidence presented, you must decide what losses are reasonably certain to occur and you may award damages for those losses only.

COMMENT

See Johnson v. Miller, 596 F. Supp. 768 (D.C. Colo. 1984); *see also Far W. Fed. Bank, S.B. v. Dir., Office of Thrift Supervision*, 787 F. Supp. 952 (D. Or. 1992); *Far W. Fed. Bank, S.B. v. Office of Thrift Supervision*, 119 F.3d 1358 (9th Cir. 1997).

7.6.3   Duty to Mitigate

Any person who claims damages as a result of an alleged wrongful act on the part of another has a duty under the law to "mitigate" those damages. This means that the person allegedly harmed must take advantage of any reasonable opportunity the person allegedly harmed may have had under the circumstances to reduce or minimize the loss or damage.

If you find that the plaintiff, to minimize the plaintiff's loss, failed to seek out or take advantage of opportunities that were reasonably available to the plaintiff under the circumstances, then you must reduce the amount of the plaintiff's damages by the amount the plaintiff could have reasonably gained if the plaintiff had taken advantage of such opportunity. The defendant bears the burden of proving that the plaintiff failed to mitigate plaintiff's damages.

COMMENT

See Bloomfield Fin. Co. v. Nat'l Home Life Assurance Co., 734 F.2d 1408 (10th Cir. 1984); *but see Fed. Deposit Ins. Corp. v. Baker*, 739 F. Supp. 1401 (C.D. Cal. 1990) (holding regulators owed duty to public and not to defendant directors, officers, and outside appraisers of state-chartered, federally insured savings and loan); *Life Care Ctrs. of Am. v. Charles Town Assocs. Ltd. P'ship*, 79 F.3d 496 (6th Cir. 1996); *Ford v. GACS, Inc.*, 265 F.3d 670 (8th Cir. 2001).

7.6.4 Damages Not Apportioned

Even if you find that the plaintiff is entitled to recover damages against more than one defendant, you must return a verdict in a single sum against all defendants you find to be liable. That is, there is only one loss to the plaintiff and correspondingly only one damage award. Therefore, even if you find more than one defendant liable, you are not to divide the damages among the defendants. Rather, you must return one damage award against all those you find liable.

COMMENT

See 3 William M. Fletcher, *Cyclopedia of the Law of Private Corporations* § 1002, at 716 (perm. ed. 1994).

7.6.5 Punitive Damages

7.6.5.a Decision to Award Punitive Damages

If you find for the plaintiff and against the defendant and you have determined that the defendant must pay damages, then you should consider whether the conduct that led to your decision also subjects the defendant to punitive damages. To award punitive damages, you must find that the defendant's conduct that proximately caused actual [or nominal] damages to the plaintiff was the result of actual malice, wanton conduct, or oppressive conduct, as measured by the instructions I will give you.

COMMENT

This charge represents the modern view of damages. *See, e.g., State Farm Mut. Auto. Ins. Co. v. Campbell,* 538 U.S. 408 (2003); *Rabun v. Kimberly-Clark Corp.,* 678 F.2d 1053 (11th Cir. 1982); *Christman v. Voyer,* 595 P.2d 410 (N.M. Ct. App. 1979); *Wussow v. Commercial Mechanisms, Inc.,* 279 N.W.2d 503 (Wis. Ct. App. 1979); *Restatement (Second) of Torts* § 908 (1979); 45 Am. Jur. 2d *Interference* § 62 (1999 & Supp.2003). Counsel should note that although generally punitive damages will be awarded upon a showing of malice, wantonness, or oppressiveness, this principle is not universal and may as well be affected by statute in a particular jurisdiction.

Most states require that the jury find liability and actual, or at least nominal, damages before punitive damages are allowed. *See* Richard C. Tinney, Annotation, *Showing of Actual Damages to Support Award of Punitive Damages,* 40 A.L.R. 4th 11 (1985 & Supp. 2002); 45 Am. Jur. 2d *Interference* § 62 (1999 & Supp. 2003); *Am. Bus. Interiors, Inc. v. Haworth, Inc.,* 798 F.2d 1135 (8th Cir. 1986). *But see Platte v. Whitney Realty Co.,* 538 So. 2d 1358 (Fla. Dist. Ct. App. 1989) (punitive damages recoverable although actual damages could not be proved). For a discussion of the prerequisite of a verdict for actual damages, see the comment to § 7.6.5.b *infra*. For the requirement of malicious, wanton, or oppressive conduct, see §§ 7.6.5.c, 7.6.5.d, and 7.6.5.e *infra*.

7.6.5.b   Nominal Damages

The award of only a nominal sum with respect to the specific losses claimed by the plaintiff will not prevent your awarding punitive damages if you find that the award of punitive damages is justified under these instructions.

COMMENT

In most states the jury must make a finding of liability and actual, or at least nominal, damages before punitive damages are allowed. *See* Richard C. Tinney, Annotation, *Showing of Actual Damages to Support Award of Punitive Damages*, 40 A.L.R. 4th 11 (1985 & Supp. 2002); 45 Am. Jur. 2d *Interference* § 62 (1999 & Supp. 2003); *Am. Bus. Interiors, Inc. v. Haworth, Inc.*, 798 F.2d 1135 (8th Cir. 1986). *But see Platte v. Whitney Realty Co.*, 538 So. 2d 1358 (Fla. Dist. Ct. App. 1989) (punitive damages recoverable although actual damages could not be proved).

In most jurisdictions, an award of nominal damages will suffice for this purpose. *See, e.g., Taylor v. Sandoval*, 442 F. Supp. 491 (D. Colo. 1977); *Tennant v. Vazquez*, 389 So. 2d 1183 (Fla. Dist. Ct. App. 1980); *Christman v. Voyer*, 595 P.2d 410 (N.M. Ct. App. 1979). *But see Wussow v. Commercial Mechanisms, Inc.*, 279 N.W.2d 503 (Wis. Ct. App. 1979). *See generally* Richard C. Tinney, Annotation, *Showing of Actual Damages to Support Award of Punitive Damages—Modern Cases*, 40 A.L.R. 4th 11 (1985 & Supp. 2002).

7.6.5.c   Actual Malice

You may find the defendants' conduct to have been undertaken with actual "malice" sufficient to enable you to award punitive damages if you find it to have been prompted or accompanied by personal ill will, spite, or hatred, either toward the plaintiff individually or toward all persons in one or more groups or categories of which the plaintiff is a member.

COMMENT

Generally, courts require proof of facts tending to establish actual, as opposed to legal, malice to justify an award of punitive damages. *See* 45 Am. Jur. 2d *Interference* § 62 (1999 & Supp. 2003); *Norwood Easthill Assocs. v. Norwood Easthill Watch*, 536 A.2d 1317 (N.J. Super. Ct. App. Div. 1988); *Anthony Pools, Inc. v. Charles & David, Inc.*, 797 S.W.2d 666 (Tex. App. 1990); *Bellefonte Underwriters Co., Inc. v. Brown*, 663 S.W.2d 562 (Tex. App. 1984). Even if not required, actual malice is always an important factor in an award of punitive damages. *See, e.g., Universal City Studios, Inc. v. Nintendo Co.*, 615 F. Supp. 838 (S.D.N.Y. 1985), *aff'd*, 797 F.2d 70 (2d Cir.), *cert. denied*, 479 U.S. 987 (1986); *Int'l Wood Processors Corp. v. Power Dry, Inc.*, 593 F. Supp. 710 (D.S.C. 1984); *Edward Vantine Studios, Inc. v. Fraternal Composite Serv., Inc.*, 373 N.W.2d 512 (Iowa Ct. App. 1985).

7.6.5.d   Wanton Conduct

You may also award punitive damages if you find that the defendants' conduct was "wanton," that is, that the conduct was undertaken in reckless or callous disregard of, or indifference to, the rights of one or more persons, including the plaintiff.

COMMENT

See King v. G.D. Van Wagenen Co., 717 F. Supp. 667 (D. Minn. 1989); *Liston v. Home Ins. Co.*, 659 F. Supp. 276 (S.D. Miss. 1986); *Universal City Studios, Inc. v. Nintendo Co.*, 615 F. Supp. 838 (S.D.N.Y. 1985), *aff'd*, 797 F.2d 70 (2d Cir.), *cert. denied*, 479 U.S. 987 (1986); *Ramona Manor Convalescent Hosp. v. Care Enterprises*, 225 Cal. Rptr. 120 (Cal. Ct. App. 1986).

7.6.5.e   Oppressive Conduct

You also may award punitive damages if, from all of the evidence, you find that the defendants' conduct was "oppressive," that is, that the conduct was done in a way or manner that injured, damaged, or otherwise violated the rights of the plaintiff with unnecessary harshness or severity, as by misuse or abuse of authority or power, or by taking advantage of some weakness, disability, or misfortune of the plaintiff.

COMMENT

See Barnes Group, Inc. v. C & C Prod., Inc., 716 F.2d 1023 (4th Cir. 1983); *Rabun v. Kimberly-Clark Corp.,* 678 F.2d 1053 (11th Cir. 1982); *Int'l Wood Processors Corp. v. Power Dry, Inc.,* 593 F. Supp. 710 (D.S.C. 1984), *aff'd,* 792 F.2d 416 (4th Cir. 1986).

7.6.5.f   Amount of Punitive Damages Award

If you decide that punitive damages are appropriate in this case based upon my prior instructions, you should award the amount of punitive damages that, in your sound judgment, will justly punish the defendants for their behavior and dissuade the defendants and others from acting the same way in future, similar situations.

In fixing the amount of punitive damages, you may consider the following factors:

1. the character of the defendants' act(s);

2. the nature and extent of the harm to the plaintiff that the defendants caused or intended to cause; and

3. the defendants' financial condition.

The amount of any punitive damages should bear a reasonable relationship to the injury, harm, or damage caused by the defendants. You must also keep in mind that the amount of such punitive damages, when awarded, must be fixed with calm discretion and sound reason. Punitive damages must not be awarded, or fixed in amount, based upon any sympathy, bias, or prejudice you may feel toward any party in the case.

[If evidence of "other acts" or harm against other parties has been allowed, add the following: Some of the evidence you have heard concerned conduct by the defendant that was not the proximate cause of the damages claimed by the plaintiff in this case. Although you may consider this evidence for any bearing upon the defendants' state of mind in causing damages claimed by the plaintiff in this case, you are not to punish the defendants for conduct relating only to parties other than the plaintiff.]

[If evidence of the defendants' financial condition has been allowed, add the following: You have heard evidence of the defendants' financial condition. You are not to consider the defendants' financial condition in deciding whether to award punitive damages, but you may consider it in fixing the amount of punitive damages to the extent that the actual [or nominal] damages are insufficient to justly punish the defendants for their behavior or dissuade the defendants or others from acting the same way in future, similar situations.]

COMMENT

See State Farm Mut. Auto. Ins. Co. v. Campbell, 538 U.S. 408 (2003); *Cooper Indus., Inc. v. Leatherman Tool Group, Inc.*, 121 S. Ct. 1678 (2001); *BMW of N. Am., Inc. v. Gore*, 116 S. Ct. 1589 (1996); *Jannotta v. Subway Sandwich Shops, Inc.*, 125 F.3d 503 (7th Cir. 1997); *Fed, Deposit Ins. Corp. v. W.R. Grace & Co.*, 877 F.2d 614 (7th Cir. 1989), *cert. denied*, 110 S. Ct. 1524 (1990); *Aldrich v. Thomson McKinnon Sec., Inc.*, 756 F.2d 243 (2d Cir. 1985); Damages—Modern Cases, 40 A.L.R. 4th 11 (1985 & Supp. 2002).

A state may not impose damages on a defendant for actions undertaken in other states that do not violate the other states' laws. *BMW*, 116 S. Ct at 1597 (1996). Similarly, a "defendant's dissimilar acts, independent from the acts upon which liability was premised, may not serve as the basis for punitive damages." *State Farm*, 123 S. Ct. 1523.

A defendant's financial condition as a factor in setting punitive damages is generally accepted. *See, e.g., Miller v. Rukoff-Sexton, Inc.*, 845 F.2d 209 (9th Cir. 1988) (the defendant's net worth was admissible for setting punitive damages); *Hollins v. Powell*, 773 F.2d 191 (8th Cir.) (reducing punitive damage award in light of defendant's limited resources), *cert. denied*, 475 U.S. 1119 (1985); *Rupert v. Sellers*, 368 N.Y.S.2d 904 (N.Y. App. Div. 1975) (in bifurcated trial, evidence of the defendants' net worth should be considered after special verdict). *See generally* Annotation, *Punitive Damages: Relationship to Defendant's Wealth As a Factor in Determining Propriety of Award*, 87 A.L.R. 4th 141 (1991 & Supp. 2002). Some states, such as Hawaii, even have statutes making the financial condition of the defendant relevant to the amount of punitive damages awardable. Others, like New York, protect the defendant from possible prejudice at trial through the use of a bifurcated trial procedure. *See Aldrich v. Thomson McKinnon Sec.,*

Inc., 589 F. Supp. 683 (S.D.N.Y. 1984). However, the Supreme Court has cautioned that the financial condition of the defendant may not be used to create bias against big businesses or to permit an award that is unrelated to the actual damages. *State Farm,* 123 S. Ct. at 1525 ("the wealth of a defendant cannot justify an otherwise unconstitutional punitive damage award."). Recent commentators have argued that the defendant's financial condition is only relevant in cases involving non-economically motivated torts. *See, e.g.,* Andrew L. Frey, *No More Blind Man's Bluff on Punitive Damages: A Plea to the Drafters of Pattern Jury Instructions,* 29 Litig. 24 (Summer 2003). In cases where the defendant was motivated by profits, they argue, compensatory damages are sufficient to act as a deterrent. *Id.*

Chapter Eight
Misappropriation of Trade Secrets

Daniel J. Gleason*

---

* Daniel J. Gleason is a partner at Nutter McClennen & Fish LLP, World Trade Center West, 155 Seaport Blvd., Boston, MA 02210, and may be reached at (617) 439-2000 or dgleason@nutter.com.

8.1   Introduction

Although there has been no sea change in the law of trade secrets misappropriation since the last edition of this book, continuing evolution has brought the law into closer correspondence with policies outlined in the Uniform Trade Secrets Act (14 U.L.A. 437 (1990 & Supp. 1992) [hereinafter UTSA]). The UTSA has been enacted, with modifications, by 44 states and the District of Columbia. Only five states—Massachusetts, New Jersey, New York, Pennsylvania, and Texas—follow the increasingly outmoded common law of trade secrets as set forth in the *Restatement of Torts* § 757, cmts. (1939).[1]

In 1995, the American Law Institute enacted sections 39 to 45 of the *Restatement (Third) of Unfair Competition*. These new sections purport to replace section 757 of the *Restatement of Torts* and to apply to both statutory and common law. Notwithstanding, courts following the common law continue to cite with frequency the old *Restatement* provisions.

In several key areas, the new *Restatement* aligns itself with the UTSA, departing from the previous *Restatement*. For example, the new *Restatement* does not require a trade secret to be continuously used in a business to warrant protection. Also, under section 40 of the new *Restatement*, improper acquisition alone is an actionable misappropriation; it is not necessary to show either use or disclosure of the trade secret. Section 45 of the new *Restatement* also permits a plaintiff to recover *both* the plaintiff's pecuniary loss *and* the defendant's pecuniary gain, so long as there is no double recovery. In addition, the new *Restatement* does not limit the award of a reasonable royalty only to cases

---

1. Wyoming is the only state that has neither explicitly followed section 757 nor adopted a version of the UTSA. Nonetheless, Wyoming does protect trade secrets information and appears to follow the common law definition of trade secret, embodied in the *Restatement of Torts*. *See* Campen v. Stone, 635 P.2d 1121 (Wyo. 1981); Ridley v. Krout, 180 P.2d 124 (Wyo. 1947).

where other forms of damages cannot be determined. *Restatement (Third) of Unfair Competition* § 45 cmt. g. (1995).

Given the growing predominance of the UTSA approach to trade secrets and analogs in the *Restatement (Third) of Unfair Competition*, this chapter provides model jury instructions that are based on the UTSA, as it has been applied by courts nationwide. While differences in application of the UTSA among states will be noted, distinctions for the five non-UTSA states are addressed only in footnotes.

The following states have adopted a form of the UTSA: Alabama, Ala. Code § 8-27-1 et seq. (1993) (effective Aug. 12, 1987); Alaska, Alaska Stat. § 45.50.910 et seq. (Michie 1995) (effective Sept. 2, 1988); Arizona, Ariz. Rev. Stat. § 44-401 et seq. (1994) (effective Apr. 11, 1990); Arkansas, Ark. Code Ann. § 4-75-601 et seq. (Michie 1994) (effective Mar. 12, 1981); California, Cal. Civ. Code § 3426 et seq. (Deering 1970 & Supp. 1996) (effective Jan. 1, 1985); Colorado, Colo. Rev. Stat. § 7-74-101 et seq. (1990 & Supp. 1995) (effective July 1, 1986); Connecticut, Conn. Gen. Stat. § 35-50 et seq. (1987 & Supp. 1996) (approved June 23, 1983); Delaware, Del. Code Ann. tit. 6, § 2001 et seq. (1993) (effective Apr. 15, 1982); District of Columbia, D.C. Code Ann. § 36-401 et seq. (1990) (effective Mar. 16, 1989); Florida, Fla. Stat. Ann. § 688.1 et seq. (West 1984 & Supp. 1988) (effective Oct. 1, 1988); Georgia, Ga. Code Ann. § 10-1-760 et seq. (1994 & Supp. 1995) (effective July 1, 1990); Hawaii, Haw. Rev. Stat. § 482B-1 et seq. (1985 & Supp. 1992) (effective July 1, 1989); Idaho, Idaho Code § 48-801 et seq. (Michie 1977 & Supp. 1995) (effective July 1, 1993); Illinois, 765 Ill. Comp. Stat. Ann. 1065/1 et seq. (West 1993 & Supp. 1996) (effective Jan. 1, 1988); Indiana, Ind. Code § 24-2-3-1 et seq. (1996) (effective Sept. 1, 1982); Iowa, Iowa Code § 550.1 et seq. (1987 & Supp. 1996) (effective Apr. 27, 1990); Kansas, Kan. Stat. Ann. § 60-3320 et seq. (1994) (effective July 1, 1981); Kentucky, Ky. Rev. Stat. Ann. § 365.880 et seq. (1988 & Supp. 1990) (effective July 13, 1990); Louisiana, La. Rev. Stat. Ann. § 51:1431 et seq. (West 1987 & Supp. 1996) (approved July 19, 1981); Maine, Me. Rev. Stat. Ann. tit. 10, § 1541 et seq. (West 1980 supp. 1995) (effective

May 22, 1987); Maryland, Md. Code Ann., Com. Law § 11-1201 et seq. (1990 & Supp. 1995) (effective July 1, 1989); Michigan, Mich. Comp. Laws Ann. § 445.1901 et seq. (West 1998) (effective Oct. 1, 1998); Minnesota, Minn. Stat. § 325C.01 et seq. (1995 & Supp. 1996) (effective Aug. 1, 1980); Mississippi, Miss. Code Ann. § 75-26-1 et seq. (1972 & Supp. 1995) (effective July 1, 1990); Missouri, Mo. Rev. Stat. § 417.450 et seq. (1995 & Supp. 2001) (effective Aug. 28, 1995); Montana, Mont. Code Ann. § 30-14-401 et seq. (1995) (effective Oct. 1, 1985); Nebraska, Neb. Rev. Stat. § 87-501 et seq. (1994) (effective July 9, 1988); Nevada, Nev. Rev. Stat. § 600A.010 et seq. (1987 & Supp. 2001) (effective Mar. 5, 1987); New Hampshire, N.H. Rev. Stat. Ann. § 350-B:1 et seq. (1995 & Supp. 1995) (effective Jan. 1, 1990); New Mexico, N.M. Stat. Ann. § 57-3A-1 et seq. (Michie 1995) (effective Apr. 3, 1989); North Carolina, N.C. Gen. Stat. § 66-152 et seq. (1995) (effective July 1981); North Dakota, N.D. Cent. Code § 47-25.1-01 et seq. (1978 & Supp. 1995) (effective July 1, 1983); Ohio, Ohio Rev. Code Ann. § 1333.61 et seq. (Anderson 2001) (effective July 20, 1994); Oklahoma, Okla. Stat. tit. 78, § 85 et seq. (1995) (effective Jan. 1, 1986); Oregon, Or. Rev. Stat. § 646.461 et seq. (1988) (effective Jan. 1, 1988); Rhode Island, R.I. Gen. Laws § 6-41-1 et seq. (1992) (effective July 1, 1986); South Carolina, S.C. Code Ann. § 39-8-10 et seq. (Law. Co-op. 1992 & Supp. 1997) (effective May 21, 1997) (replacing prior version of UTSA); South Dakota, S.D. Codified Laws § 37-29-1 et seq. (Michie 1994) (effective July 1, 1988); Tennessee, Tenn. Code Ann. § 47-25-1701 et seq. (2000) (effective July 1, 2000); Utah, Utah Code Ann. § 13-24-1 et seq. (1996) (effective May 1, 1989); Vermont, Vt. Stat. Ann. tit. 9 § 4601 et seq. (1995 & Supp. 1996) (effective July 1, 1996); Virginia, Va. Code Ann. § 59.1-336 et seq. (Michie 1992 & Supp. 1995) (effective July 1, 1986); Washington, Wash. Rev. Code § 19.108.10 et seq. (1989 & Supp. 1996) (effective Jan. 1, 1982); West Virginia, W. Va. Code § 47-22-1 et seq. (1995) (effective July 1, 1986); Wisconsin, Wis. Stat. § 134.90 (1989 & Supp. 1995) (effective Apr. 24, 1986).

The following states have not adopted the UTSA and instead look to the common law of trade secrets as embodied by section

757 of the *Restatement of Torts:* Massachusetts, New Jersey, New York, Pennsylvania, and Texas. *See, e.g., Lehman v. Dow Jones & Co.,* 783 F.2d 285 (2d Cir. 1986) (citing *Eagle Comtronics, Inc. v. Pico, Inc.,* 453 N.Y.S.2d 470 (App. Div. 1982)); *J.T. Healy & Son, Inc. v. James A. Murphy & Son, Inc.,* 260 N.E.2d 723 (Mass. 1970); *Sun Dial Corp. v. Rideout,* 108 A.2d 442 (N.J. 1954); *Felmlee v. Lockett,* 351 A.2d 273 (Pa. 1976); *Hyde Corp. v. Huffines,* 314 S.W.2d 763 (Tex.), *cert. denied,* 358 U.S. 898 (1958). While Massachusetts does address trade secrets by statute, Mass. Gen. Laws ch. 93, §§ 42, 42A (1969 & Supp. 1983), the statute is not even loosely based on the UTSA, and Massachusetts courts tend to rely far more heavily on the common law than on the statute.

Although the vast majority of jurisdictions have adopted a version of the UTSA, courts do look to common law trade secrets cases, section 757 of the *Restatement of Torts,* and/or sections 39 to 45 of the *Restatement (Third) of Unfair Competition* as "helpful guidance," even when the UTSA is faithfully applied. This practice is not necessarily contradictory because the UTSA was intended to codify the common law and is based on the better reasoned *Restatement* cases. *See* UTSA, Prefatory Note. This chapter will refer to common law guidelines where they have been especially useful to courts.

Keep in mind that where state case law is sparse, courts have often relied on decisions of sister states that have also adopted the UTSA, as the UTSA encourages. UTSA § 8.

Two major public policies drive trade secret misappropriation law: the desire to maintain commercial standards of ethics among business competitors, and the desire to allow for as much free competition and entrepreneurial activity as possible. Both the UTSA and the common law evince an attempt to accommodate these sometimes conflicting public policies by according trade secrets protection only when a wrongdoer has acquired a trade secret through improper means or has used or disclosed information in violation of a confidential relationship (or other duty owed a plaintiff). *See, e.g.,* UTSA § 1; *Restatement of Torts* § 757 cmt. a. The law does not protect the owner of a trade secret from competitors who acquire or strive to acquire a trade secret through proper means, such as independent invention, reverse engineering, a gift or purchase from the owner, observation of an object on public display, or independent research of publicly available written information, in trade directories or patent filings or the like. *See, e.g.,* UTSA § 1 cmt.; *Restatement of Torts* § 757 cmt. a.

Although particular jurisdictions may emphasize one element of the tort over another, or define elements somewhat differently, all jurisdictions essentially require that a plaintiff prove the following to prevail on a misappropriation of trade secrets claim:

1. that a trade secret existed in which plaintiff had ownership rights when defendant committed the acts complained of by plaintiff;

2. that defendant acquired the trade secret (a) through improper means, (b) through plaintiff's disclosure of the trade secret to defendant under a confidential relationship, or (c) under other circumstances giving rise to a duty;

3. if acquisition was not through improper means, that defendant used or disclosed the trade secret without plaintiff's permission; and

4. that (a) plaintiff suffered harm as a direct and proximate result of defendant's use or disclosure of plaintiff's trade secret, or (b) defendant gained from such use or disclosure.

Proof in this area is intensely fact-specific, making it difficult for courts to formulate precise standards to define a trade secret and its tortious misappropriation. Bear in mind that even if courts claim to apply objective standards and require minimum showings of proof, they will inevitably "balance" and "weigh" a host of competing factors to determine whether a trade secret exists and whether misappropriation occurred. Most courts apply a rigorous trade secret definitional threshold, requiring the right holder to establish a property interest in the information before considering whether the other elements of a misappropriation case are present. *See, e.g., Buffets, Inc. v. Klinke*, 73 F.3d 965 (9th Cir. 1996) (applying Washington law); *Group One, Ltd. v. Hallmark Cards, Inc.*, 254 F.3d 1041 (Fed. Cir. 2001) (applying Missouri common law); *Koch Eng'g Co. v. Faulconer*, 610 P.2d 1094 (Kan. 1980); *Electro-Craft Corp. v. Controlled Motion, Inc.*, 332 N.W.2d. 890 (Minn. 1983); *Rycoline Prods., Inc. v. Walsh*, 756 A.2d 1047 (N.J. Super. Ct. App. Div. 2000); *Lowndes Prods., Inc. v. Brower*, 191 S.E.2d 761 (S.C. 1972). A minority of courts focus foremost on the relational history between the parties and whether a misappropriation can be found, often with little or no analysis of whether a trade secret exists in the first place. *See, e.g., E.I. DuPont de Nemours & Co. v. Christopher*, 431 F.2d 1012 (5th Cir. 1970); *Henkle & Joyce Hardware Co. v. Maco, Inc.*, 239 N.W.2d 772 (Neb. 1976); *Kamin v. Kuhnau*, 374 P.2d 912, 916 (Or. 1962); *Hyde Corp. v. Huffines*, 314 S.W.2d 763 (Tex.), *cert. denied*, 358 U.S. 898 (1958)

Better-reasoned cases, however, focus first on the threshold question: Does a trade secret exist that requires protection? This approach is eminently logical, because regardless of whether the parties ever stood in a confidential relationship, there can be no liability for misappropriation absent the existence of a trade secret. *See generally* 2 R. Callmann, *The Law of Unfair Competition, Trademarks and Monopolies* § 14.02 (4th ed. 1992). The model jury instructions have been drafted with insights of this nature in mind.

Instructions generic to the jury process—for example, as to plaintiff's burden of proof, the use of circumstantial evidence, and the standard of certainty required for prospective damages—are not covered here, as they are not peculiar to trade secrets law.

8.2 Prima Facie Case

To recover on the trade secret claims plaintiff has made in this case, plaintiff must prove each of the following four elements by a preponderance of the evidence:

1. that plaintiff possessed a trade secret;

2. that defendant acquired the trade secret (a) by using improper means, (b) through a confidential relationship with plaintiff, or (c) under other circumstances giving rise to a duty not to use or disclose the trade secret without plaintiff's permission;

3. if acquisition was not through improper means, that defendant used or disclosed the trade secret without plaintiff's permission; and

4. that (a) plaintiff suffered harm as a direct and proximate result of defendant's use or disclosure of plaintiff's trade secret, or (b) defendant obtained benefit from such use or disclosure.

I will go over each of these elements more specifically in the following instructions.

If after you consider all of the evidence you find that plaintiff has proven each of these elements in accordance with the legal requirements as I describe them to you, then your verdict must be for the plaintiff and you will consider the amount of monetary damages to be awarded to plaintiff, by following the instructions that I will give you relating to damages.

If, on the other hand, you find that plaintiff has not proven one or more of these elements, then your verdict must be for the defendant.

COMMENT

Despite the varying formulations courts use to establish the elements of a prima facie case for misappropriation of trade secrets, "the criteria are essentially the same in all instances." 1 Melvin F. Jager, *Trade Secrets Law* § 5:5, at 5-24 (2002) (and cases cited therein).

Under the UTSA, unlike at common law, improper acquisition alone is sufficient to establish liability for misappropriation. UTSA § 1(2); *see, e.g., Minuteman, Inc. v. Alexander*, 434 N.W.2d 773 (Wis. 1989); *see also* Richard J. Cipolla Jr., *A Practitioner's Guide to Oklahoma Trade Secrets Law, Past, Present and Future: The Uniform Trade Secrets Act*, 27 Tulsa L.J. 137 n.152 (1991) (damages available for improper acquisition alone, as acquisition may diminish indirect value of trade secret). *But see* Ala. Code §§ 8-27-3, 4 (1993) (improper disclosure or use in addition to acquisition required for liability under Alabama act); *Ins. Assocs. Corp. v. Hansen*, 782 P.2d 1230 (Idaho 1989) (even if plaintiff possessed trade secret, claim fails without proof of use). However, where acquisition has not been improper, as in the case of an employee who initially receives information by proper means, then proof of use or disclosure will be required. *See* comment to § 8.5, *infra*.

8.3 Definition of Trade Secret

Before you consider defendant's actions, you must find that plaintiff possessed a trade secret. Broadly speaking, a trade secret may consist of any formula, pattern, device, program, method, technique, process, or compilation of information, including a customer list. However, to prove that particular information is entitled to special protection as a "trade secret," plaintiff must show:

1. that the information at issue is indeed secret;

2. that plaintiff has taken reasonable measures to protect the secrecy of the information; and

3. that the information is sufficiently valuable to confer a competitive advantage on plaintiff over its business rivals.

COMMENT

Section 1(4) of the UTSA provides that

> "Trade Secret" means information, including a formula, pattern, compilation, program, device, method, technique, or process, that:
>
> > (i) derives independent economic value, actual or potential, from not being known to, and not being readily ascertainable by, proper means by other persons who can obtain economic value from its disclosure or use, and
> >
> > (ii) is the subject of efforts that are reasonable under the circumstances to maintain its secrecy.

The language of some statutes will vary slightly from the UTSA, and changes in the jury instruction may be advisable to accommodate particular statutory language. *See, e.g.,* Ala. Code § 8-27-2 cmts. (1993 & Supp. 1995) (trade secret defined as information that (a) is used or intended for use in trade or business, (b) is included or embodied in a formula, pattern, compilation, computer software, drawings, device, method, technique, or process, (c) is not publicly known or generally known in the relevant trade or business, (d) cannot be readily ascertained or derived from publicly available information, and (e) has significant economic value); Alaska Stat. § 45.50.940(3) (Michie 1995) (trade secret defined as information that is secret and has economic value because not generally known or readily ascertainable); Colo. Rev. Stat. § 7-74-102(4) (1990 & Supp. 1995) (trade secret definition differs from UTSA in that information *must* relate to plaintiff's business and there is no requirement that type of secrecy-preserving measures employed be reasonable; definition encompasses "the whole or any portion or phase of any scientific or technical information, design . . . procedure . . . improvement, confidential business or financial information, listing of names, addresses or telephone numbers, or other information relating to any business or profession which is secret and of value"); Conn. Gen. Stat. § 35-51(d) (1987 & Supp. 1996) (adding "drawing, cost data and customer list" to UTSA definition); Ga. Code Ann. § 10-1-761(4) (1994 & Supp. 1995) and 765 Ill. Comp. Stat. Ann. 1065/2(d), cmts. (West 1993 & Supp. 1996) (in addition to types of information listed in UTSA, Georgia and Illinois acts add information, including, "but not limited to," technical or nontechnical data, a drawing, financial data, financial plans, product plans, or list of actual or potential customers or suppliers; also, under Illinois act, term "program" meant to cover computer programs and term "information" intended to include know-how and ideas used in computer science and biotechnology); Iowa Code § 550.2(4) (1987 & Supp. 1996), Me. Rev. Stat. Ann. tit. 10, § 1542(4) (West 1980 & Supp. 1995), Neb. Rev. Stat. § 87-502(4) (1994), Nev. Rev. Stat. § 600A.030 (1987 & Supp. 2001), Va. Code Ann. § 59-1-336 (Michie 1992 & Supp. 1995), and W. Va. Code § 47-22-1(d) (1995) (these statutes broaden trade secret definition by explicitly making list of types of information nonexclusive; in addition, Nebraska statute adds "drawing" and "code" to list of information that may constitute trade secret); Minn. Stat. § 325c.01(5) (1995 & Supp. 1996) (adds the words "information or computer software, including a formula . . . " to definition of trade secret); N.C. Gen. Stat. § 66-152(3) (1995) (specifies that trade secret is business or technical information, and also adds "compilation of information" to UTSA definition); Ohio Rev. Code Ann. § 1333.61(D) (Anderson 2001) (adds "any business information or plans, financial information, or listing of names, addresses, or telephone numbers"); Or. Rev. Stat. § 646.461(4) (1988) (adds drawing, cost data, and customer list to UTSA definition of trade secret); S.C. Code Ann. § 39-8-20(5)(b) (Law. Co-op. 1992 & Supp. 1997) ("A trade secret may consist of a simple fact, item, or procedure, or a series or sequence of items or procedures which, although individually could be perceived as relatively minor or simple, collectively can make a substantial difference in the efficiency of a process or the production of a product, or may be the basis of a marketing or commercial strategy. The collective effect of the items and procedures must be considered in any analysis of whether a trade secret exists and not the general knowledge of each individual item or procedure.").

Many courts rely on the well-known six "factors"—originally enunciated in the *Restatement of Torts*—to evaluate whether a trade secret exists:

1. the extent to which the information is known outside of plaintiff's business;

2. the extent to which it is known by employees and others involved in plaintiff's business;

3. the extent of measures taken by the plaintiff to guard the secrecy of the information;

4. the value of the information to plaintiff and plaintiff's competitors;

5. the amount of effort or money expended by plaintiff in developing the information; and

6. the ease or difficulty with which the information could be properly acquired or duplicated by others.

Restatement of Torts § 757 cmt. b. (1939); *see, e.g., Enterprise Leasing Co. of Phoenix v. Ehmke*, 3 P.3d 1064, 1069 n.6 (Ariz. Ct. App. 1999); *Saforo & Assocs., Inc. v. Porocel Corp.*, 991 S.W.2d 117 (Ark. 1999); *Bond v. Polycycle, Inc.*, 732 A.2d 970, 973-74 (Md. Ct. Spec. App. 1999); *Wilmington Star-News, Inc. v. New Hanover Reg'l Med. Ctr.*, 480 S.E.2d 53, 56 (N.C. Ct. App. 1997); *State ex rel. Besser v. Ohio State Univ.*, 732 N.E.2d 373 (Ohio 2000).

The requirements of secrecy, reasonable measures to protect secrecy, and competitive advantage found in this model instruction are distilled from these six oft-cited *Restatement* factors.[2]

According to the *Restatement (Third) of Unfair Competition*: "A trade secret is any information that can be used in the operation of a business or other enterprise and that is sufficiently valuable and secret to afford an actual or potential economic advantage over others." *Restatement (Third) of Unfair Competition* § 39 (1995).

---

2. An additional requirement noted by the *Restatement of Torts* but accorded little prominence even in common law states is that a trade secret be continuously used in the plaintiff's business. The UTSA, the *Restatement (Third) of Unfair Competition*, and states adopting the UTSA have all rejected the continuous use requirement. Accordingly, information that was not in use at the time of defendant's actions, as well as information that has never been put to use, including so-called "negative" information, may constitute a trade secret. *See, e.g.*, Glaxo, Inc. v. Novopharm, Ltd., 931 F. Supp. 1280 (E.D.N.C. 1996), *aff'd*, 110 F.3d 1562 (4th Cir. 1997) ("A trade secret need not necessarily be comprised of positive information, such as a specific formula, but can include negative, inconclusive, or sufficiently suggestive research data that would give a person skilled in the art a competitive advantage he might not otherwise enjoy . . . ."); Courtesy Temp. Serv., Inc. v. Camacho, 272 Cal. Rptr. 352 (Cal. Ct. App. 1990) (customer list held protectable even when part of extensive research in compilation of list included finding entities that would not subscribe to plaintiff's services); State *ex rel*. Besser v. Ohio State Univ., 732 N.E.2d 373, 378-79 (Ohio 2000) (draft asset purchase agreement, even though relating to a single event, not precluded from being a trade secret).

The *Restatement of Torts* defines trade secret as follows:

> A trade secret may consist of any formula, pattern, device or compilation of information which is used in one's business, and which gives him an opportunity to obtain an advantage over competitors who do not know or use it. It may be a formula for a chemical compound, a process of manufacturing, treating or preserving materials, a pattern for a machine or other device, or a list of customers. *Restatement of Torts* § 757 cmt. b (1939).

8.3.1 Secrecy

To determine that a trade secret exists you must first decide whether the information was indeed secret when defendant's allegedly wrongful conduct occurred. Matters that are generally known to the public at large or to people in a trade or business are not trade secrets. Nor can information be considered a trade secret if it would be ascertainable with reasonable ease from publicly available information. In addition, a trade secret must possess enough originality so that it can be distinguished from everyday knowledge.

Absolute secrecy is not necessary for information to qualify as a trade secret. There is no requirement that no one else in the world possess the information. Rather, a plaintiff must demonstrate that the information was known only to it or to a few others who have also treated the information as a trade secret.

COMMENT

Although neither the UTSA nor the *Restatement* specifically require a finding of "novelty," courts routinely require some degree of novelty or originality for information to be accorded trade secret status. Although information need not evince the same degree of novelty required for patent protection, it must possess sufficient originality to separate it from everyday knowledge or knowledge commonly used by people in a trade or business. *See, e.g., Buffets, Inc. v. Klinke*, 73 F.3d 965 (9th Cir. 1996); *Northup v. Reish*, 200 F.2d 924 (7th Cir. 1953); *BBA Nonwovens Simponsville, Inc. v. Superior Nonwovens, LLC*, 303 F.3d 1332 (Fed. Cir. 2002); *Electro-Craft Corp. v. Controlled Motion, Inc.*, 332 N.W.2d 890 (Minn. 1983); *Dionne v. Southeast Foam Converting & Packaging, Inc.*, 397 S.E.2d 110, 113-14 (Va. 1990).

To determine whether information is secret, the courts in UTSA states generally focus on whether the information is generally known or readily ascertainable using proper means. *See Capital Asset Research Corp. v. Finnegan*, 160 F.3d 683 (11th Cir. 1998) (information on property values and determining bid amounts not trade secret under Georgia law because any experienced bidder could and likely would compile it from publicly available information); *Fleming Sales Co. v. Bailey*, 611 F. Supp. 507 (N.D. Ill. 1985) (holding information known throughout an industry not protectable regardless of secrecy measures employed); *Wal-Mart Stores, Inc. v. P.O. Mkt., Inc.*, 66 S.W.3d 620 (Ark. 2002) (business plan combining generally known or readily ascertainable economic principles not protectable as trade secret); *Essex Group, Inc., v. Southwire Co.*, 501 S.E.2d 501 (Ga. 1998) (system uniquely integrating readily ascertainable elements protectable as trade secret); *Home Pride Foods, Inc. v. Johnson*, 634 N.W.2d 774*Home Pride* (Neb. 2001) (customer list will not be protected when it contains "mere identities and locations of customers that anyone could easily identify as possible customers" but will be protected "where time and effort have been expended to identify particular customers with particular needs or characteristics"); *Weins v. Sporleder*, 569 N.W.2d 16 (S.D. 1997) (feed product composed of well-known feed materials that could be easily reverse-engineered by chemical analysis not worthy of trade secret protection); *see also Scott v. Snelling & Snelling, Inc.*, 732 F. Supp. 1034 (N.D. Cal. 1990); *Colorado Supply Co. v. Stewart*, 797 P.2d 1303 (Colo. Ct. App. 1990), *cert. denied*, 1991 Colo. LEXIS 708 (Colo. Oct. 7, 1991); *Xpert Automation Sys. Corp. v. Vibromatic Co.*, 569 N.E.2d 351 (Ind. Ct. App. 1991); *Electro-Craft Corp. v. Controlled Motion, Inc.*, 332 N.W.2d 890 (Minn. Ct. App. 1985); *State ex rel. Besser v. Ohio State Univ.*, 732 N.E.2d 373 (Ohio 2000).

According to the *Restatement (Third) of Unfair Competition*, circumstantial evidence that information is not readily ascertainable can include precautions taken by claimant to preserve the secrecy of the information, the willingness of licensees to pay for disclosure of the secret, unsuccessful attempts by defendant and others to duplicate the information by proper means, and resort by defendant to improper means of acquisition. *Restatement (Third) of Unfair Competition* § 39, cmt. f. (1995).

Some courts have found posting on the Internet to be persuasive evidence that the information in question is generally known. *See Religious Tech. Ctr. v. Lerma*, 908 F. Supp. 1362 (E.D. Va. 1995) (finding that once a trade secret is posted on the Internet, it is effectively part of the public domain); *Hoechst Diafoil Co. v. Nan Ya Plastics Corp.*, 174 F.3d 411 (4th Cir. 1999) (dicta); *but see* Nev. Rev. Stat. § 600A.055 (1987 & Supp. 2001) (providing that information posted on the Internet shall not cease to be a trade secret so long as (1) the owner obtains an injunction within a reasonable time after discovering that the trade secret has been posted and (2) the trade secret is actually removed within a reasonable time after the injunction is issued by the court).

The California and Illinois statutes do not include the requirement that trade secret information not be readily ascertainable by proper means. Under these statutes, therefore, a trade secret may consist of information that could be legally obtained. The "readily ascertainable" standard is, however, available as a defense in both states. *See* Cal. Civ. Code § 3426 *et seq.*, cmts. (Deering 1970 & Supp. 1996); 765 Ill. Comp. Stat. Ann. 1065/2(a), cmts. (West 1993 & Supp. 1996); *Rockwell Graphic Sys. v. Dev. Indus.*, 730 F. Supp. 171 (N.D. Ill. 1990), *rev'd on other grounds,* 925 F.2d 174 (7th Cir. 1991); *Gillis Associated Indus., Inc. v. Cari-All, Inc.*, 564 N.E.2d 881 (Ill. App. Ct. 1990).

8.3.1.a   Independent Discovery

A trade secret may be protected even though others have discovered the secret through their own efforts. The mere fact that more than one person has obtained the trade secret through proper means does not mean that the information is not secret or that the defendant may not be held liable for obtaining the trade secret through improper means.

COMMENT

On occasion, the defendant may claim that independent discovery by an entity other than plaintiff is evidence that the information was not really secret. Where there is such a case, the above instruction should be used. *See Restatement (Third) of Unfair Competition* § 40 cmt. a (1995) ("Since neither novelty nor absolute secrecy is a prerequisite for protection as a trade secret, each of several independent discoverers can have a proprietary interest in the same information.") (internal citation omitted); 2 Roger M. Milgrim, *Milgrim on Trade Secrets* § 7.02.1.c (2003).

8.3.2   Reasonable Measures to Protect Secrecy

Plaintiff must prove that it took reasonable measures to protect the secrecy of its trade secret. There is no precise definition of what "reasonable measures" are; what is reasonable depends on the situation. Factors you may wish to consider in evaluating whether "reasonable measures" were taken could include the following:

1. whether plaintiff made it a practice to inform its employees or others involved with its business that the information was a trade secret and/or was to be kept confidential;

2. whether plaintiff required employees or others involved with its business to sign confidentiality agreements regarding the information or agreements not to compete in areas that could use the information;

3. whether plaintiff restricted access to the information on a "need to know" basis; and

4. whether plaintiff generally maintained tight security to protect the alleged trade secret, and did not voluntarily disclose it to others, except in confidence.

COMMENT

This instruction lists four of the most commonly discussed measures for protecting the secrecy of trade secret information, but ultimately the test is not readily defensible in terms of whether any one (or even any group) of specific factors is present or absent and to what degree. Relevant factors will most often depend on particular case facts. Some factors listed here may not be relevant at all, and, in some circumstances, factors not listed here may be enough to establish reasonable secrecy measures. This list, then, is not meant to be, and cannot be, comprehensive. *See Tubos de Acero de Mex., SA v. Am. Int'l Inv. Corp.*, 292 F.3d 471 (5th Cir. 2002) (under Louisiana law, no requirement that "extreme and unduly expensive procedures be taken to protect trade secrets") (citation omitted); *Sheets v. Yamaha Motors Corp.*, 849 F.2d 179 (5th Cir. 1988) (holding reasonable security measures not taken when plaintiff publicly displayed product containing alleged trade secret, installed alleged trade secret in other products without instructing customers not to disclose it, and allowed others to take pictures and examine product without requiring confidentiality agreements), *aff'd in part and rev'd in part*, 891 F.2d 533 (5th Cir. 1990), *reh'g denied*, 897 F.2d 528 (5th Cir. 1990); *Surgidev Corp. v. Eye Tech., Inc.*, 828 F.2d 452 (8th Cir. 1987) (secrecy measures found adequate when information shared with employees only on need-to-know basis, employees on notice that information secret and required to sign nondisclosure agreements, and visitor access restricted in areas containing information); *CVD, Inc. v. Raytheon Co.*, 769 F.2d 842 (1st Cir. 1985), *cert. denied*, 475 U.S. 1016 (1986) ("Heroic measures to ensure secrecy are not essential, but reasonable precautions must be taken."); *E.I. DuPont de Nemours & Co. v. Christopher*, 431 F.2d 1012 (5th Cir. 1970) (holding reasonable security measures do not require plaintiff to build impenetrable fortress around its construction site to shield secrets from competitor's aerial photography); *United Centrifugal Pumps v. Cusimano*, 708 F. Supp. 1038 (W.D. Ark. 1988) (adequate measures to maintain secrecy include disclosure only upon execution of confidentiality agreement, limited access to location where trade secret used, surveillance of files containing information, and computer information accessible only by special password); *Anaconda Co. v. Metric Tool & Die Co.*, 485 F. Supp. 410 (E.D. Pa. 1980) ("Although the secrecy maintained was by no means absolute, it was such that except by the use of improper means, defendant would have had difficulty in acquiring the information."); *Allied Supply Co. v. Brown*, 585 So. 2d 33 (Ala. 1991) (holding adequate security measures not taken when employees had free access to customer lists, lists not marked "confidential," and many copies available within company); *Tyson Foods, Inc. v. Conagra, Inc.*, 79 S.W.3d 326 (Ark. 2002) (holding corporate code generally requiring employee confidentiality inadequate measure to confer trade secret status on nutrient profile known by hundreds of managers); *Morlife, Inc. v. Perry*, 66 Cal. Rptr. 2d 731 (Cal. Ct. App. 1997) (finding restricted computer access, confidentiality contract, and employee handbook prohibiting disclosure adequate measures to protect secrecy of customer information); *Network Telecomms., Inc. v. Boor-Crepeau*, 790 P.2d 901 (Colo. Ct. App. 1990) (trade secret found to exist when information given to employees only on need-to-know basis, employees advised that information was trade secret, and access to company plant controlled and limited); *Elm City Cheese Co. v. Federico*, 752 A.2d 1037 (Conn. 1999) (despite absence of other precautionary measures, family-run company employed adequate measures to protect secrecy where information available only to family and close personal friend and trusted advisor); *Spottiswoode v. Levine*, 730 A.2d 166, 175, n.7 (Me. 1999) (listing factors to use in determining whether efforts to maintain secrecy are reasonable); *J.T. Healy & Son, Inc. v. James A. Murphy & Son, Inc.*, 260 N.E.2d 723 (Mass. 1970) (reasonable security precautions include "constant warnings to all persons to whom the trade secret has become known and obtaining from each an agreement, preferably in writing, acknowledging its secrecy and promising to respect it"); *Fred's Stores of Miss., Inc. v. M & H Drugs, Inc.*, 725 So. 2d 902 (Miss. 1998) (finding steps to maintain secrecy, while not elaborate, to be reasonable under the circumstances); *Hildreth Mfg., L.L.C. v. Semco, Inc.*, 785 N.E.2d 774 (Ohio Ct. App. 2003) (no reasonable measures to protect information when limited access policy not adhered to, no employees required to sign non-disclosure agreements, and no set document destruction policy); *Omega Optical, Inc. v. Chroma Tech. Corp.*, 800 A.2d 1064 (Vt. 2002) (security measures not adequate where no internal policies concerning confidentiality, nondisclosure, or noncompetition); *Dicks v. Jensen*, 768 A.2d 1279 (Vt. 2001) (burden on plaintiff to demonstrate that he "pursued an active course of conduct designed to inform his employees that such secrets and information were to remain confidential") (quoting *Jet Spray Cooler, Inc. v. Crampton*, 282 N.E.2d 921 (Mass. 1972)); *Boeing Co. v. Sierracin Corp.*, 738 P.2d 665 (Wash. 1987) (secrecy measures adequate even though information disclosed to Federal Aviation Administration, because information not available to public on demand).

The requirement that reasonable measures be taken to protect a trade secret may be decreasing in importance. *See Restatement (Third) of Unfair Competition* § 39, cmt. g (1995) (not including reasonable measures to maintain secrecy in definition of trade secret and stating, "[I]f the value and secrecy of the information are clear, evidence of specific precautions taken by the trade secret owner may be unnecessary."); *see also* Nev. Rev. Stat. § 600A.032 (1987 & Supp. 2001) (creating a presumption of reasonable efforts to maintain secrecy so long as owner marks information or item "confidential," "private," etc.; presumption may only be rebutted by clear and convincing evidence that owner did not take reasonable efforts).

8.3.3   Competitive Advantage

A trade secret must be valuable either to plaintiff or to its business rivals in the sense that, as long as it is secret, the information provides plaintiff with an actual or potential competitive business advantage over its rivals. To help you determine whether plaintiff enjoyed either an actual or potential competitive advantage, you may consider such things as:

1. the degree to which the information was generally known or readily ascertainable by others;

2. the extent to which plaintiff used or uses the information in its business;

3. whether the information allows plaintiff to earn increased profits or operate its business more efficiently;

4. what gain or benefits defendant's business obtained from the information;

5. what money, effort, and time plaintiff expended to develop the information; and

6. the ease or difficulty of acquiring or duplicating the information through independent development, research of publicly available information, or taking apart and analyzing a product properly acquired to learn its secrets (a process called "reverse engineering").

COMMENT

The factors listed in the model instruction include factors most commonly referred to by the courts. Depending upon circumstances of a particular case, some may not be relevant at all, or others, not listed here, may establish the requirement of competitive advantage.

The UTSA requires that the information "derive independent economic value, actual or potential, from not being known to, and not being readily ascertainable by proper means by, other persons who can obtain economic value from its disclosure or use." UTSA § 1(4). To determine whether information has "independent economic value" under the UTSA, most courts look to whether the information gives plaintiff a "competitive advantage."[3] *See, e.g., Religious Tech. Ctr. v. Wollersheim*, 796 F.2d 1076 (9th Cir. 1986); *Secure Serv. Tech., Inc. v. Time & Space Processing, Inc.*, 722 F. Supp. 1354 (E.D. Va. 1989); *Electro-Craft Corp. v. Controlled Motion, Inc.*, 332 N.W.2d 890 (Minn. Ct. App. 1983), *appeal after remand*, 370 N.W.2d 465 (Minn. Ct. App. 1985); *see also Surgidev Corp. v. Eye Tech., Inc.*, 828 F.2d 452 (8th Cir. 1987) (defendant's intention to use plaintiff's information is circumstantial proof of economic value); *In re R & R Assocs., Inc.*, 119 B.R. 302 (Bankr. M.D. Fla. 1990) (information has independent economic value when plaintiff spent considerable time, effort, knowledge, and expense compiling information and when information secret and not available from other sources); *United Centrifugal Pumps v. Cusimano*, 1988 U.S. Dist. LEXIS 11012, at *13 (W.D. Ark. 1988) (information has independent economic value when competitor would have to spend at least as much time, effort, and money as plaintiff had expended to obtain information using proper means); *Morlife, Inc. v. Perry*, 66 Cal. Rptr. 2d 731 (Cal. Ct. App. 1997) (stating that "a customer list can be

---

3. The *Restatement of Torts* requires that the information "give [the holder of it] an opportunity to obtain an advantage over competitors who do not know or use it." *Restatement of Torts* § 757 cmt. b (1939). Proof under the old *Restatement* is thus very similar to proof under the UTSA, though the language differs. *See, e.g.*, Rohm and Haas Co. v. Adco Chem. Co., 689 F.2d 424, 430-31 (3d Cir. 1982) (evidence of plaintiff's competitive advantage included fact that plaintiff derived four highly successful products from information in dispute and that defendant tried for years to duplicate plaintiff's manufacturing process without success); FMC Corp. v. Spurlin, 596 F. Supp. 609 (W.D. Pa. 1984) (holding showing of competitive advantage necessary for trade secret protection); Sheridan v. Mallinckrodt, Inc., 568 F. Supp. 1347 (N.D.N.Y. 1983) (plaintiff's manufacturing process conferred competitive advantage on plaintiff because it required less attention from machine operators and made it easier to detect defects in plaintiff's products, thus helping to control production costs).

found to have economic value because its disclosure would allow a competitor to direct its sales efforts to those customers who have already shown a willingness to use a unique type of service or product as opposed to a list of people who only might be interested"); *Elm City Cheese Co. v. Federico*, 752 A.2d 1037, 1053-54 (Conn. 1999) (business model as a whole enabled company to occupy a unique and competitively advantageous niche in its industry); *Aries Info. Sys., Inc. v. Pacific Mgmt. Sys. Corp.*, 366 N.W.2d 366, (Minn. Ct. App. 1985) (computer program had independent economic value because not generally known, available only through plaintiff, and plaintiff generated extensive revenues from sale of program); *Restatement (Third) of Unfair Competition* § 39 cmt. e (1995) (evidence of value may include the amount of resources invested by plaintiff in producing the information, precautions taken by plaintiff to protect the secrecy of the information, the willingness of others to pay for access to the information, plaintiff's use of the trade secret in the operation of its business, and benefits realized by the owner through use of the information).

8.4   Acquisition by Defendant

You must determine whether defendant acquired the trade secret under circumstances where defendant owed a duty to plaintiff. Defendant would have a duty to plaintiff if defendant acquired the information, (a) by using improper means, (b) through a confidential relationship with plaintiff, or (c) under other circumstances where a duty is imposed by law. Let me discuss each of these with you in detail.

8.4.1   Improper Means

"Improper means" in acquiring a trade secret can arise in three types of circumstances: (a) where defendant itself has obtained the trade secret by its own improper conduct, (b) where defendant has obtained the trade secret from a third party who acquired the trade secret by improper means, and (c) where defendant induced another to obtain the trade secret by improper means. It would be improper for a defendant to acquire trade secret information by theft, bribery, trespass, misrepresentation, or corporate espionage, such as wiretapping. It would also be improper for defendant to acquire the information from a third party who either used improper means to acquire the information or breached a duty of confidentiality in disclosing the information. Where defendant has acquired the information from a third party in one of these circumstances, defendant's conduct is only improper if defendant knew or should have known that it was acquiring a trade secret belonging to another. Lastly, it would be improper for defendant to induce another to either use improper means to acquire the information or to breach a duty of confidentiality that person owed to plaintiff.

Since improper means can cover a wide variety of circumstances, it may be helpful to identify situations that the law would *not* consider "improper means." It is not improper to acquire information through independent development, research of public resources (such as, for example, trade directories, patent filings, or even the telephone book), or purchase of a product that contains trade secrets and then disassembling it to analyze those secrets (a process called "reverse engineering"). Similarly, a party who obtains information by mistake, or without knowledge or reason to know that the information is a trade secret, has not acquired the trade secret through improper means.

COMMENT

This model instruction deals with acquisition through improper means, such as corporate espionage and theft. *See E.I. DuPont de Nemours & Co. v. Christopher,* 431 F.2d 1012 (5th Cir. 1970) (holding competitor who attempted to discover DuPont's trade secrets through aerial photography of DuPont plant under construction liable for wrongful acquisition of trade secrets). In reality, these situations are far less common than acquiring the information through lawful means, such as in the context of a confidential relationship, and then misusing the information. An example would be a former employee competing or sharing information with a new employer. The classic example of a confidential relationship that is often implied-at-law is that of employee to employer. *See* comment to § 8.4.2, *infra.*

This definition of "improper means" might be considered somewhat less comprehensive than the definition used by the UTSA, in that the instruction excludes "breach . . . of duty to maintain secrecy," which is included in the UTSA. *See* UTSA § 1(1). Because these instructions address acquisition of the secret first, and then wrongful disclosure or use, a breach of duty to maintain secrecy is not treated as acquisition by "improper means." Subsequent instructions on wrongful use and disclosure cover this concept.

Note that the UTSA's definition of "improper means" ("[t]heft, bribery, misrepresentation, breach or inducement of a breach of duty to maintain secrecy, or espionage through electronic or other means") is subject to variation in statutes that are based on the UTSA. *See, e.g.,* Ala. Code § 8-27-2(2) (1993) ("improper means" also includes trespass and other deliberate acts committed for purpose of gaining access to information by means of "electronic, photographic, telescopic or other aids to enhance normal human perception" when owner has reasonable expectation of privacy); 765 Ill. Comp. Stat. Ann. 1065/2(a), cmts. (West 1993 & Supp. 1996) ("improper means" also includes "breach of a confidential relationship or other duty to maintain secrecy" and any conduct improper under circumstances); N.C. Gen. Stat. § 66-152 (1995) (term "improper means" not used; rather, violation of statute includes only acquisition, use, or disclosure of plaintiff's trade secret without plaintiff's express or implied authority); S.C. Code Ann. § 39-8-20(1) (Law. Co-op. 1972 & Supp. 1997) ("improper means" also includes "breach or inducement of a breach of . . . duties imposed by the common law, statute, contract, license, protective order, or other court or administrative order"). The practitioner should consider these variations when formulating this instruction.

The UTSA imposes liability for mere acquisition of a trade secret using improper means; neither disclosure nor use of the trade secret is required for liability to attach.[4] *See* comments to §§ 8.2, *supra*, and 8.5, *infra*. Thus, if the misappropriation claim is based on improper acquisition alone, the misappropriation instruction should end here, to be followed by the damages instructions. *But see* Ala. Code § 8-27-3 cmt. (1993) (stating that requirements for proof of misappropriation codify common law, and no liability for improper acquisition alone).

---

4. However, the UTSA does impose additional liability when a defendant that has improperly acquired a trade secret uses or discloses that information. UTSA § 1(2)(ii)(A). In imposing liability for mere acquisition, without disclosure or use, the UTSA differs from the *Restatement of Torts*, under which use or disclosure is always required.

8.4.2   Confidential Relationship

You must determine whether defendant acquired the information through a confidential relationship with plaintiff.

To determine whether the trade secret was disclosed to defendant through a confidential relationship, you may consider whether, based on the dealings between the parties, defendant knew or should have known that plaintiff expected the information to be kept secret and whether plaintiff's expectation was reasonable.

At times an agreement about confidentiality will be express, as when there is a written agreement between the parties specifying that defendants will not disclose or use the information unless authorized to do so. At other times an agreement about confidentiality will be implicit in the circumstances of the parties' dealings. You may find a confidential relationship existed between the parties based either on an express agreement between the parties or one implied from the circumstances of their dealings.

COMMENT

This model instruction, or portions, should be used if there is an issue about whether an express or implied-in-fact confidential relationship exists (often not disputed by the parties). The relevant inquiry involves classic jury issues, such as what the parties subjectively believed about the nature of their relationship and what a reasonable person would have believed under the circumstances.

However, some confidential relationships are commonly implied as a matter of law (except when the parties expressly contract otherwise), including employer-employee relationships, joint venture or partnership relationships, or prospective licensee-licensor relationships. *See generally* 1 Roger M. Milgrim, *Milgrim on Trade Secrets* §§ 3.01-3.03 (2003). Whether a confidential relationship is to be implied as a matter of law is typically a question of law for the court and not the jury.

See Surgidev Corp. v. Eye Tech., Inc., 648 F. Supp. 661 (D. Minn. 1986), *aff'd,* 828 F.2d 452 (8th Cir. 1987) (plaintiff can prove confidential relationship by presenting proof of express contract or continuous trusting relationship that gives rise to duty not to disclose); *Vacco Indus., Inc. v. Van Den Berg,* 6 Cal. Rptr. 2d 602 (Cal. Ct. App. 1992) (essence of misappropriation claim is breach of faith or confidence); *Elm City Cheese Co., Inc. v. Federico,* 752 A.2d 1037, 1052-53 (Conn. 1999) (confidential relationship where defendant was plaintiffs' close personal friend, trusted advisor, and personal accountant); *H. E. Butt Grocery Co. v. Moody's Quality Meats, Inc.*, 951 S.W.2d 33 (Tex. App. 1997) ("Trade secret information disclosed pursuant to negotiations for the sale of a business are disclosed under a duty of confidence imposed as a matter of law."); *Omega Optical, Inc. v. Chroma Tech. Corp.*, 800 A.2d 1064 (Vt. 2002) (requiring "something more than the mere employer-employee relationship to establish a duty of confidentiality"; employee must know or have reason to know the information is confidential) (and cases cited therein); *Ed Nowogroski Ins., Inc. v. Rucker,* 971 P.2d 936 (Wash. 1999) ("The employment relationship is a confidential relationship which gives rise to a post-employment duty not to disclose trade secrets.").

8.4.3   Other Circumstances Where Duty Imposed by Law

There are times when a party acquires trade secret information innocently, and only later comes under a duty to plaintiff. One example would be when the trade secret is acquired by mistake or accident, when defendant does not have reason to believe it belongs to another. Another example would be when defendant buys information from someone, without having any reason to know that the information is stolen. In innocent situations such as these, a duty is only imposed on defendant if and when defendant either knows or has reason to know (i.e., is on notice) that the trade secret belongs to another and has been wrongfully acquired.

If you determine that defendant acquired plaintiff's trade secret innocently, you must next decide whether defendant ever learned or was put on notice that its acquisition of the trade secret occurred by mistake or by accident, or through a third party that had used improper means or breached a confidential relationship. If you determine that defendant either learned or should have known that the trade secret information had come to it through improper means, then defendant's duty to plaintiff would begin only on the date when defendant first acquired such knowledge.

COMMENT

The UTSA codifies the common law rule that one who acquires a trade secret by accident, mistake, or from a third party without knowledge that such person is under a duty not to use or disclose the information, owes no duty to plaintiff until put on actual or constructive notice of plaintiff's rights. Even once the good faith acquirer is put on actual or constructive notice, it might still be exempted from liability—at least to an extent—if it has materially and prejudicially changed its position in reliance on the information. *See* comment to § 8.5, *infra*.

The following state statutes differ slightly from the UTSA: Or. Rev. Stat. § 646.461(2) (1988) (Oregon statute does not discuss liability for disclosure or use of trade secret acquired by accident or mistake); Va. Code. Ann. § 59.1-336 (1995) and Wis. Stat. § 134.90 (1995) (these acts impose liability if, when defendant used or disclosed trade secret, defendant knew, or had reason to know, that it acquired its knowledge of trade secret by accident or mistake; irrelevant whether defendant's disclosure or use was before or after defendant materially changed defendant's position).

See Restatement (Third) of Unfair Competition § 40 cmt. d (1995) (among facts that might be relevant in establishing defendant's actual or constructive knowledge are defendant's knowledge of any precautions against disclosure taken by trade secret owner, defendant's familiarity with industry customs or practices that would justify an assumption that disclosure by a third person was unauthorized, information known to defendant regarding nature of relationship between trade secret owner and person from whom defendant acquired the secret, and any direct communications to defendant from trade secret owner).

8.5   Wrongful Use or Disclosure

You must determine whether defendant wrongfully used or wrongfully disclosed the trade secret in question.

A defendant who has acquired trade secret information by improper means has no right to use or to disclose the information in any way whatsoever. Thus, any use or disclosure by a defendant who has acquired a trade secret by improper means is wrongful.

A defendant who originally acquired information through a confidential relationship may not disclose such information in any way that goes beyond the scope of authorization it received from plaintiff regarding use and disclosure. That is, a person receiving trade secret information in confidence may use or disclose the information only in strict accordance with the understanding under which the information was given to the person. Any other use or disclosure is wrongful.

A person who comes into possession of trade secret information without realizing that it has been, for example, acquired through improper means, or who acquires the information by mistake or accident not having reason to believe that it belongs to another, is authorized to use that information so long as the person does not know, and has no reason to know, that the information in fact belongs to another or that use is not authorized. By the same token, once a defendant has reason to believe such information belongs to another, then it is wrongful for the defendant to use or disclose the information.

COMMENT

A defendant who has acquired plaintiff's trade secret information by mistake or accident, or without knowledge of a third party's use of improper means or breach of a confidential relationship, is not liable for any use or disclosure of a trade secret before receiving actual or constructive notice of plaintiff's rights in the information. When defendant has, in good faith, paid fair value for the secret, or materially changed its position in detrimental reliance before receiving such notice, then, to the extent that to subject defendant to liability would be inequitable, defendant is also immune to liability for defendant's future use or disclosure. *See* UTSA § 3(a), cmt.; *Restatement of Torts* § 758 (1939). Because the questions of whether defendant changes its position in material reliance before receiving notice, and whether it would be inequitable to hold defendant liable for future use and disclosure under such circumstances are more appropriate for a judge than a jury, they have been excluded from these jury instructions.

While improper acquisition alone can be a basis for liability under the UTSA, where acquisition of the trade secret is not improper, use or disclosure in violation of a duty must still be proven.[5] *See* UTSA § 1(2); comments to §§ 8.2, 8.4.1, *supra; e.g., Morlife, Inc. v. Perry*, 66 Cal. Rptr. 2d 731 (Ct. App. 1997); *Ed Nowogroski Ins., Inc. v. Rucker*, 971 P.2d 936, 942-43 (Wash. 1999). *See generally* Restatement *(Third) of Unfair Competition* § 40 cmt. b (noting that the cases requiring proof of wrongful use or disclosure are typically those in which the information was properly acquired through a confidential relationship).

Note that the "inevitable disclosure" doctrine, which gained popularity after *Pepsico, Inc. v. Redmond*, 54 F.3d 1262 (7th Cir. 1995), is not addressed in these instructions because it is an equitable doctrine used in determining appropriateness of injunctive relief. However, circumstantial evidence can be sufficient to prove use to a jury. *See Restatement (Third) of Unfair Competition* §

---

5. In contrast to the UTSA, the *Restatement of Torts* requires a finding of use or disclosure by defendant, or that defendant will likely use or disclose plaintiff's trade secret in the future, to impose liability on defendant. *See* Hunter v. Fisons Corp., 776 F.2d 1 (5th Cir. 1985) (holding existence of trade secret or confidential relationship immaterial if defendant did not use information); Abraham Zion Corp. v. Lebow, 593 F. Supp. 551 (S.D.N.Y. 1984) (holding plaintiff must prove commercial use by defendant to establish liability), *aff'd*, 761 F.2d 93 (2d Cir. 1985).

40 cmt. c ("[P]roof of the defendant's knowledge of the trade secret together with substantial similarities between the parties' products or processes may justify an inference of use by the defendant.").

8.6   Compensatory Damages

If you find that defendant is liable to plaintiff for its conduct, then you should consider whether plaintiff has suffered monetary damages as a result. You should address the issue of damages, however, only if you first determine that defendant is liable to plaintiff on any of the bases we have discussed previously.

As with issues of liability, plaintiff has the burden to prove to you that it has suffered harm due to the wrongful conduct of defendant. You may look at damages from several perspectives: (1) actual loss to plaintiff, (2) benefits gained by defendant, and (3) a reasonable royalty.

Let me now go over each of these types of damages.

8.6.1 Plaintiff's Actual Losses

Plaintiff claims that it has suffered actual monetary loss from misuse of its trade secrets. This actual loss can include both out-of-pocket expenses and lost profits. If you find, for example, that plaintiff would have realized profits from using trade secrets in its business that it has lost due to the wrongful conduct of defendant, then you may measure damages by the amount of such lost profits for the particular periods of time that I will cover with you in a moment.

COMMENT

See comments that follow model instructions relating to all damages instructions.

8.6.2   Defendant's Benefit

In measuring plaintiff's damages, you may also consider what benefit defendant has gained from misuse of plaintiff's trade secrets. Regardless of whether you find that plaintiff itself suffered losses, if you find that defendant benefited from using a trade secret belonging to plaintiff, then you may award the monetary value that you attribute to those benefits as the measure of plaintiff's damage.

It may be that only one of these measures of damages (i.e., plaintiff's losses or defendant's benefit) is necessary to fully compensate plaintiff. However, you are also entitled to combine both plaintiff's losses and defendant's gains in determining the measure of damages to award plaintiff, so long as you follow the guidelines I am about to give you.

These two approaches to damages—plaintiff's losses and defendant's gains—while different in some respects, may overlap. That is, it may be that defendant profited from particular sales that plaintiff would have made had defendant not competed using the trade secrets. In that situation, the two ways of approaching damages that I have just described would measure the identical damages—whether viewed as plaintiff's loss or defendant's gain. The law does not permit a plaintiff to recover twice for the same damages. Thus, you may include as damages *both* plaintiff's lost profits *and* defendant's gain *only* if and to the extent that they do not overlap in this way. Stated in other words, if you were to include lost sales in calculating plaintiff's losses because defendant made the sales, then the value of those same sales should be excluded from any calculation of defendant's gains that you may make.

COMMENT

See comments following instructions relating to all damages instructions.

8.6.3 Royalties

Plaintiff is claiming damages in the form of a royalty.

You may measure damages in terms of a royalty, but only if you find that plaintiff has presented evidence of what a reasonable royalty would be. A reasonable royalty is the price that would be agreed upon by a willing buyer and a willing seller for the use made of the trade secret by defendant. You may only award a royalty to cover the time period during which damages apply, which I will discuss with you in a moment.

Some of the factors you may consider in determining the amount of a reasonable royalty include:

1. the price that has been paid in the past for use of the trade secret;

2. the total value of the secret to plaintiff, including its development costs, if any;

3. the uses for the information that the defendant had in mind; and

4. the time and effort that would have been required before the defendant or another competitor could have acquired or likely acquired the same or equivalent information through proper means.

COMMENT

See comments following instructions relating to all damages instructions.

8.6.4　Time Period for Damages

Plaintiff would be entitled to damages running only for as long as (1) you find that plaintiff's trade secret would be entitled to protection, plus (2) an additional period, if any, that you find that the trade secret afforded defendant a competitive advantage, such as providing defendant a head start in its business.

COMMENT REGARDING DAMAGES INSTRUCTIONS GENERALLY

Rather than referring to plaintiff's damages merely as "lost profits," plaintiff's damages have here been described in terms of "losses," to include not only lost profits but also detriments such as loss of direct overhead and general and administrative expenses resulting from defendant's misappropriation. As for defendant's illicit gains, while many cases speak in terms of "unjust enrichment," and some speak of "profits," the model instructions describe these concepts as "gains" or "benefits"— terms more likely to be meaningful to a juror.

The measure of a reasonable royalty will vary by jurisdiction, and practitioners are advised to review the specific standards adopted by their law. The list of factors cited in the model instruction on a reasonable royalty is not meant to be comprehensive; rather, it refers to the more common measures of a reasonable royalty courts have used.

Of course, lost profits, unjust enrichment, gains, or other benefits are not consistently applied across jurisdictions, and may be subject to differing standards according to state law. For example: What costs should be deducted from gross revenues to calculate lost profit damages? Who has the burden of proving the deductions from gross revenues that are appropriate to calculate defendants' gains? Care should be given to use terms that are accepted in a given jurisdiction.

The generally less stringent burden imposed on a plaintiff when proving damages, as opposed to proving liability, will also vary by jurisdiction and has accordingly not been covered.

Under the UTSA, a plaintiff is entitled to both its actual loss and defendant's unjust enrichment, to the extent they do not overlap.[6] UTSA § 3(a). *But see* N.C. Gen. Stat. §§ 66-154(b) (damages available either for plaintiff's losses or defendant's unjust enrichment, whichever is greater); *Saforo & Assocs., Inc. v. Porocel Corp.*, 991 S.W.2d 117 (Ark. 1999) (holding that plaintiff may recover the greater of his own lost profits or defendant's gain but not a combination of the two); *cf. Home Pride Foods, Inc. v. Johnson*, 634 N.W.2d 774 (Neb. 2001) (despite statute that tracks UTSA, finding ambiguity over whether Nebraska follows UTSA or either/or approach to damages).

The UTSA permits damages in the form of a reasonable royalty "in lieu of" damages in any other form.[7] UTSA § 3(a). Despite the technical "in lieu of" requirement, it seems unlikely that a court would deny the recovery of out-of-pocket losses merely because a reasonable royalty was the chosen form of relief.

Under some statutes, reasonable royalty damages are awarded by the court and are available only if neither plaintiff's lost prof-

---

6. This approach is in contrast to the *Restatement of Torts*, which takes an either/or approach to measuring damages—plaintiff may recover the greater of plaintiff's lost profits or defendant's gains. *See, e.g.*, Sperry Rand Corp. v. A-T-O, Inc., 447 F.2d 1387 (4th Cir. 1971) (plaintiff may recover either lost profits or defendant's unjust enrichment); Curtiss-Wright Corp. v. Edel-Brown Tool & Die Co., 407 N.E.2d 319 (Mass. 1980) (holding that higher amount of plaintiff's profits or defendant's unjust enrichment is proper measure of damages).

7. Under the *Restatement of Torts*, royalty damages are available only if neither plaintiff's lost profits nor defendant's gain can be shown. *See, e.g.*, Molex, Inc. v. Nolen, 759 F.2d 474 (5th Cir. 1985) (reasonable royalty measure of damages remedy applied); University Computing Co. v. Lykes-Youngstown Corp., 504 F.2d 518, 538-39 (5th Cir. 1974) (listing factors to be considered in determining reasonable royalty measure of damages).

its nor defendant's unjust enrichment can be proven. *See* Cal. Civ. Code § 3426.3(b) (Deering 1970 & Supp. 1996); Ga. Code Ann. § 10-1-763(a) (1994 & Supp. 1995); 765 Ill. Comp. Stat. Ann. 1065/4(a) (West 1993 & Supp. 1996); Ind. Code § 24-2-3-4(b) (West 1993 & Supp. 1996); *see also* Va. Code Ann. § 59.1-338 (Michie 1992 & Supp. 1995) (allowing award of reasonable royalty if such amount greater than any other provable measure of damages); Wis. Stat. § 134.90(4) (1989 & Supp. 1995) (providing for reasonable royalty award to be awarded by court, if this sum is greatest provable amount of damages).

The Alabama, Alaska, Arkansas, Connecticut, Delaware, Idaho, Louisiana, Minnesota, Montana, North Dakota, and Washington acts *do not* provide for a reasonable royalty measure of damages.

In contravention of the maxim that every wrong is compensable, the UTSA provides that a plaintiff cannot recover from a defendant that materially and prejudicially changed its position in reliance on a trade secret prior to acquiring knowledge of the misappropriation, where such recovery would be "inequitable."[8] UTSA § 3(a). *But see* Alaska Stat. § 45.50.915 (1995) and Cal. Civ. Code § 3426.3 (Deering 1970 & Supp. 1996) (declining to exempt a defendant that has materially changed its position from liability for damages). The North Carolina and South Carolina statutes provide greater detail on the damages impact of a good faith acquirer that materially changes its position. N.C. Gen. Stat. § 66-154(a)(2) (1995) (if a good faith acquirer has acquired inventory through knowledge or use of the trade secret in question, he can dispose of the inventory without payment or royalty; if use of the trade secret by a good faith acquirer has no adverse economic effect upon the owner of the trade secret, the only available remedy shall be injunction against disclosure); S.C. Code Ann. § 39-8-40(A) (Law. Co-op. 1992 & Supp. 1997) (a material

---

8. The UTSA does, however, provide that an injunction may issue to condition future use of the trade secret by such a defendant on payment of a reasonable royalty. UTSA § 2(b).

and prejudicial change in position before acquiring knowledge or reason to know of misappropriation may not only render full monetary recovery inequitable, but may also form the basis for reducing monetary recovery).

In addition, the following statutes vary slightly from the UTSA on damages or contain greater or less detail: Ala. Code §§ 8-27-4(1)(b), (c) (1993) provides for monetary damages equal to defendant's profits and any other benefits to defendant attributable to misappropriation *and* plaintiff's actual damages resulting from misappropriation, if actual damages not duplicative of defendant's profits; to prove defendant's profits, plaintiff must present proof of defendant's gross revenues; defendant then has burden of proving its deductible expenses and other elements of profit not attributable to misappropriation); Or. Rev. Stat. § 646.465(2) (1988) (provides for actual loss and unjust enrichment; however, total amount of damages shall not be less than amount of reasonable royalty); Wis. Stat. § 134.90(4) (1989 & Supp. 1995) (court may award damages).

8.7 Exemplary Damages

[No model instructions provided.]

COMMENT

Depending on whether plaintiff is pursuing a trade secrets claim based on a contract or tort theory of recovery, plaintiff may be able to recover exemplary or punitive damages. Although generally not awarded in contract actions, punitive damages are available in many states under tort theories. The UTSA standard for obtaining punitive damages under a tort theory of trade secret misappropriation is whether defendant acted willfully and maliciously in misappropriating plaintiff's trade secret. The measure of punitive damages available to plaintiff varies from state to state, and practitioners are advised to review the standard for the particular state involved. *See generally* 1 Melvin F. Jager, *Trade Secrets Law* § 7:23 (2002) (and cases cited therein); 2 Roger M. Milgrim, *Milgrim on Trade Secrets* § 15.02[3][i] (2003) (and cases cited therein); M.A. Rosenhouse, *Proper Measure and Elements of Damages for Misappropriation of Trade Secret*, 11 A.L.R. 4th 12 § 36 (1982).

Under the UTSA, the *court* may grant exemplary damages. UTSA § 3(b). Hence, there would be no jury instruction given. Nonetheless, some state statutes allow the jury to grant such damages. *See, e.g.*, Colo. Rev. Stat. § 7-74-104(2) (1990 & Supp. 1995) (court *or jury* may award exemplary damages, not to exceed monetary damages awarded); N.C. Gen. Stat. § 66-154(c) (1995) ("trier of fact" has discretion to award punitive damages). Two states, Alabama and Oregon, do not specify whether the court or the jury may award damages. Ala. Code § 8-27-4 (1993); Or. Rev. Stat. § 646.465(3) (1988). All state statutes provide for exemplary damages, except for Arkansas, Louisiana, Michigan, and Nebraska.

The UTSA permits exemplary damages of up to twice the amount of compensatory damages. UTSA § 3(b). However, the amount of exemplary damages recoverable may vary by state. *See, e.g.*,

Ala. Code § 8-27-4 (1993) (exemplary damages cannot exceed amount awarded for lost profits or other monetary damages, but shall not be less than $5,000); Minn. Stat. § 325C.04 (1995 & Supp. 1996) (court may award exemplary damages in amount it deems just and equitable); Miss. Code Ann. § 75-36-7(2) (1972 & Supp. 1995), Mo. Rev. Stat. § 417.457(2) (1995), and Mont. Code Ann. § 30-14-404(2) (1995) (no limit on exemplary damages specified); N.C. Gen. Stat. § 66-153(c) (1995) (no limit on punitive damages in North Carolina Trade Secrets Protection Act, though limited elsewhere); Ohio Rev. Code Ann. § 1333.63(B) (Anderson 2001) (punitive or exemplary damages not to exceed three times award for compensatory damages); Vt. Stat. Ann. tit. 9 § 4603(b) (1995 & Supp. 1996) (no limit on punitive damages); Va. Code Ann. § 59.1-338(B) (Michie 1992 & Supp. 1995) (exemplary or "punitive" damages limited to amount stated in Uniform Act or $350,000, whichever is less).

Table of Cases

Aldrich v. Thomson McKinnon Sec., Inc., 589 F. Supp. 683 (S.D.N.Y. 1984) 60; 110; 149; 213; 315; 382

Aldrich v. Thomson McKinnon Sec., Inc., 756 F.2d 243 (2d Cir. 1985) 59; 108; 148; 212; 314; 338; 381

Alexander v. Certified Master Bldr. Corp., 43 F. Supp. 2d 1242 (D. Kan. 1999) 305

Allen & O'Hara, Inc. v. Barrett Wrecking, Inc., 898 F.2d 512 (7th Cir. 1990) 5; 45

Allen v. Leybourne, 190 So. 2d 825 (Fla. Dist. Ct. App. 1966) 12

Allen v. Sanders, 337 S.E.2d 428 (Ga. Ct. App. 1985) 333

Allfast Fastening Sys. v. Briles Rivet Corp., 16 F. Supp. 2d 1154 (C.D. Cal. 1998) 181

Allied Supply Co. v. Brown, 585 So. 2d 33 (Ala. 1991) 402

Allwaste, Inc. v. Hinson, 65 F.3d 1523 (9th Cir. 1995) 254

Alpo Petfoods, Inc. v. Ralston Purina Co., 720 F. Supp. 194 (D.D.C. 1989), *aff'd in part, vacated in part*, 913 F.2d 958 (D.C. Cir. 1990) 160

Alyeska Pipeline Serv. Co. v. Aurora Air Serv., Inc., 604 P.2d 1090 (Alaska 1979) 66; 94

Am. Bus. Interiors, Inc. v. Haworth, Inc., 798 F.2d 1135 (8th Cir. 1986) 52; 68; 72; 103; 104; 141; 143; 206; 207; 308; 309; 375; 376

Am. Cyanamid Co. v. Elizabeth Arden Sales Corp., 331 F. Supp. 597 (S.D.N.Y. 1971) 16

Am. Footwear Corp. v. Gen. Footwear Co., 609 F.2d 655 (2d Cir. 1979), *cert. denied*, 445 U.S. 951 (1980) 229

Am. Greetings Corp. v. Dan-Dee Imports, Inc., 619 F. Supp. 1204 (D.N.J. 1985) 180; 229

Am. Greetings Corp. v. Dan-Dee Imports, Inc., 807 F.2d 1136 (3d Cir. 1986) 181

Am. Ins. Co. v. Franc, 111 Ill. App. 382 (Ill. App. Ct. 1903) 139

Am. Life Ins. Co. v. Parra, 63 F. Supp. 2d 480 (D. Del. 1999) 280

Arbour v. Hazelton, 534 A.2d 1303 (Me. 1987) 269

Aries Info. Sys., Inc. v. Pacific Mgmt. Sys. Corp., 366 N.W.2d 366 (Minn. Ct. App. 1985) 407

Arkansas v. Texas, 346 U.S. 368 (1953) 7

Arlington Heights Nat'l Bank v. Arlington Heights Fed. Sav. & Loan Ass'n, 229 N.E.2d 514 (Ill. 1967) 79

Art Metal-U.S.A., Inc. v. United States, 753 F.2d 1151 (D.C. Cir. 1985) 113; 114; 118; 120; 122; 134

Arthur D. Little Int'l, Inc. v. Dooyang Corp., 928 F. Supp. 1189 (D. Mass. 1996) 279

Artus Corp. v. Nordic Co., 512 F. Supp. 1184 (W.D. Pa. 1981) 224; 225

Aschinger v. Columbus Showcase Co., 934 F.2d 1402 (6th Cir. 1991) 341

Asermely v. Allstate Ins. Co., 728 A.2d 461 (R.I. 1999) 289

Ashburn v. Miller, 326 P.2d 229 (Cal. Ct. App. 1958) 292

Asia Inv. Co., Ltd. v. Borowski, 184 Cal. Rptr. 317 (Cal. Ct. App. 1982) 94

Associates in Adolescent Psychiatry, S.C. v. Home Life Ins. Co., 941 F.2d 561 (7th Cir. 1991) 250

Astor Chauffeured Limousine v. Runnfeldt Inv. Corp., 910 F.2d 1540 (7th Cir. 1990) 280

Atkinson v. Anadarko Bank & Trust Co., 808 F.2d 438 (5th Cir.), *cert. denied,* 483 U.S. 1032 (1987) 244

Atlas Pile Driving Co. v. DiCon Fin. Co., 886 F.2d 986 (8th Cir. 1989) 244; 250

Audio Fidelity, Inc. v. High Fidelity Recordings, Inc., 283 F.2d 551 (9th Cir. 1960) 221

AUSA Life Ins. Co. v. Ernst & Young, 206 F.3d 202 (2d Cir. 2000) 302

Ausley v. Bishop, 515 S.E.2d 72 (N.C. 1999) 273

AutoZone, Inc. v. Tandy Corp., 174 F. Supp. 2d 718 (D. Tenn. 2001) 159

B.C. Morton Int'l Corp. v. FDIC, 199 F. Supp. 702 (D. Mass. 1961) 116

Bellefonte Underwriters Co., Inc. v. Brown, 663 S.W.2d 562 (Tex. App. 1984) 55; 144; 208; 310; 377

Bennett v. E.F. Hutton Co., Inc., 597 F. Supp. 1547 (D. Ohio 1984) 338

Berger v. Sec. Pac. Info. Sys., 795 P.2d 1380 (Colo. App. 1990) 273

Berkowitz v. Baron, 428 F. Supp. 1190 (S.D.N.Y. 1977) 283

Bernard v. Commerce Drug Co., 964 F.2d 1338 (2d Cir. 1992) 173

Besett v. Basnett, 389 So. 2d 995 (Fla. 1980) 292

Besser v. Ohio State Univ., State ex rel, 732 N.E.2d 373 (Ohio 2000) 395 n.2; 398

Beyda v. USAir, Inc., 697 F. Supp. 1394 (W.D. Pa. 1988) 12

Big O Tire Dealers v. Goodyear Tire & Rubber Co., 408 F. Supp. 1219 (D. Colo. 1976), *modified on other grounds*, 561 F.2d 1365 (10th Cir. 1977), *cert. dismissed*, 434 U.S. 1052 (1978) 101; 121; 122; 125; 163; 164; 166; 173; 175; 196; 198; 200; 221

Binkewitz v. Allstate Ins. Co., 537 A.2d 723 (N.J. Super. Ct. App. Div. 1988) 131

Blake v. Levy, 464 A.2d 52 (Conn. 1983) 67; 78

Blank v. Kirwan, 703 P.2d 58 (Cal. 1985) 66; 74

Blatty v. New York Times Co., 728 P.2d 1177 (Cal. 1986), *cert. denied*, 485 U.S. 934 (1988) 123

Blisscraft of Hollywood v. United Plastics Co., 294 F.2d 694 (2d Cir. 1961) 192

Bloomfield Fin. Co. v. Nat'l Home Life Assurance Co., 734 F.2d 1408 (10th Cir. 1984) 373

Bloomfield v. Neb. State Bank, 465 N.W.2d 144 (Neb. 1991) 340

Blue Bell, Inc. v. Farah Mfg. Co., 508 F.2d 1260 (5th Cir. 1975) 192

Blue Ribbon Feed Co. v. Farmers Union Cent. Exch. Inc., 731 F.2d 415, 421 (7th Cir. 1984) 203

BMW of N. Am., Inc. v. Gore, 116 S. Ct. 1589 (1996) 59; 108; 148; 212; 314; 381

Boeing Co. v. Sierracin Corp., 738 P.2d 665 (Wash. 1987) 403

Courtesy Temp. Serv., Inc. v. Camacho, 272 Cal. Rptr. 352 (Cal. Ct. App. 1990) 395 n.2

Craig v. First Am. Capital Res., Inc., 740 F. Supp. 530 (N.D. Ill. 1990) 332

Cramer v. Gen. Tel. & Elec. Corp., 582 F.2d 259 (3d Cir. 1978), *cert. denied,* 439 U.S. 1129 (1979) 350

Credit Alliance Corp. v. Arthur Anderson & Co., 483 N.E.2d 110 (N.Y. 1985) 284

Creta, In re, 271 B.R. 214 (B.A.P. 1st Cir. 2002) 302

Crockett v. Sahara Realty Corp., 591 P.2d 1135 (Nev. 1979) 92

Crosby v. Beam, 47 Ohio St.3d 105, 548 N.E.2d 217 (Ohio 1989) 341

Crosby v. Rogers, 30 S.E.2d 248 (Ga. 1944) 338

Crowe v. Domestic Loans, Inc., 130 S.E.2d 845 (S.C. 1963) 32

Cuisinarts, Inc. v. Robot-Coupe Int'l Corp., 580 F. Supp. 634 (S.D.N.Y. 1984) 203

Cundiff v. Umfleet, 21 S.W.3d 127 (Mo. Ct. App. 2000) 319

Cunningham v. PFL Life Ins. Co., 42 F. Supp. 2d 872 (N.D. Iowa 1999) 280

Curtiss-Wright Corp. v. Edel-Brown Tool & Die Co., 407 N.E.2d 319 (Mass. 1980) 423 n.6

CVD, Inc. v. Raytheon Co., 769 F.2d 842 (1st Cir. 1985), *cert. denied,* 475 U.S. 1016 (1986) 402

Cytanovich Reading Ctr. v. Reading Game, 208 Cal. Rptr. 412 (Cal. Ct. App. 1984) 156

Dairy Stores v. Sentinel Publ'g, 516 A.2d 220 (N.J. 1986) 132

Dale Sys. v. Gen. Teleradio, 105 F. Supp. 745 (S.D.N.Y. 1952) 114

Daly v. Nau, 339 N.E.2d 71 (Ind. Ct. App. 1975) 48

Damon v. Sun Co., 87 F.3d 1467 (1st Cir. 1996) 272

Danann Realty Corp. v. Harris, 157 N.E.2d 597 (N.Y. App. 1959) 293

Daniels v. Dean, 833 P.2d 1078 (Mont. 1992)

Eversharp, Inc. v. Pal Blade Co., 182 F.2d 779 (2d Cir. 1950) 114

Exxon Corp. v. Allsup, 808 S.W.2d 648 (Tex. App. 1991) 78

F. L. Mendez & Co. v. Gen. Motors Corp., 161 F.2d 695 (7th Cir. 1947) 101

Faberge, Inc. v. Saxony Prods., Inc., 605 F.2d 426 (9th Cir. 1979) 179

Fabrica, Inc. v. El Dorado Corp., 697 F.2d 890 (9th Cir. 1983) 188

Falls v. Sporting News Publ'g Co., 714 F. Supp. 843 (E.D. Mich. 1989), *on remand from* 834 F.2d 611 (6th Cir. 1987), *aff'd*, 899 F.2d 1221 (6th Cir. 1990) 137

Falls v. Sporting News Publ'g Co., 834 F.2d 611 (6th Cir. 1987), *aff'd*, 899 F.2d 1221 (6th Cir. 1990) 140

Fane v. Zimmer, Inc., 927 F.2d 124 (2d Cir. 1991) 368

Fantaco Enter., Inc. v. Iavarone, 555 N.Y.S.2d 921 (N.Y. App. Div. 1990) 67; 92

Far W. Fed. Bank, S.B. v. Dir., Office of Thrift Supervision, 787 F. Supp. 952 (D. Or. 1992) 372

Far W. Fed. Bank, S.B. v. Office of Thrift Supervision, 119 F.3d 1358 (9th Cir. 1997) 372

Farm Bureau Policy Holders & Members v. Farm Bureau Mut. Ins. Co. of Ark., Inc., 984 S.W.2d 6 (Ark. 1998) 270

Farmland Indus., Inc. v. Grain Bd. of Iraq, 904 F.2d 732 (D.C. Cir. 1990) 29

Feaheny v. Caldwell, 437 N.W.2d 358 (Mich. Ct. App. 1989) 30

Feak v. Marion Steam Shovel Co., 84 F.2d 670 (9th Cir. 1936) 293

Fed. Deposit Ins. Corp. v. Baker, 739 F. Supp. 1401 (C.D. Cal. 1990) 367; 373

Fed. Deposit Ins. Corp. v. Boone, 361 F. Supp. 133 (W.D. Okla. 1972) 347; 353

Fed. Deposit Ins. Corp. v. Carter, 701 F. Supp. 730 (C.D. Cal. 1987) 367

Fed. Deposit Ins. Corp. v. Schuchmann, 235 F.3d 1217 (10th Cir. 2000) 342; 357

Grogan v. Garner, 498 U.S. 279 (1991) 241

Gross v. Sussex, Inc., 630 A.2d 1156 (Md. App. 1993) 294

Grosvenor Properties Ltd. v. Southmark Corp., 896 F.2d 1149 (9th Cir. 1990) 31

Group One, Ltd. v. Hallmark Cards, Inc., 254 F.3d 1041 (Fed. Cir. 2001) 389

Grove Holding Corp. v. First Wis. Nat'l Bank of Sheboygan, 12 F. Supp. 2d 885 (E.D. Wis. 1998) 279

GTFM, Inc. v. Solid Clothing, Inc., 215 F. Supp. 2d 273 (S.D.N.Y. 2002) 201

Guastella v. Wardell, 198 So. 2d 227 (Miss. 1967) 286

Gulf Oil Corp. of Penn. v. Newton, 31 A.2d 462 (Conn. 1943) 283

H. E. Butt Grocery Co. v. Moody's Quality Meats, Inc., 951 S.W.2d 33 (Tex. App. 1997) 413

H.J., Inc. v. Int'l Tel. & Tel. Corp., 867 F.2d 1531 (8th Cir. 1989) 5; 23

H.J., Inc. v. Northwestern Bell Tel. Co., 492 U.S. 229 (1989) 254

H.L. Hayden Co. v. Siemens Med. Sys., Inc., 879 F.2d 1005 (2d Cir. 1989) 51

Hall v. Edge, 782 P.2d 122 (Okla. 1989) 280

Hamilton-Brown Shoe Co. v. Wolf Bros. & Co., 240 U.S. 251 (1916) 201

Handy v. Beck, 581 P.2d 68 (Or. 1978) 287

Hanley v. Cont'l Airlines, Inc., 687 F. Supp. 533 (D. Colo. 1988) 15

Hanson Trust PLC v. ML SCM Acquisition, Inc., 781 F.2d 264 (2d Cir. 1986) 359; 360

Harman v. Willbern, 374 F. Supp. 1149 (D. Kan. 1974), *aff'd,* 520 F.2d. 1333 (10th Cir. 1975) 348; 355; 356

Haroco, Inc. v. Am. Nat'l Bank & Trust Co., 747 F.2d 384 (7th Cir. 1984), *aff'd on other grounds,* 473 U.S. 606 (1985) 243; 261

Harp v. Appliance Mart, Inc., 827 P.2d 1209 (Kan. Ct. App. 1992) 157

J. Eck & Sons, Inc. v. Reuben H. Donnelley Corp., 572 N.E.2d 1090 (Ill. App. Ct. 1991)

J.T. Healy & Son, Inc. v. James A. Murphy & Son, Inc., 260 N.E.2d 723 (Mass. 1970) 387; 403

Jacobs Mfg. Co. v. Sam Brown Co., 792 F. Supp. 1520 (W.D. Mo. 1992), *aff'd in part and rev'd in part*, 19 F.3d 1259 (8th Cir. 1994) 274

Jacobs v. Freeman, 163 Cal. Rptr. 680 (Cal. Ct. App. 1980) 275

Jannotta v. Subway Sandwich Shops, Inc., 125 F.3d 503 (7th Cir. 1997) 59; 109; 148; 212; 314; 381

Japan Telecom, Inc. v. Japan Telecom Am. Inc., 287 F.3d 886 (9th Cir. 2002) 169

Jarvis Christian Coll. v. Nat'l Union Fire Ins. Co., 197 F.3d 742 (5th Cir. 1999) 342

Jean Patou, Inc. v. Jacqueline Cochran, Inc., 201 F. Supp. 861 (S.D.N.Y. 1962), *aff'd*, 312 F.2d 125 (2d Cir. 1963) 154; 226

Jeffrey v. Cathers, 104 S.W.3d 424 (Mo. Ct. App. 2003) 130

Jet Spray Cooler, Inc. v. Crampton, 282 N.E.2d 921 (Mass. 1972) 403

Jimenez v. Chrysler Corp., 74 F. Supp. 2d 548 (D.S.C. 1999) 307

Joba Constr. Co. v. Burns & Roe, Inc., 329 N.W.2d 760 (Mich. Ct. App. 1982) 67; 73

John R. Cowley & Bros., Inc. v. Brown, 569 So. 2d 375 (Ala. 1990) 273

Johnson v. Miller, 596 F. Supp. 768 (D.C. Colo. 1984) 372

Johnston v. Wilbourn, 760 F. Supp. 578 (S.D. Miss. 1991) 254

Jones v. H.F. Ahmanson & Co., 460 P.2d 464 (Cal. 1969) 342

Jones v. Harper, 55 F. Supp. 2d 530 (S.D.W.V. 1999) 336

Jones v. O'Connell, 458 A.2d 355 (Conn. 1983) 78

Joseph v. Norman LaPorte Realty, Inc., 508 So. 2d 496 (Fla. Dist. Ct. App. 1987) 284

Joy v. North, 692 F.2d 880 (2d Cir. 1982), *cert. denied sub nom. Citytrust v. Joy*, 460 U.S. 1051 (1983) 350

Minuteman, Inc. v. Alexander, 434 N.W.2d 773 (Wis. 1989) 390

Mirabito v. Liccardo, 5 Cal. Rptr. 2d 571 (Cal. Ct. App. 1992) 339

Misany v. United States, 873 F.2d 160 (7th Cir. 1989) 17

Mitchell v. Aldrich, 163 A.2d 833 (Vt. 1960) 67

Mobil Oil Corp. v. Cook, 494 S.W.2d 926 (Tex. App. 1973) 73

Mobius Mgmt. Sys., Inc. v. Fourth Dimension Software, Inc., 880 F. Supp. 1005 (S.D.N.Y. 1994) 160

Modern Prods., Inc. v. Schwartz, 734 F. Supp. 362 (E.D. Wis. 1990) 117; 134

Moldea v. New York Times Co., 22 F.3d 310 (D.C. Cir. 1994) 115

Molex, Inc. v. Nolen, 759 F.2d 474 (5th Cir. 1985) 423 n.7

Moloney v. Centner, 727 F. Supp. 1232 (N.D. Ill. 1989) 15

Mooney v. Johnson Cattle, Inc., 634 P.2d 1333 (Or. 1981) 50

Moore Bus. Forms, Inc. v. Ryu, 960 F.2d 486 (5th Cir. 1992) 198

Moore v. Eli Lilly & Co., 626 F. Supp. 365 (D. Mass. 1986) 262

Morex S.P.A. v. Design Inst. Am., Inc., 779 F.2d 799 (2d Cir. 1985) 227

Morlife, Inc. v. Perry, 66 Cal. Rptr. 2d 731 (Cal. Ct. App. 1997) 402; 416

Morrison v. Nat'l Broad. Co., 266 N.Y.S.2d 406 (N.Y. App. Div. 1965), *rev'd on other grounds*, 227 N.E.2d 572 (N.Y. 1967) 117; 134; 136

Morton-Norwich Prods., Inc., In re, 671 F.2d 1332 (C.C.P.A. 1982) 223

Mr. Gasket Co. v. Travis, 299 N.E.2d 906 (Ohio Ct. App. 1973) 161; 221

Mulford v. Computer Leasing, Inc., 759 A.2d 887 (1999) 346

Musick v. Burke, 913 F.2d 1390 (9th Cir. 1990) 245

Mutual of Omaha Ins. Co. v. Novak, 836 F.2d 397 (8th Cir. 1987) 198

Nader v. Allegheny Airlines, Inc., 445 F. Supp. 168 (D.D.C. 1978) 307

Najem v. Classic Cadillac Atlanta Corp., 527 S.E.2d 259 (Ga. 1999) 289

Nat'l Collegiate Athletic Ass'n v. Hornung, 754 S.W.2d 855 (Ky. 1988) 45

Nat'l Football League Props., Inc. v. New Jersey Giants, Inc., 637 F. Supp. 507 (D.N.J. 1986) 155; 229

Nat'l Lampoon, Inc. v. Am. Broad. Cos., 376 F. Supp. 733 (S.D.N.Y.), *aff'd*, 497 F.2d 1343 (2d Cir. 1974) 180

Nat'l Ref. Co. v. Benzo Gas Motor Fuel Co., 20 F. 2d 763 (8th Cir.), *cert. denied*, 275 U.S. 570 (1927) 113; 122

Natural Footwear, Ltd. v. Hart Schaffner & Marx, 760 F.2d 1383 (3d Cir.), *cert. denied*, 474 U.S. 920 (1985) 157

Navajo Mfg. Co. v. Camp, 1995 WL 311792 (Minn. Ct. App. 1995) 301

Nazeri v. Mo. Valley Coll., 860 S.W.2d 303 (Mo. 1993) 23

NCC Sunday Inserts, Inc. v. World Color Press, Inc., 759 F. Supp. 1004 (S.D.N.Y. 1991) 16; 17

Neapolitan, United States v., 791 F.2d 489 (7th Cir.), *cert. denied*, 479 U.S. 939 (1986) 260

Neder v. United States, 527 U.S. 1 (1999) 250

Needham v. White Lab., Inc., 847 F.2d 355 (7th Cir. 1988) 368

Nelson v. Taff, 499 N.W.2d 685 (Wis. Ct. App. 1993) 297; 299; 300

Nesler v. Fisher & Co., 452 N.W.2d 191 (Iowa 1990) 67

Neterer v. Slabaugh, 548 N.E.2d 832 (Ind. Ct. App. 1990) 26

Network Telecomms., Inc. v. Boor-Crepeau, 790 P.2d 901 (Colo. Ct. App. 1990) 403

Neville v. Higbie, 20 P.2d 348 (Cal. Ct. App. 1933) 118

New England Butt Co. v. Int'l Trade Comm'n, 756 F.2d 874 (D.C. Cir. 1985) 155; 189

New York Times Co. v. Sullivan, 376 U.S. 254 (1964) 21; 134

Newport Elecs., Inc. v. Newport Corp., 157 F. Supp. 2d 202 (D. Conn. 2001) 155

Nolte v. Pearson, 994 F.2d 1311 (8th Cir. 1993) 247

Roadmaster Indus., Inc. v. Columbia Mfg. Co., 893 F. Supp. 1162 (D. Mass. 1995) 321

Roberts v. Gen. Motors Corp., 643 A.2d 956 (N.H. 1994) 95

Robinson, United States v., 763 F.2d 778 (6th Cir. 1985) 245

Rockwell Graphic Sys. v. Dev. Indus., 730 F. Supp. 171 (N.D. Ill. 1990), *rev'd on other grounds*, 925 F.2d 174 (7th Cir. 1991) 399

Rodonich v. House Wreckers Union, 627 F. Supp. 176 (S.D.N.Y. 1985) 261

Rohm and Haas Co. v. Adco Chem. Co., 689 F.2d 424 (3d Cir. 1982) 406 n.3

Rolley v. Younghusband, 204 F.2d 209 (9th Cir. 1953) 192

Rose v. Bartle, 871 F.2d 331 (3d Cir. 1989) 245

Roy v. Coyne, 630 N.E.2d 1024 (Ill. App. Ct. 1994) 6

Roy v. Cunningham, 731 P.2d 526 (Wash. Ct. App. 1986) 94

Roy v. Woonsocket Inst. for Sav., 525 A.2d 915 (R.I. 1987) 20

Rupert v. Sellers, 368 N.Y.S.2d 904 (N.Y. App. Div. 1975) 59; 108; 148; 212; 314; 381

Rusk Farms, Inc. v. Ralston Purina Co., 689 S.W.2d 671, 679 (Mo. Ct. App. 1985) 67

Russow v. Bobola, 277 N.E.2d 769 (Ill. App. Ct. 1972) 321

Rycoline Prods., Inc. v. Walsh, 756 A.2d 1047 (N.J. Super. Ct. App. Div. 2000) 389

S. Atl. Ltd. P'ship of Tenn. v. Riese, 284 F.3d 518 (4th Cir. 2002) 334

S. Cal. Dist. Counsel v. Shepherd of Hills Evangelical Lutheran Church, 144 Cal. Rptr. 46 (Cal. Ct. App. 1976) 279

S.C. Johnson & Son, Inc. v. Johnson, 175 F.2d 176 (2d Cir.), *cert. denied*, 338 U.S. 860 (1949) 173

Saforo & Assocs., Inc. v. Porocel Corp., 991 S.W.2d 117 (Ark. 1999) 394; 423

Salinas v. United States, 522 U.S. 52 (1997) 258

Univ. Computing Co. v. Lykes-Youngstown Corp., 504 F.2d 518 (5th Cir. 1974) 423 n.7

Upjohn Co. v. Riahom Corp., 650 F. Supp. 485 (D. Del. 1986) 49

Va. Bd. of Pharm. v. Va. Citizens Consumer Council, Inc., 425 U.S. 748 (1976) 116

V.C. Video, Inc. v. Nat'l Video, Inc., 755 F. Supp. 962 (D. Kan. 1990)

V.S.H. Realty, Inc. v. Texaco, Inc., 757 F.2d 411 (1st Cir. 1985) 275

Vacco Indus., Inc. v. Van Den Berg, 6 Cal. Rptr. 2d 602 (Cal. Ct. App. 1992) 413

Varwig v. Anderson-Bethel Porsche-Audi, Inc., 141 Cal. Rptr. 539 (Cal. Ct. App. 1977) 284

Vaughn v. Gen. Foods Corp., 797 F.2d 1403 (7th Cir. 1986) 278

Ventura Travelware, Inc. v. Baltimore Luggage Co., 322 N.Y.S.2d 93 (N.Y. App. Div. 1971), aff'd, 328 N.Y.S.2d 811 (N.Y. App. Div. 1972) 182

Verizon Directories v. Yellow Book USA, Inc., 309 F. Supp 2d 401 (E.D. N.Y. 2004) 137

Verkin v. Melroy, 699 F.2d 729 (5th Cir. 1983) 72; 78

Victoria Bank & Trust Co. v. Brady, 811 S.W.2d 931 (Tex. 1991) 67; 69; 87; 89; 94

Vietri Homes, Inc., Matter of, 58 B.R. 663 (Bankr. Del. 1986) 331

Village Supermarket, Inc. v. Mayfair Supermarkets, Inc., 634 A.2d 1381 (N.J. Super. Ct. Law Div. 1993) 83

Vision Sports, Inc. v. Melville Corp., 888 F.2d 609 (8th Cir. 1988) 182

VNA Plus, Inc. v. Apria Healthcare Group, Inc., 29 F. Supp. 2d 1253 (D. Kan. 1998) 278

Voilas v. Gen. Motors Corp., 170 F.3d 367 (3d Cir. 1999) 290

Volkswagenwerk Aktiengesellschaft v. Rickard, 492 F.2d 474 (5th Cir. 1974) 170

W. Des Moines State Bank v. Hawkeye Bancorporation, 722 F.2d 411 (8th Cir. 1983) 203; 204

W. T. Rogers Co., Inc. v. Keene, 778 F.2d 334 (7th Cir. 1985) 188; 189

W. Technologies v. Sverdrup & Parcel, Inc., 739 P.2d 1318 (Ariz. Ct. App. 1986) 45

W.L. Gore & Assocs., Inc. v. Totes, Inc., 788 F. Supp. 800 (D. Del. 1992), *amended*, 1992 U.S. Dist. LEXIS 8055 (D. Del. 1992) 160

Wallace Int'l Silversmiths, Inc. v. Godinger Silver Art Co., Inc., 916 F.2d 76 (2d Cir.), *cert. denied*, 499 U.S. 976 (1991) 188

Wal-Mart Stores, Inc. v. P.O. Mkt., Inc., 66 S.W.3d 620 (Ark. 2002) 398

Wal-Mart Stores, Inc. v. Sturges, 52 S.W.3d 711 (Tex. 2001) 82; 88; 89

Walt Disney Prods. v. Air Pirates, 581 F.2d 751 (9th Cir. 1978), *cert. denied sub nom. O'Neill v. Walt Disney Prods.*, 439 U.S. 1132 (1979) 220

Walters v. First Fed. S&L Ass'n, 641 P.2d 235 (Ariz. 1982) 280

Walters v. First Nat'l Bank, 855 F.2d 267 (6th Cir. 1988), *cert. denied*, 489 U.S. 1067 (1989) 250

Warner Bros. v. Gay Toys, Inc., 658 F.2d 76 (2d Cir. 1981) 227

Warner v. Buck Creek Nursery, Inc., 149 F. Supp. 2d 246 (W.D. Va. 2001) 37

Waste Conversion Sys., Inc. v. Greenstone Indus., Inc., 33 S.W.3d 779 (Tenn. 2000) 31

Waste Distillation Tech., Inc. v. Blasland & Bouck Eng'rs, P.C., 523 N.Y.S.2d 875 (N.Y. App. Div. 1988) 139

Wedgewood Carpet Mills, Inc. v. Color-Set, Inc., 254 S.E.2d 421 (Ga. Ct. App. 1979) 12

Weins v. Sporleder, 569 N.W.2d 16 (S.D. 1997) 398

Weitzman v. Stein, 436 F. Supp. 895 (S.D.N.Y. 1977) 290

Wells Fargo Bank v. Ariz. Lab., Teamsters and Cement Masons, 38 P.3d 12 (Ariz. 2002) 23; 323; 324

Welter v. Seton Hall Univ., 579 A.2d 332 (N.J. Super. Ct. App. Div. 1990) 97

Wembley, Inc. v. Diplomat Tie Co., 216 F. Supp. 565 (D. Md. 1963) 220

Wiseheart v. Zions Bancorp., 49 P.3d 1200 (Colo. Ct. App. 2002) 324

Wishnick v. Frye, 245 P.2d 532 (Cal. App. 1952) 271

Witte Transp. Co. v. Murphy Motor Freight Lines, Inc., 193 N.W.2d 148 (Minn. 1971) 74; 77

WLWC Ctrs., Inc. v. Winners Corp., 563 F. Supp. 717 (M.D. Tenn. 1983) 175

Wochnick v. True, 356 P.2d 515 (Or. 1960) 299; 300

Wolf v. Brungardt, 524 P.2d 726 (Kan. 1974) 324

Womack v. McDonald, 121 So. 57 (Ala. 1929) 137

Woodward v. Dietrich, 548 A.2d 301 (Pa. Super. Ct. 1988) 285; 287

Wussow v. Commercial Mechanisms, Inc., 279 N.W.2d 503 (Wis. Ct. App. 1979) 52; 54; 102; 104; 141; 143; 162; 205; 207; 307; 309; 375; 376

Wysong and Miles Co. v. Employers of Wausau, 4 F. Supp. 2d 421 (M.D.N.C. 1998) 287

Xpert Automation Sys. Corp. v. Vibromatic Co., 569 N.E.2d 351 (Ind. Ct. App. 1991) 398

Yaindl v. Ingersoll-Rand Co., 422 A.2d 611 (Pa. 1980) 68

Yeomans v. Lysfjord, 327 P.2d 957 (Cal. Ct. App. 1958) 333

Yiakas v. Savoy, 526 N.E.2d 1305 (Mass. App. Ct.), *review denied*, 529 N.E.2d 1346 (Mass. 1988) 15

Young v. Johnson, 538 So. 2d 1387 (Fla. Dist. Ct. App. 1989) 271

Youngblood v. Mock, 238 S.E.2d 250 (Ga. Ct. App. 1977) 337

Youst v. Longo, 729 P.2d 728 (Cal. 1987) 72; 73

Yurevich v. Sikorsky Aircraft Div., 51 F. Supp. 2d 144 (D. Conn. 1999) 278

Zanakis-Pico v. Cutter Dodge, Inc., 47 P.3d 1222 (Haw. 2002) 320

Zatarains, Inc. v. Oak Grove Smokehouse, Inc., 698 F.2d 786 (5th Cir. 1983) 170

Zee-Bar, Inc.-N.H. v. Kaplan, 792 F. Supp. 895 (D.N.H. 1992) 250

Index

I